JAMES HILLER is a member of the Department of History at the Memorial University of Newfoundland.
PETER NEARY is a member of the Department of History at the University of Western Ontario.

The first comprehensive history of Newfoundland was published in 1793, but a century and a half passed before the first university course in the history of the island was offered there. During the past fifteen years there has been growing activity in the subject. This volume is the work of six scholars who have either studied or taught at the Memorial University of Newfoundland. Some have done both.

The book has two broad aims. First, to point out the major themes of modern Newfoundland history currently being examined, and to offer a number of new interpretations of economic and political development in the last two centuries. Second, to supplement the standard works that are readily available to students. In some areas it provides additional details; in others, it bridges wide gaps.

The themes considered include: an introduction to the writing of Newfoundland history; the transition from the purely maritime economy of the nineteenth century to the mixed oceanic and inland resource economy of the twentieth, and the difficulties this involved; the decline of the traditional cod fishery in the nineteenth century; Newfoundland's rejection of confederation in 1869; the limitations imposed by the fisheries agreements Britain negotiated with France and the United States; the consequences of the decision to reject confederation and diversify the local economy; the growth of the Fishermen's Protective Union; the political atmosphere of the 1920s; party politics in the post-confederation period; and, finally, the collapse of Newfoundland's oldest industry, the saltfish trade, and the province's integration into the North American economy.

This is a book intended for both regional specialists and general students of Canadian history. It provides a valuable resource about a province of rapidly growing importance.

EDITED BY
JAMES HILLER AND PETER NEARY

Newfoundland in the Nineteenth and Twentieth Centuries: essays in interpretation

UNIVERSITY OF TORONTO PRESS

Toronto Buffalo London

© University of Toronto Press 1980
Toronto Buffalo London
Printed in Canada

Canadian Cataloguing in Publication Data

Main entry under title:

Newfoundland in the nineteenth and twentieth centuries

Bibliography: p.
Includes index.
ISBN 0-8020-6391-8 pa. ISBN 0-8020-5486-2 bd.
I. Newfoundland – History.   2. Newfoundland –
Politics and government.   3. Newfoundland –
Economic conditions.   I. Hiller, James K., 1942-
II. Neary, Peter, 1938-

FC2161.N49   971.8   c80-094088-1
FI122.N49

Contents

Preface vii

The Writing of Newfoundland History: An Introductory Survey / 3
PETER NEARY

Newfoundland's Traditional Economy and Development to 1934 / 17
DAVID ALEXANDER

The Newfoundland Salt Cod Trade in the Nineteenth Century / 40
SHANNON RYAN

Confederation Defeated: The Newfoundland Election of 1869 / 67
JAMES HILLER

The French and American Shore Questions as Factors in Newfoundland
History / 95
PETER NEARY

The Railway and Local Politics in Newfoundland, 1870–1901 / 123
JAMES HILLER

W.F. Coaker and the Balance of Power Strategy: The Fishermen's Protective
Union in Newfoundland Politics / 148
IAN MCDONALD

Newfoundland Politics in the 1920s: The Genesis and Significance of the Hollis
Walker Enquiry / 181
R.M. ELLIOTT

Party Politics in Newfoundland, 1949–71: A Survey and Analysis / 205
PETER NEARY

The Collapse of the Saltfish Trade and Newfoundland's Integration into the North American Economy / 246
DAVID ALEXANDER

Select Bibliography / 269

Index / 283

Contributors / 290

Preface

The purpose of this volume is twofold – to point out the major themes of modern Newfoundland history that are currently being studied by historians of the province, and to supplement the standard works that are readily available to students. The collection both provides more detailed examinations of specific subjects and bridges some yawning gaps. It is designed both for the regional specialist and the general student of Canadian history, and the editors have, therefore, sought to balance originality with breadth and comprehensiveness. 'To˙ some inland Canadians,' Principal George M. Grant of Queen's University wrote in 1898, 'with little appreciation of the importance of the maritime element in a nation or of the sea ... it is a matter of indifference whether Newfoundland unites with Canada or remains out in the cold.'* It is with a like concern that this collection has been put together.

The first and most prominent theme examined here is the transition from the purely maritime economy of the nineteenth century to the mixed oceanic and inland resource economy of the twentieth century. That this transition was fraught with difficulty, the boosterism of some nineteenth-century publicists notwithstanding, is made clear in David Alexander's 'Newfoundland's Traditional Economy and Development to 1934,' while Shannon Ryan concentrates on and analyses the decline of the traditional cod fishery in the face of severe market competition. The Newfoundlanders of the 1860s did not necessarily perceive this decline as a permanent condition and their confidence in the economic future of the colony had much to do with their rejection of confederation in 1869, a subject which is dealt with in James Hiller's first essay. Newfoundland's sense of separateness was further enhanced by the frustrations imposed on her freedom of action by the Anglo-French and Anglo-American fisheries agreements, which are examined in Peter Neary's paper 'The French and American Shore Questions as Factors in

*'Newfoundland and Canada,' *Canadian Magazine* 11, no. 6 (October 1898): 467.

Newfoundland History.' In 'The Railway and Politics in Newfoundland, 1870–1901,' James Hiller explores the consequences of the decision to reject confederation and diversify the local economy. The strains created by these developments were in part responsible for the growth of the Fishermen's Protective Union after 1908, a phenomenon whose political consequences are examined in the late Ian McDonald's essay. R.M. Elliott pursues the political theme, and the results of the failure to broaden and diversify the economy sufficiently, in her study of the increasingly seedy political atmosphere of the 1920s, which culminated in the suspension of responsible government in 1934. The last two items in the collection survey the political economy of the post-confederation period. 'Party Politics in Newfoundland, 1949–71' examines the nature of Liberal power in the new Canadian province and the mounting crisis that led to that party's demise beginning with the federal election of 1968. David Alexander's 'The Collapse of the Saltfish Trade and Newfoundland's Integration into the North American Economy' relates the fate of Newfoundland's most ancient industry to the continentalist leitmotif of Canada's post-war economic history.

All the writers represented in this volume have either studied or taught – some have done both – at the Memorial University of Newfoundland. As colleagues and friends of the late Ian McDonald, we record here our deep sense of loss at his early death. It is fitting that his last essay should be published in this familiar company.

This book has been published with the help of a grant from the Social Science Federation of Canada, using funds provided by the Social Sciences and Humanities Research Council of Canada, a grant to the University of Toronto Press from the Andrew W. Mellon Foundation, and a grant from the Vice President's Research Fund at Memorial University. The maps were prepared in the Memorial University Cartographic Laboratory.

J.K.H.
P.F.N.

NEWFOUNDLAND IN THE NINETEENTH AND TWENTIETH CENTURIES: ESSAYS IN INTERPRETATION

Abbreviations

CHR	*Canadian Historical Review*
CJEPS	*Canadian Journal of Economics and Political Science*
CO	Colonial Office (records at Public Record Office, London, and microfilm copies)
JHA	Newfoundland, *Journal of the House of Assembly*
NQ	*Newfoundland Quarterly*
PANL	Provincial Archives of Newfoundland and Labrador

The Writing of Newfoundland History:
An Introductory Survey

PETER NEARY

Newfoundland history is a very old subject; indeed, the first systematic and comprehensive account of the Newfoundland past appeared as early as 1793, just two years after the enactment of the legislation which led to the division of the old province of Quebec into Upper and Lower Canada.[1] Moreover, if Newfoundland historiography does not exhibit the sharply defined schools that can be found in, say, the historiography of French Canada, it does contain a considerable range of opinion and at least some controversy. Thus John Reeves, the author of the 1793 work, *History of the Government of the Island of Newfoundland*, addressed himself to a question that has been central to the writing of Newfoundland history ever since, namely, the relationship between the ancient transatlantic fishery of the West Country of England and the colonization of Newfoundland. Reeves published the first volume of his two-volume *History of the English Law* in 1785. In 1790 he was made chief justice of Newfoundland after a court of judicature had been established there. In 1794 he gave evidence before a committee of the House of Commons that was enquiring into the affairs of Newfoundland. It was in connection with this enquiry that he produced his history of Newfoundland. He identified 'the West Country merchants with villainy,' blaming them 'for every evil, real or imagined, which existed upon the island.'[2]

The next writer to attempt a systematic history of the island was an Anglican divine, the Reverend Lewis Amadeus Anspach, who arrived in Newfoundland in October 1799. Between 1802 and 1812 Anspach served in the District of Conception Bay at Harbour Grace and Carbonear as a missionary for the Society for the Propagation of the Gospel. In the former year he was also appointed to the local magistracy. As a missionary Anspach claimed great success for his work: in 1810, for example, he wrote that whereas in Bay de Verde District the Sabbath had formerly been spent 'in profanation and vice,' it was now being observed 'in an orderly manner.'[3] Not surprisingly, his missionary enthusiasms spilled over into his writing of history. Thus his immensely readable and useful *History of the Island of Newfoundland*, published in London in 1819, was undertaken to remedy the neglect of Newfoundland by 'historians and geographers.' His explanation for this neglect reveals the bias of his work: 'Newfoundland has hitherto been little known, because it has not forced itself upon the notice of the historiographer by deeds of cruelty, or by intestine divisions or external attempts which endangered the safety or the peace of its neighbours; but, on the contrary, like the source of the Nile, unobserved and unknown, it silently distributed subsistence to a considerable portion of the inhabitants, and particularly of the *poor* of both hemispheres.'[4] Newfoundland had been 'the object of frequent and obstinate contests among the principal maritime powers of Europe' because it was 'a mine of treasure far more valuable than the boasted mines of Peru, because more really advantageous to its possessor and to mankind in general.'[5]

Anspach's successor in the genealogy of Newfoundland historians was another clergyman, this time a Congregationalist, the Reverend Charles Pedley (1820–72). Pedley was born in Staffordshire and studied at Rotherham College. In 1849 he became minister at Chester-le-Street in County Durham. Ten years later he went to St John's at the behest of the Colonial Missionary Society. In 1863 he published in London *The History of Newfoundland from the Earliest Times to the Year 1860.* His work was based in part on records which had been made available to him by the governor of the day, Sir Alexander Bannerman. The 'principal design' of his work was 'to furnish, so far as possible, a connected and intelligible narration of the progress of the island in more recent times, so as to afford some answer to the very natural questions – How did the colony arrive at its present state? How did it pass from a mere fishery to the rank of a colony? Whence, and in what circumstances, were its inhabitants introduced? How originated and grew the religious distinctions which have now such a marked place in their condition? How were the different institutions, legislative, legal, and educational, brought into existence, and consolidated into the shape in which they appear at this day?'[6] The emphasis in Pedley's work on 'religious distinctions' well reflected his times. He arrived in Newfoundland just after responsible government had been inaugurated and while the sectarian feeling this event had engendered was still rife. Moreover, he was living in St John's when the rioting, some of it sectarian, and constitutional crisis of 1861 occurred. His work reflects the strain of nineteenth-century local thought which held that the granting of responsible government had been a mistake.

After Pedley the stream of Newfoundland historical writing broadens considerably and it is at last possible to talk about 'groups of historians' and 'schools' of historical writing. Between the appearance of his work and the turn of the century the writing of Newfoundland history was dominated by authors whose purpose, to use the words of the best known of them, Daniel Woodley Prowse, was 'booming Newfoundland and making her attractions known.'[7] One such writer was Philip Tocque, who in 1878 published in Toronto *Newfoundland: As It Was and as It Is in 1877*. Tocque was born in Carbonear, Conception Bay, in 1814. He taught school in Newfoundland and in 1846 published his first book, *Wandering Thoughts and Solitary Hours*. After studying at Berkeley Divinity School in Connecticut he entered the Anglican ministry in 1864. He subsequently served in Nova Scotia, Massachusetts, Quebec, and Ontario, where he died in 1899. The 'design' of Tocque's work was to become a hardy perennial in Newfoundland historiography: it was 'to show the British and American reader that Newfoundland is something more than a mere fishing station, as well as to make Newfoundlanders themselves better acquainted with their own country.'[8] Tocque's work also exhibited a strain of émigré romanticism that would be echoed by many later writers about Newfoundland. 'The grand object of all sound history,' he wrote, 'should be to place the simple truth before the reader. I have made this book out of myself, out of my life. I have derived it from observation, from my relations of friendship, and of neighbourhood; have picked it up from the roads; above all, I have found it in the recollections of my youth. To know the history and life of the people of Newfoundland, I had but to interrogate my memory.'[9]

Tocque had an energetic clerical counterpart on the St John's literary scene in the person of Moses Harvey. Born in Armagh, Harvey was ordained in 1844. From 1852 to 1877 he was rector of St Andrew's Free Presbyterian Church in St John's. In 1891 he became a fellow of the Royal Society of Canada. Most of Harvey's writing has an historical bent but in two works he addressed himself particularly to the history of his adopted homeland. In 1883 he and Joseph Hatton, an English writer, published in London *Newfoundland the Oldest British Colony: Its History, Its Present Condition and Its Prospects in the Future*. In 1890 his later work, *A Short History of Newfoundland*, appeared in a revised edition. Harvey's great contemporary, Prowse, was the first native-born writer to attempt a truly comprehensive history of Newfoundland. Born at Port de Grave, Conception Bay, in 1834, Prowse joined the colonial bench in 1869. An energetic essayist, commentator, publicist, lecturer, and observer of the human condition, he reached the peak of his literary career in 1895 with the publication in London of his massive *A History of Newfoundland from the English, Colonial, and Foreign Records*, easily the most comprehensive and ambitious work of its kind undertaken to that time. Both Harvey and Prowse celebrated the maritime past of Newfoundlanders; but they were both also very much concerned in their work to foster the rising interest in Newfoundland in railway construction and the concomitant industrial development of land resources. If the past had a lesson, it was that Newfoundland would prosper by change in this direction to supplement her historic oceanic economy. As this extract from the American edition of his 1883 work amply demonstrates, Harvey was a 'progressive' historian with a vengeance.

Newfoundland has now entered on a course of self-development, and has at length got fairly into the groove of progress. Her prospects were never so bright and cheering as at the present hour. She has at length obtained the grand lever of all progress – a railway, which will extend year by year, open up the fertile lands for settlement, and produce a material and social revolution which will be conducive to the advancement of her people. Mining is rapidly extending and home industries are multiplying. A considerable rill from the great stream of emigration rushing past her shores to the West will speedily be directed to her fertile valleys. She is now free and self-governed, and her people feel that their destinies are in their own hands. What her political future may be, in the ages to come, it would be vain to conjecture. The duty of the present hour is to turn to account those great natural advantages which have lain dormant so long, and thus raise the country to a higher level of prosperity and social progress. Should this volume help forward such results, in any humble measure, the labor bestowed on it will be more than recompensed.[10]

Harvey's 'earnest hope' for his work was that it would 'prove useful, not only in diffusing correct and reliable information abroad, but also in leading the people of Newfoundland to think more highly of the land of their birth or adoption, to entertain a firmer confidence in its future, and to cherish more warmly that patriotic spirit which is the mainspring of all true progress.'[11]

Prowse was less rhapsodic in his purpose; thus he characterized his work as 'an attempt to describe how England's first colony, Newfoundland, was founded and developed; to show the influence of its discovery on the making of England. My plan has been to cite contemporary documents, for the most part hitherto unpublished.'[12] Yet his account of the history of his own times parallels that of Harvey:

notwithstanding great fluctuations in the fisheries, and disasters like the great fires of 1817, 1846, and the last terrible calamity of the 8th day of July, 1892, and worst of all the financial crisis of 1894, the Colony has progressed; her resources in minerals and timber are being greatly developed, railways are being extended, steam communication and telegraph lines are promoting civilization and advancement. The immense resources of the great island have been only, as it were, tapped here and there. Agriculture is slowly progressing. A greater impetus will be given to the Colony when the railway to Port-aux-Basques and a steam ferry across the Gulf brings us into closer connexion with America, and the strong current of progress and prosperity in the Dominion and the United States. Besides our splendid fisheries, timber, and minerals, Newfoundland is without a rival as a sporting country; with increased facilities of communication we should become the playground of America. With her vast resources, her temperate climate, and her unique position, the future of this ill-used and down-trodden Colony should be brighter than it has been of yore.[13]

The Book of Newfoundland, edited by J.R. Smallwood (St John's, vols. 1 and 2, 1937; vols. 3 and 4, 1967; vols. 5 and 6, 1975), would richly embroider this tradition.

On the whole, twentieth-century historians have been more reluctant to write 'general' histories than were their nineteenth-century predecessors. But there are – textbooks, 'shorter' and 'concise' histories excluded – at least three works belonging to this century that can be so described. These are J.D. Rogers, *Newfoundland* (Oxford 1911), A.B. Perlin, *The Story of Newfoundland* (St John's 1959), and St John Chadwick, *Newfoundland: Island into Province* (Cambridge 1967). A barrister by profession, Rogers undertook his work as part of an 'Historical Geography of the British Colonies' being published by the Clarendon Press. Rogers detected 'two or three essential characteristics' in Newfoundland history. The first of these was 'an immobility ... and a fixity of character in the Newfoundlander, which is unique in colonial history. Somersetshire, Devonshire, and Irish peasants are there and have been there from the first or almost from the first, preserving their ancient types, partly it is true by constant movements between their old and new homes, and partly also from other causes.' The second distinguishing characteristic of Newfoundland historically was 'the uncertainty of its fate.' 'For three hundred years, that is to say, during the whole of its colonial life, the colony has been menaced with complete or partial extinction; not by force but by incessantly reiterated arguments. From the very beginning until the very end of its life clever people proved over and over again almost to demonstration that the colony ought not to exist.'[14] 'Down to 1757' Rogers based his history on primary materials 'chiefly gathered from the Record Office and the Manuscript Department of the British Museum'; after 1757 he was 'thrown back on contemporary writers, on Blue books, and on those second-hand authors, who have had access to first-hand authorities which I have not had.' On his differences with previous historians, Rogers had 'neither room nor taste for discussion.' 'History,' he wrote, 'has only to do with the movement of events.'[15]

Albert Perlin, the author of the first of the two general histories written since Newfoundland became a Canadian province in 1949, was born in St John's in 1901 and educated at Bishop Feild College. A businessman and journalist, he was a prominent and influential commentator on Newfoundland affairs for many years. His history was 'born of an affection for Newfoundland' and was 'put together in the hope that it may help a little to create a larger and more sympathetic understanding of this province, its past struggles and present problems.'[16] His work harks back to that of Prowse and Harvey and the other enthusiasts of the local history as progress school. St John Chadwick, the author of *Newfoundland: Island into Province* (Cambridge 1967), the latest, if somewhat conventional, history of Newfoundland, was born in 1915. A career diplomat, he became the first director of the Commonwealth Foundation in London in 1966. Chadwick's purpose was to produce 'a history which, in reviewing and reassessing the facts already known, carries the story further and attempts a picture in the round of Newfoundland's struggle both to obtain a place in the colonial sun and to achieve a quasi-independent status; in short a modern history of Newfoundland from discovery to federation.'[17]

While university research and publication in the field of Newfoundland history is of comparatively recent origin, it exhibits considerable scope and diversity. As might be expected, given Newfoundland's transatlantic connections, there has been a long-standing interest in the Newfoundland past in the universities of the United Kingdom. As noted above, Rogers' history was published in Oxford at the Clarendon Press. In 1915 the Cambridge University Press published James P. Howley's *The Beothucks or Red Indians: The Aboriginal Inhabitants of Newfoundland*, a book that remains the most authoritative work ever undertaken on the history of the indigenous people of the Island of Newfoundland.[18] In 1930 the same press published the *Canada and Newfoundland* volume in its *History of the British Empire*. Three chapters of this volume were devoted to Newfoundland. The first of these, entitled 'Newfoundland to 1783,' was written by A.P. Newton, one of the general editors of the series and the Rhodes professor of imperial history at the University of London. The other Newfoundland chapters were by Sir C. Alexander Harris, a former governor of Newfoundland and sometime scholar of Christ's College, Cambridge.

That Newton should have undertaken part of the Newfoundland work himself reflected his encouragement of graduate work in the Newfoundland field at the University of London. Altogether five theses on Newfoundland history were completed under his direction. His students included Gordon O. Rothney, who went on to preside over the inauguration of graduate studies in history at the Memorial University of Newfoundland, and A.H. McLintock, a New Zealander, who in 1941 published *The Establishment of Constitutional Government in Newfoundland, 1783–1832: A Study of Retarded Colonization* in the 'Imperial Studies' series of the Royal Empire Society. The foundation laid by Newton was built upon by his successor Gerald S. Graham, much of whose own work on the history of seapower in the North Atlantic was relevant to the history of Newfoundland. Graham supervised doctoral theses on Newfoundland topics by Gertrude Gunn and Ian McDonald. In 1966 Gertrude Gunn published *The Political History of Newfoundland, 1832–1864* in the 'Canadian Studies in History and Government' series of the University of Toronto Press.

The first thesis ever written at Oxford on the history of Newfoundland was submitted by W.L. Morton for the B LITT degree in 1935. His subject was 'Newfoundland in Colonial Policy, 1775–1793.' Morton's successors in the field at Oxford have included H.B. Mayo, F.F. Thompson, S.J.R. Noel, and Keith Matthews. Thompson's Oxford work led to the publication in 1961 of *The French Shore Problem in Newfoundland: An Imperial Study* by the University of Toronto Press, again in its 'Canadian Studies in History and Government' series. In 1971 S.J.R. Noel published *Politics in Newfoundland* in the 'Canadian Government Series,' also of the University of Toronto Press. Based on his Oxford D PHIL thesis, which had been supervised by A.F. Madden of Nuffield College, this work brought the writing of modern Newfoundland history to a new level of maturity and sophistication. Keith Matthews' D PHIL thesis, which was completed in 1968 and entitled 'A History of the West of England–Newfoundland Fishery,' has made a similar mark on the earlier period.

At Cambridge Alan Cooke, James Hiller, and Frederick Jones have completed doctoral theses on Newfoundland and Labrador topics.[19] In 1956, the Cambridge economic historian C.R. Fay published *Life and Labour in Newfoundland* and, in 1961, *Channel Islands and Newfoundland.* Elsewhere in the United Kingdom the names of two scholars stand out when the Newfoundland field is considered: J.A. Williamson of Bristol University and David Quinn of Liverpool University. In Williamson's extensive bibliography the following items are of particular Newfoundland interest: *The Voyages of the Cabots and the English Discovery of North America under Henry VII and Henry VIII* (London 1929) and *The Cabot Voyages and Bristol Discovery under Henry VII* (Cambridge 1962). Quinn's published work includes *The Voyages and Colonising Enterprises of Sir Humphery Gilbert* (London 1940); *Sebastian Cabot and Bristol Exploration* (Bristol 1968); and (with Neil Cheshire) *The New Found Land of Stephen Parmenius* (Toronto 1972). In 1969 Gillian T. Cell, one of Quinn's former students, published *English Enterprise in Newfoundland, 1577–1660.*

In France the ancient quarrel over fishing rights on the Newfoundland coast occasioned four dissertations during the period 1900–5 – two at the University of Rennes and one each at the University of Paris and the University of Poitiers. In 1900 the prolific French historian Henry Harrisse published *Découverte et évolution cartographique de Terre-Neuve et des pays circonvoisins 1497–1500–1769.* His extensive bibliography includes many other Newfoundland references. A recent major French work is Ch. de La Morandière, *Histoire de la pêche française de la morue dans l'Amérique septentrionale* ... (3 vols., Paris 1962–6).

In the United States theses dealing in whole or in part with subjects in Newfoundland history have been completed at more than ten universities but little published work has come out of them. Notable exceptions are Charles B. Judah, *The North American Fisheries and British Policy to 1713* (Urbana 1933) and R.G.

Lounsbury, *The British Fishery at Newfoundland, 1634–1763* (New Haven 1934), the latter based on a doctoral thesis completed at Yale. Three scholars working in the United States have, however, contributed a great deal to our understanding of Newfoundland's diplomatic history. John Bartlet Brebner, *North Atlantic Triangle: The Interplay of Canada, the United States and Great Britain* (New Haven 1945) in the 'Carnegie Series on the Relations of Canada and the United States' contains many Newfoundland references. C.C. Tansill, *Canadian-American Relations, 1875–1911* (New Haven 1943) in the same series deals with the settlement in 1910 of the North Atlantic fisheries dispute but has, for the most part, been superseded by more recent work. An invaluable source for Newfoundland's role in a crucial period of Anglo-American relations is C.S. Campbell, *Anglo-American Understanding, 1898–1903* (Baltimore 1957).

As might be expected, academic interest in Newfoundland history at 'mainland' Canadian universities has been sporadic. Newfoundland history as such is not taught at any Canadian institution other than Memorial; indeed, courses in the history of the Atlantic Provinces as a whole are rare in Canadian universities outside the region itself. Fads in the Canadian historical world tend to follow the latest crisis of confederation or, with a five- to ten-year time lag, the latest wave of opinion in the United States. Since the Atlantic Provinces have never shaken the foundations of the nation or offered a suitable model for the application of ideas derived from American history, interest in their past has remained slight in other parts of the country. On the whole whatever commitment there has been has arisen out of the concern of individuals rather than the decided policies of departments or universities. Two scholars stand out for their Newfoundland work – Harold A. Innis of the University of Toronto and W.S. MacNutt of the University of New Brunswick, the former for *The Cod Fisheries: The History of an International Economy* (rev. ed., Toronto 1954), and the latter for *The Atlantic Provinces: The Emergence of Colonial Society, 1712–1857* (Toronto 1965) in the 'Canadian Centenary Series.' At the level of graduate research the pickings are somewhat leaner. Nevertheless there are theses on various aspects of Newfoundland history scattered throughout the libraries of at least half a dozen Canadian universities outside the Atlantic region. In the Maritime Provinces theses on a variety of Newfoundland subjects can be found in the libraries of Acadia and St Francis Xavier universities. On the other hand little of the graduate research done in the field either at these or other Canadian universities has found its way into print. Two notable exceptions are F.W. Rowe, *The History of Education in Newfoundland* (Toronto 1952) and John Mannion, *Irish Settlements in Eastern Canada: A Study of Cultural Transfer and Adaptation* (Toronto 1974), the latter a strikingly original work. Gradually, however, Newfoundland historical writing is being integrated with that of Canada as a whole. Three readily available bibliographical guides which direct the student of Canadian history to Newfoundland material are W.F.E. Morley, *The Atlantic Provinces* (Toronto 1967); Claude Thibault, *Bibliographica Canadiana* (Toronto 1973), and J.L. Granatstein and Paul Stevens (eds.), *Canada since 1867: A Bibliographical Guide* (2nd ed., Toronto 1977). The first of these is very comprehensive but the second greatly flawed. The third contains an excellent chapter on 'Atlantic Canada' by W.B. Hamilton. His imaginative *Local History in Atlantic Canada* (Toronto 1974) is equally rewarding.

The most important Canadian scholarly journals have all published papers on Newfoundland topics, if somewhat fitfully. Since *Acadiensis* reappeared in 1971 most of the important work is to be found in its pages. Other national journals, past and present, of special interest to the student of the province's history and affairs include: *Canadian Historical Review, Canadian Journal of Economics and Political Science, Canadian Journal of Political Science, Journal of Canadian Studies*, and *Dalhousie Review*. In keeping with the Canadian sense of manifest destiny, Newfoundland subjects were frequently given special attention in dominion reference works long before the island and Labrador entered confederation in 1949. For example, W.S. Wallace (ed.), *The Macmillan Dictionary of Canadian Biography*, 3rd ed. (Toronto 1963), which was first published in 1926, contains useful biographical information on many Newfoundland figures. Canada's great wartime interest in Newfoundland was reflected in the publication in 1946 of the influential *Newfoundland: Economic, Diplomatic and Strategic Studies*, edited by R.A. MacKay for the Royal Institute of International Affairs.

Finally, one topic in Canadian history – the history of confederation itself – has inevitably drawn 'mainland' Canadian historians into the study of at least some aspects of Newfoundland history. The historian of confederation who probably gives Newfoundland the most extensive coverage in his work is P.B. Waite. His *Life and Times of Confederation*, 2nd ed. (Toronto 1962) is soundly based on the relevant Newfoundland sources.

In Newfoundland itself academic interest in Newfoundland history is of surprisingly recent vintage. Although Memorial University College was founded in 1924, it was not until the academic year of 1943–4 that a course on the history of Newfoundland was taught there. The introduction of the subject at the college was the work of A.M. Fraser; his inaugural course covered the period 1832–1939 and laid 'special emphasis ... on constitutional development and external relations.'[20] This course was given every year until 1950 but, surprisingly, for the first few years of Memorial's life as a degree-granting institution – it was given this status in 1949 – Newfoundland history was not part of the curriculum. Finally, in the academic year 1955–6 Fraser's pioneering work was taken up by Gordon O. Rothney, his successor as Memorial's sole professor of history. The 1955–6 calendar not only held out the prospect of History 221 – 'History of Newfoundland; a Survey, from 1497 to the Present' – but also promulgated regulations for the MA degree in history.[21] From its inception at Memorial graduate work in history was almost entirely concerned with the history of Newfoundland. In 1959 Leslie Harris was awarded the first MA degree in history ever given at Memorial for a thesis entitled 'The First Nine Years of Representative Government in Newfoundland.' Since then more than twenty MA theses have been completed at Memorial in the field of Newfoundland history. In 1971 the development of historical study at Memorial reached a new level of achievement when the Maritime History Group was formed there under the leadership of Keith Matthews and David Alexander.[22] The launching of this important venture coincided with a growing interest at the university in the social and economic history of Newfoundland as opposed to the constitutional and diplomatic history which had dominated the work done in the 1950s and 1960s. David Alexander's *The Decay of Trade: An Economic History of the Newfoundland Saltfish Trade, 1935–1965* (St John's 1977) exemplifies the new genre.

During the last decade the work of historians at Memorial has been considerably enriched by the work of scholars in other disciplines at the university. In the English Department E.R. Seary, G.M. Story, William Kirwin, D.G. Pitt, and Patrick O'Flaherty have been especially active. Memorial's Folklore Department, established in 1968, has an extensive archive and a comprehensive graduate program. Historians of the province have also benefitted greatly from the creation at Memorial in 1961 of an Institute of Social and Economic Research. While the work of this institute has been mainly sociological and anthropological, its growing list of publications suggests many leads for the historian to follow. To date the institute has published more than twenty volumes. Its 1977 publication edited by John Mannion, *The Peopling of Newfoundland: Essays in Historical Geography* (St John's 1977), is an excellent introduction to the important regional work of the university's geographers. The study of Newfoundland history has been further advanced by the publication program of the Newfoundland Historical Society. Since 1966 the society has had a publication entitled *Aspects*, which is included in each issue of the *Newfoundland Quarterly*. Edited by Leslie Harris, *Aspects* has maintained a consistently high quality.

Needless to say the entire study of Newfoundland history at Memorial and elsewhere has benefitted enormously from the growth and development of the Provincial Archives. Three Memorial historians – Gordon O. Rothney, Harvey Mitchell, and William H. Whiteley – were instrumental in the establishment of the archives, which opened at the university in 1956 with the assistance of a grant from the Carnegie Foundation. Harvey Mitchell has contributed an account of the early days of the archives to the *American Archivist* (21 [1958]: 43–53). The archives is now located in the Colonial Building in St John's and is the repository of an increasingly well organized and growing body of material. The archives has issued an inventory of its holdings and has published in mimeographed form both a newsletter and a document reprint series. The work of local historians has also been assisted by the growth of the Centre for Newfoundland Studies at Memorial University. This centre was opened in 1964 and presided over for many years by Agnes O'Dea, who was also closely associated with the founding of the Newfoundland archives. Her Newfoundland bibliography, which is available on cards in the centre (and forthcoming in published form), is an indispensable research guide. The centre also contains an excellent collection of both published and unpublished writing on the province's history. The Hunter Library at the St John's Arts and Culture Centre houses another good Newfoundland collection. A local organization which has both benefitted from and encouraged historical research is the Newfoundland Historic Trust. The writing of Newfoundland history is today characterized by vigorous scholarly activity on many fronts. It is to be hoped that the present collection will introduce the general Canadian audience to the work that is in progress in one of the most lively regional fields in the country.

NOTES

1 Because of the magnitude and great diversity of historical writing about Newfoundland and Labrador I have confined myself here, as far as possible, to two types of writers: those who have undertaken 'general' histories of the region and academic historians. In the former category I have excluded writers whose work is essentially derivative, including the authors of 'concise' or 'shorter' histories, particularly those designed for school use. My approach to the academic historians has been to show where Newfoundland history has been studied and why. Since Labrador is the subject of an excellent published bibliography – Alan Cooke and Fabian Caron (comp.), *Bibliography of the Quebec-Labrador Peninsula*, 2 vols. (Boston 1968) – I have not dealt with its historiography in detail here. In listing titles I have, with a few exceptions, confined myself to published work. The select bibliography below includes all the titles mentioned here that refer to the nineteenth and twentieth centuries.
2 Keith Matthews, 'Historical Fence Building: A Critique of the Historiography of Newfoundland,' *NQ* 74, no. 1 (1978): 22.
3 C.F. Pascoe, *Two Hundred Years of the S.P.G. ...* , 2 vols. (London 1901), 1: 93.
4 L.A. Anspach, *History of the Island of Newfoundland* (London 1819), viii–x.
5 Ibid., viii.
6 Charles Pedley, *The History of Newfoundland from the Earliest Times to the Year 1860* (London 1863), ch. 1, 2.
7 Quoted in G.M. Story, 'Judge Prowse: Historian and Publicist,' *NQ* 78, no. 4 (winter 1972), 23.

8 Philip Tocque, *Newfoundland: As It Was and as It Is in 1877* (Toronto 1878), preface.
9 Ibid.
10 Moses Harvey and Joseph Hatton, *Newfoundland, the Oldest British Colony ...* (London 1883), preface to the American edition (Boston 1883), xi.
11 Ibid., xii.
12 D.W. Prowse, *A History of Newfoundland from the English, Colonial, and Foreign Records* (London 1895), introduction, xiii.
13 Ibid., xx–xxi.
14 J.D. Rogers, *Newfoundland* (Oxford 1911), preface, iv–v.
15 Ibid., ix.
16 A.B. Perlin, *The Story of Newfoundland* (St John's 1959), preface.
17 St John Chadwick, *Newfoundland: Island into Province* (Cambridge 1967), preface, xi.
18 In 1974 this work was reprinted in Coles Canadiana Collection. A geologist by profession, Howley was Alexander Murray's successor as director of the Newfoundland geological survey. Recent work on Newfoundland's Indian peoples includes the following: Ralph Pastore, *The Newfoundland Micmacs* (St John's 1978); Frederick W. Rowe, *Extinction: The Beothuks of Newfoundland* (Toronto 1977); L.F.S. Upton, 'The Extermination of the Beothucks of Newfoundland,' *CHR* 58 (1977): 133–53, and 'The Beothucks: Questions and Answers,' *Acadiensis* 7, no. 2 (1978): 150–5. The remarkable Howley family produced two other writers of distinction: Richard and Michael. The latter's *Ecclesiastical History of Newfoundland* (Boston 1888) remains the standard work on the much neglected history of the Roman Catholic Church. For a highly original recent article on the early history of that church in Newfoundland see R.J. Lahey, 'The Role of Religion in Lord Baltimore's Colonial Enterprise,' *Maryland Historical Magazine* 72 (1977): 492–511. Unfortunately, what published comment there is on the history of the church since 1855 concentrates on the political role of the hierarchy. This has produced a narrow, one-dimensional view of modern Catholic Newfoundland – a portrayal which invites the broadening attentions of intellectual, social, and economic historians. W.F. Ryan's *The Clergy and Economic Growth in Quebec (1896–1914)* (Quebec 1966) suggests many Newfoundland parallels that cast serious doubt on the conservative characterization of the church which flows from strictly political study.
19 The most comprehensive work attempted in Newfoundland in this century on the history of Labrador is W.G. Gosling, *Labrador: Its Discovery, Exploration, and Development* (London 1910). Gosling was born in Hamilton, Bermuda, in 1863. He arrived in St John's in 1881 and enjoyed a successful business career there. He served as mayor of the city from 1916 to 1919. His work on Labrador was undertaken at the behest of Sir Wilfred Grenfell, who had become an international celebrity through his various activities in northern Newfoundland and Labrador. Gosling's 'design' was 'to preserve the knowledge of the incidents which took place in the past, and which are likely to have

some value in the development of the country in the future. That may tend to the protection and amelioration of the native races of Indians and Eskimos, to the betterment of the comparatively few white settlers, to the development and conservation of its marvellous fisheries, the framing of proper laws for the governance of the thousands of Newfoundland, Canadian and American fishermen who frequent its coasts, to excite an interest in this neglected country, and to assist Dr. Grenfell, who has been working for these same ends for the past sixteen years with a single-minded devotion which excludes all other interests' (preface, viii).

20 Memorial University College, *Calendar*, 1943–4, 46.

21 Memorial University, *Calendar*, 1955–6, 110–11.

22 The study of Newfoundland history is but one aspect of the work of the Maritime History Group. The group's archival holdings are now the fourth largest in Canada. The nucleus of this archive, which is located at Memorial University, is a collection of shipping records. These were transferred to St John's from the Public Record Office, London, in 1971 and consist of 'The agreement on account of crew' (crew lists) for the period 1861–1913. The collection covers the whole British empire. A computer index to these records has now been completed and is available from the office of the group at Memorial University. The Maritime History Group also has an enquiry and document reproduction service. At present the major research project of the members of the group is a study of Atlantic Canadian shipping. For an example see David Alexander and Gerry Panting, 'The Mercantile Fleet and its Owners: Yarmouth, Nova Scotia, 1840–1889,' *Acadiensis* 7, no. 2 (1978): 3–28.

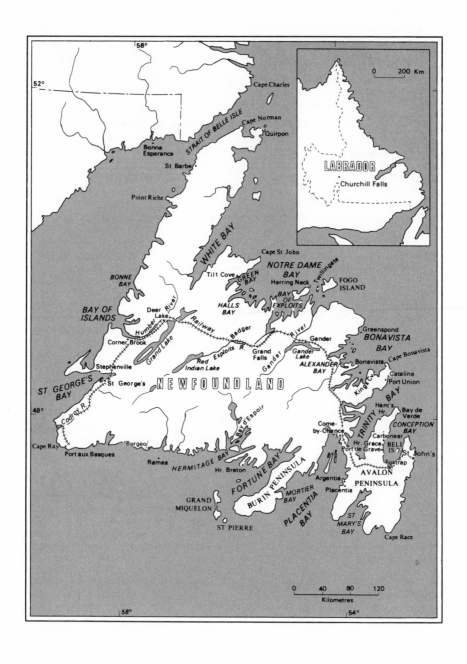

58°
52°
Cape Charles
STRAIT OF BELLE ISLE
Cape Norman
Quirpon
Bonne
Esperance
St Barbe
Point Riche

0   200 Km
LABRADOR
Churchill Falls

WHITE BAY
Cape St John
Tilt Cove
GREEN BAY
NOTRE DAME BAY
Herring Neck
Twillingate
FOGO ISLAND
BONNE BAY
BAY OF ISLANDS
Deer Lake
HALLS BAY
BAY OF EXPLOITS
Humber River
Railway
Badger
Red Indian Lake
Exploits R.
River
Grand Falls
Gander
Gander Lake
Greenspond
BONAVISTA BAY
Corner Brook
Grand Lake
Gander
ALEXANDER BAY
Bonavista
Cape Bonavista
Stephenville
NEWFOUNDLAND
Catalina
Port Union
ST GEORGE'S BAY
St George's
Kings C.
TRINITY BAY
Hant's Hr.
Bay de Verde
48°
Codroy R.
Bay d'Espoir
Come-by-Chance
CONCEPTION BAY
Carbonear
Hr. Grace
Port de Grave
BELL IS.
St. John's
Cape Ray
Burgeo
Foxtrap
Port aux Basques
Ramea
HERMITAGE BAY
Hr. Breton
FORTUNE BAY
BURIN PENINSULA
MORTIER BAY
Argentia
Placentia
AVALON PENINSULA
GRAND MIQUELON
PLACENTIA BAY
ST MARY'S BAY
ST PIERRE
Cape Race

0   40   80   120
Kilometres

58°
54°

Newfoundland's Traditional Economy and Development to 1934

DAVID ALEXANDER

The price of being a country is willingness to bear a cross. For Germany it is the cross of beastliness; for Russia it is stolidity; the United States must rise above material wealth; and Canada is required to find a national identity. The burden which Newfoundland has carried is to justify that it should have any people. From the Western Adventurers of the seventeenth century to Canadian economists in the twentieth, there has been a continuing debate as to how many, if any, people should live in Newfoundland. The consensus has normally been that there should be fewer Newfoundlanders – a conclusion reached in the seventeenth century when there were only some 2,000 inhabitants, and one which is drawn today when there are over 500,000.

Newfoundland's economic history has centred on valuation of its natural resource endowment in relation to the size of its population. The particular object of debate has been (and still is) the size and well-being of the traditional or rural economy, and the likelihood that it could expand extensively at acceptable standards of life, or that other sectors can be developed to absorb labour exports from the traditional sector. The economic characteristics of a traditional economy can be stated simply enough. Labour and natural resources, or 'land,' are the most important factors of production, and capital plays a very minor role. If it is assumed that land is a constant, then the average output of labour is a simple function of the ratio of labour to land. Thus, if the population expands and the ratio increases, then average per capita output falls; that is, standards of living fall. If it is further assumed that the economy is closed to emigration, then the prospects are those of deteriorating standards to a very low level of physical security and comfort. To make matters still more depressing, a once-and-for-all technical improvement in the traditional economy (say the introduction of the cod trap) which shifts average per capita output upwards, is of little long-term benefit, for

Reprinted with minor editorial changes from *Acadiensis* 5, no. 2 (1976): 56–78, by permission.

the gains in living standards will be eaten away by the likelihood of strengthened population growth: one ends up with a larger economy, but not necessarily a more prosperous one. The only routes to a long-run improvement in living standards are a widening resource base and technical change (including organizational changes such as the growth of domestic and international market activity).[1] These assumptions imply a movement away from the traditional economy with capital growth (both reproducible and human) defining the growth of total and per capita income.

The stark features of this simple model obviously fail to capture accurately the complexities of Newfoundland's economic history. Yet it does identify some realities of its economic problems and, what is just as important, perceptions of the problems. When Newfoundland's traditional economy reached an apparent limit to extensive expansion in the second half of the nineteenth century, a struggle was waged to expand the resource base and modernize both the structure of production and the composition of output. This campaign ended in collapse and that collapse led directly to union with Canada. In 1949 the effort to 'develop' was resumed under new constitutional dress. But the historical record sketched in this essay suggests that confederation did not introduce any especially new perceptions of Newfoundland's economic problems and potential, and some might argue that it simply reinforced a depressing tendency to neglect the province's most obvious natural resource – the sea.

At the time of its discovery Newfoundland's fishery was an international open-access resource, exploited by fleets from France, Portugal, and Spain. At this time (unlike today) the volume of factors of production available to exploit the resource, the primitive techniques, and the size of the markets meant the resource base was in no danger of overexploitation in the sense of significant reductions in maximum sustainable yield. For the continental countries, the adoption of a 'green cure' (transport in salt bulk) meant the issue of settling Newfoundland did not arise, since the island was mainly a convenient watering and repair station. But this was not the case with the west of England fishery, which developed in the second half of the sixteenth century.[2] Whether in response to relatively high costs of salt or to local tradition, the West Country fisherman pursued a light-salted, sun-dried fishery at Newfoundland. Land resources were consequently important to the Westcountrymen, as wood was needed for flakes and stages, and shore facilities for drying. The consequences of this technology were two-fold: first, an undignified annual rush by the west of England fishing boats to Newfoundland to claim *seasonal* property rights over the best fishing 'rooms': and secondly, opposition to establishment of 'plantations' or any other settlement of the island, whether by Englishmen or foreigners, which would prejudice seasonal claims to ownership over essential land inputs.

The short fishing season and poor winter employment opportunities in Newfoundland, as well as the grim agricultural potential, favoured a migratory fishery; but very slowly in the course of the seventeenth and eighteenth centuries the difference in the rates of return between a migratory and a settled fishery shifted in favour of the latter. Rising European shipping costs and the development of regular and lower cost supplies of food and other imports from the North American colonies were critical factors in this shift. Nonetheless the growth of a resident population was painfully slow. In 1650 it was around 2,000 and by 1750, with sharp fluctuations, reached only 6,000. The turning point came in the second half of the eighteenth century. The French fishery declined after the Seven Years' War and the New England fishery following the American revolution, and neither fully recovered until the end of the Napoleonic Wars. By the end of the century the West Country merchants had translated an international migratory fishery at Newfoundland into a colonial industry in Newfoundland. Between 1750 and 1804 Newfoundland's population grew at an annual rate of 2.3 per cent reaching over 20,000 and in the next twelve years doubled to 40,000, implying a high growth rate per annum.[3]

The transition from a British fishery at Newfoundland to a Newfoundland fishery was significant in two ways. It meant the foundation of a new country in the world, for while it is customary (at least in Newfoundland) to claim a history of many hundreds of years, it is more realistic to view Newfoundland as one of the nineteenth-century countries of European settlement. Secondly, while there was always a possibility (however remote up to the nineteenth century) that an expanding migratory fishery would deplete an open-access resource, there was now a better possibility that a settled traditional economy would expand to the point of impoverishing a country.

The inshore salt cod industry dominated Newfoundland's economic history in the nineteenth century and continued to be the single most important source of employment and market income well into the twentieth. Table 1 is the basis for suggesting that in terms of the gross value of (export) production, prices, and physical output, there were three long cycles running between 1815 and 1934: the first covering 1815/19 to 1850/4, the second between 1855/9 to 1895/9, and a third between 1900/4 to 1930/4. Mean volumes, prices, and export values tended to be higher in each period, but as table 2 indicates, fluctuations around the means were extreme, especially with respect to prices and export values. It is clear that prices were more volatile than physical production, and that on a quinquennial basis gross export values were less stable than either output or prices. The industry was obviously an unstable one upon which to found a country's external earnings and such a large fraction of its national income, and it is hardly surprising that with responsible government politicians launched an effort to widen the country's production base.

TABLE 1

Quinquennial averages and variations in salt cod export: volumes, prices, and gross values 1815/19 to 1930/34

Period	Volumes (000 quintals)			Prices ($ per quintal)			Gross export value (000 dollars)		
	$\bar{X}$	S	V	$\bar{X}$	S	V	$\bar{X}$	S	V
1815–19	1,018	50	5%	3.90	1.07	27%	2,968	1,429	48%
1820–24	883	30	3	2.46	0.23	9	2,175	224	10
1825–29	923	37	4	2.08	0.11	5	1,942	174	9
1830–34	763	110	14	2.42	0.32	13	1,840	326	18
1835–39	788	65	8	2.78	0.04	1	2,193	201	9
1840–44	944	59	6	2.79	0.13	5	2,637	216	8
1845–49	963	115	12	2.66	0.16	6	2,547	226	9
1850–54	955	108	11	2.61	0.38	15	2,454	161	—
1855–59	1,205	128	11	3.33	0.34	10	4,008	605	15
1860–64	1,172	140	12	2.65	0.50	14	4,218	266	6
1865–69	969	81	8	3.86	0.45	12	3,731	450	12
1870–74	1,273	175	14	3.93	0.02	0.5	5,026	896	18
1875–79	1,134	132	12	3.88	0.31	8	4,354	432	10
1880–84	1,460	70	5	3.82	0.13	3	5,582	615	11
1885–89	1,192	112	9	3.66	0.52	14	4,316	374	9
1890–94	1,101	70	6	3.60	0.04	1	3,957	461	12
1895–99	1,224	81	7	2.89	0.16	5	3,549	559	16
1900–04	1,302	78	6	4.19	0.03	0.6	5,562	289	5
1905–09	1,574	112	7	n/a	n/a	n/a	n/a	n/a	n/a
1910–14	1,346	122	9	5.66	0.51	9	7,583	599	8
1915–19	1,517	250	16	9.35	2.80	30	15,650	6,030	41
1920–24	1,499	183	12	8.67	2.29	26	13,265	4,974	37
1925–29	1,398	162	12	8.37	0.76	9	11,587	584	5
1930–34	1,179	52	4	5.90	1.87	32	7,010	2,464	35

SOURCE: Calculated from Government of Newfoundland. *Historical Statistics of Newfoundland* (St John's 1970), vol. 1, table K-7

NOTES: $\bar{X}$ = arithmetic mean, $\bar{S}$ = standard deviation, $\bar{V}$ = coefficient of variability ($V = S/X. 100$)

Although high volumes, prices, and export values characterized the cod fishery in the first years of the century, output volumes grew by only 0.08 per cent per annum from the mid-1820s to mid-1850s and in four out of six quinquennia were below the trend for 1805/9–1915/19. During the same period prices rose by only 0.13 per cent per annum and in five quinquennia were below trend for 1820/4–1900/4. Accordingly, the value of cod exports grew by only 0.9 per cent per annum and in all six quinquennia was below trend for 1805/9–1900/4.[4] Over the

TABLE 2
Mean values of quinquennial coefficients of variation for the salt
cod industry

Period	Volumes %	Prices %	Gross values %
1815/19–1930/34	8.88	11.09	15.57
1855/59–1895/99	9.33	7.50	12.11
1900/04–1930/34	9.43	17.77	21.83

same period population grew at slightly over 2.5 per cent per annum, and the apparent depression of the first half of the century would appear worse if the initial benchmark for measurements was the values of 1811/15 – a quinquennium when many people were encouraged to migrate to Newfoundland. But it does not follow necessarily that for the economy as a whole the productivity of labour and living standards were falling. It is possible that a decline in per capita export values was compensated by a general decline in unit costs of imports, for while a U.S. wholesale price index for farm products rose from 59 in 1826/30 to 84 in 1851/5 (with a dip to 55 in 1841 /5), a United Kingdom merchandise export price index fell from 169 in 1826/30 to 104 in 1851/2.[5] Moreover, within Newfoundland the rapid growth of the seal fishery softened the depression in the cod fishery, and it is also a reasonable hypothesis that over the period some fraction of total domestic expenditure was shifted from imports to domestic production. In addition to the non-market output which a rural community could generate through increasing familiarity with its environment, the very rapid growth of St John's (reaching some 20 per cent of the population by 1857) suggests development of import-substituting commodity and service production.

Between the grant of responsible government in 1855 and the mid-1880s, Newfoundland's basic industry flourished, although there were always bad years, frequently coupled with indifferent ones. But prices grew by 1.17 per cent per annum in 1850/4–1880/4 and were above the trend referred to earlier in every quinquennia. Volumes grew by 1.25 per cent per annum and were above trend in four out of six quinquennia. Accordingly, over the same interval, export values grew by 2.14 per cent per annum and were above the trend in each quinquennium. Over the period 1857/84 population growth decelerated to an annual rate slightly over 1.7 per cent. Furthermore, while according to the censuses the labour force (occupied population) was growing at just over 2 per cent per annum, the male fishing labour force grew by only 1.7 per cent. Thus, the industry's share in total employment fell from 90 per cent in 1857 to 82 per cent in 1884, and the implication (under the assumption of constant factor proportions) is a modest growth in total productivity. The trend in living standards, however, is unclear. The U.S. wholesale price index for farm products rose sharply from 83 in 1856/60 to 117 and 130 in the two quinquennia of the 1860s, then fell to 86 in 1880/4. The UK merchandise export price index moved in the same direction, rising from 110 in 1856/60 to a plateau of about 126 in the three quinquennia between 1861 and 1875 and then falling off to 93 in 1881/5. But whatever the implications of the terms of trade for living standards, behind the growth rates for the fishing economy an alarming situation was emerging. The absolute level of employment in the fishing industry grew from some 38,500 men in 1857 to around 60,400 in 1884, and fishing rooms in use expanded from some 6,000 to around 10,500.[6] This meant that the average volume of production per fisherman was falling from around 30 quintals in the 1850s and 60s to a low of some 23 quintals in the late 1880s, after which there was a modest recovery.[7] We know little about trends in man-hours among fishermen and the growth of employed capital, and it is therefore difficult to be certain about changes in labour and total factor productivity. But contemporaries were convinced that the traditional fishing economy had reached a limit to extensive growth.

The size of national income produced by this traditional economy is impossible to estimate precisely. In 1884 the value of all exports was $6.6 million and almost all of this was accounted for by fish products – notably salt codfish and oil, while the remainder consisted of mineral and other primary product shipments.[8] Primary employment (the export sector) accounted for 87 per cent of the labour force, the secondary sector some 10 per cent and the service sector some 3 per cent.[9] If we assume that the value of output in the secondary and tertiary sectors was a proportional fraction of their labour forces to the *realized* output of the primary sector, then the realized national income would be around $7.5 million.[10] There was a great deal of production in rural Newfoundland, however, that did not move through markets. In the late 1930s it was estimated that income in kind amounted to some 55 per cent of the value of fish exports.[11] If the same proportion of non-market income was produced in 1884, then this would add some $4.1 million to the realized national income, for a total national income of some $11.6 million and a per capita income of around $60. Probably this is a low estimate. If realized income accounted for, say, only around half of a *fishing family*'s total income, then the output of factors in the secondary and tertiary sectors should be at least doubled (otherwise there would have been migration from the urban to rural sector), yielding a realized national income of $8.4 million and a total national income of around $12.5 million. Even this figure may underestimate the national income, for despite the strains of the depression period, impressionistic evidence suggests the economy was less oriented to markets in the nineteenth century than during the 1930s. At the later date a smaller fraction of the labour force was geographically and occupationally situated to generate income in kind and consumption patterns were by then more oriented through taste and availability of cash towards marketed foodstuffs and manufactures. Thus as an 'outside' estimate, if we impute an income in kind at least equal in value to that of primary exports, then the estimate of national income rises to around $15 million with income per capita of $75.[12]

Even if this high estimate is accepted, then it is clear that Newfoundland's traditional economy was by no means an affluent component of the North Atlantic world. Comparisons are fraught with dangers, but as a rough indicator, it can be noted that Canada's per capita national income in 1880 (without adjustment for income in kind) was around $135.[13] It is probably true that with a more sophisticated and market oriented economy, the burden of capital depreciation and taxation on personal incomes was higher in Canada than in Newfoundland at this time; nonetheless the gap in average material well-being must have been substantial.

Newfoundland's traditional economy underwent a crisis in the late 1880s and 1890s. Export prices for salt codfish sank from $3.82 a quintal in 1880/4 to $2.89 in 1895/9 – a collapse of around 32 per cent. Production volumes also fell from about 1.5 million quintals in 1880/4 to some 1.2 million in 1895/9 – a 20 per cent decline. Accordingly, industry gross earnings sagged from $5.6 million to $3.6 million – a decline of 36 per cent.[14] But the impact on the real level of national income and per capita consumption was probably less severe than these figures suggest. Table 3 represents a rough indicator of Newfoundland's terms of trade up to the end of World War I for the fishing sector. It suggests that the terms of trade actually moved in Newfoundland's favour in the two quinquennia 1884–94 relative to the 1870s and first half of the 1880s, although there was a sharp deterioration during 1895–9. But the point remains that employment levels reached in 1884 could not be maintained, quite apart from the additional burden of absorbing into the traditional economy increments from natural increase. The male labour force engaged in catching and curing fish fell back from an historic peak of 60,000 in 1884 to just under 37,000 in 1891. Employment inched up again during the prosperous first decade of this century and reached almost 44,000 in 1911; but then it began a slow decline to some 35,000 in 1935.[15]

The sharp decline in employment in the traditional economy after 1884, and its relative stability during the first half of this century, was achieved in part through the absorption of labour into other sectors; but a major contribution also came through slower rates of growth of population and labour force. Whereas in 1874–84 population grew at a rate of 2.1 per cent per annum, it was close to stationary in 1885–91 at 0.3 per cent and remained below 1 per cent per annum until World War II[16] Deceleration of population growth was not principally a function of changes in fertility or mortality. The crude birth rate was around 30 per thousand in 1884, 33 in 1891, and 35 in 1901. The crude death rate, which was 14 per thousand in 1884, rose to 22 in 1891 and fell back to 15 in 1901.[17] Throughout

TABLE 3
Terms of trade for the traditional economy

Period	Index of salt cod prices 1913 = 100	UK merchandise export index 1913 = 100	Terms of trade with UK exports/imports	Canadian export price index 1913 = 100	Terms of trade with Canada exports/imports	USA merchandise export index 1913 = 100	Terms of trade with USA exports/imports	Country share in Newfoundland imports %			All-country weighted index of terms of trade
								UK	Canada	USA	
1870–74[a]	69	130	53	78	88	n/a	n/a	40	30	30	67
1875–79[a]	68	110	62	83	82	n/a	n/a	40	30	30	70
1880–84	67	99	68	84	80	102	66	40	30	30	71
1885–89	65	87	75	81	80	88	74	39	36	35	77
1890–94	63	87	72	84	75	81	78	35	41	24	75
1895–99	51	80	64	78	65	71	72	33	35	32	67
1900–04	74	81	91	86	86	83	89	29	38	33	88
1905–09	n/a	91	n/a	96	n/a	91	n/a	25	37	38	n/a
1910–14	100	96	104	100	100	98	102	26	35	39	102
1915–19[b]	165	n/a	n/a	180	92	168	98	11	42	47	96
1920–24[c]	153	236	65	178	86	117	131	24	44	33	97
1925–29	148	164	90	158	94	138	107	23	44	33	97
1930–34	104	130	80	106	98	97	107	20	44	36	98
1935–39	82	135	61	117	70	113	73	26	40	34	69
1940–44[d]	172	n/a	n/a	142	121	250	69	7	60	33	100
1945–49[e]	281	300	94	222	127	252	112	5	60	35	120

[a] Calculated with 1881–85 distribution of trade between the three trading partners, and with the USA the 1880–84 terms of trade

[b] Calculated with 1910–14 terms of trade with the UK

[c] Calculated with 1923–24 only as weights

[d] Calculated with 1935–39 UK terms of trade

[e] Calculated with 1945–48 only as weights

SOURCES: *Historical Statistics of Newfoundland*, table κ-7; DBS *Newfoundland, Statistical Background*, table 98: *Historical Statistics of Canada*, series 184-95 and J108-17; *Historical Statistics of the United States*, series U21-44; Mitchell, *Abstract of British Historical Statistics*, ch. 11, table 15

the 1920s and 1930s the crude birth rate was above 20 per thousand – in the high twenties during the relatively prosperous 1920s and the low twenties during the depression – while the crude death rate fluctuated around 12 per thousand.[18] It follows that population and labour force growth could only have been held down by substantial net emigration. Trends in net migration can be estimated by noting population levels at census periods and imputing what the population would have been with no migration at the estimated rate of natural increase. By this method, net immigration at an annual average of less than 1,000 prevailed between 1869 and 1884. But from 1884 to 1935 a large flow of emigrants began. Between 1884 and 1901 it probably ranged between 1,500 to 2,500 per year, and from 1901 to 1945 between 1,000 to 1,500 per year.[19]

It is clear that the 1880s is an important benchmark in Newfoundland's economic history. The traditional economy reached a limit to its extensive growth and further development was perceived as a function of the emergence of modern resource industries, with emigration acting as a mechanism to balance a labour force growing faster than employment opportunities. Since the acquisition of responsible government in 1855, the ever pressing task which confronted ministries was to raise market incomes in the traditional sector and to substitute domestic job creation for the humiliating, costly, and enervating mechanism of emigration. Indeed, during the decades when the traditional economy was approaching its maximum extensive growth, government had begun to search for a development strategy which would reduce the rate of inshore fishery expansion and initiate its relative decline. The most famous statement of this goal was the report of the committee headed by William Whiteway,[20] which declared that 'no material increase of means is to be looked for from our fisheries, and ... we must direct our attention to the growing requirements of the country.'[21] The strategy the committee proposed contained the essential features of the national development policy pursued by all nineteenth-century territories of European settlement.[22] Through railway technology the country would be shaken free from dependence upon coastal resources, and a moving frontier of inland settlement would open export sectors in agriculture and minerals – resources whose existence in Newfoundland was confirmed by geological survey. There was also a hint in the committee's report that St John's would provide a market for country products, and, presumably with the growth of the latter, would emerge as a centre of domestic manufacturing. At one stroke, a blow was dealt to the one-product export economy and the income leakages resulting from high foreign trade dependence. In general, Newfoundland's economic problem was seen not as an actual or approaching overabundance of labour relative to resources, but of labour relative to resources currently being exploited.

In the latter part of the nineteenth century this strategy was pursued with a legislative ferocity which took second place to no developing country. In 1873 a Homestead Law was passed to encourage 'Agriculture and the more speedy settlement of the Wilderness' and the Companies Corporation Act provided the legal framework for establishing limited liability companies in manufacturing, mining and commerce. In 1875 a system of bounties was introduced to speed up land clearance and cultivation. Two years later there was an 'Act for the Encouragement of Manufacturing' providing subsidies on imports of flax, cotton, and wool used in fishing gear and textiles. An act of 1880 offered large blocks of land to licensees who would settle farming families. In the same year the receiver general was authorized to issue debentures for construction of a railway from St John's to Notre Dame Bay, and in the next year the first railway contract was brought down for a line to Halls Bay with branches to Conception Bay. The 1880 session also introduced one of many bounty schemes to encourage ship-building for the bank fishery, and legislation was passed in 1882 providing assistance to New York promoters to establish the Newfoundland Dock Company – the railway and drydock being the two great infrastructure investments of the late nineteenth century.[23]

The 1882 session included a flight of fancy, in legislation for the 'Great American and European Short Line Railway.' It provided the promoters with incentives to build a southern line from St John's to the southwest coast, there to link up by steamer with railways to be built or running rights to be acquired, through eastern Canada and the United States – a scheme perhaps no more ridiculous in its historical context than the Canadian dream of an imperial transportation link between Europe and the Orient. In any case, it was an early manifestation of Newfoundland's continuing fascination with its supposed locational advantages in the North Atlantic. In 1884 an act closely modeled on Canadian legislation provided for the survey of Newfoundland into townships, sections, and quartersections, with a further development of homesteading, mining, and forestry law. This was followed two years later by an 'Act for the Promotion of Agriculture' which established agricultural districts under the direction of a superintendent and staff to direct settlement, road building and other public works as well as the promotion of scientific agriculture. In 1889 these measures were supplemented by the establishment of a Board of Agriculture to supervise local agriculture societies, and found a model farm to introduce improved stock, seeds, and farm equipment.[24] In 1896 the trans-insular railway was completed, but the decade saw the projection of fresh schemes, including a line from the Canadian border to the Labrador coast.

Throughout the late nineteenth century the St John's newspapers followed the progress of secondary manufacturing, giving close attention to technical accomplishments, the level of employment, and the likelihood of staunching imports.

Gaden's Ginger Ale Factory was applauded for beating out imported mineral waters. The carriage factory of Messrs W.R. Oke and Sons was hailed for developing a wooden tricycle for the French consul which could be marketed at a quarter the cost of steel models. Archibald's Tobacco Works, employing some 120 people, produced a Newfoundland plug tobacco. Stained glass, with designs in a national idiom, was made by the Newfoundland Glass Embossing Company. Newfoundland fruit was bottled in a new factory on Mundy Pond Road and samples were sent to the queen with the hope of acquiring a royal appointment. Boots and shoes were turned out in a plant at Riverhead in St John's employing close to 150 people, and since its work could 'compare more than favourable with work turned out in any part of the world' it was anticipated that imports would be reduced.[25] The seriousness with which manufacturing development was viewed was symbolized by a government decision in 1891 to fund an industrial exhibition at St John's 'for the encouragement of the national and mechanical products of this colony.'[26]

Like Canada's National Policy, Newfoundland's first development strategy envisioned a moving frontier of agricultural settlement (facilitated by investments in inland transportation) linked to an initially protected and subsidized industrial sector. The results were disappointing. Improved acreage doubled from 36,000 acres in 1874 to 86,000 in 1901, but on a per capita basis this meant a growth from only 0.28 acres to 0.32.[27] Similarly, there was modest growth in the livestock population – from 90,000 cows and cattle to 148,000, and from 180,000 sheep to 350,000 – but the country had hardly made a dent in its domestic import bill and certainly had not emerged as one of the world's frontiers of agricultural investment.[28] In the industrial sector the value of factory output per capita grew from only $10 in 1884 to $12 in 1901 and $14 in 1911.[29] It is, accordingly, a reasonable conclusion that agriculture and secondary manufacturing developments brought no important shifts in the composition of output. Nonetheless, the structure of employment in the country was significantly different in 1911 compared with 1884, as shown in table 4. Between these dates almost 30 per cent of the labour force – a growing labour force – was shifted out of fishing and into other occupations. Over half of this 30 per cent represented small gains to defined primary, secondary, and service occupations, while the other 13 per cent was accounted for by the census aggregate 'others.' This category likely included workers in a variety of personal service occupations, although the sharp increase in the category between 1884 and 1891 suggests another analysis which supports its allocation to secondary employment. Between 1884 and 1891 railway construction and a number of urban service projects got underway, and the upswing in the category 'others' probably reflects the emergence of a large labour force in transportation, communications, public utilities, and construction. If this is so,

TABLE 4
Distribution of the labour force 1857–1935

	1858	1869	1874	1884	1891	1901	1911	1921	1935
Labour force	43,251	47,024	53,309	73,796	56,984	67,368	82,426	80,327	88,710
Primary	94%	90%	89%	87%	70%	69%	63%	59%	55%
Agriculture	4	4	2	2	3	4	4	4	5
Fishing	89	84	86	82	64	61	53	51	⎱ 48
Lumbering	1	1	1	2	1	2	3	3	⎰
Mining	–	1	–	0.5	2	2	2	1	2
Secondary	5	9	10	10	22	23	27	28	24
Mechanics	5	4	4	5	5	5	7	6	7
Factory workers	–	–	–	–	2	1	2	2	–
Others	–	5	6	5	15	17	18	20	17
Service	1.9	1.6	1.5	3.8	7.9	8	11	12	22
Professional	0.3	0.4	0.4	0.4	2	2	2	2.6	3.6
Merchants	1.6	1.3	1.1	1.2	1.4	1.5	1.6	1.3	⎱ 8.7
Clerical	–	–	–	2.2	3.4	3.5	5.6	6.2	⎰
Government	–	–	–	–	–	–	–	–	7.3

SOURCE: *Tenth Census of Newfoundland and Labrador*, 1935, pt 1, vol. 2
NOTE: A 'modern' occupational classification was introduced in the 1935 census which renders comparisons with previous years difficult. The category 'others' for 1935 includes employees in electric power, construction, transportation, and unspecified areas. Prior to 1935 employees in personal service were enumerated under 'others' insofar as they were recorded at all. The error would hence inflate secondary employment and deflate service employment in earlier years relative to 1935.

then a large share of employment diversification in this period was secured by a flow of public, and largely foreign private funds, into capital projects. Indeed it was two of the largest of these investments – the Bell Island iron mine and the Harmsworth newsprint plant at Grand Falls – which accounted for the decline in fish products as a percentage of exports (despite rising values from 1900) from over 90 per cent in the 1880s to less than 70 per cent by the opening of the war.

It is very probable that gross domestic product grew substantially in real terms between the mid-1880s and 1911. But the gains to gross national product and to personal incomes would be less dramatic; for both the railway, the new resource industries, and the expanding urban services must have increased the gross investment ratio and introduced for the first time into the Newfoundland economy substantial payments abroad for technology, capital, and entrepreneurship.

The assumptions guiding Newfoundland's first development strategy were akin to those shaping the nineteenth-century territories of settlement. The weight of development was to be assumed by Newfoundlanders – native born and immigrants – accumulating capital and absorbing modern technology through the formation and expansion of small agricultural and industrial enterprises. Their efforts would be complemented by footloose entrepreneurs who, with government backing, would tackle large and complex capital investments. These assumptions began to give way by the beginning of the twentieth century. It is true that interest in native Newfoundland enterprise remained strong in the St John's newspapers. For example, in 1912 excitement built up over the prospect of a rubber goods factory employing 'all local capital,' but it was abandoned when it was found that 'the smallest plant which could be established ... would produce enough stock in about four to five weeks to accommodate the demand.'[30] It was also suggested at various times that factory hands should boycott merchants who carried imported lines when local products were available.[31] But the bulk of development legislation from the turn of the century was devoted not to the stimulation of local enterprise, but to a search for foreign direct investment firms to develop modern resource industries through a package of advanced management and technology.

The reasons for this shift are clear. The original development strategy had failed. The high cost of land clearance and fertilization of an acidic soil made the land marginal to Newfoundlanders and the European migrants who flooded into the prairie lands of Australia and South and North America. With manufacturing, the size of the domestic market doomed firms to suboptimal scale, and the absence of an industrial tradition in the country among capitalists and workers made it unlikely that Newfoundland firms would overcome the difficulties of entering foreign markets to achieve optimum scale. The remaining avenue to development was primary manufacturing industries, where possession of a scarce natural resource provided cost advantages for entry into international markets. Unlike the fishing industry, however, the minimum size of the firm in modern resource-based manufacturing was large, and Newfoundland, with its tiny national income, had neither the savings, the entrepreneurs, nor the skilled workers to launch and control such developments.

The resulting wedding between Newfoundland and the international corporation can be traced back to the nineteenth-century contracts for railways, the drydock, and the Bell Island mines. But the volume of such contracts accelerated with the successful Anglo-Newfoundland Development Company agreement in 1905 for a paper-mill at Grand Falls. In the following year the Marconi Company was given a monopoly over telegraphy in return for a commitment to improve the island's communications. In 1910 the 'Coal Development Act' provided the Newfoundland Exploration Syndicate with tariff guarantees on coal imports if the company established a commercial mine. A similar inducement was given in 1910 to the Newfoundland Oil Fields Limited of London. In 1911 the British-Canadian Explosives Company, also of London, was offered protection to establish a manufacturing plant of sufficient capacity at least to supply local demand. In the same year an agreement was reached with the International Carbonizing Company to manufacture peat fuel, and two Maine promoters were offered various inducements to build five cold storage plants for fish products. In the next year the American-Newfoundland Pulp and Paper Company of Grand Rapids, Michigan, entered into an agreement for a pulp- and paper-mill at Deer Lake. In 1913 the Orr Newfoundland Company was empowered to construct five reduction plants to manufacture glue and fertilizer from dogfish, while the Canadian North Atlantic Corporation revived an old vision of a railway from Quebec City to the Labrador coast.[32]

The war years slowed down but did not staunch the flood of industrial promotions. In 1915 the Newfoundland-American Packing Company received concessions for cold storage facilities to pack freshwater fish, fruits, and berries, and the Newfoundland Products Corporation was launched to manufacture fertilizers on the Humber. In the first year of peace the St George's Coal Fields Company revived the prospect of domestic coal supplies. In 1920 the St Lawrence Timber, Pulp and Steamship Company offered prospects for the development of pulp mills on Bonne Bay, while the Terra Nova Sulphite Company was planning a similar facility at Alexander Bay. In 1921 the D'Arcy Exploration Company was granted leases for oil exploration, while the Pulp and Paper Corporation of America proposed mills in Labrador – probably only to acquire rights to export pulpwood and pit-props. In 1923 an agreement with the Newfoundland Power and Paper Corporation resulted in the mill at Corner Brook – one concrete success. In 1924 the Newfoundland Milling Company was founded to mill cereals with a guarantee of a twenty-year monopoly and tariff protection. In 1929 the Newfoundland Mines and Smelters Limited was granted concessions over a large part of the Avalon to mine and process lead, copper, zinc, and other ores. In 1930 one of the most imaginative – and enduring – schemes was launched by the Great Lakes-Atlantic Newfoundland Company for a transshipment port at Mortier Bay. In the last years, as the edifice of responsible government slipped away, the Terra Nova Oils Company was granted privileges to distil for export.[33]

Each of the agreements had common threads. Any provision for Newfoundland equity participation, either public or private, was absent. The Newfoundland government provided concessions in the form of crown land grants, drawbacks on duties on new construction materials, machinery, and raw materials, tax holidays, and where applicable, the promise of protective tariffs. In return for these privileges, the companies promised to employ Newfoundland labour wherever possible and to invest certain minimum amounts over specified time periods – a guarantee which was commonly extended for further grace periods by amending legislation. But for all the hopes and efforts embodied in these agreements, few resulted in any investment and still fewer in any permanent additions to the country's productive capacity.

In contrast to the late nineteenth century, legislation involving Newfoundland entrepreneurship was remarkably scarce and, with two exceptions, unoriginal. In 1908 the Model Farm Act provided for an agricultural experimental station to undertake original and applied research. In 1917 the Newfoundland Knitting Mills and the Riverside Woolen Mills, both apparently Newfoundland firms, were given relief from import duties on machinery and raw materials and a limited subsidy for fifteen years. In 1928 a Harbour Grace merchant was given a three-year monopoly to establish a shark oil industry – a trade perhaps better fitted to some of the foreign concessionaires. A more promising direction was offered in the Tourist Commission Act of 1927 which established a public corporation drawing revenues from a tax on hotels, steamships, and similar enterprises to promote a tourist traffic and a 'wider knowledge of the colony's natural resources.' Undoubtedly the most important legislation in these years seeking to upgrade the efficiency and returns to Newfoundland enterprise was the two acts which made up the Coaker Regulations.[34] The acts established national quality controls in the production of saltfish and an organized approach in the markets for all Newfoundland output. Regrettably, the regulations foundered on divisions within the trade and were repealed in the following year.[35] It was not until the economic collapse of the 1930s, when prospects of attracting foreign capital for resource development dried up, that attention to fishery legislation revived. In the interval Newfoundland's position as the world's largest exporter of salt cod weakened in the face of a growing competitiveness in Scandinavia and the development of national fishing fleets in traditional importing countries.[36]

'No colony of the British Empire,' it was stated in 1910, 'has made such progress in recent years as has Newfoundland.' It was 'one of the most progressive states in the Western hemisphere' and 'no people in the world maintain a more comfortable and contented existence than the Newfoundland fishermen ...'[37] Twenty years later, on the eve of Newfoundland's economic and political collapse, Joseph Smallwood wrote at length of the country as a budding industrial Michigan set down in a North Atlantic Arcadia.[38] But the structural transformation, so often planned, predicted, and seen, had not in fact arrived. Between 1911 and 1935 Newfoundland's population grew from 243,000 to 290,000, an annual rate of 0.8 per cent as compared with about 1.7 per cent in Canada. As a consequence of emigration, the labour force grew more slowly than population at an annual rate of 0.3 per cent whereas in Canada it grew faster than population at slightly over 1.8 per cent.[39] In other words, the demographic trends were not those of a country which had surmounted a development hump into modern economic growth.

The foreign trade statistics appeared, superficially, to indicate considerable growth and diversification. Exports and re-exports grew from $11.7 million in 1906/10 to a peak of $40.0 million in 1929/30, or from about $50 per capita to around $135, while fishery products fell from some 80 per cent to 40 per cent of total exports.[40] Indeed, per capita exports from Newfoundland were higher than in Canada, which stood at $40 in 1911 and $115 in 1929. But given the small volume of domestic production for home consumption, Newfoundland needed very high levels of exports per capita to emulate the North American pattern of consumption which, as Smallwood noted, was increasingly emulated and desired.[41] Moreover, the gains to levels of consumption from rising per capita exports could not have been very great since, as table 3 suggests, the export price indices of countries from which Newfoundland drew most of her imports rose by 40 to 60 per cent between the immediate pre-war years and the second half of the 1920s. Secondly, duties as a percentage of imports rose from around 20 per cent to 28 per cent over the period,[42] and expenditures for servicing foreign debt rose from 20 per cent of revenue in 1919–20 to 35 per cent in 1929–30.[43] Thirdly, the per capita value of exports in pre-war Newfoundland reflected much more realistically returns for consumption to factors of production in Newfoundland than was the case by the late 1920s. The new resource industries in mining and forest products, which accounted for over 55 per cent of the value of exports in 1929–30, required substantial payments out of the gross value of sales for capital depreciation, payments to foreign suppliers of intermediate inputs and non-resident management and ownership. For the same reason, the apparent diversification of the economy is misleading. Newfoundland had progressed from a domestically owned one-product export economy to a substantially foreign owned three-product export economy, for in 1929–30 some 98 per cent of exports were accounted for by fish, forest, and mineral products.

Diversification of output for the export economy had no dramatic impact on the distribution of the labour force. In table 4 the apparently strong growth in service employment and the decline in secondary shares between 1911 and 1935 is largely a statistical illusion arising either from a failure to enumerate personal service before 1935, or its allocation to 'others' in earlier periods. The table suggests a continuation of long-run trends rather than sharp discontinuities. Relative to the labour force, primary employment was declining, service employment was increasing, but secondary employment was stabilizing at around 20 to 25 per cent of labour force. This was the share reached in the 1890s when the modern transportation, communications, and construction labour force began to emerge. Fishing and lumbering in 1935 continued to employ almost half the labour force, while factory and shop employment, despite the paper-mills and electrical power stations, still employed only about 7 per cent, while all occupations in the service sector showed small relative gains. The modern resource industries attracted to Newfoundland since the turn of the century had had a much greater impact on the composition of domestic product than on the structure of the labour force. The *trends* in labour's sectoral allocation were the same as those affecting other countries in the western world,[44] but the strength of demand for labour in Newfoundland's non-primary sectors and the growth of labour productivity in the primary sector had generated a much slower pace of transition than elsewhere. Thus, while the employment trends were toward the 'modern' allocation, at each date the secondary sector and, to a lesser degree, the service sector were more weakly developed.

Table 5 compares the sectoral allocation of employment with distribution of earnings in 1935 and gives the resulting sectoral average per capita earnings. The table is misleading as to the share in earnings of the fishing industry in 'normal' times, since the price collapse of fish products was more severe than in other export industries. Still, even if the export value of fish products for 1928/9 (some $16 million) is allocated entirely to labour income in Newfoundland and no adjustment is made for depressed earnings in other sectors – obviously a gross bias in favour of the fishing industry in normal times – the sector would have received only about 45 per cent of earnings, and per capita earnings would have stood at around $350. It is more likely that in good years some 35 to 40 per cent of earnings went to this sector which, according to the 1935 census, directly and indirectly employed and supported some 40 per cent of the population. It is true that fishermen had to outfit themselves from earnings, but it is also the case that non-market income was more available to the rural than the urban labour force. The best guess is that in normal times standards of living for the mass of workers in the fishing sector did not differ sharply from those for the mass of workers in other sectors of the economy. If this is so, then the reason for the small absolute decline of the fishing labour force in the first half of the twentieth century is not simply a function of employment potential

34 Alexander

TABLE 5
Occupations and earnings in Newfoundland 1935

	% total employment	% total earnings	Per capita earnings
All industries	(88.710)	($24,952,700)	($280)
Forestry, fishing, trapping	48%	24%	$ 140
Services	15	19	350
Professional (male)	1.3	5.4	830
Public administration (male)	2.3	6	750
Personal service (female)	6.5	2	60
Unspecified	8	4	140
Trade	7	16	640
Manufacturing	7	14	610
Transportation and communication	5	10	500
Agriculture	5	4	155
Construction	3	4	350
Mining	2	4	500
Electric power	0 (0.3)	1	1,100
Finance	0 (0.2)	1	1,350

SOURCE: Calculated from *Tenth Census of Newfoundland and Labrador*, 1935
NOTE: All calculations are rounded in the major breakdowns to the nearest 1%

in other sectors. The critical fact is that the economy as a whole could not provide sufficient employment for the growing population and potential labour force, necessitating emigration from *both* urban and rural sectors. With stronger growth in secondary and tertiary sectors the level of emigration would have fallen, but it would have required a massive boom in demand for secondary and service output and a correspondingly sharp rise in per capita earnings in those sectors to have attracted large amounts of labour out of the primary sector.

The Newfoundland government struggled with the prospect of bankruptcy during the early years of the depression, and finally surrendered independence and dominion status early in 1934. The commission appointed from Britain a year earlier to review the causes of impending collapse attributed it largely to the irresponsibility of politicians in the management of public funds.[45] But from its own evidence it is difficult to make the case that there was a riot of spending. Revenues grew steadily from $8.4 million in 1920/21 to $11.6 million in 1929/30, but current expenditures actually declined from $8.9 million to $7.2 million and in every year between were under $7 million.[46] It is true that the budget was in surplus only in 1924/5, whereas it was in surplus in every year after 1922 in Canada; but the great development expenditures of the Canadian government were over by the 1920s, whereas in the twenty-eight years between 1885 and 1913 the

Canadian budget had been in deficit in all but six of those years.[47] In 1933 the per capita public debt in Newfoundland stood at around $344 compared with $540 for all levels of government in Canada,[48] which given relative income levels implied a heavier burden in Newfoundland.[49] Analysis of the Newfoundland public debt in 1933 shows that 35 per cent was attributable to development of the railway; 60 per cent was accounted for by the railway and other development expenditures on fisheries, agriculture, schools, roads, urban development, and similar accounts; that over 70 per cent was chargeable to these and the war debt; and finally that the lion's share of borrowings made to cover budget deficits was in order to keep the railway operating.[50]

Whatever the peccadillos of its politicians, Newfoundland's collapse was not the result of corruption or even unwise, as distinct from unfruitful, spending of public funds. With the grant of responsible government, Newfoundland had set out to replicate the economic performance of its continental neighbours. The levels and patterns of North American consumption were the goal, and it is not surprising that development strategies to achieve it were imported as well. From hindsight, some of the reasons for failure are apparent. The matter of scale was crucial, for it was only by the output of massive volumes of several primary products and the simultaneous enlargement of domestic markets that servicing of development expenditures could be covered, a measure of isolation from the swings of international prices secured, and dependence upon external capital markets reduced. Newfoundland was unfortunate. The economy was too narrowly based to benefit from war demand in 1914–18 and at best only a small commodity trade surplus was achieved. Moreover, unlike Canada, Newfoundland had to finance much of her war effort by borrowing in London and New York. The economy emerged from the war without a sharply diversified structure or increased capacity, with a casualty-ridden labour force, and an increased external debt.

In the 1920s weak primary product prices offered no relief, and unlike Canada the country could not escape from the treadmill of external borrowing to service existing debt and to seek the elusive breakthrough into modern economic growth and structure. Hence the country was extremely vulnerable in the face of the international economic crisis which was steadily building throughout the 1920s. Newfoundland's export earnings dropped by 22 per cent in 1930/1–1934/5 over their level in 1925/6–1929/30 – a rather modest decline compared with the almost 50 per cent collapse in Canada's foreign earnings in 1931–5 over 1925–9.[51] But the smaller percentage decline had a much greater impact on Newfoundland since a larger share of national income was derived from foreign trade, the fishing industry (which was the most important in terms of payment to resident factors) was most severely hit, and government revenues, out of which payments on development capital had to be met, were almost entirely derived from customs.

Emulation of the style of life and the development strategies by which the new continental countries had achieved it resulted in ruin for Smallwood's 'New Newfoundland.' For the impatient public servants of the 1933 royal commission, it was a case of a 'people misled into the acceptance of false standards' and a 'country sunk in waste and extravagance.'[52] A blunter conclusion was reached in the 1940s by MacKay and Saunders: 'the Newfoundland economy cannot, in normal times, provide the revenue required to supply the Island with the public services demanded by a Western people.'[53] In short, Newfoundland was not a fit place for white men, or at least very many of them.

E.H. Carr has suggested that history rarely repeats itself because man is conscious of the past.[54] But in Newfoundland the past has not been well understood and the range of choice has been severely restricted. After the 1934 collapse succeeding decades have brought a repetition of earlier development cycles. During commission government in the 1930s and 1940s, attention reverted to improving the efficiency and expanding the capacity of indigenous enterprise; in the 1950s and 1960s, as a province of Canada, there was a further round on 'infrastructure' investment and strenuous efforts to woo international capital and corporations. In the 1970s the province confronted the highest per capita debt and burden of taxation and the lowest credit rating in Canada. Almost half of provincial revenues are transfers from the federal government, and consumer expenditure and private investment is heavily supported by direct and indirect federal expenditures and transfers. The level of unemployment hovers around 20 per cent of a labour force with a low participation rate, and many of the province's hard-won industrial projects, such as the electric reduction plant, the linerboard mill and the oil refinery, are either heavily subsidized or operating at a loss. The Labrador mineral and hydro-electric projects have not generated major returns to the province and their prospect for further expansion is now dim. On the island and coastal Labrador a large rural population remains, reluctant to move to the mainland, and dependent upon the tattered remnants of a once great fishing industry wrecked by unfavourable trends in the international economy and hopelessly ineffective national trade and fisheries policies.[55] As Newfoundlanders once hoped that paper and mining companies would finally bring prosperity, they now await the discoveries of international oil companies on the Labrador coast.

If there are lessons from the past, however, they suggest that the province's natural potential lies on the sea, not the land, and that international resource corporations will not effect the economic transformation so long awaited. It might be wiser for Newfoundland to define and accept more modest goals and expectations, or perhaps more accurately, different ones. The development which a country achieves is not simply a quantitative measure of real output, but a qualitative valuation of the levels and patterns of consumption secured with that output, and its mental independence from valuations made by other influential countries. A tropical island will be poor no matter how much fish, fruit, sunshine, and leisure its economy can provide, if its people want, or are persuaded to want, cars and apartment towers. It is possible Newfoundland could develop a more prosperous economy and more self-confident society if its people adjusted to a pattern of consumption somewhat different from that of the mainland, and its labour and capital were more effectively linked to its obvious natural endowment.

NOTES

1 See C.H. Fei and Gustav Ranis, 'Economic Development in Historical Perspective,' *American Economic Review* 59 (1969): 386–400.
2 On this point see Keith Matthews, 'A History of the West of England–Newfoundland Fishery' (unpublished D PHIL thesis, Oxford 1968).
3 Calculated from figures in Shannon Ryan, 'Collection of CO 194 Statistics' (unpublished manuscript, Centre for Newfoundland Studies, Memorial University, 1970).
4 Calculated from Government of Newfoundland, *Historical Statistics of Newfoundland and Labrador* (St John's 1970), vol. 1, table K-7.
5 Calculated from Department of Commerce, *Historical Statistics of the United States* (Washington 1962), series E1–12; and B.R. Mitchell and P. Deane (eds.), *Abstract of British Historical Statistics* (Cambridge 1962), ch. 11, table 15. It is a reasonable assumption that wholesale prices for Canadian farm products, which Newfoundland bought, moved in directions similar to the American.
6 *Tenth Census of Newfoundland and Labrador*, 1935, pt 1, vol. 2, 87.
7 Calculated from ibid.
8 Parzival Copes, 'Role of the Fishing Industry in the Economic Development of New-foundland' (unpublished manuscript, Centre for Newfoundland Studies 1970), table 3.
9 Calculated from *Tenth Census of Newfoundland*.
10 By 'realized' output is meant that fraction which enters into markets. For estimates of 'National Cash Income' in this period see Steven D. Antler, 'Colonialism as a Factor in the Economic Stagnation of Nineteenth Century Newfoundland: Some Preliminary Notes' (unpublished manuscript, Centre for Newfoundland Studies 1973), table 3.
11 R.A. MacKay (ed.), *Newfoundland: Economic, Diplomatic and Strategic Studies* (Toronto 1946), appendix B.
12 More accurately, this is an estimate of total domestic income as no allowance has been made for depreciation and the balance of net property income from abroad.
13 Calculated from M.C. Urquhart and K.A.H. Buckley (eds.), *Historical Statistics of Canada* (Toronto 1965), series E2.4-244.
14 Calculated from *Historical Statistics of Newfoundland*, table K-7.
15 Calculated from *Tenth Census of Newfoundland*.

16 *Historical Statistics of Newfoundland*, table A-1.

17 Calculated from *Census of Newfoundland*, 1901, table J, 17. The sharp increase in the death rate in 1891 may represent an unusual year or a weakness in the census.

18 Dominion Bureau of Statistics (hereafter DBS), *Province of Newfoundland, Statistical Background* (Ottawa 1949), tables 21, 22.

19 Sources for these estimates are the *Census of Newfoundland*, 1901, 1911, and 1935; and DBS, *Newfoundland, Statistical Background*, table 23. Michael Staveley, 'Migration and Mobility in Newfoundland and Labrador: A Study in Population Geography' (unpublished PH D thesis, University of Alberta 1973), 71, also concludes that a flood of emigration began around 1884.

20 William Whiteway, born Devon, 1828; lawyer and politican; entered politics as a Conservative in 1859; premier, 1878–85, 1889–94, 1895–7; died St John's, 1908.

21 'Report of the Select Committee to Consider and Report upon the Construction of a Railway,' *JHA*, 1880, 126.

22 For a discussion of this point see A.J. Youngson, 'The Opening up of New Territories,' *Cambridge Economic History* (Cambridge 1966), vol. 6, pt I, ch. 3.

23 For the statutes embodying these provisions see *Statutes of Newfoundland*, 36 Vict., c.7, c.8; 38 Vict., c.18; 40 Vict., c.10; 43 Vict., c.3. c.4; 44 Vict., c.2; 43 Vict., c.5; and 45 Vict., c.3.

24 See ibid., 45 Vict., c.4; 47 Vict., c.2; 49 Vict., c.3; and 52 Vict., c.8.

25 I am grateful to Mrs B. Robertson of the Newfoundland Historical Society for drawing my attention to these references. See *Daily Colonist* (St John's), 1 April, 13 Sept. 1886; 9 July 1887; 8 Oct. 1888; 4 June 1889.

26 54 Vict., c.10.

27 Calculated from *Census of Newfoundland*, 1911, vol. 1, table 21.

28 Ibid., table 22.

29 Ibid., table 23. Some large firms, however, did not report, such as Reid-Newfoundland, Angel Engineering, and A. Harvey.

30 *Daily News* (St John's), 16 Jan. 1912.

31 *Evening Telegram* (St John's), 9 July 1908.

32 See *Statutes of Newfoundland*, 5 Ed. VII, c.9, c.8; 10 Ed. VII, c.23, c.24; 1 Geo. V, c.11, c.20, c.22; 2 Geo. V, c.8, c.14.

33 Ibid., 6 Geo. V, c.3, c.4; 9 & 10 Geo. V, c.25; 11 Geo. V, c.2, c.6; 12 Geo. V, c.8, c.9; 14 Geo. V, c.1; 15 Geo. V, c.1; 20 Geo. V, c.12; 21 Geo. V, c.6; 22 Geo. V, c.5; 23 & 24 Geo. V, c.5.

34 Ibid., 8 Ed. VII, c.7; 8 Geo. V, c.1. c.2; 18 Geo. V, c.1; 11 Geo. V, c.25. c.27.

35 See Ian McDonald, 'Coaker the Reformer: A Brief Biographical Introduction,' in J.R. Smallwood (ed.), *The Book of Newfoundland*, vol. 6 (St John's 1975), 71–96.

36 See G.M. Gerhardsen and L.P.D. Gertenbach, *Salt Cod and Related Species* (Rome: Food and Agricultural Organization 1949).

37 'The Golden Age of Newfoundland's Advancement' (1910), 1, 8. Internal evidence suggests this to be a Harmsworth promotional pamphlet.

38 J.R. Smallwood, *The New Newfoundland* (New York 1931).

39 The Canadian rate is calculated for the employed population, 1911–31. The dependency ratio was not, however, remarkably different. Both countries had heavy child dependency ratios of 35 per cent in Newfoundland in 1935 and 31 percent in Canada for 1931. That the Newfoundland ratio was not more unfavourable may be attributable to the apparently higher infant mortality rate (see DBS, *Newfoundland, Statistical Background*, table 24) and differing marriage and fertility patterns. Whatever the explanation, the occupied labour force was 34 percent of the population in 1911 and only 30 per cent in 1935.

40 DBS, *Newfoundland, Statistical Background*, table 97.

41 Smallwood, *New Newfoundland*, 211.

42 DBS, *Newfoundland, Statistical Background*, table 97.

43 Dominions Office, Newfoundland Royal Commission, *Report*, 1933 (Cmd. 4480), 57, 63.

44 See Simon Kuznets, *Modern Economic Growth* (New Haven 1966), ch. 3.

45 1933 Commission *Report*, 43.

46 Ibid., 57, 63.

47 Calculated from *Historical Statistics of Canada*, series 621–4 and 626–44.

48 Calculated from 1933 Commission *Report*, 253; *Historical Statistics of Newfoundland*, table A-1, and *Historical Statistics of Canada*, series 696–710.

49 In Canada in 1933 debt charges of all governments as a percentage of revenues amounted to 40 per cent as compared with 63 per cent for Newfoundland in 1932–3. Calculated from *Historical Statistics of Canada*, series 662–82, 683–710, and 1933 Commission *Report*, 57, 63.

50 Calculated from 1933 Commission *Report*, 253.

51 Calculated from DBS, *Newfoundland, Statistical Background*, table 97, and *Historical Statistics of Canada*, series F242–5.

52 1933 Commission *Report*, 43.

53 MacKay, *Newfoundland*, 190.

54 *What is History?* (New York 1972), 84–9.

55 See David Alexander, *The Decay of Trade: An Economic History of the Newfoundland Saltfish Trade, 1935–1965* (St John's 1977), and below.

The Newfoundland Salt Cod Trade in the Nineteenth Century

SHANNON RYAN

At the beginning of the twentieth century the ancient maritime economy of Newfoundland was slowly being eroded by the forces of modernization and industrialization. One hundred years earlier, Newfoundland had been a 'fishing ship anchored on the Grand Banks' with a small, generally unwanted, resident population – fewer than 20,000 people in 1803 (see table 1). By 1901 the population had increased to over 220,000 and the annual migration of English fishermen to the Newfoundland coast had long since ceased. Thus, it was during the nineteenth century that Newfoundland outport society was formed. That society consisted of semi-independent, though often exploited, fishermen; it was served by English, Scottish, Jersey, and local importing-exporting firms. Outport people were almost totally dependent on the sea for their livelihood and the production of dried codfish was their main economic activity. The seal fishery, which utilized another resource, commenced at the beginning of the century, and the seal oil industry flourished during its middle decades but declined sharply after 1870 because of overharvesting.

The origins of what is referred to as 'traditional' in the present-day culture of Newfoundland can, for the most part, be traced to the way of life that developed in the nineteenth-century outports around these two great maritime pursuits. Since the beginning of the twentieth century urban centres have arisen based on mining, pulp and paper manufacturing, the establishment of American military bases, and the centralization programs of successive governments. St John's has expanded rapidly as a centre of commerce, higher education, and government. This 'new Newfoundland' has risen within the context of the traditional fishing economy. Accordingly, it can only be understood by first examining the history and legacy of that economy, particularly of its formative nineteenth-century period.

A version of this paper was presented at the 1973 annual meeting of the Canadian Historical Association.

TABLE 1
Population 1803–1901

Year	Number	Year	Number
1803	19,034	1845	96,295
1809	25,157	1857	124,288
1815	40,568	1869	146,536
1820	42,535	1874	161,374
1825	55,504	1884	197,335
1836	74,993	1891	202,040
		1901	220,249

SOURCES: Figures for 1803–25 are from Shannon
Ryan, 'Collection of CO 194 Statistics' (unpublished
paper, Centre for Newfoundland Studies, Memorial
University 1970); all others are from Newfoundland
census reports.
NOTE: Figures for 1857–1901 include Labrador.

THE COLLAPSE OF THE WEST COUNTRY FISHERY

At its inception the Newfoundland cod fishery had been migratory in nature,
carried on by mutually hostile groups of European fishermen. The English involvement centred on the West Country; from this region fishing ships and crews
journeyed to Newfoundland each spring and returned with their catch in the
autumn.[1] As stages, flakes, and other fishing facilities became more extensive,
caretakers were left behind to care for this property during the winter. These
people, together with the occasional deserter and the remnants of several colonization attempts, became the first permanent residents. Simultaneously, some
fishermen, known as bye-boat men, began the practice of leaving their boats in
Newfoundland and finding transportation for themselves and their crews to and
from the West Country on board fishing ships. By the early eighteenth century this
bye-boat fishery, the resident fishery, and the ship fishery from the West Country
were all well established, but the migrants still greatly outnumbered the residents.

During the eighteenth century the cod fishery and the various groups associated
with it experienced many ups and downs. The resident fishery flourished in war
time when the migratory fishermen were unable to travel across the Atlantic either
because of the dangers of the passage or because of impressment. Between 1710
and 1715, for example, the population of Newfoundland increased from about
2,400 to over 4,000; again, between 1750 and 1764 it rose from about 8,225 to
nearly 16,000. Post-war depressions, however, caused severe problems for residents and always brought about a halt in population growth, if not a decline. For

instance, the number of inhabitants declined betweeen 1715 and 1720 from over 4,000 to fewer than 2,500, and during the period 1764–70 it declined from nearly 16,000 to just over 11,000. By contrast, the migratory fishery, being well supplied with ships, sailors, and fishermen released from naval service, always recovered after the wars. This pattern was repeated several times during the century; nevertheless the resident fishery, which had the advantage of being less expensive, had become the more important by the end of the century. By the time of the Napoleonic Wars the migratory fishery had been severely weakened and this conflict brought it to an end.

The outbreak of the Peninsular War in 1808 opened up large markets in Iberia for Newfoundland. Moreover, the War of 1812, by forcing the United States of America out of much of the dried cod trade, gave an additional stimulus to the Newfoundland-based fishery, while further disrupting the West Country migratory fishery. The production of dried cod increased rapidly between 1808 and 1815, and prices went up with the highest level being reached in 1813. This general prosperity in Newfoundland led to greater capital investment. It also stimulated a rapid growth in the local population, though there was a lag between the production and price rises and the population growth. Another related development was a sizable increase in the number of commercial enterprises in St John's; these quickly became powerful rivals to the English and Jersey firms in Newfoundland and Labrador and eventually forced them all out. Combined with the collapse of the West Country fishery, this development set Newfoundland on the road to full colonial status.

PRODUCTION TRENDS

The decade of economic expansion in the fishery that occurred just prior to 1815 was not to be matched in Newfoundland for many years. After 1815 a long period of stagnation began which, except for temporary advances, most notably in the late 1850s, lasted until the early 1870s. From then until the end of the century production was maintained at a significantly higher level; thus during the thirty-year period ending in 1900 dried cod exports averaged over 1,200,000 quintals annually, compared with an average of less than 1,000,000 quintals during the period 1810 to 1870 (see table 2). But this picture of alternating periods of growth and stagnation changes if one examines the population figures for the century (table 1). The increase in dried cod exports is much less than the increase in population. There was, therefore, a marked decline in the per capita export of dried cod as the century progressed – from 29.2 quintals in 1815 to 5.6 quintals in 1901. Since the dried cod industry continued to be the mainstay of the economy, this decline was serious indeed. Moreover, the decline in per capita production was not offset by an

TABLE 2
Newfoundland dried cod exports 1801–1900

Year	Annual average number of quintals	Year	Annual average number of quintals
1801–05	589,270	1851–55	959,126
1806–10	743,688	1856–60	1,188,616
1811–15	935,450	1861–65	912,849
1816–20	883,387	1866–70	812,827
1821–25	920,607	1871–75	1,184,028
1826–30	927,993	1876–80	1,181,777
1831–35	737,805	1881–85	1,423,209
1836–40	841,525	1886–90	1,143,469
1841–45	961,260	1891–95	1,206,368
1846–50	980,340	1896–1900	1,248,880

SOURCES: Ryan, 'Collection of CO 194 Statistics'; Blue Books, 1836–1850; *JHA*, 1852–1901
NOTE: All figures are rounded to the nearest whole number. See also David Alexander, 'Newfoundland's Traditional Economy and Development to 1934,' tables 1 and 3

increase in the price of fish; indeed, towards the end of the century there was a serious decline in price.[2]

TYPES OF FISHING

External factors were of primary importance in these developments, but they can only be fully understood if the internal structure of the Newfoundland industry is first examined. The Newfoundland cod fishery had four major branches during the nineteenth century: the inshore, Labrador, bank, and winter fisheries. The inshore fishery grew out of the resident fishery that had developed in Newfoundland as the migratory fishery declined, and it was the most important of the four. During the eighteenth century the inshore fishery had been prosecuted for the most part by planters (fishermen who owned property, buildings, boats, and equipment) and their crews. This remained the case at least until 1820. During the 1820s and 1830s the planter fishery declined, never to recover, and a corresponding contraction in the average size of individual fishing operations is evident. It would seem that these changes were related to marketing problems and changes in commercial organization. Patrick Hogan, a commentator on the fisheries, offered some evidence on this point later in the century:

Up to the year 1836 the fisheries of this country were conducted not alone under British law, but also in accordance with certain usages which were adopted from time to time, and which grew with the trade, and were found necessary to its well working. One of these rules was, the current supplier furnished the planter with all requirements necessary for the prosecuting of the voyage, viz., nets, lines, provisions, etc.; in return the supplier got the entire voyage, large or small, at current rates. On receipt of which he paid all the wages, bait, boat hire, freight, and gave the planter a moderate supply for the winter, even if he had no work, which he generally had to give him. In 1836 the merchants, for the first time, refused to pay the wages, falling back on British law, and discarding the usages of the fishery, the planter being in debt after the summer; this was the small end of the wedge that divided, from that day to this [1882], the supplier and supplied; the planter, unable to depend on the supplier, as formerly, for his winter supply, was driven, and has been driven, ever since, to consult the first law of nature, self preservation, and hard to blame him, in the face of a long winter. The wages not being secured to the servants, they declined serving the planters, at sea or on shore, the fishery suffered in consequence, there being no shoremen to cure the fish as formerly. Women were called in, who pickled the fish, producing an inferior article which ruined the character of our fish in foreign markets.[3]

This letter not only indicates that the planters and their servants were being replaced by independent fishermen during the 1830s; it also suggests that this was caused by a squeeze in the profit margins of the merchants.[4] Yet there was little change in the methods being used in the industry. Hand-lines, cod jiggers, bultows (trawl lines), and cod seines were used throughout the century with individual fishermen being confined to the first two. During the last quarter of the century the cod trap was introduced and may have helped to increase the catch after 1870. But not even this major innovation was sufficient to arrest the decline.

South coast fishermen had the benefit of a winter fishery to supplement their summer voyage. Beginning in January small vessels were fitted out to fish on the banks near the south coast; the fish taken in this manner would be cured in the spring and exported in late May and early June.[5] Since these fishing banks were close by and the voyages short, this fish was cured as a regular light-salted product. The Labrador fishery developed during the nineteenth century, deriving from the migratory fishery practised by east coast (particularly Conception Bay) fishermen on the 'North Shore' of the island during the Napoleonic Wars. This area between Cape St John and Quirpon was part of the French Shore, and was quickly utilized when war forced French withdrawal. When the French returned after 1815, the Newfoundland fishermen were forced to move further north and exploit the Labrador fisheries which, though more expensive than the North Shore fisheries, were profitable when prosecuted in combination with the seal fishery.

From the beginning the men and ships that took part in the North Shore and Labrador fisheries were the same ones engaged in sealing, and the two must be considered together. Seals had previously always been harvested by landsmen, and it was not until 1793 that ships began sailing from Newfoundland in search of the herds.[6] Thereafter the industry expanded rapidly; during the war years the annual value of seal oil exports was £20,000 to £60,000. When compared with the value of dried cod exports, which probably exceeded £600,000 per year on average during the same period, seal oil accounted for only a small portion of the total export trade. But the industry grew tremendously during the following decades. Most of the expansion in sealing occurred in the St John's–Conception Bay region, with the Conception Bay area controlling the major part of the industry until steam vessels were introduced, a development that coincided with a decline in the harvest. In 1818 the harvest was 165,622 seals. In 1822, 368,336 seals were taken and in 1831, 601,742. Seal oil exports increased from 1,397 tons in 1815 to an average of over 7,500 tons during the four-year period ending in 1833. This writer has calculated that dried cod and seal oil exports respectively were valued at about £453,000 and £159,000 in 1830, and £360,000 and £197,000 in 1831. This high level of production in the sealing industry was maintained until the 1860s when a decline became apparent. The decline accelerated after 1880; during the ten-year period ending in 1900 the value of sealing exports was only about one-third what it had been for the ten-year period ending in 1859.

The growth of the sealing industry early in the century provided extensive employment for a large number of ships and men. By 1827 there were 290 ships and 5,418 men engaged in the industry; in 1857 these figures reached a peak of 370 and 13,600. The average size of the sealing vessels also increased. After 1863, when steam vessels participated in the seal fishery for the first time, the number of sailing vessels declined. By 1882 the steam fleet had increased to twenty-five while only twenty to thirty small sailing vessels were involved. By that year the number of men employed had declined to about 5,000. The introduction of steamers required a larger capital expenditure and allowed St John's to monopolize the industry for the first time. Only Harbour Grace of all the outports was able to remain active in the seal fishery and even there the decline was drastic: 53 ships and 2,825 men in 1870; 17 ships and 1,515 men in 1880, and, at a time of general decline in the industry, 3 ships (steamers) and 600 men in 1890. St John's sent 10 ships and 1,200 men in 1870; 24 and 5,089 in 1880; and 15 ships and 3,399 men in 1890. At the same time the percentage of Newfoundland exports consisting of seal products declined steadily from an average of 24 per cent during the period 1850–59 to an average of 9 per cent during the period 1890–99.[7] The whole Newfoundland economy was affected by this change but the Conception Bay outport economy most of all. In this area prosperity had been built on the interaction of the sealing and Labrador enterprises.

In terms of men, ships, and commercial organization the Labrador fishery was basically similar to the island fishery but there were important differences. Two types of fishermen from Newfoundland were involved: those who journeyed to Labrador and established themselves on shore, catching and curing their fish in the one place, were known as stationers; those who lived on board their ships and moved along the coast to the various fishing grounds were called floaters. The floaters generally brought their fish back to the island to be dried; many also owned fishing rooms at Labrador and could operate as stationers or floaters at will depending on the circumstances.[8] Unlike island fish, which was salted at a rate of about ten quintals of fish per hogshead of salt and had to be dried carefully and at the right moment, Labrador fish was heavily salted. Although some stationers may have produced a light-salted product, because of the migratory nature of the Labrador fishery the amount must have been small.

The Labrador fishery itself was not sufficiently productive to support completely those engaged in it. But since it employed the same men and ships as did the seal fishery it expanded during the early part of the century, remained at a fairly high level throughout the middle decades, and only declined with the decline in the seal fishery. In 1848, for instance, over 400 registered vessels, besides boats of between 10 and 30 tons, were engaged in the Labrador fishery, most of them from Conception Bay. Harbour Grace was the major Labrador fishing and sealing outport in this bay. No early figures are available on trade there, but in 1867, 90 Harbour Grace ships went to the Labrador fishery and 36 of them had also taken part in the seal fishery. Fourteen other ships that had been engaged in the seal fishery were used during that summer to transport supplies to Labrador and to bring back dried cod for export. But by the years 1896–1900 the Harbour Grace–Labrador fleet had declined to an average of 37 ships; these ships were much smaller than those of the late 1860s (53 tons compared with 80 tons) and carried on average some 3,000 fewer people.[9] Although figures for the production of Labrador fish do not exist for the pre-1874 period, during the years 1874–8 the average annual quantity exported from Labrador was nearly 300,000 quintals; this increased during the next five-year period to about 375,000 quintals per annum. But during the following eight years the average annual export was just a little over 200,000 quintals and there was little improvement during the remainder of the century.[10] After the commercial crisis of 1894 St John's firms curtailed their Labrador business, and it was reported in 1897 that 'Bowring, Job, Tessier, Baird, Bennett, Rogerson, Goodfellow, and Others' had cut out nearly all their Labrador supplying.[11]

As the Labrador and seal fisheries declined, it became obvious to both business and government that the bank fishery would have to be developed. There had been a west of England and local bank fishery in the eighteenth century and a few ships from the island had been engaged in this fishery earlier in the century. Yet it was not until 1876 that the government initiated a bounty system to encourage the local bank fishery.[12] Under the stimulus of this and a ship-building bounty the bank fishing expanded. It reached its peak in 1889 when 330 vessels were involved and over 230,000 quintals of fish were caught.[13] Thereafter it declined swiftly.

Of these various fisheries the island's inshore fishery was the most important, employing more men and producing more and better fish than the other branches. But the Labrador fishery, in conjunction with the seal fishery, was also of major importance to the St John's–Conception Bay–Trinity Bay area. Although the winter fishery provided a supplementary source of income for fishermen on the south coast, it was of minor overall importance, as was the bank fishery, which flourished only for a short while on the northeast, east, and southeast coasts.

LOCAL COMMERCIAL ORGANIZATION

Whatever the source, fish had to be exported if Newfoundland was to live. The internal organization of the Newfoundland fish trade as it existed in 1815 had its origin in the commercial organization of the west of England migratory fishery. The British businessmen who first became involved in the Newfoundland fishery were the shipowners and captains from the west of England. As fishing premises became larger, caretakers were left behind, and these caretakers eventually evolved into agents and clerks, collecting fish from the residents for shipment and distributing equipment and supplies in return. Then as wars and transportation costs made the migratory fishery less profitable, these establishments concentrated on bringing in immigrants and supplies and exporting fish and cod oil.[14] By the end of the eighteenth century exporters such as the Poole merchants on the northeast coast, and the Hunts and Newmans from Dartmouth on the south coast, had solidly entrenched themselves in this next phase of the dried cod fishery. They provided the fishermen with the necessary food, supplies, and equipment, generally on credit, and collected their dried fish and cod oil in payment. Large premises were needed since plenty of storage space was necessary and nearly all services had to be provided locally. For example, Newman and Company's relatively small establishment at Burgeo had a total of 43 employees in 1859, including a storekeeper, understorekeeper, joiner, cooper, cooper apprentice, master of the voyage, culler, cook, sawyer, two shoremen, nine youngsters, six boat masters, seven midshipmen, and eleven foreshipmen.[15] Besides these men, this establishment could and did borrow other tradesmen, such as blacksmiths and sail makers, from the company's large establishment in Harbour Breton, and when extra help was needed to dry fish or load and unload ships, labourers could be hired from the community. Firms like Newman and Company were distinguished by the fact that they supplied the fishermen directly and operated through agents who were appointed by the British owners. By the end of the Napoleonic Wars these establishments, with their headquarters usually in the west of England, Liverpool, London, Greenock, Waterford, or the Channel Islands, had set up operations along the Newfoundland coast, except the French Shore, and were expanding their control.

During the Napoleonic Wars another somewhat different commercial structure was being formed with its headquarters at St John's. It was at this time that St John's 'became the Emporium of the Island and changed its character from a fishery to a considerable commercial town.'[16] The social, economic, and political boost that the war gave St John's enabled it to become the centre of trade and commerce, and competition between St John's and the large outport firms began. St John's firms began supplying small outport traders and merchants and thus avoided the merchant-fishermen relationship that continued to hamper the old outport firms. In 1849, while discussing the decline in certain forms of litigation in the outports, James Simms, the attorney general, wrote:

One great cause that has operated to diminish the utility of these courts through the long series of years, has been, that in fact they became less required for at the time when this Species of Court exercised its ambulatory functions under the denomination of Surrogate Courts, there might be counted between St John's and Fortune Bay, throughout the Harbours of the Southern Settlements upwards of thirty mercantile establishments of importing, exporting and supplying Merchants surrounded by their numerous planters, dealers and fishermen – whereas now within these extensive limits there is only one or at most two, such Establishments existing. And in the Northern District beyond Conception Bay, very few of the once great number of such Mercantile houses are now remaining, for St John's has become, through the process of thirty years, the emporium of the Island, and absorbed to a great extent the supplying of planters and fishermen, where of course they resort spring and fall for supplies and for the settlement of accounts.[17]

By 1850, therefore, the trend towards the centralization of commerce in St John's was almost complete and although a few firms, such as Newman, William Cox, and the Slades, survived for some time they did not handle a large part of the trade. Their presence finally came to an end when Newman and Company left in 1907 after over 300 years in the Newfoundland fish trade.

There are several reasons why the St John's exporters were relatively successful. In the first place, their principal partners resided on the island and could keep a close watch on their operations, while the outport firms continued to use agents to operate their establishments. Few of these agents could be expected to devote the time and energy to the business that became increasingly necessary as the profit margin decreased. Newman and Company survived in Newfoundland for so long chiefly because of their ruthless efficiency in dealing with their agents, their painstaking scrutiny and careful examinations of account books, and their specific and detailed instructions regarding all matters. Thomas R. Job made it quite clear how the St John's merchant felt about agents when he wrote: 'The business under one's own supervision is hazardous enough nowadays without leaving it to servants.'[18]

Related to the changing focus of commerce, of course, was the gradual with-drawal of the St John's merchants from the actual operation of retail establishments in the outports. For example, Job Brothers and Company ceased the operation of their business in Hant's Harbour in 1864[19] and Baine Johnston and Company withdrew from Harbour Breton in 1871.[20] This process brought with it a change from the old merchant-fishermen credit relationship to a St John's merchant–small outport merchant or trader–fisherman one. It was much easier for the large firms to control these small outport merchants and traders than it was to control thousands of individual fishermen. This willingness on the part of the St John's merchants to supply traders who could go anywhere along the coast trading for fish was the major complaint that the outport firms had against St John's.[21] Newman and Company and others like them could see no advantage in selling goods at wholesale prices to traders and small merchants who could then compete with their suppliers in the retail trade. To make matters worse for the outport firms, the number of traders would increase during periods of high market demand, thereby reducing the profit margin for all concerned. Few traders, however, would bother to operate when markets were poor and prices low, circumstances which put pressure on the outport firms to buy all the fish and supply all the credit. The whole system was extremely favourable to the St John's merchants and played havoc with the business of the outport firms. As a consequence, by 1882 Newman and Company was probably the only establishment left that was still operating under the old system.[22]

But the St John's firms also had problems, the decline in the seal fishery being among the most important. The St John's (and Conception Bay) firms prosecuted the seal fishery to its fullest extent; it was a very lucrative business until the 1870s and remained fairly lucrative for many decades thereafter. An example of their dependence on this industry can be seen in the papers of the Job family business for the period 1810–85. An overall loss of £9,000 in 1864 is explained by the note 'Seal Voyage very bad.' Similarly, the above average profits of £15,000 and £18,000 in 1869 and 1871 are explained by notes indicating very successful seal voyages. The St John's firms were able, through questionable financial arrange-ments with the two local banks, to continue operating throughout the profit squeeze of the 1880s, but the suspension of business by the Union and the Commercial banks in 1894 precipitated a major business and financial catastrophe. Some major firms, such as John Munn and Company, Thorburn and Tessier, and Edward Duder and Company, which owed the banks $520,000, $458,000, and $668,676 respectively were forced to liquidate.[23] Other firms such as Baine Johnston and Company, which owed the Union Bank $618,000, were able to reach a compromise on their debts.[24] On the basis of a superficial examination of the situation it seems that the economic crisis of 1894 resulted from an increasing dependence on the fairly static cod fishery which faced increasingly difficult market conditions. The decline of the seal fishery, the general lack of diversification in the economy, the withdrawal of capital from the fish trade by several of the larger firms, and the widespread and even illegal use of bank financing by the businesses were all symptomatic of this malaise.[25]

There were several technological developments which had an impact on the fish trade, but for the most part these failed to stop or reverse the downward trend in the dried cod industry; in fact one advance in technology – the introduction of steamers – may have hastened this decline. The use of bultows was probably the first major innovation in the traditional hook and line fishery; by 1850 their use had become an issue, with fishermen disagreeing whether they were beneficial or harmful.[26] Although the bultow may have been an improvement, exports did not increase because of its use. During the 1860s the telegraph was brought to many parts of the island and together with the transatlantic cable enabled the exporters to keep a closer watch on the markets; information or instructions could now be telegraphed in a matter of hours, whereas formerly letters often took months to reach their destinations. The use of steam to ship fish resulted in the export of much larger cargoes than ever before with resultant market gluts. Exporters, therefore, began to compete to get the first shipments to market, which brought about a deterioration in cure. Another development of this period was the invention of the cod trap by Captain W.H. Whiteley at Bonne Esperance in 1866.[27] In 1868 the Canadian government prevented him from using it and it was not until 1876 that this ruling was reversed. As in the case of the bultow, it is difficult to ascertain the effects of this invention on the industry.[28] It may have been responsible for the increased production during the last decades of the century, but it too failed to reverse the downward trend of per capita production. Technological change may have slowed the decay of the cod fishery but it certainly did not stop it.

As per capita production declined during the century, the quality of the Newfoundland product declined also. The factors that caused inferior cure can be divided into those over which the fisherman had direct control, and those beyond his control. The former were certainly of more importance and there were many complaints throughout this period of the fisherman's carelessness and deceit. The fisherman was often to blame for any problems in the process of splitting, salting, and drying, but in the end it was the income from his product that determined the amount of time, effort, and money that he would put into his catch. Every exporter had his own cullers, who graded fish, and his own standards, which were liberal when demand was high and stringent when it was low. In addition the exporters were forced to compete with each other in difficult market conditions and consequently no uniform standards were possible. With such fluctuations, fishermen often felt that it was better to concentrate on catching fish rather than on curing, since a large quantity of a poorly cured product often brought a larger reward than a smaller quantity of a well-cured product. In addition to this, many fish buyers began purchasing fish tal qual[29] during the second half of the century. This practice seems to have been largely confined to Labrador fish; Nicholas Smith, an experienced stationer in the Labrador trade, maintains that this procedure was introduced to save time after the introduction of steamers to transport the Labrador fish to market.[30] This was in essence a marketing rather than a production problem, extreme laissez-faire practices making such a development inevitable as marketing became difficult. The major factor influencing the curing process was one over which the fisherman had no control – the weather – but except in a few seasons this did not cause any major problems. Like catch failure, poor weather was a factor in limited areas or for limited periods of time but it was never important enough to permanently injure the industry.

MARKETS

Developments outside Newfoundland were clearly much more fundamental than these internal problems. With her growing population and continued dependence on the cod fishery, Newfoundland had not only to hold her existing markets but increase them. Unfortunately, she not only failed to expand her trade, but in several cases she lost some of her most important markets. The fact that this happened while the total world production of dried cod and the demand for it was rapidly increasing is a significant comment on the problems besetting the Newfoundland fish trade throughout the century. Although information is scarce in this regard, it is apparent that the total world demand for dried cod increased during the century. The population increase of the major markets – Spain, Portugal, and Brazil – was quite substantial. An examination of one major port, Bilbao, shows that imports of dried cod between 1815 and 1828 averaged well under 100,000 quintals per year compared with over 400,000 between 1882 and 1886.[31] In addition, world markets during the period 1815 to 1819 were almost completely supplied by Newfoundland's average exports of 944,998 quintals per year while Norway's share of these markets amounted to an annual average of 184,175 quintals. But during the ten-year period ending in 1889, Newfoundland exported an annual average of 1,320,131 quintals; Norway's share, in the meantime, had

TABLE 3
Newfoundland's exports of dried cod to the major markets (quintals): 1803–33

Year	Spain, Portugal, and Italy	British Europe	British West Indies	British America	USA	Brazil	Total
1803	381,519	102,638	64,248	3,082	31,362	—	582,849
1804	425,446	41,480	41,590	15,757	35,169	—	559,442
1805	377,293	65,979	81,488	22,776	77,983	—	625,519
1806	438,918	84,241	100,936	32,555	116,159	—	772,809
1807	262,366	130,400	103,418	23,541	155,085	—	674,810
1808	154,669	208,254	115,677	40,874	56,658	—	576,132
1809	326,781	292,068	133,359	41,894	16,117	—	810,219
1810	—	—	—	—	—	—	—
1811	611,960	139,561	152,184	18,621	1,214	—	923,540
1812	545,451	67,020	91,864	4,121	—	2,600	711,056
1813	727,739	50,701	119,354	14,389	—	—	912,183
1814	768,010	55,791	97,249	24,712	—	2,049	947,811
1815	952,116	46,116	159,233	24,608	588	—	1,182,661
1816	770,693½	59,341½	176,603	37,443	2,545	—	1,046,626
1817	681,559	79,746	150,827	20,656	2,848	—	935,636
1818	560,632	57,258	116,716	—	—	—	751,818
1819	606,689	57,737	126,995	3,762	—	13,067	808,250
1820	626,644	81,014	139,484	19,741	—	7,723	874,606

TABLE 3 (*Concluded*)

Year	Spain, Portugal, and Italy	British Europe	British West Indies	British America	USA	Brazil	Total
1821	699,349	95,935	127,105	26,686	–	14,817	963,892
1822	726,400	73,931½	88,181	22,090	–	13,681	924,283½
1823	631,089	65,140	118,414	27,324	636	16,201	858,813
1824	723,438	65,592	126,625	28,221	104	39,703	963,683
1825	512,389	146,106	137,561	32,285	–	64,025	892,366
1826	687,200	93,739	105,410½	57,945	54	49,665	994,013½
1827	533,092	118,738	146,033	44,831	–	34,088	876,782
1828	586,155	112,696	123,611	48,201	–	63,569	934,232
1829	474,236	156,378	158,493	54,998	–	84,713	928,818
1830	560,620	125,449	129,525	35,875	–	54,650	906,119
1831	425,427	89,051	110,801	61,215	–	40,387	726,881
1832	426,673	62,359	127,687	58,585	–	32,078	707,382
1833	515,880	89,765	136,830	73,637	3,668	47,407	867,187

SOURCE: Ryan, 'Collection of CO 194 Statistics'

TABLE 4
Newfoundland's exports of dried cod to the major markets (quintals): 1857–1900

Year	Spain	Portugal	Italy	British West Indies	Brazil	Total
1857	266,775	206,076	144,754	118,997	368,205	1,392,322
1858	120,127	149,603	54,048	78,351	394,092	1,038,089
1859	239,552	113,323	56,902	87,850	358,568	1,105,793
1860	259,406	204,285	45,008	132,841	268,937	1,138,544
1861	262,092	182,125	51,427	123,919	232,219	1,021,720
1862	274,737	267,806	54,098	95,916	203,400	1,080,069
1863	209,740	136,956	37,138	75,432	163,528	811,777
1864	242,768	182,390	47,780	97,908	154,518	849,339
1865	173,714	201,559	28,842	67,287	178,462	801,339
1866	182,940	165,795	25,782	83,105	149,749	716,690
1867	171,543	198,294	19,550	102,453	171,456	815,008
1868	150,128	150,316	25,184	100,799	98,426	688,063
1869	170,628	206,027	68,948	83,570	201,212	874,106
1870	211,222	167,589	62,146	86,461	249,425	930,204
1871	218,864	191,545	65,511	77,978	255,708	957,488
1872	185,551	231,102	31,254	92,366	246,292	916,843
1873	247,710	197,045	42,968	81,159	266,577	999,637
1874	259,064	254,656	70,202	105,579	326,969	1,249,320
1875	139,031	208,405	48,014	82,717	275,482	888,489
1876	161,983	150,829	53,947	63,791	228,470	757,218
1877	109,888	150,228	23,716	75,417	292,129	760,446
1878	77,916	150,026	39,383	57,459	268,455	694,339
1879	157,942	182,967	50,242	66,821	362,429	994,334
1880	109,856	170,872	46,179	82,847	395,044	985,134
1881	139,882	236,617	56,190	96,395	471,244	1,173,510
1882	166,489	362,033	80,830	67,486	312,078	1,027,269
1883	158,828	332,030	61,097	85,011	295,094	1,163,934
1884	133,872	318,820	45,941	88,758	375,089	1,197,637
1885	92,336	362,084	47,891	82,865	259,818	1,034,710
1886	115,630	370,257	36,049	102,829	294,267	1,088,004
1887	139,536	215,518	28,400	82,033	315,150	913,145
1888	123,672	260,520	25,422	77,439	276,058	953,537
1889	87,736	267,231	15,622	112,392	262,501	889,574
1890	65,574	208,474	16,850	107,173	218,833	774,294

TABLE 4 (*Concluded*)

Year	Spain	Portugal	Italy	British West Indies	Brazil	Total
1891	90,660	219,129	39,773	101,383	250,663	947,575
1892	86,695	198,568	35,394	93,176	255,347	795,549
1893	70,841	190,903	27,575	71,385	352,160	900,744
1894	29,546	187,335	20,121	73,697	356,929	898,359
1895	42,404	247,099	43,734	93,575	342,692	1,026,636
1896	60,424	352,214	40,374	112,328	338,193	1,150,297
1897	20,396	298,501	29,473	98,403	321,910	980,573
1898	28,632	235,368	16,838	107,250	402,724	951,234
1899[a]	24,793	211,991	38,726	102,489	464,531	1,266,336
1900	67,380	226,366	24,114	68,166	458,240	1,300,622

SOURCE: *JHA*, 1858–1901, appendices. The amount exported from Newfoundland and Labrador to smaller insignificant markets are not included in this table.
NOTE: [a]In the figures for 1899 and 1900 it appears likely that the Labrador cod exports are included.

grown to an average of 1,165,416.[32] At the same time, other producers had also substantially increased their exports (see tables 3 and 4).

Newfoundland's export trade did not keep pace with the increase in world demand. The actual quantity exported to Portugal, for a time the major market, and to Italy did not change very much; but other producers increased their business in these markets. In Spain the quantity of fish purchased from Newfoundland declined substantially while total Spanish consumption increased to the advantage of other producers, particularly Norway. The markets in the West Indies remained fairly stable, although here also others expanded at Newfoundland's expense. Brazil, not a traditional Newfoundland market, was the only country where the purchase of Newfoundland fish grew considerably during the century.

Italy had always been the least important of the three European markets and this continued to be the case during the nineteenth century, although that country provided a major market for the cod and salmon produce of Labrador. Throughout the Napoleonic War period Italy bought little Newfoundland fish and this remained true during the 1820s and 1830s, when only about 30,000 quintals were sold in that area annually.[33] The situation improved thereafter and by 1850 Newfoundland was supplying over 115,000 quintals out of a total Italian consumption of over 180,000.[34] Exports declined again during the second half of the century.

Portugal had always been a major market for Newfoundland fish and continued as such throughout the century, although there were great fluctuations in this trade.

During the Peninsular War, Portugal was probably buying as much as 300,000 quintals per year (somewhat less than Spain) and although the actual quantity declined after the war, Portugal's share increased so that by 1833 she was buying about 73 per cent of Newfoundland's annual exports of about 480,000 quintals to Spain, Portugal, and Italy.[35] Between 1833 and 1857 the Newfoundland-Portuguese trade declined but it increased again in the 1860s and by the early 1880s Portugal was once again importing over 300,000 quintals of the island's fish. There was a decline after this resurgence but Portugal continued to buy a substantial quantity of fish from Newfoundland during the remainder of the century.

Spain had been Newfoundland's best customer during the Napoleonic Wars but she was certainly the island's greatest disappointment afterwards. Throughout the Peninsular War Spain bought most of Newfoundland's exports; in 1813, for example, she purchased 400,000 quintals.[36] After the war this trade declined and by 1833 the quantity of Newfoundland fish being bought by Spain had dropped as low as 100,000 quintals annually.[37] But a revival of trade doubled this amount by the late 1850s and Spain remained, on the whole, a good customer until the mid 1870s, when a serious and rapid decline began. It continued for the rest of the century and as a result Spain became a fourth-rate importer of Newfoundland cod.

The other traditional market for Newfoundland fish was the British West Indies; here, there were few major changes during the century. Newfoundland had expanded into this market after the American War of Independence and exports increased in the early years of the century to over 120,000 quintals annually by the early 1830s. There was a decline during the second half of the century which was probably offset by sales of fish to other West Indian islands and to Nova Scotia.[38]

The most extraordinary development in the Newfoundland fish trade during the nineteenth century was the growth of Brazil as a major market. After 1808, when it became possible to ship fish directly to Brazil, Newfoundland became the chief supplier of that country. This trade developed slowly during the early decades of the century but by 1848 approximately 100,000 quintals were being exported annually to Brazil.[39] There was a rapid growth during the following decade and by the late 1850s the quantity had tripled. This was followed by a decline in the 1860s but a rapid recovery in the 1870s continued, with few exceptions, to the end of the century, so that by 1900 Brazil was buying almost 400,000 quintals annually.

There are many reasons why the countries mentioned above were the major markets for Newfoundland dried cod. With warm climates they all needed an easily preserved, high protein food; none of them produced a sufficient quantity of livestock for their own needs. The major cities to which dried cod was exported were also major sea ports and more easily supplied by sea than by land. Moreover, these markets were able to purchase this inexpensive food with their own exports of wine, olive oil, fruit, nuts, salt, and minerals from the Mediterranean, cotton and coffee from Brazil, and sugar from the West Indies. In addition they lacked major fishing grounds of their own. Brazil is a special case in that she depended on dried beef – both local and Argentinian – for a high proportion of her protein needs; but over 75 per cent of her immigrants (at least after 1874) came from Italy, Portugal, and Spain and no doubt brought their food preferences with them: 'An obsession for cod fish or bacalhau' was one.[40] In addition there was a great increase in the production of cotton and coffee in the coastal parts of Pernambuco and San Salvador after 1850, and 'Brazil was caught up in a frenzy of uneven growth and modernization that affected every aspect of national life.'[41] Thus, there was a common need for a low-priced high protein food which could be stored and transported without deterioration. Newfoundland's light-salted hard-dried cod fish was well suited to meet this need.

Each market, however, had its own preferences, which meant that different types of dried cod were in demand in different places. As the firm of Punton and Munn explained in 1856, 'Our largest and best fish find the best sale in Portugal, Spain, and Italy whereas the smallest and driest cured are taken off in large quantities for Brazil leaving the inferior qualities for the West India Islands.'[42] Besides these major differences, there were other differences, particularly in Spain and Italy where the southern ports preferred a drier fish than the northern ports; in the latter, a moister, more heavily salted fish could be sold. In addition there were degrees of quality and size within the major divisions, which added up to well over twenty grades of fish in all.[43]

The fact that these markets were willing and able to purchase increasing amounts of dried cod during the nineteenth century encouraged other producers to enter the trade. Although it is impossible to establish definitely the causal relationship between producer and consumer, an examination of the increase in competition is a necessary preliminary to a study of the internal developments within each market.

COMPETITORS

Besides Newfoundland, the dried cod producers of the nineteenth century were Iceland, the United States of America, Nova Scotia, France, and Norway. Iceland, France, and Norway sold most of their exported fish in Europe while American and Nova Scotian exports were generally sent to the West Indies. None of these countries, as far as can be ascertained, sold much fish to Brazil during this period. Newfoundland's competitors were not all of equal stature; their trade varied from the virtually insignificant quantities of Iceland to the extremely large amounts produced and sold by Norway.

Iceland, the United States, and Nova Scotia were the least important of Newfoundland's competitors. Iceland's total exports reached 85,000 quintals by mid century but most was sold in Denmark.[44] In 1897, however, Iceland was selling 60,000 quintals annually in Genoa where only 50,000 quintals of Labrador fish were being sold.[45] The American cod fishery, although large, did not affect the sale of Newfoundland fish to any great extent for most of its production went to the large domestic market. Nova Scotia's fishery, like that of Newfoundland, had expanded during the Napoleonic Wars. Although Nova Scotia did not compete with Newfoundland in European markets, she did compete effectively in the British and foreign West Indian markets. Over 200,000 quintals went from Nova Scotia to the former in 1840 while only 14,000 were sent to the latter. The British West Indian market declined somewhat in importance during the following decades while the foreign West Indies' trade increased substantially. In 1864 the figures were approximately 161,000 and 106,000 quintals respectively out of a total sale of approximately 310,000 quintals. After 1869 Nova Scotia's fishery expanded, rising to nearly 800,000 quintals a year by 1888; thereafter, it declined rapidly to less than 600,000, where it remained for the rest of the century. The greater part of this product continued to be sold in the British and Spanish West Indies.[46] Although Nova Scotia was probably instrumental in keeping down the price of West Indian fish, neither she nor the other two competitors mentioned above caused the Newfoundland mercantile establishments any concern. Moreover, they were not involved, at least to any significant extent, in Spain, Portugal, or Brazil.

Although France's fishery recovered after the Napoleonic Wars, it was not until the second half of the century, particularly during the 1880s, that it offered serious competition to Newfoundland. There is evidence that between 1850 and 1880 some French fish were being sold in traditional Newfoundland markets but competition from France became stiffer after 1880. A marked decline in Newfoundland exports to Naples, Bilbao, Valencia, Alicante, and Leghorn was accompanied by a major increase in the sale of French fish in these ports. After 1886, however, the French suffered several setbacks, although they remained one of Newfoundland's most important competitors.[47]

Unlike France, Norway began competing with Newfoundland in the dried cod markets immediately after the Napoleonic Wars, and the expansion of her trade was rapid. By the 1850s her exports to Spain had reached 400,000 quintals annually and Brazil was purchasing about 40,000 quintals annually from her.[48] Norwegian exports to Spain continued to grow and by 1898 northern Spain (Bilbao and Santander) alone was buying about 550,000 quintals annually.[49] Portugal was now also buying Norwegian fish, taking 150,000 to 250,000 quintals annually.[50] Although it is difficult to explain fully this expansion in the Norwegian fishery, several things are obvious. The Norwegian government assisted every aspect of the fishing industry, from production to marketing. The major fishing grounds are fairly concentrated along Norway's coast and the fish migration pattern results in a longer fishing season than in Newfoundland. Again, Norway's more heavily salted fish found particular favour in the northern Spanish market and huge shipments to this region resulted in a decrease in average shipping charges. All things considered, Norway could and did produce large quantities of cheaper fish, probably because both the standard and the cost of living were lower there than in Newfoundland during most of the century.[51] In any case, as Norway's share of world production rose, Newfoundland's declined considerably and by 1900 Norway had become Newfoundland's major competitor in the dried cod trade.

CONDITIONS OF TRADE

By examining the export trade of all these dried cod producers it can readily be seen that the total world production rose significantly throughout the century. Although it must be taken for granted that even the smallest producers influenced the markets to some extent, this increase was not simply a function of supply. The demand side must also be taken into account. Here the tariff regulations of the importing countries are of great importance. If the duties were universally low, it kept down the consumer price and increased profits for all producers. If, on the other hand, the duties were universally high, the profit margin was low, as the producers tried to keep the fish within the consumer's purchasing power. This situation could be harmful to all producers; in such cases the country with the lowest production costs and/or highest government assistance had the advantage. Another tariff consideration was the preferential duty, by which a particular fish-consuming country would give an advantage in its market to a particular fish-producing country in return for a reciprocal trading concession. The discriminatory duty was a somewhat different arrangement; in this case a higher duty was placed on the produce of one or more countries putting it, or them, at a disadvantage. Unfortunately for Newfoundland exporters, their tariff problems were not treated with the dispatch that other producers often received from their governments. As a result, the colony seems to have lost more than it gained from the tariff arrangements and rearrangements that occurred during the century. Besides tariff regulations there were, of course, other factors influencing the fish trade. These included clearance charges, quarantine laws, shipping regulations, wars, revolutions, depressions, droughts, and other political, economic, and social upheavals. Since it would require a very detailed study to examine fully all the individual factors that determined the quantity, quality, and price of fish imported by the markets in any one year, only those developments which had major, unmistakable results on the trade will be mentioned here.

The British West Indies and Italy were the least important of Newfoundland's major markets during the nineteenth century. Not surprisingly, their relative unimportance is reflected in a lack of information on developments within these markets that may have affected their imports from Newfoundland. The nature of the British West Indian market, with its demand for very inexpensive fish, combined with the competition of American and Nova Scotian producers, made it difficult for Newfoundland exporters to earn profits in this area. This market declined somewhat in importance during the second half of the century probably because of the repeal of the Navigation Acts in 1846. But a small increase in exports to the foreign West Indies, combined with the development of a market in Nova Scotia itself for Newfoundland fish, offset this decline. The Newfoundland-Italian fish trade was also of a comparatively minor nature (bearing in mind its importance to the Labrador cod and salmon fisheries), and there does not seem to have been much Italian interference regarding imports of Newfoundland cod. In 1816 the duty at Naples was fixed at 9s. 8d. per quintal; although this was fairly high, it did not cause much alarm since Italy purchased little fish. It is not known at the moment what changes, if any, were made in this 1816 tariff, but since the cod exporters remained silent on the subject, except for the occasional perfunctory complaint, it probably stayed much the same throughout the country. On the other hand, it was reported in 1898 that taxation was high in Italy and the people poor and that for these reasons the bounty-supported French fish could be sold more easily than the Newfoundland product.[52] This could explain the growth in the French fish trade during the latter years of the century. Although governmental interference in the British West Indies and Italy did not affect the amount of cod purchased from Newfoundland, the very nature of the demands of these markets placed Newfoundland at a disadvantage and prevented the island from deriving any benefit from the increase in consumption in these two areas.

The Brazilian government also interfered little with the import of Newfoundland dried cod during the century, although there were other problems in this market. An agreement between Great Britain and Brazil in 1808 established the duty on British goods entering Brazil at a reasonable 15 per cent.[53] This was revised upward in 1844 but shortly thereafter the duty on cod was reduced considerably so that by 1881, except for the period of increased duties for revenue purposes during the Paraguayan War (1865–70), it had declined to 3s. 3d. per quintal.[54] This low duty partly explains why so much Newfoundland fish was imported by Brazil during this period. After the establishment of a republic in 1889, however, the Brazilian economy deteriorated and fish duties were sharply increased to 7s. 7d. per drum (128 lb). A decline in imports of Newfoundland fish resulted.[55]

Newfoundland exports of dried cod to Portugal were hampered by several developments in that country during the century. There was a decline in the

Portuguese economy early in the century caused, at least in part, by the dislocation of Portugal's traditional trade with Brazil. This encouraged both an increase in tariffs for revenue purposes and stimulated the development of a local fishery. During the period 1810–33, Newfoundland produce received preferential treatment under the Anglo-Portuguese commercial treaty of 1810 which established an ad valorem duty of 15 per cent.[56] By the 1830s Portugal was '... regarded as the mainstay of their [the exporters'] fishery,' taking about 350,000 quintals annually.[57] In 1834 there was a reduction in the duties paid by other countries and in 1835, after the expiration of the treaty, there was a sharp increase in the tariff, to be followed by others. By the late 1850s exports of dried cod from Newfoundland to Portugal had declined to an annual average of only 168,322 quintals. From 1896, Norwegian fish was given preference of 10d. per quintal and soon captured a large portion of the market.[58]

In 1836 the National Fishing Company of Portugal was formed at Lisbon. In spite of tariff protection this company does not seem to have been a success. From 1884, however, the government began to encourage actively the formation of a Portuguese banking fleet in Lisbon.[59] By 1900 the amount of fish being landed by this fleet amounted to about one-third of that being sold by Newfoundland. It does not seem that this competition was a significant factor in Newfoundland's market difficulties, any more than the temporary irritations to trade caused by civil war, cholera, or clearance charges. The major difficulty lay in the area of tariff regulations. The cessation of preferential treatment was a severe blow to the island's trade. Subsequent increases in duty diminished profit margins and opened the way for Norway's cheaper fish.

Though Spain increased her total import of dried cod during the nineteenth century, Newfoundland's exports to this market declined. Among many developments in Spain encouraging a movement towards French and Norwegian fish, the most important was the manipulation of the tariff. Like Portugal, Spain suffered an economic depression during the early nineteenth century as her colonial empire disappeared and her revenue decreased. Fish duties were increased drastically, from 3s. 8d. per quintal in 1808 to 14s. per quintal in 1822.[60] At the same time the price of dried cod declined by about 4s. per quintal, giving an advantage to the cheaper Norwegian product, which quickly displaced Newfoundland fish in northern Spain. Between 1813 and 1833 Newfoundland exports to Spain declined from about 400,000 quintals annually to about 100,000 quintals annually.[61] A more moderate tariff of 1841 reduced fish duties, but introduced a flag differential to encourage Spanish shipping. By the late 1850s exports of Newfoundland cod to Spain had more than doubled, partly as a result of the new tariff, partly as a result of growth in the Spanish economy. The flag differential annoyed Newfoundland exporters, however, since Spain supplied most of its own shipping in the Newfoundland cod trade up to the 1860s.[62] The differential disappeared with the introduction of a lower tariff in 1868, but in 1877 a differential tariff policy was adopted, and in 1882 Norway and France were given a significant preference over Newfoundland.[63] In the last decades of the century, Newfoundland exports to Spain steeply declined. A major market had been lost.[64]

Several conclusions can be drawn from this brief survey of the important nineteenth-century dried cod markets. In Portugal and Spain the loss of colonial revenues resulted in changes in tariff regulations that made it more difficult for Newfoundland to sell a high-priced product. Moreover, the very nature of her cod fishery and the price of her product made it difficult for Newfoundland to compete successfully with Norway in the sale of fish to northern Spain. Yet developments in the Spanish and Portuguese markets differed greatly. High Spanish tariffs nearly wiped out the import of Newfoundland fish early in the century, while differential duties introduced between 1877 and 1882 destroyed the recovery that had taken place at mid-century in this trade. In Portugal the situation was somewhat different; here, the removal in 1833 of the preferential treatment that had been granted Newfoundland fish in 1810 caused a decline in the Portuguese-Newfoundland fish trade. The situation in Brazil was different again. There the only serious problems confronting Newfoundland related to internal disturbances rather than tariff changes. In any case the growth of this market more than compensated for the problems that existed there. All things considered, Spain's tariff policy was probably the most important market problem of the century for Newfoundland, with Portugal's tariff changes also being quite serious.

CONCLUSION

In general Newfoundland's position as a major dried cod exporter was adversely affected by external factors during the nineteenth century. Other producers, notably Norway, increased their production of cod and moved into markets that had previously belonged to Newfoundland. The demand for the island's hard-dried, light-salted fish expanded only in Brazil while most of Europe became more and more inclined to buy the Norwegian product. The result was that while world production of dried cod increased per capita export of the product from Newfoundland continued to decline. This decline affected every facet of Newfoundland life. Its seriousness is self-evident when it is considered that Newfoundland's population increased five fold during the century and that the stagnating cod fishery remained the major economic activity. Rapid population growth in the context of a stagnant fishing economy led to an increase in government poor relief. This in turn led to an increase in customs duties in order to provide revenue. Although customs revenue averaged only 5 per cent of the value of imports during the years 1836–41, it had increased to 23 per cent by the period 1890–1914.[65] Yet despite this increase in revenue, the public debt also increased rapidly, particularly after 1880 when the government became involved in railway building in an attempt to diversify the economy. Throughout the latter part of the century the business establishment was forced to retrench and the wiser, major firms became wholesale suppliers in St John's. This general retrenchment made it possible for the Fishermen's Protective Union to prosper on the northeast coast after 1908, a development that shook the Newfoundland political edifice to its foundations. Economic adversity was also responsible for the interest which Newfoundland showed towards confederation with Canada in the 1860s and 1890s. Everything considered, the drift of the fishery during the nineteenth century into greater and greater economic difficulties must be counted among the basic themes of modern Newfoundland history.

NOTES

1 For the history of this fishery to 1815 see Keith Matthews, 'A History of the West of England-Newfoundland Fishery' (unpublished D PHIL thesis, Oxford 1968). For statistical information on this period see Shannon Ryan, 'Collection of CO 194 Statistics' (unpublished paper, Centre for Newfoundland Studies, Memorial University 1970). These statistics are incomplete but trends can be detected from them. They are most useful in considering long-term developments. See also John Mannion (ed.), *The Peopling of Newfoundland: Essays in Historical Geography* (St John's 1977).

2 In addition, a brief study of the cost of various items throughout the century does not indicate any appreciable decline in the cost of living. It must also be remembered that the tariff was increased considerably towards the end of the century as the government tried to cover its expenditures (see *JHA*, 1850–1900, appendices).

3 *JHA*, 1882, appendix, 615–19.

4 It is also important to note that at this time the government began a system of poor relief which provided food for the poor during the winter.

5 One company which engaged in this trade, Newman and Company, had some difficulty explaining to buyers that this product was not fish from the previous year's catch (see PANL, Newman Hunt papers, Letterbook 68, 81–3).

6 CO 194/129, LeMarchant to Grey, 4 May 1848.

7 Shannon Ryan, 'The Newfoundland Cod Fishery in the Nineteenth Century' (unpublished MA thesis, Memorial University 1971), 16–26.

8 Most stationers operated south of Cape Harrison while the floaters went as far north as Cape Chidley.

9 Harbour Grace Museum, Collection of the late Martin R. Lee of Placentia, Newfoundland, 'Book of Coasting and Fishing Ships Cleared from Harbour Grace.'

10 *JHA*, appendices, Export statistics.

11 Maritime History Group Archives Memorial University, Baine Johnston letterbook,
    1893–98, 169–70, 5 February 1897 (letters from J.C. Hepburn, managing director, to
    his partners in Scotland). The Bell Island iron ore mines, which opened in 1895,
    provided work for unemployed sealers and Labrador fishermen, particularly those in the
    Harbour Grace area. They thus broadened the economic base of the Conception Bay
    region.

12 *JHA*, 1877, appendix, 21.

13 Ibid., 1890–9, appendices.

14 Cod oil or train oil was produced from cod livers and on average equalled about 10 per
    cent of the value of the dried cod.

15 PANL, Newman Hunt papers, Letterbook 64, 121–4.

16 CO 194/55, Governor R.G. Keats' report on Newfoundland for the year ending 10
    Oct. 1814.

17 CO 194/131, Simms to LeMarchant, 23 June 1849.

18 PANL, Job family papers, Thomas R. Job to his father, 16 Dec. 1864.

19 Ibid.

20 PANL, Newman Hunt papers, Letterbook 65, 334, 21 Nov. 1871.

21 Ibid., Letterbook 67, 233–6, 1882.

22 Ibid., 225–8, 23 May 1882.

23 *Times and General Commercial Gazette* (St John's), 30 Jan. 1895, and *The Crown* vs
    The Directors and Manager of the Commercial Bank of Newfoundland (St John's 1895).
    See also *The Crown* vs *The Directors of the Union Bank of Newfoundland* (St John's
    1895).

24 *Times and General Commercial Gazette*, 30 Jan. 1895.

25 In a speech to the House of Assembly, 11 May 1897 (printed in the *Evening Telegram*
    (St John's), 1–2 June 1897), Premier Whiteway gave examples of the withdrawal of
    capital from the fish trade. The deaths of John Munn, Arthur Duder, and Allan
    Goodridge had resulted in a shortage of working capital because large legacies went to
    their dependents; Charles P. Hunter, Walter Grieve, and James Grieve had withdrawn a
    substantial amount of capital from Baine Johnston and Company, and Robert and
    Thomas Job and Stephen Rendell had done the same at Job Brothers and Company.
    These withdrawals may have been an important factor, but it is not possible to ascertain
    whether they were different from previous ones. Moreover, the general economic
    situation in the early 1890s may have precipitated exceptionally large withdrawals
    rather than vice versa.

26 See *JHA*, appendices, for many petitions requesting that bultows be banned on the
    grounds that they destroyed mother fish.

27 Captain George Whiteley, 'How the Cod Trap Was Invented,' *Western Star* (Corner
    Brook), 1 July 1949.

28 In a petition to the Canadian Department of Marine and Fisheries in 1876 requesting

permission to use the trap, Whiteley claimed that it had increased his annual production of cod from 100 to 3,000 quintals. Needless to say, other factors may have contributed to this increase. This petition, dated 15 Aug. 1876, is in the possession of Dr W.H. Whiteley, Department of History, Memorial University.

29 A flat rate for a quantity of fish without culling.

30 Nicholas Smith, *Fifty-Two Years at the Labrador Fishery* (London 1936), 17–18.

31 Information about the 1815–28 period was provided by Keith Matthews from the *Newfoundland Gazette* (St John's), 22 Sept. 1829. Information about the 1882–86 period was taken from statistics gathered from the trade reports of British consuls by James Hiller.

32 There is a reason to believe that Norway's share of the trade continued to increase during the 1890s, although figures could not be obtained for this period.

33 Ryan, 'Newfoundland Cod Fishery,' 119.

34 CO 194/137, W. Petre (Rome) to W.L. Bulwer, 2 July 1852.

35 Ryan, 'Newfoundland Cod Fishery,' 120–1.

36 CO 194/60, Report of the Select Committee on Newfoundland Trade, 1817.

37 Leslie Harris, 'The First Nine Years of Representative Government in Newfoundland' (unpublished MA thesis, Memorial University 1959), 94.

38 See the customs records in the *JHA*, 1857–1900, appendices.

39 Ryan, 'Newfoundland Cod Fishery,' 125; CO 194/130, Chamber of commerce to secretary of state, 11 March 1848.

40 Simon Kuznets et al. (eds.), *Economic Growth: Brazil, India, Japan* (Durham, NC 1955), 256; William Lytle Schurz, *Brazil: The Infinite Country* (New York 1961), 123.

41 Herman G. James, *Brazil after a Century of Independence* (New York 1925), 294; Pollie E. Poppino, *Brazil: The Land and People* (New York 1968), 200.

42 Collection of the late Martin R. Lee of Placentia, Newfoundland, Punton and Munn letterbook, 1855–7, Punton and Munn to Waterman and Ryan, 29 Oct. 1856.

43 Interview with Stephen Hogan, Carbonear, 21 April 1972. Mr Hogan worked for over forty years as a fish culler and foreman for a major salt fish establishment.

44 *JHA*, 1868, appendix, 840, 'Report of Vice Consul J.R. Crowe, Christiania, on the Fisheries, Trade and General Features of Iceland for the years 1865–1866 to Lord Stanley.'

45 *Report of the Trade Commissioners on the Mediterranean Markets, Etc.* (St John's 1898), 13.

46 Ruth Fulton Grant, *The Canadian Atlantic Fishery* (Toronto 1934), 16–17.

47 See Ryan, 'Newfoundland Cod Fishery,' 146–51. Since the French had rights on part of the Newfoundland coast they were frequently made a scapegoat for the problems of the Newfoundland government and exporters during the second half of the century. The French Shore fishery in Newfoundland declined rapidly after 1880 and France gave up her rights on the island's coast in 1904 (see below, 113–14).

48 *JHA*, 1861, appendix, 31.

49 *Report of the Trade Commissioners*, 25.

50 Ibid., 19–20.

51 Norway produced klipfish and stockfish. The former was salted and dried and it was this fish that competed most successfully in Newfoundland's traditional markets. Stockfish was dried without salt during the early spring and was sold in northern Europe and the Baltic region.

52 *Report of the Trade Commissioners*, 16.

53 Joao Pandia Calogeras, *A History of Brazil*, trans. and ed. Percy Alvin Martin (Chapel Hill 1939), 145.

54 PANL, Chamber of Commerce minute book, 1868–75, vol. 5, Annual report, 4 Aug. 1869; CO 194/201, Chamber of Commerce to Earl Kimberley, 19 Nov. 1881.

55 Cologeras, *Brazil*, 200, 256–95.

56 PANL, Chamber of Commerce minute book, 1834–41, vol. 1, Chamber of Commerce to George Richard Robinson, MP, London, 20 Nov. 1834.

57 CO 194/89, Chamber of Commerce to the secretary of state for the colonies, 25 July 1834; CO 194/88, Governor's observations on the fishery for 1833.

58 CO 194/236, Foreign Office to Colonial Office, 6 Oct. 1896; CO 194/239, Foreign Office to Colonial Office, 2 Sept. 1897.

59 *Report of the Trade Commissioners*, 17–18.

60 CO 194/94, Chamber of Commerce to the secretary of state for the colonies, 26 Jan. 1836; CO 194/87, Chamber of Commerce to the secretary of state for the colonies, June 1834.

61 Harris, 'First Nine Years of Representative Government,' 94.

62 D.W. Prowse, *History of Newfoundland* (London 1895) 452–4.

63 CO 194/204, Chamber of Commerce to Earl Kimberley, 9 Sept. 1882; Foreign Office to Colonial Office, 4 Aug. 1882; PANL, Chamber of Commerce annual reports, 1849–84, Annual report for 1884.

64 See also Jamie Vincent Vives, *An Economic History of Spain*, trans. Frances M. Lopez-Morillas (Princeton 1969), especially 690–711.

65 See Ryan, 'Newfoundland Cod Fishery,' 199.

Confederation Defeated:
The Newfoundland Election of 1869

JAMES HILLER

It is entirely possible that Newfoundland would not have been represented at the Quebec conference had not Hugh Hoyles,[1] the colony's premier, approached Charles Tupper in the summer of 1864, when visiting his wife's family in Halifax.[2] Tupper blandly told Hoyles that Newfoundland had not been invited to Charlottetown because of 'the belief that was generally entertained, that Newfoundland had no wish to become a party' to the proposed union, but it is more likely that the possibility had not crossed his mind, nor that of any other future father of confederation.[3] On the other hand, Newfoundland had shown no interest in mainland moves towards Maritime or federal union. The 1864 legislative debates contain no reference to the matter, and the newpaper editors were silent. So far as one can tell, Hoyles acted entirely on his own initiative. He was invited to Charlottetown, prudently declined on the grounds that he had to return home to bid farewell to his old political ally Governor Bannerman, and submitted Macdonald's subsequent invitation to Quebec to his government.[4]

Hoyles' exclusively Protestant Conservative party, which had the support of the most important merchants, had come into office in 1861 when Bannerman had unceremoniously dismissed the mainly Catholic Liberals led by John Kent.[5] This action precipitated a severe crisis, characterized by rioting in parts of Conception Bay and St John's, and active political intervention by both Anglican and Roman Catholic bishops.[6] Once settled in power, however, the Conservatives put religious cries aside. Showing themselves to be, on the whole, cautious, moderate, and honest, their leaders maintained from the outset that effective and progressive government would depend upon the reconciliation of Protestant and Catholic, Conservative and Liberal, after the bitter fights of the 1850s. Hoyles can hardly have expected the Liberals to coalesce with the premier who had ousted them from office, but he kept cabinet posts symbolically open for them, and adopted fair and moderately nationalistic policies to which little exception could be taken.[7] His

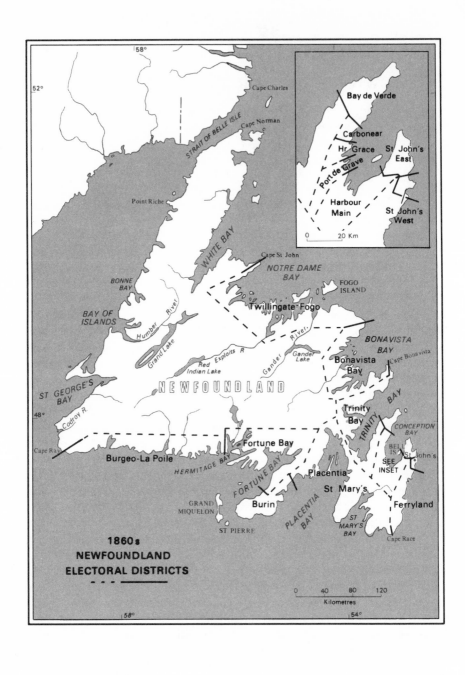

52°

58°

Cape Charles

STRAIT OF BELLE ISLE

Cape Norman

Cape St John

Point Riche

WHITE BAY

NOTRE DAME BAY

FOGO ISLAND

BONNE BAY

Humber River

Twillingate · Fogo

BAY OF ISLANDS

Grand Lake

Red Indian Lake

Exploits R.

Gander River.

Gander Lake

BONAVISTA BAY

Cape Bonavista

N E W F O U N D L A N D

Bonavista Bay

ST GEORGE'S BAY

48°

Codroy R.

Trinity Bay

CONCEPTION BAY

TRINITY BAY

Cape Race

Fortune Bay

BELL IS. St John's SEE INSET

Burgeo-La Poile

HERMITAGE BAY

FORTUNE BAY

Placentia

St Mary's

Ferryland

GRAND MIQUELON

Burin

PLACENTIA BAY

ST MARY'S BAY

ST PIERRE

Cape Race

**1860s
NEWFOUNDLAND
ELECTORAL DISTRICTS**

- - - ━━━

0   40   80   120
Kilometres

58°

54°

Inset:

Bay de Verde

Carbonear

Hr Grace

St John's East

Port de Grave

Harbour Main

St John's West

0   20 Km

government's reaction to attending the Quebec conference was entirely in character. Union was a national question, and should not be treated as a party matter; thus
the delegation should be bi-partisan and denominationally balanced. There had
been no local debate on confederation in any forum, thus the delegates could make
no binding commitment.[8] It was all very cautious, moderate, and reasonable.
Frederick Carter,[9] the respected speaker, would represent Conservatives and
Protestants; Ambrose Shea,[10] one of the leading and most energetic members of
the opposition, Liberals and Catholics.

There is no need to summarize yet again the proceedings of the Quebec
conference. Suffice it to say that the Newfoundland delegates became caught up in
the spirit of the occasion, made enthusiastically confederate speeches at Quebec,
Toronto, and Montreal, and arrived back in St John's on 14 November.[11] The
resolutions which they had signed were printed in the local press on 1 December
and debate on the issue that was to dominate local politics for the next five years
began.[12]

It soon became clear that two important groups were opposed to federation.
These were the major merchants of St John's and Conception Bay, who effectively
dominated the local economy, and the Roman Catholic population. There were, of
course, members of both groups who supported confederation from the start, but
the overwhelming majority of each expressed either outright hostility or deep
reservations. Foreshadowed in newspaper debate and correspondence, the character of the opposition became clearly defined when the legislature opened in January
1865. No vote on the Quebec resolutions was asked for or taken, but in debating a
clause in the throne speech calling for a 'calm examination' of the question and in
subsequent discussion the assembly showed itself almost evenly divided.[13] Eight
of the thirteen Liberals and five of the seventeen Conservatives spoke against
confederation, all of the latter being merchants.[14] The sixteen members favouring
union in principle, if not on the Quebec terms, included most of the lawyers and
smaller businessmen, and five Liberals – John Kent, Ambrose Shea, his two
co-members from Placentia–St Mary's district, and his brother Edward. The
majority of speakers in the largely mercantile Legislative Council declared themselves undecided or opposed.[15]

In these circumstances it was clearly impossible for the government to push for a
definite decision, as it had originally intended.[16] In the opinion of both Hoyles and
Governor Anthony Musgrave,[17] it was better to have no decision than an adverse
one, and given events in the Maritimes, speed no longer seemed essential. In any
case, the government was under pressure from outside the legislature to avoid
precipitate action. On 10 February the Commercial Society drafted a clearly
anti-confederate petition asking for more information and an election on the
issue.[18] The next day an impressive array of Water Street aristocrats addressed a

well-attended public meeting, where a similar petition was unanimously approved.[19] Hoyles conceded the point on 14 February, when he moved a resolution in the assembly establishing that confederation would be decided by the electorate.[20]

The next election was due in the fall of 1865, and the leading confederates probably hoped that its results would provide the necessary *imprimatur*. When the session closed, Hoyles retired from politics to the bench, and was succeeded as premier by Carter, who had no difficulty in persuading Kent and the Shea brothers to join his government. This move had the effect of emasculating the Liberals and strengthening the confederate wing of the Conservatives, besides creating a strong, pan-sectarian administration, which could hope to split the Catholic vote. Carter and his new allies of course justified the amalgamation in loftier terms, arguing in essence that 'Sectarianism had been tried and found wanting,'[21] and that the critical state of the colony demanded a strong government of all the talents.[22] The sincerity of these protestations need not be doubted; however, the anti-confederate press was right to howl in disbelief when the *Newfoundlander* claimed: 'Into the consideration of the arrangements for the coalition Government the idea of Confederation has never entered.'[23] Confederation was not a major issue in the 1865 election, though, because the new government had no wish to make it one. The situation in the Maritimes remained uncertain, the Conservatives divided, the merchants and Catholics hostile. A visitor to St John's found confederation 'a very sore subject ... the feeling against it being much more unanimous than in either New Brunswick, Nova Scotia or Cape Breton.'[24] Time was needed, the confederates thought, to allow reason to work on the minds of the electorate; then, as Edward Shea put it, 'the conversion will be easy and complete.'[25] But even he must have had private doubts about his own district of Ferryland, where he had thought it prudent to retire from the contest after being burned in effigy.[26] In the absence of any significant opponents, Ambrose Shea delivered the three Placentia seats, but in St John's East John Kent found it necessary to assure his constituents that 'no matter what my private convictions may be, I must renounce the advocacy of a measure at variance with the opinions of those on whom I rely for Parliamentary support.'[27] Of the thirteen members elected for predominantly Catholic districts in 1865, only four were confederates; had confederation been a central issue, none would have succeeded.[28]

Though 93 per cent of the Catholic population was native born, it was still very Irish in character and orientation.[29] The priests and schoolteachers were for the most part Irish born and trained, and it is hardly surprising that they looked at the world through the prism of past and contemporary Irish prejudices. Newfoundland Catholics of Irish descent, with few exceptions, accepted the view that the troubles of the homeland derived exclusively from the Act of Union. Confederation was viewed as a proposal to re-enact in a colonial context that infamous piece of legislation. 'The Confederation or Union ... of a small country with a large one is pretty much in the nature of a conquest,' wrote Thomas Talbot, an Irish-born schoolmaster and journalist, 'the relation between them must always be that of slave and master.' The Irish Union demonstrated the point – it had resulted in 'the almost total destruction of the Irish people as a Nation.'[30] 'In proportion as Ireland was made to suffer, Newfoundland would have to suffer also,' echoed the ancient Peter Brennan.[31] '[H]ow has Ireland been under her Union with England?' asked John Kavanagh.

Had she gained any benefits by that? How has it fared with that lovely land of the sun, which might be said, for its fertility, to be flowing with milk and honey – that land whose sons are brave, and its daughters virtuous, who sent forth saints and heroes to instruct man and combat tryants ... Was Ireland benefitted by the union? On the contrary, she lost everything ... she sank far below the level of a petty province, and is now steeped in misery and want ... With this fact before our eyes, let us, in the name of everything that is good, retain that great boon [responsible government] which the mother country bestowed on us ...[32]

This line of argument, casting Canada in the role of England, had an immense emotional force which Catholic confederates could not weaken. Ambrose Shea desperately stressed his O'Connellite credentials, and denied that any parallel could be drawn with Ireland since Newfoundland would join the union on just, negotiated terms.[33] But it was to no avail. To the Catholic mind, union spelled ruin, and its advocates were traitors.

On the whole, the Catholic community in Newfoundland was satisfied with the status quo and was loath to take any action that might destroy it. They had their own, state-funded schools – to the chagrin of the High Church Anglicans who wanted the same – and, in theory, a fair share of government patronage. Through the Liberal party they had fought for and won responsible government, widely perceived as local Home Rule. Change might well be for the worse. There was fear, for instance, that the denominational school system would be destroyed. Even Bishop John Mullock[34] of St John's, who ought to have known better, thought that 'the education of our people [might] be taken out of the hands of the local clergy and transferred to a Board in a remote Province notorious for its anti-Catholic spirit ...'[35] In a chauvinistic outburst, Robert Parsons, editor of the *Patriot*, claimed that the Newfoundland school system, 'probably the best in the world,' would be 'broken up, and we should be compelled to adopt the Canadian system.'[36] Canada – meaning, in local parlance, Canada West – was seen as a hotbed of militant Orangeism, whose spread would accompany confederation to the detriment of the Catholic population. Hitherto, said Talbot, Newfoundland had been mercifully free of both Orangemen and Fenians, but 'Let the Canadians come down here, and let us go up there, and very soon we should have both Fenian and Orange lodges established here.'[37] Better continued independence than the importation of new religious feuds.

Linked with such arguments were patriotic effusions celebrating the glories of Newfoundland and denigrating Canada. A typical example can again be culled from the prolific Talbot:

there is not a country in the world so happily circumstanced as is Newfoundland, and so open to the influences of civilization. She is situated between Europe on the one side, and the United States on the other ... she is in constant communication, through the medium of her commerce, with ... these two great and civilized Continents of the world; she lies on the pathway of both, with the full radiance of all their civilization flashing upon her; and ... she is asked to surrender herself to Canada, a country placed outside the current of civilization, shut out by natural barriers from the Commerce of the world, and influenced in her civilization only by her association with the polar bear.[38]

Such inflated rhetoric was the common coin of all anti-confederates, but it was especially relevant to the Catholics in that it reinforced their belief that in Newfoundland they had built a society which should not be despised, in a country which, though underdeveloped, had great economic potential.

In the face of such deeply felt anti-confederate feeling, the 'easy and complete' conversion of which Edward Shea spoke could only have been effected had the Catholic church chosen to make common cause with the Catholic confederates. In both Nova Scotia and New Brunswick (from 1866) bishops urged Irish Catholics to vote for confederation, and the *Newfoundlander* (edited by Edward Shea) gave prominence to their efforts. But the Newfoundland bishops, Mullock of St John's and John Dalton[39] of Harbour Grace, did not follow the trend. As Irishmen long settled in Newfoundland they shared the prejudices of their flocks, and such evidence as exists indicates that both were opposed to confederation.[40] Neither bishop made any direct public statement on the issues, probably because they had no wish to revive sectarian animosity which, by the later 1860s, had died down significantly. Their withdrawal from active politics after the rowdy crisis of 1861 – for which Mullock had to bear at least some of the blame – made possible the denominational accommodation promoted by Hoyles and completed by Carter. Yet Mullock was a mercurial, outspoken man who, had he believed in it, would have fought for confederation. He did not need to fight against it; it was sufficient to leave the largely anti-confederate priesthood alone, and deny his support to Kent and the Sheas, politicians with whom he had always had uneasy relations. The position of the small band of middle-class Catholic confederates was therefore extremely weak, and their hope of gaining support slim. Lacking episcopal approval they were fair game for virulent anti-confederate attacks which exposed their lack of influence. The elderly Kent, nearing the end of a tortuous political career with prestige tarnished by the events of 1860–1, was no longer the populist of the 1830s and commanded little loyalty. The Sheas, though respected for their talents, were not trusted, and Ambrose in particular was thought to be more concerned with his own and his relations' ambitions than with the good of party or colony:

> I'm a cute old codger, fond of tin,
> And Ambo is my name;
> Tho' very few can take me in,
> At length I've lost my game.
> Sure, you'd think 'twould be a splendid hit,
> And worthy Castlereagh,
> To sway the country every bit,
> And then get dubbed Lord Shea.[41]

If the key to winning the Catholic districts was the support of the priesthood, the key to the predominantly Protestant constituencies was the support of the merchants who supplied the fisheries and otherwise provided employment. The Protestant clergy did not possess the same degree of influence as their Catholic counterparts, and were in any case less inclined to become openly embroiled in politics.[42] The influence of the merchant, on the other hand, was considerable. Running the fisheries on a credit system, he could exert pressure on his dealers at outfitting time in the spring, and again at settling-up time in the fall. Outfits and supplies could be refused or curtailed, debts suddenly called in. Their attitude was obviously crucial.

The initial reaction of the trade was almost unanimously hostile, and was neatly summarized in the report of the St John's Chamber of Commerce for 1865:

So far as this Chamber is aware the project of a Confederation ... was devised as a means of relieving Canada from the political difficulties which have for some time past embarrassed the action of the Legislature, and also of affording more available resources for repelling any act of agression upon that Province on the part of the adjoining republic and of providing access to the Atlantic Seabord at all seasons ... for its products through territory under its own government ... the latter two [objects] ... would apparently confer proportionate advantages on the Provinces of New Brunswick and Nova Scotia, but it is difficult to see what interest this Colony can have in any one of these objects to justify the sacrifice of its independent legislative position and the assumption of a share of the enormous expenditure that must be incurred for the support of the General Government; for the erection of efficient defensive works ... for the maintenance of a Military and Naval force ... and ... for the construction of many public works of advantage to the Provinces only.

These expenditures ... would necessitate the imposition of a very high tariff ... which would press with peculiar and unequal severity on this Colony ...

It is moreover to be apprehended that the operation of such a tariff would divert much of our commerce from its accustomed and most convenient and advantageous channels, by compelling our Importers to have recourse not to the cheapest markets ... but to the Confederated Provinces ...

It [confederation] can open no new or more extensive market for the products of our fisheries, nor does it hold out the prospect of developing new resources within the Colony or of extending those we now possess.[43]

In short, the purposes for which the union had been conceived were irrelevant to Newfoundland, and there was no point in paying higher taxes and dislocating trade to benefit the mainland – sentiments enthusiastically applauded by the Catholic anti-confederates.[44]

Isolated on the periphery of the continent, Newfoundlanders felt no threat to their security, which they assumed would be forever safeguarded by the British government. '[A]s long as Great Britain maintains her supremacy on the Sea, and has any possessions to protect in North America,' wrote Newman and Company, 'we need not fear molestation, at any rate Canada could not help us.'[45] Though St John's was rattled by the occasional scare, Fenianism was not regarded as a danger, and there was no mistrust of the United States. Many Newfoundlanders had relatives living there, even at this comparatively early date, and for economic reasons most merchants wanted as close and untroubled a relationship with the USA as possible. One of the threats of union was involvement in Canadian quarrels which would damage the chance of continued reciprocity, quite apart from costing Newfoundland dearly in terms of money and men.[46]

Newfoundland merchants had relatively little to do with the mainland provinces, which took only about 5 per cent of the colony's exports and provided about 16 per cent of its imports. The markets for Newfoundland produce were in southern Europe, the West Indies, and Brazil; imports came mainly from the United States and Britain, which together provided 70 per cent of the colony's needs.[47] To businessmen operating in this Atlantic economy it appeared essential that trade remain as free as possible, unhampered by tariffs that were high or protective. Engaged in a somewhat precarious business, they must be free to buy and sell where they would, keeping costs as low as possible. Confederation made no economic sense because the other provinces did not represent a promising market for imports or exports. Further, there was the threat of a tariff that would be high – to finance schemes dreamt up by the notoriously spendthrift Canadians for their own benefit – and also protective. Newfoundland merchants' costs would rise as a result, and they would lose the freedom to import from traditional markets. What Canada could not supply would be expensive, because subject to a protective duty. Had the Canadian tariff of 1864 been applied to the Newfoundland imports of the same year, taxes would have risen by nearly 44 per cent.[48] Even if remodelled to meet the needs of the Atlantic region, merchants did not see how taxes could fail to rise significantly, given the commitments of the future federal government. Confederation looked like a poor speculation.

Confederate counter-arguments seemed weak, because they could point to no immediate or tangible benefit. Though confederates were prepared to argue interminably about tariff levels and comparative costs, their most usual reply was to point to the appalling state of the colony and enquire what solution the merchants could offer if they rejected confederation, which at least offered a chance for material and cultural improvement. Many came close to saying that Newfoundland was in such straits that any change would be for the better.[49]

Newfoundland's economic condition, which contrasted so painfully with the relative prosperity of the Maritimes, was caused by a series of poor seal and cod fisheries beginning in the late 1850s, and complications in the Spanish and Brazilian fish markets. The catch of seals declined between 1856 and 1864, with 1862 and 1864 being particularly disastrous years, and did not approach the level of the early 1850s until 1870. Similarly, the catch of cod declined between 1857 and 1868, and though the worst failures were in the inshore fishery, the industry as a whole fared badly in the mid 1860s.[50] Over the same period the population increased by about 19.5 per cent (approximately 24,000), and since no other sector of the economy expanded, the per capita fish export fell steeply while expenditures on poor relief climbed.[51] Between 1861 and 1865, relief payments absorbed, on average, 23 per cent of current revenue before slightly improved conditions and firmer administration by Carter stopped the spiral.[52] In response to poor fisheries and difficult markets, most merchants cut back on their credit business. '[I]t is not our duty,' wrote Newman and Company, 'to maintain Paupers.'[53] It was the duty of the government, and the merchants found it safer and more profitable to let the government look after the problem of fishermen who could not earn enough to buy a winter's diet. As a result, winter supply on credit became exceptional, and summer credit more difficult to obtain.[54] Poverty was endemic. Anglican missionary reports from all over the island comment monotonously on fishery failures, potato blight, short supplies, high food prices, and sickness. 'At no time during my residence of more than twenty years ...,' wrote the Reverend Bertram Jones from Harbour Grace in 1864, 'has the condition of the whole people been more deplorable than it is this winter.'[55]

There was fairly general agreement that the ultimate cure lay in economic diversification. The Conservative governments of the 1860s, as a result, attempted to stimulate mining and agriculture – by instituting a geological survey (1864), and by a scheme of bounty payments for the clearing and cultivation of waste lands (1866) which, it was hoped, would induce people to move to the heads of the bays and combine fishing with agriculture and lumbering.[56] Such initiatives had no immediate results. The area of cultivated land actually declined between the census years of 1857 and 1869, apparent confirmation of the contention that the agricultural traditions of the first generation immigrants largely died with them, their children being content with subsistence farming in a land where soils are poor and acidic, the market was small, and the fisheries left little time for tending fields and flocks.[57] The Geological Survey certainly stimulated interest in the island's mineral potential, but only one mine opened – at Tilt Cove in Notre Dame Bay – and that exploited an ore body discovered in the late 1850s. The more radical Liberals pressed for greater government initiative, urging the Conservatives to subsidize industry, provide tariff protection, and begin large-scale public works.[58] In essence free traders, the latter were not prepared to do more. In their view it was up to private capital to take the initiative.[59] The fact was, though, that local capital was loath to diversify out of the fisheries. Charles Fox Bennett,[60] the eventual anti-confederate leader, was the only merchant in this period who invested significantly in new ventures, possessing besides a share of the Tilt Cove copper mine, a foundry, a brewery and a distillery. Why, it was asked, had not others done the same?

One possible answer was that the merchants, as importers, were naturally averse to the development of import substitutes; another was that in the absence of a protective tariff or an extensive drawback system, it was cheaper to import boats and nets, for instance, than to invest in their local manufacture; a third, widely accepted at the time, was that since many local houses were branches of English and Scottish firms, profits were drained out of the country leaving Newfoundland capital poor.[61] There was an element of truth in each of these points. As a group, the merchants were cautious and conservative; they were more concerned with the stability of their firms, and the creation of some personal wealth out of a hazardous trade, than with the long-term development of the economy of a colony in which few of them would lay their bones. But critics took no account of the fact that merchants had large amounts of capital tied up in the fishery – in premises, inventory, and debts – and had little surplus cash for speculation in enterprises which, in a period of depression, were sure to lose money and in which they had no expertise. If government was not to intervene, and if the merchants were not prepared to diversify, how was stagnation to end?

One answer was confederation, and its supporters urged insistently that union would remove the colony's curse, the great impediment to economic diversification, its isolation from the rest of the world. Better communications, better government would create the climate in which businessmen would begin to invest in the colony. This rather dubious argument did not convince the merchants: if Newfoundland was worth investing in, men would have done so already – and why expect Canadian investment, when most Canadians hardly knew where Newfoundland was, and were borrowing abroad for their own purposes? In their view confederation would create an additional impediment to diversification by raising costs. They could not, however, show how diversification might be achieved, arguing only that taxation and government expenditure should be reduced, and that better times would bring about the desired change.[62] While agreeing on most points, the merchants' Liberal allies could not accept the passive role envisaged for government, a disagreement which spotlighted a fundamental divergence between the two wings of the nascent anti-confederate party, as well as a basic point of agreement among Conservatives, whether or not they favoured confederation.

The Liberal anti-confederates were among those who had fought most fiercely for the grant of responsible government in the 1850s, and they believed in it as a potential agency for promoting reform and progress. They were prepared to admit that there was a case for retrenchment and purification, but not that the system should be abandoned, or infused with principles that would reduce a government's sphere of action. The Conservatives, though, were prepared to admit that responsible government had been a failure. 'Moving within the restricted circle of local politics,' said Carter, 'no matter what comparative amount of political skill a local government could possess, they must be powerless, as any have been powerless to confer any signal and enduring benefit upon the country.' The constitution was cumbersome and expensive, unsuited to so small a colony.[63] Many merchants agreed with him, even if unprepared to accept confederation as the cure. Charles Bennett, who had served on the Executive Council in pre-responsible government days, was especially extreme in his condemnation of responsible government and advocated a return to crown colony status. 'The sooner we get rid of the House of Assembly, and make Newfoundland a Crown Colony, the better,' he wrote, 'for there are but few persons among us who can afford to pay the taxes.'[64] Thus the anti-confederate party emerged as a strange coalition of left and right, those espousing the maintenance of responsible government on principle, and those who hated responsible government but had to argue for its maintenance from a belief that confederation would bring catastrophe.[65] The alliance between Liberal Catholic politicians and the Protestant Tories of Water Street did not go unremarked – Daniel Prowse thought it a 'wonderful and affecting sight' to see these old enemies form 'a solemn league and covenant' – and confederates derived enjoyment from watching Bennett, who had bitterly opposed the introduction of responsible government, pose as the champion and defender of Newfoundland's rights and liberties.[66]

Though united in opposition to confederation in 1864 and 1865, the mercantile community was clearly split on the issue by 1869 when the promised appeal to the electorate finally took place. The fundamental cause appears to lie with the muddled mercantile response to the economic future of the colony. The attitude of Bennett and his friends was basically Micawberish – economize, and something would turn up. But as economic depression continued wearily year after year, it was a point of view increasingly difficult to maintain. The confederate position, which offered a reduction in the cost of local government and the chance of economic recovery, became increasingly attractive as a result. Stephen Rendell, manager of the large St John's firm of Job Brothers, was originally anti-confederate; in 1869, he told the assembly:

... many who were at first opposed ... are now at all events quiet, and think it best to 'accept the situation,' make the best terms we can, and get instead of our present expensive local government, something cheaper, less cumbersome ... This he believed was the general idea that was entertained by those connected with the commerce of the country ... In our present condition we were now perfectly helpless and could do nothing of ourselves.[67]

Economic depression bred confederates out of pessimism and a sense of helplessness.

There were of course other factors. Fears of excessive taxation and trade dislocation were probably lessened by the character of the federal tariff, although there is no direct evidence on this point. A feeling of inevitability appears to have been growing, especially after Nova Scotia's acquiescence in the union, and it was strengthened by an awareness that the imperial government was determined that the colonies should accept the full implications of internal responsibility. '[W]e must look upon Confederation as a foregone conclusion ...,' lamented J.S. Clift of St John's. 'Were we to hesitate ... a pressure would be brought to bear on us that would leave no other alternative.'[68] A final and telling factor in the local context was the character of the anti-confederate coalition. Though Charles Bennett, the emerging leader, was a respected figure in the community, he had always been something of an outsider, and his followers were, for the most part, politically and culturally alien to the mercantile elite. In the last analysis, what troubled many of the Protestant gentry of the colony was the prospect of working with their old religious and political enemies. Sooner Carter and his confederates, who were at least respectable and moderate, than Bennett and his following of dangerously volatile Irishmen – 'leagued with the disaffected rabble,' as one critic said.[69]

In the early months of 1869, then, the prospects for confederation looked favourable. Draft terms of union passed through the legislature without difficulty, and the acquiescence of the merchants seemed final when, on 6 March, Robert Prowse failed to find a seconder for an anti-confederate motion at a meeting of the Commercial Society.[70] The Catholics still appeared obdurate, but in the absence of powerful opposition it seemed likely that Shea could at least win the Placentia seats, thus ensuring that confederation would not be carried by Protestants alone. It is not surprising, therefore, that Carter was urged to call a spring election to coincide with the issuing of fishery supplies. He refused on the grounds that it would be unfair.[71] This remarkably high-minded decision, deriving in part from overconfidence, and in part from a genuine conviction that there was no room for trickery or deceit when the future of a country was at stake, was fatal to confederate chances. During the summer of 1869 the situation was changed by two factors. First, the economy showed signs of improvement. A reasonable seal fishery was followed by a much improved catch of cod – the best since 1858 – accompanied by fair average prices. The upturn was not so dramatic that poverty was banished from the land, but it was sufficient to dispel much of the pessimism that had pervaded the colony during the sixties, and to allow many fishermen to eliminate or reduce their debts so that, as Governor Stephen Hill complained, they could feel 'more or less free and in consequence … [able to] adopt opinions in opposition to the Merchants.'[72] Secondly, Carter's delay in calling the election allowed Bennett and his allies to begin a vigorous and strident campaign, which profited from improved economic conditions, mobilised all anti-confederate elements – Catholic, Liberal, and mercantile – and placed the confederates very much on the defensive. When Hill arrived to replace the blithely optimistic Musgrave in early August, he found that the Protestant vote was no longer securely confederate, and that members of the government 'entertain[ed] grave doubts as to the result of the Elections proving favourable …'[73] Indeed, Carter and Shea must already have realized that the election was lost.

Of the thirty seats in the assembly, thirteen represented the predominantly Roman Catholic districts of the southeast.[74] Reason had so obviously failed to work on the minds of these voters that only four confederate candidates could be found. In St John's East, a Methodist clockmaker was soundly trounced, obtaining votes only in the few Protestant outharbours.[75] In Placentia–St Mary's Ambrose Shea led a slate against Charles Bennett. At Paradise he was advised not to land; at Oderin he was sent on his way with flags at half-mast and three groans; at Placentia he was met by priest and people bearing pots of pitch and bags of feathers, and the moaning of cow horns. His defeat was overwhelming.[76]

Given the division of mercantile opinion, results in the Protestant districts were less predictable. There was, however, one foregone conclusion in the two-seat district of Twillingate-Fogo. The sitting members, William Whiteway – the future premier – and Thomas Knight,[77] faced the combined anti-confederate opposition of the area's two dominant employers. These were the fishery supply house of Muir and Duder, which during the 1860s had come to dominate the Notre Dame Bay business, and the mining company at Tilt Cove.[78] The anti-confederate candidates represented the two interests: Charles Duder the fishery business, Smith McKay, Bennett's partner, the mine. It is not to be wondered at that Whiteway appeared on the hustings trying 'to be merry but it wouldn't do, his face seemed care-worn,' while Knight stayed up the bay canning salmon.[79] They collected only a quarter of the vote.

In other east coast districts the contests were more evenly balanced, even though the preponderance of mercantile influence was in favour of the confederates. Without exception, all the major Conception Bay merchants worked on Carter's behalf and as a result both Carbonear and Harbour Grace (three seats) were won by the confederates, though not without some hard campaigning. Their influence was also decisive in Bay de Verde, where John Bemister, a Carbonear merchant, beat his opponent with the active help of his relative, the Methodist clergyman, who no doubt had an interest in aiding the defeat of a former Methodist, recently turned Anglican.[80] The merchants were unable, however, to deliver the single-member district of Brigus–Port de Grave, where the election was unusually violent. Though the confederate candidate, R.J. Pinsent, had been born in the district of a prominent Conception Bay family he was hampered by the death in 1866 of the district's principal merchant, an event which had caused a political vacuum. When he appeared at Port de Grave in the company of John Munn, largest of the bay merchants, they 'were ... hooted and pelted with stones, sods and filth.' Later in his hazardous campaign Pinsent narrowly avoided ambush, and he was showered with stones and insults with some regularity. Had not troops been sent into the area, it is doubtful that he would have got the 101 votes that he did.[81]

The confederates' loss at Brigus, and the narrow majority at Harbour Grace, indicate that along with the Catholic minority in Conception Bay, many Protestant planters[82] and fishermen were passionately anti-confederate, and, given the economic climate of 1869, unafraid to show it. In Harbour Grace, the confederates fielded John Munn himself and W.S. Green, a prominent Bay Roberts merchant, against the relatively undistinguished opposition of J.L. Prendergast, a small Catholic merchant, and Captain Robert Dawe, a Bay Roberts sealing master. Their victory was narrow, and if the anti-confederate *Courier* can be believed, Munn found it necessary to spend £50 on 'ardent spirits,' close his business, and refuse to pay wages until the polls were declared.[83] It is evident that, had not the Conception Bay merchants used their influence to the fullest, anti-confederates would have swept the board.

In Trinity Bay (three seats) the confederate slate represented mercantile influence. Stephen Rendell, a sitting member, had once managed the Job Brothers' establishment at Hant's Harbour. The business there was, by 1869, run by Ellis Watson, another candidate, who was probably supplied by Jobs. The third candidate was Thomas Ridley of Harbour Grace, who operated branches at Catalina and Heart's Content.[84] Against this impressive trio the anti-confederates ran Stephen March, a locally born St John's merchant, and Robert Alsop, a failed businessman who was nevertheless able to exert considerable influence as chairman of the Board of Works, a position from which Carter did not remove him until just before the election.[85] They were backed by the principal firms of the town of Trinity, Grieve and Bremner and Brooking and Company. The election was hard fought, and very close, the confederates taking two seats, and the anti-confederates one.

Bonavista Bay (three seats) fell to the antis, although the confederates had probably counted on victory. The Protestant vote was almost equally divided. The principal firm in the bay, Brooking and Company, had branches at Bonavista and, more importantly, Greenspond. The local manager, J.L. Noonan, headed the anti-confederate slate, which also had the support of the St John's based firm of J. and W. Stewart. This influence was countered by Ridley's of Harbour Grace, which maintained a small operation at Greenspond and exerted a considerable amount of influence over the town of Bonavista and the southern shore of the bay from its branch at Catalina. The large local traders of Bonavista such as Michael Ryan and Jabez Saint – who dealt with the confederate St John's firm of Baine, Johnston, and Company[86] – were also active on the confederate side. Victory was given the anti-confederates by the Catholic voters living in and around King's Cove, whose natural antipathy to union was sharpened by the fact that one of the confederate candidates, Michael Carroll, had had to close his business there the previous autumn, causing some hardship. The sole confederate vote at King's Cove came from the Anglican minister who, alone among confederates in the village, was allowed to go to the polls.[87]

Of the three predominantly Protestant districts on the south coast, only one was contested. Burgeo–La Poile was handed to the confederates since the anti-confederate – T.R. Smith, Bennett's St John's manager – failed to be properly nominated.[88] In Fortune Bay, the confederates did not oppose the election of the sitting member, Thomas Bennett, an English Harbour trader held in considerable local respect. The dominant firm in the area, Newman and Company of Harbour Breton, was probably anti-confederate (although Governor Hill claimed the opposite) and a confederate would also have had to contend with the hostility of the merchants on the French island of Saint-Pierre.[89]

The Newfoundland–Saint-Pierre trade has never been studied in any detail, but its volume was probably growing during the 1860s with the expansion of the bank fishery, which in turn created a demand for fresh bait. Bankers coming from France would habitually touch at Saint-Pierre to load fresh herring, supplied by Newfoundland fishermen, before making their first voyage. Newfoundlanders traded bait – as well as firewood and game – for supplies which were smuggled back to the island. The merchants of Saint-Pierre prospered as middlemen in this traffic, and Newfoundland fishermen profited from lower prices. Their mutual fear was that confederation would end this trade through the efficient enforcement of customs and fisheries laws. The available evidence indicates that the most politically active of the Saint-Pierre merchants was J.P. Frecker, who did all he could to ensure the defeat in Burin district of his brother-in-law Edward Evans, a Grand Bank merchant, and Frederick Carter, who had inherited this difficult seat from Hoyles.

The Burin election was the closest contest of all. Carter and Evans had to contend not only with Frecker, but also with the overt hostility of the Catholic priest, whose flock comprised 38 per cent of the population. Prominent antis campaigning on Bennett's behalf in the neighbouring district of Placentia–St Mary's made frequent incursions, and Carter was further handicapped by the necessity of his speaking on behalf of candidates elsewhere in the island. There is no evidence that the confederates received a significant amount of mercantile support, and there may well be truth in the *Courier*'s accusation that they had to encourage and exploit an adverse Protestant reaction to the strident campaigning of the local Catholics – a common enough tactic in a district where the electorate was fairly equally divided into Methodists, Anglicans, and Catholics.[90] In the event, the confederates won by five votes – proxies from Frenchman's Cove, whose authors were immediately visited by one of Frecker's agents and bidden to repair at once to Burin and change their minds. This they did, and the returning officer obligingly altered the poll book. Carter, however, persuaded him to change it back, fought off his opponents' charges that he had received pauper votes as well, and returned in triumph to St John's with the hapless returning officer in tow.[91]

The final election result gave the confederates nine seats, the antis twenty-one.[92] The analysis presented above has attempted to show that this was brought about by two basic factors: the implacable opposition of the mass of Catholic voters to any scheme of union, and a division in mercantile ranks which made it impossible for Carter to carry all the Protestant seats. It does not, however, account for the close margins by which all victorious confederates won their seats. There was, obviously, a powerful groundswell of anti-confederate sentiment that was by no means confined to the Catholic districts. It has already been suggested that one cause of this was the improvement in the fisheries, which removed the apathy that was the confederates' best ally. Another was the fact that, on the Labrador coast in the summer of 1869, Newfoundland fishermen imbibed the anti-confederate opinions of Nova Scotians.[93] Licking their wounds after the election, confederates added two others: the abolition of able-bodied poor relief in 1868, and the highly emotional character of the anti-confederate campaign.

By proclamation in June 1868 the government confined relief to the sick, infirm, destitute widows, and orphans.[94] This measure was almost universally applauded by the colonial elite as a means of reducing expenditure and removing the pauperism that was thought to be demoralizing the populace. In the poverty-stricken outports it was predictably unpopular. At Fogo the magistrates offered a reward for the apprehension of those 'who did wilfully and maliciously besmear the said Proclamation with *Cow dung* – thereby offering a gross and malicious insult to the Governor and Government of Newfoundland.'[95] That Carter should risk such a move so near to a crucial election shows how much more he and his government were concerned with satisfying the traditional moulders of opinion than with gratifying the electorate. It was, as he later admitted, a bad political mistake. 'If anything could have kept the late government in power,' said Carter in 1870, 'that thing would be [*sic*] the continuance of pauper relief.'[96] Likewise, Pinsent believed that 'hundreds throughout the country would have voted for confederation if they could, as usual, have received the customary dole ...'[97] Governments associated with, and thought to have contributed to, hard times are usually unpopular; Carter's was no exception.

Confederates were agreed, however, that the character of the campaign was of greater significance. Carter complained bitterly of irresponsible rumour-mongering; people had been told 'they would be sold into slavery. They had even been told that their young children would be rammed into guns, their young men taken away. Even the taking of the Census, it was said, was for the ... information of the Canadian government.'[98] Captain Edward White, a sealing skipper of Greenspond background who campaigned for the confederates in Bonavista Bay, said he had often been asked: 'are our gardens to be sold; are our hoops, poles to be taxed; and some assured him they were told if they had a pig to be killed, they should send to Canada for a person to come and kill it, who would take half for his portion.'[99] The antis worked on the ignorance, credulity, and conservatism of rural Newfoundland and without difficulty created a deep fear of Canada and confederation against which 'Influence ... was ineffectual.'[100] '[I]t was better to bide as us be,' said McKay's seconder at Twillingate, 'than to sill the country and have the "Kennedy's" a comin down to make slaves of us.'[101] Robert Kent, a prosperous St John's merchant, was laughed at by the labourers on his wharf who declared 'they got enough of union at home.'[102] The cries of excessive taxation, conscription, and selling the country 'so bewildered the poor people that they did not know whether they were standing on their heads or their heels.'[103] The confederates' position was difficult, for, as Nicholas Stabb remarked, it was far easier to inspire terror than remove it.[104] Rational argument was certainly attempted, and the electorate was provided with elaborate assurances that taxation would be reduced and the economy improved; but in the end, the confederates had to fight with the same weapons, confusing the issue even more. If the antis attacked them as a coterie of place-hunting lawyers, they in turn were branded as the reactionary dupes of a mining monopolist. If the antis bewailed the loss of the British connection, the confederates lambasted them as closet annexationists. The more the antis played on the prejudices of the Catholic voter, the more confederate candidates and newspapers played up the threat of a Catholic political ascendancy should Bennett win. The antis did not have a monopoly on exaggeration and slander. Nevertheless, it was they who set the tone of the campaign, turning it into a lusty brawl in which they held the superior weapon – fear of the unknown.

Confederation could only have been won had Carter been willing to abandon the pledge given by Hoyles in 1865 that the electorate would be consulted or, alternatively, had he been prepared to fight the election in the spring of 1869 and mount an overtly anti-Catholic campaign. There were fears that the mistrusted Ambrose Shea would persuade Carter to merely pass an address through the legislature, as provided for by the British North America Act, but the latter reaffirmed his policy on several occasions. For example, at a meeting in St John's in October 1867, he stated before a hostile audience that confederation would occur only 'if the people wanted it ... and that was *his* solemn promise and determination ... (Loud cheers for Mr. Carter).'[105] He was not prepared to follow Tupper's example, believing, like his opponent Thomas Glen, that the 'constitution was granted, not to the House of Assembly, but to the people of Newfoundland, and ... the people were entitled to be consulted ...'[106] For the same reasons, he was not disposed to allow a spring election in 1869. The sectarian cries that were used by some confederate candidates in the election were the result of desperation rather than part of a planned strategy. An overtly sectarian campaign would have been abhorrent to Carter not only because a great question was to be decided, but also because it would have negated the basis of his coalition government, which enjoyed the support of many members of the Catholic bourgeoisie. He had denounced sectarian politics as sterile and, like many others, was haunted by memories of the violently sectarian battles of the 1850s and earlier, and their spectacular culmination in 1861. Given his principles, Carter had no alternative but to put the question in the fall of 1869.

Such justifications for Carter's actions should not obscure the fact that he lacked the dynamism imparted by personal ambition and thus tended to shy away from bold and decisive political action. He was temperamentally unable to turn the confederate campaign into a crusade, or to indulge in the sharp practice that might have brought success. From a Canadian perspective, which views confederation as an unquestionable good, Carter may seem to be a rather colourless failure; but it was his character which, from a Newfoundland point of view, made him an ideal premier for the later 1860s and gave him an important place in the country's history. Respected, trusted, honest, and broad-minded, Carter was the only politician who could heal the divisions created by previous battles and pave the way for party politics based on issues other than religion. His great achievement was the establishment of the principle of denominational power sharing, a development which, though possessing harmful side effects, at least prevented Newfoundland from developing into a transatlantic Ulster.

Many confederates were bitter in defeat. Claiming that the election had been carried 'by means the most fraudulent and flagitious,' they argued that the result did not represent the 'rational and dispassionate judgment of the community,' and was therefore not a true verdict.[107] Governor Hill agreed with this assessment; supplying the Colonial Office with details of the uniquely rowdy election at Brigus, he suggested to Granville that Newfoundland be thrust into confederation by imperial order in council. The Colonial Office demurred.[108] Besides the legal impossibility was the traditional insistence that the consent of the colonies involved was essential. 'I should deprecate anything like using violence,' Blackwood had minuted in 1866, when Musgrave suggested the application of pressure. 'This scheme of Union is the offspring of the Colonies. It is not initiated or forced on them by H.M. Govt.'[109] Newfoundland was in any case thought to be less vital to the success of the scheme than any other colony, and officials were worried lest imperial bullying should lead to difficulties over the French Shore – the interminable question around which all Colonial Office thinking about Newfoundland revolved.[110] From the lack of any significant reaction in London to the results of the 1869 election it can be deduced that the officials felt sooner or later confederation would happen; in the meantime Newfoundland's political isolation posed no problem.

Ottawa reacted in a similar manner. Newfoundland had never been viewed as a vital component of the confederation, and Canadian politicians had taken no active interest in Carter's campaign. There had been no delegations to the colony, no ministerial visits, no funds. Newfoundland was 'of no importance to Canada,' Macdonald told Lisgar, and the terms of union had been too generous. A reaction would soon occur.[111] An unidentified member of his cabinet told the French consul at Québec that 'il ne fera une seule démarche pour ramener les récalcitrants; il se bornera à attendre ... "Terre-Neuve est trop pauvre pour persister longtemps dans cette opposition," ajoutait ce Ministre, "et la faim nous la fera ramener".'[112]

Given what had occurred in Nova Scotia and New Brunswick, and the fact that Carter commanded the support of most of the colony's able politicians, the supposition that confederation had only been postponed was not unreasonable. It

TABLE 1
Social characteristics of candidates for the 1869 election

| | Total cands. | Age[a] | | Occupation | | |
		Ave	Median	Mchnts & Busnsmen	Professions	Other
Confeds	20	49.4	47	13 (65%)	6 (25%)	1
Antis	27	54.5	55.5	15 (55.6%)	7 (25.9%)	5

| | Birthplace[b] | | | Residence | | Denomination[c] | | |
	British Isles	BNA	Nfld	St John's	Other	RC	CE	Dissent
Confeds	10	1	8 (42%)	10 (50%)	10	4 (20%)	9	7
Antis	8	4	13 (52%)	20 (74.1%)	7	9 (34.6%)	9	8

[a]Ages known for 17 confederates, 20 anti-confederates
[b]Birthplace known for 19 confederates, 25 anti-confederates
[c]Denomination known for all confederates, 26 anti-confederates

was based, however, on the expectation that the Newfoundland confederates would remain active supporters of union, and this was not to be the case. Within a few years they had decided to accept the obvious: that the electorate was overwhelmingly opposed to union, and was likely to remain so unless some compelling reason for changing its mind emerged. To remain wedded to confederation was to accept perpetual exclusion from office. Thus the Conservatives abandoned confederation, and having managed to convince the voters that the matter was indeed closed, regained control of the government in 1874. The basis from which all governments now had to work was the colony's continued independence. Newfoundland began to take independent, nationalistic attitudes towards such questions as the North Atlantic fisheries, reciprocity, and the French Shore, much to the annoyance of both Ottawa and London. The confederates of the 1860s, then, became the nationalists of the late nineteenth century, but they never lost the continental orientation that had in part distinguished them from the antis. Thus when Carter and Whiteway looked for ways to develop the local economy, they took Macdonald as the exemplar and launched into a program of railway building designed to open up the 'hidden resources' of the interior. There was no attempt to create an indigenous development strategy, with the result that a tiny political unit became burdened with a huge development debt, gradually sank into insolvency, and after a decent interval, confederation. In this sense the nineteenth-century confederates succeeded; in the short term they failed because most Newfound-

TABLE 2
1869 election – summary of results

District	Population[a]	RC[a] Prot.%	Turnout[b] %	Confederate candidates	Anti-confederate candidates
Twillingate/Fogo	13,067	15 / 85	70.3%	W.V. Whiteway (208), T. Knight (83)	C. Duder (1,025), S. McKay (1,063), J.L. Noonan (697), W.M. Barnes (650), F. Winton (657)
Bonavista Bay	11,560	20.9 / 79.1	77.1	J.H. Warren (539), J.T. Burton (537), M. Carroll (515)	R. Alsop, S. March
Trinity Bay	13,817	10 / 90	87.8	S. Rendell, T.H. Ridley, E.C. Watson	R. Reader
Bay de Verde	7,057	24.5 / 75.5	70.9	J. Bemister	F. Taylor
Carbonear	5,633	42 / 58	80.2	J. Rorke	J.L. Prendergast, R. Dawe
Harbour Grace	12,740	32.6 / 67.4	82.5	J. Munn, W.S. Green	J.B. Wood (735)
Brigus–Port de Grave	7,546	25.3 / 74.7	87.8	R.J. Pinsent (101)	W.P. Walsh (1,327), J.A. Jordan (1,325), R.J. Parsons, Sr (1,298)
St John's East	17,204	75.2 / 24.8	65.9	W.T. Parsons (412)	P. Brennan, T. Talbot, H. Renouf[c]
St John's West	11,646	65.4 / 34.6	No contest	–	J.I. Little, J. Kennedy
Harbour Main	6,542	76.2 / 23.8	No contest	–	T. Glen, T. Badcock
Ferryland	5,991	97.1 / 2.9	No contest	–	
Placentia/St Mary's	8,794	84 / 16	71.1	A. Shea (100), P. Barron (90), T. O'Reilly (103)	C.F. Bennett (882), R.J. Parsons, Jr (860), H. Renouf (872)

TABLE 2 (*Concluded*)

District	Population	RC[a] Prot.%	Turnout[b] %	Confederate candidates	Anti-confederate candidates
Burin	6,731	37.8 62.2	85.4	*F.B.T. Carter* E. Evans	H.C. LeMessurier J. Woods *T.R. Bennett*
Fortune Bay	5,233	24.7 75.3	No contest	–	
Burgeo–La Poile	5,119	2.8 97.2	No contest	*P. Emerson*	–
Total for colony including Labrador and French Shore	146,546			Total elected: 9	Total elected: 21

[a]Figures from 1869 census
[b]Figures derived from 1870 Blue Book; percentage is of registered voters
[c]L. Tessier (anti) was elected in 1870 to fill the St John's West seat vacated by Renouf

landers, rightly or wrongly, believed that the experiment of independence should at least be given a fair trial. 'Let us try ... .' urged Robert Parsons, 'before we seek to absorb this country in the New Dominion to become the outharbor of another province.'[113]

NOTES

1 Hugh Hoyles, born St John's, 1815; lawyer; premier and attorney general, 1861–5; chief justice, 1865–80.

2 A detailed narrative of events can be derived from the following: A.M. Fraser, 'The Issue of Confederation, 1864–70,' in R.A. MacKay (ed.), *Newfoundland: Economic, Diplomatic and Strategic Studies* (Toronto 1946); H.B. Mayo, 'Newfoundland and Confederation in the Eighteen-Sixties,' *CHR* 29 (1948): 125–42; P.B. Waite, *The Life and Times of Confederation*, 2nd ed. (Toronto 1962); E.C. Moulton, 'The Political History of Newfoundland, 1861–1869' (unpublished MA thesis, Memorial University 1960), ch. 5, 7; W.D. MacWhirter, 'A Political History of Newfoundland, 1865–1874' (unpublished MA thesis, Memorial University 1963), ch. 1; F.J. Smith, 'Newfoundland and Confederation, 1864–1870' (unpublished MA thesis, University of Ottawa 1970).

3 Minute of council, 12 Sept. 1864, *JHA*, 1865, appendix, 845.

4 Minute of council, 13 Sept. 1864, *JHA*, 1865, appendix, 846–7.

5 John Kent, born Waterford, 1805; commission merchant; premier, 1858–61.

6 E.C. Moulton, 'Constitutional Crisis and Civil Strife in Newfoundland, February to November 1861,' *CHR* 48 (1967): 251–72; John P. Greene, 'The Influence of Religion in the Politics of Newfoundland, 1850–61' (unpublished MA thesis, Memorial University 1970), ch. 6; Gertrude Gunn, *The Political History of Newfoundland 1832–1864* (Toronto 1966), ch. 11.

7 For an account of Hoyles' ministry, see Moulton, 'Political History, 1861–1869.'

8 Minute of council, 13 Sept. 1864, *JHA*, 1865, appendix, 846–97.

9 Frederick B.T. Carter, born St John's, 1819; lawyer; premier and attorney general, 1865–70, 1874–8; chief justice, 1880–1900.

10 Ambrose Shea, born St John's, 1816; merchant; member of assembly, 1848–69, 1874–87; governor of the Bahamas, 1887.

11 Their speeches at the Quebec conference on 10 Oct. 1864 can be found in 'A.A. Macdonald's Notes on the Quebec Conference, 10–29 October 1864,' printed in G.P. Browne (ed.), *Documents on the Confederation of British North America* (Toronto 1969), 129–30. The speech given by Carter to Quebec Board of Trade, printed in *Newfoundlander* (St John's), 3 Nov. 1864; at Toronto, printed in ibid., 24 Nov. 1864; by Shea at Montreal, printed in ibid., 17 Nov. 1864, which also reports their return.

12 The resolutions appeared first in the *Newfoundlander*, owned by the Shea family and edited by Ambrose's brother Edward, also a Liberal politician. Born 1820, Edward was a member of the assembly, 1848–69, and member of the Legislative Council, 1873–1913.

13 *JHA*, 1865, 2; for the assembly debate on this clause see *Newfoundlander*, 2–16, 21 Feb. 1865. For subsequent debates on confederation in 1865, see *Newfoundlander*, 9 March to 1 May 1865.

14 Stephen Rendell of Job Brothers was absent from the house, but it is known that he was anti-confederate at this time. The standings were therefore 16 favourable to confederation, 14 opposed.

15 For the Legislative Council debate on 13–14 Feb. 1865, see *Newfoundlander*, 16, 23, 27 Feb., 6, 9 March 1865.

16 Hoyles in assembly debate, 14 Feb. 1865 (ibid., 16 Feb. 1865).

17 Anthony Musgrave, born Antigua, 1828; governor of Newfoundland, 1864–9, and of British Columbia, 1869–71.

18 *Times and General Commercial Gazette* (St John's), 15 Feb. 1865. The petition was presented to the assembly, 23 Feb. 1865 ((*Newfoundlander*, 6 March 1865), and to the Legislative Council, 13 Feb. 1865 (ibid., 16, 23 Feb. 1865).

19 For various accounts of the meeting, see *Day Book* (St John's), 13 Feb. 1865; *Times and General Commercial Gazette*, 15 Feb. 1865; *Courier* (St John's), 15 Feb. 1865; *Newfoundlander*, 13 Feb. 1865; *Telegraph* (St John's), 15 Feb. 1865. Presented to assembly, 20 Feb. 1865 (see *Newfoundlander*, 3 March 1865).

20 Hoyles in assembly debate, 14 Feb. 1865 (*Newfoundlander*, 16 March 1865).

21 Ambrose Shea in assembly debate, 8 Feb. 1866 (ibid., 19 Feb. 1866).

22 See Kent, Carter in assembly debate, 8 Feb. 1866 (ibid., 19, 22 Feb. 1866, and editorial, 23 Nov. 1865). See also CO 194/174, Musgrave to Cardwell, 19 April 1865.

23 *Newfoundlander*, 27 April 1865.

24 Extract from *Edinburgh Daily Review* printed in *Times and General Commercial Gazette*, 7 Oct. 1865.

25 *Newfoundlander*, 21 Dec. 1865.

26 Ibid., 6 Nov. 1865; Archives of the Roman Catholic Archdiocese of St John's, Edward Morris diary, 11 Oct. 1865. Morris, a member of the Legislative Council, was a cousin of John Kent.

27 John Kent, 'To the Electors of the Eastern Division of the District of St. John's,' 29 Sept. 1865, printed in *Newfoundlander*, 6 Nov. 1865.

28 The predominantly Catholic districts were Placentia–St Mary's (3), Ferryland (2), St John's West (3), St John's East (3) and Harbour Main (2).

29 Figure derived from Newfoundland census of 1869.

30 Thomas Talbot, 'A Few Brief Observations on Confederation, Its Nature and Effects,' printed in *Chronicle* (St John's), 11–13 Sept. 1869.

31 Brennan in assembly debate, 1 March 1869 (*Newfoundlander*, 17 March 1869). A

merchant and bone-setter, Brennan was 80 when elected for St John's West in 1866.

32 Kavanagh in assembly debate, 28 Feb. 1865 (ibid., 20 April 1865).

33 Shea in a speech at Harbour Grace in 1869, reported in *Chronicle*, 24 Sept. 1869, and *Courier*, 25 Sept. 1869; in assembly debates, 27 Jan., 21 Feb. 1865 (*Newfoundlander*, 6 Feb., 2 March 1865).

34 John Mullock, born Limerick, 1807; coadjutor bishop, 1848; bishop of St John's, 1850–69.

35 Lenten pastoral, 1867, in *Newfoundlander*, 6 March 1867.

36 Parsons in assembly debate, 26 Feb 1869 (ibid., 12 March 1865).

37 Talbot in assembly debate, 7 March 1866 (ibid., 5 April 1866). Compare speeches by Kearney, 16 Feb. 1866, and Brennan, 1 March 1869, reported in ibid., 8 March 1866, and 17 March 1869, respectively.

38 Talbot, 'A Few Brief Observations,' *Chronicle*, 23 Sept. 1869.

39 John Dalton, born Tipperary, 1821; arrived Newfoundland, 1839; bishop of Harbour Grace, 1856–69.

40 In 1866 Dalton signed an anti-confederate petition (see Arthur Fox, 'The Merchants' 1866 Petition against Confederation,' in J.R. Smallwood (ed.), *The Book of Newfoundland*, vol. 5 (St John's, 1975), 190–3). In 1868 Mullock spoke strongly against confederation in private conversation (Edward Morris diary, 13 May 1868).

41 'Ambo's Lament,' *Chronicle*, 1 Oct. 1869.

42 Scattered evidence from the press and letters from Anglican ministers to the Society for the Propagation of the Gospel (PANL, Society papers, Series E, microfilm) suggests that the Protestant clergy was generally in favour of confederation. Edward Feild, the Anglican bishop, was cautious, however; '[L]et us not build much ... upon the proposed Confederation,' he told his flock in the spring of 1869; 'or the new laws and legislators under and by which we shall be governed. We may hope for some change for the better in our social, as well as political state. But he must have a greater faith in Dominion politics and politicians than I have, who expects to obtain much relief from that quarter' (The 'Poor Pastoral' in H.W. Tucker, *Memoir of the Life and Episcopate of Bishop Feild, D.D.* (London 1877), appendix A, 301).

43 CO 194/174, enclosure in Musgrave to Cardwell, 19 Aug. 1865.

44 For example, Parsons in assembly debate, 28 Feb. 1865 (*Newfoundlander*, 2 April 1865); Glen in assembly debate, 12 Feb. 1866 (ibid., 20 Feb. 1866).

45 PANL, Newman Hunt papers, Letterbook, 1858–65 (microfilm), Newman, Hunt and Co. (London) to J. and W. Stewart (St John's), 13 March 1865.

46 For the attitude towards Fenianism see, for example, Edward Morris diary, 23–31 March 1866; *Newfoundlander*, 12, 19 Jan. 1865; *Patriot* (St John's), 20 Oct. 1866. The attitude towards the USA can be seen in letters from C.F. Bennett to *Times and General Commercial Gazette*, 21 Nov., 5 Dec. 1868; Talbot, 'A Few Brief Observations,' *Chronicle*, 17 Sept. 1869.

47 The percentages represent averages for the period 1857–63.

48 Calculated from a table printed in *JHA*, 1865, appendix, 302–9. The average annual revenue per capita for the period 1860–4 was $4.18. Application of the Canadian tariff to the 1864 Newfoundland imports resulted in a per capita increase of $1.82.

49 For example, letter of Ambrose Shea to his constituents, 7 Feb. 1867, *Newfoundland*, 12 Feb. 1867.

50 Sir W. MacGregor, *Report of the Foreign Trade and Commerce of Newfoundland*, 1905 (Cmnd. 2480), tables 6, 8. See also above.

51 Shannon Ryan, 'The Newfoundland Cod Fishery in the Nineteenth Century' (unpublished MA thesis, Memorial University 1971), table 14, 41.

52 Figure derived from PANL Blue Books, 1861–70.

53 PANL, Newman Hunt papers, Letterbook, 1866–72, Newman, Hunt and Co. (London) to Newman and Co. (Newfoundland), 24 April 1869.

54 Glen in assembly debate, 3 Feb. 1864 (*Newfoundlander*, 18 Feb. 1864); *Day Book*, 19 May 1865; 'Tyro' to *Courier*, 21 Dec. 1867.

55 Society for the Propagation of the Gospel papers, E series, microfilm, Jones to Hawkins, 31 Dec. 1864.

56 The Act to Reduce Pauperism by Encouraging Agriculture was passed in 1866. The Conservatives also provided small bounties to encourage ship-building and bank fishing.

57 Carter in assembly debate, 21 Feb. 1866 (*Newfoundlander*, 15 March 1866); Prowse in assembly debate, 1 March 1866 (ibid., 26 March 1866).

58 For example, Talbot in assembly debate, 8 Feb. 1866 (ibid., 19 Feb. 1866); Renouf in assembly debate, 11 Feb. 1868 (ibid., 14 Feb. 1868); Parsons in assembly debate, 27 Feb. 1868 (ibid., 28 Feb. 1868).

59 Carter in assembly debate, 21 Feb. 1866 (ibid., 15 March 1866); Prowse in assembly debate, 11 Feb. 1868 (ibid., 14 Feb. 1868); Kent in assembly debate, 6 March 1868 (ibid., 11 March 1868).

60 Charles Fox Bennett, born Dorset, 1793; merchant; premier, 1870–4.

61 'Bayman' to *Courier*, 30 Dec. 1865, expressed the first suggestion. For the second see M. Kearney to *Chronicle*, 10 Nov. 1866, and in assembly debate, 12 Feb. 1866 (*Newfoundlander*, 1 March 1866); see also 'Vindex' to *Courier*, 31 Jan. 1866; *Chronicle*, 26 Feb. 1868. For examples of the third point of view, see Hogsett in assembly debate, 1 April 1867 (*Newfoundlander*, 3 April 1867); 'Comus' to *Courier*, 25 Nov. 1868.

62 See C.F. Bennett's letters to *Times and General Commercial Gazette*, 2 Nov., 4, 12 Dec. 1868.

63 Carter in assembly debate, 23 Feb. 1869 (*Newfoundlander*, 3 March 1869).

64 Bennett to *Times and General Commercial Gazette*, 11 Feb. 1867. For a comparison see Bennett to *Chronicle*, 7 Dec. 1868.

65 'Senex' to *Chronicle*, 25 Feb. 1867; 'Hampden' to ibid., 11 Oct. 1868; editorials in

ibid., 13 Feb., 20 March 1867. Bennett's reactionary attitudes goaded Thomas Glen, a leading Liberal, to reply; for their bitter exchange, see ibid., November 1868 to January 1869.

66 Prowse in assembly, 6 Feb. 1865 (*Newfoundlander*, 20 Feb. 1865).

67 Rendell in assembly debate, 4 Feb. 1869 (ibid., 10 Feb. 1809).

68 Clift in Legislative Council debate, 12 March 1869 (*Times and General Commercial Gazette*, 24 March 1869).

69 'Comus' to *Courier*, 25 Nov. 1868.

70 For the draft terms, see *JHA*, 1869, 33–6. For the final terms, see Canada, *Sessional Papers*, 1869, vol. 5, no. 51. For the report of the Commercial Society meeting see *Newfoundlander*, 10 March 1869.

71 Prescott Emerson, 'Carter: A Father of Confederation,' reprinted in J.R. Smallwood (ed.), *Book of Newfoundland*, vol. 6 (St John's 1975), 58.

72 CO 194/178, Hill to Granville, 22 Oct. 1869. Hill (1809–91) was governor of Newfoundland from 1869 to 1876.

73 Ibid., Hill to Granville, 8 Aug. 1869.

74 See note 28 above. For a social analysis of the candidates, see table 1.

75 *Patriot*, 16 Nov. 1869.

76 *Courier*, 16 Oct. 1869, and J.E. Collins, *Life and Times of the Right Honourable Sir John A. Macdonald* (Toronto 1883), 311–12. The anti-confederate majority was about 770 votes.

77 For Whiteway's career see above, 38 n20. Thomas Knight ran a small business in Green Bay and had represented the district since 1855.

78 Ryan, 'Newfoundland Cod Fishery,' 89–91. Muir and Duder absorbed the business formerly carried on by the Slades and W. Cox and Co.

79 'A Looker on at Twillingate' to *Telegraph*, 22 Dec. 1869.

80 *Courier*, 27 Nov. 1869.

81 For Pinsent's version of events, see CO 194/178, enclosures in Hill to Granville, 22 Nov. 1869.

82 See table 2.

83 *Courier*, 27 Nov. 1809. The voting figures are not known for any of the Conception Bay districts except Brigus. For Munn, see *Dictionary of Canadian Biography* (hereafter *DCB*), 10: 538.

84 For Thomas Ridley, see *DCB*, 10: 617–18.

85 For Robert Alsop, see *DCB*, 10: 8–9. The voting figures for Trinity Bay are not known.

86 'In Re Jabez Saint. 1883' in E.P. Morris (ed.), *Decisions of the Supreme Court of Newfoundland, 1874–84* (St John's 1898), 477.

87 J. T. Lawton and P. K. Devine, *Old King's Cove* (St John's 1944), 10–11, 17–18, 61–2. The Bonavista Bay results can be found in *Telegraph*, 1 Dec. 1869.

88 *Courier*, 22 Feb. 1870.

89 CO 194/178, Hill to Granville, December 1869. The last reference to confederation in the firm's correspondence is in February 1869, and was not favourable (see Newman, Hunt papers. Newfoundland letterbook, 1866–72, 150, Newman, Hunt and Co. (London) to J. and W. Stewart (St John's, 22 Feb. 1869).

90 *Courier*, 21 Jan., 8, 16 March 1870.

91 'Vindex' to *Telegraph*, 16 March 1870; *Express*, 26 Feb. 1870; *Chronicle*, 21 Nov. 1869.

92 H. Renouf was elected for both St John's West and Placentia. In 1879, Lewis Tessier (anti) was elected for the St John's vacancy. See table 2.

93 *Newfoundlander*, 15 Oct. 1869; *Courier*, 16 Oct. 1969.

94 *Newfoundlander*, 19 June 1868.

95 Public notice, July 1868 (copy in PANL, CS 2/80).

96 Carter in assembly debate, 18 Feb. 1870 (*Chronicle*, 5 March 1870).

97 Pinsent in Legislative Council debate, 3 Feb. 1870 (*Newfoundlander*, 11 Feb. 1870).

98 Carter in assembly debate, 18 Feb. 1870 (*Chronicle*, 5 March 1870).

99 White in Legislative Council debate, 9 Feb. 1870 (*Newfoundlander*, 18 Feb. 1870).

100 Pinsent in Legislative Council debate, 3 Feb. 1870.

101 'A Looker on at Twillingate' to the *Telegraph*, 22 Dec. 1869.

102 Kent in Legislative Council debate, 9 Feb. 1870 (*Newfoundlander*, 18 Feb. 1870).

103 'Retriever,' Bonavista, to *Telegraph*, 6 April 1870.

104 Stabb in Legislative Council debate, 11 Feb. 1870 (*Newfoundlander*, 15 Feb. 1870).

105 *Chronicle*, 11 Oct. 1867.

106 Glen in assembly debate, 27 Jan. 1865 (*Newfoundlander*, 2 Feb. 1865).

107 *Newfoundlander*, 10 Dec. 1869; Pinsent in Legislative Council debate, 3 Feb. 1870.

108 CO 194/178, Hill to Granville, 20 Nov. 1869; Granville to Hill, 24 Dec. 1869.

109 CO 194/175, Minute by Blackwood, 28 July 1866.

110 See, for example, ibid., minute by Rogers, 31 July 1866. In 1868 Elliott wrote that he thought the existence of the French Shore problem made it undesirable for Newfoundland to confederate – 'much embarrassment might arise if we had to deal upon those questions with so powerful a Community as Canada' (CO 194/177, minute, 3 June 1868).

111 Macdonald to Lisgar, 8 Dec. 1869, in J. Pope, *Memoirs of the Rt. Hon. Sir John A. Macdonald* (Toronto 1930), 505–6.

112 Public Archives of Canada, Ministère des Affaires étrangères, correspondance consulaire politique, Québec et Montréal, microfilm, vol. 44, 369, F. Gautier to secretary of state, 29 Nov. 1869.

113 Parsons in assembly debate, 27 Feb. 1868 (*Newfoundlander*, 28 Feb. 1868).

The French and American Shore Questions as Factors in Newfoundland History

PETER NEARY

For students of nineteenth-century British North American life the common threads running through the histories of the colonies have offered a rich and rewarding research connection. Not least among them is the obstacle which the property rights entrenched in the great constitutional and diplomatic settlements of the eighteenth century posed – or were thought by developers and liberal reformers to pose – to material advancement and constitutional reform. In Upper Canada the clergy reserves question was one of the most abrasive political issues until its settlement in 1854. In Lower Canada the problems associated with seigneurial tenure constituted a similar source of political division; while in Prince Edward Island the absentee landlord situation was resolved only after the island became part of Canada in 1873. Newfoundland has a similar theme in the French and American shore questions, but in the Newfoundland case the problems arising from the eighteenth-century inheritance were not finally resolved until the early twentieth century. The remarkable persistence of these ancient Anglo-French and Anglo-American differences helped make Newfoundlanders, in Lord Salisbury's phrase, 'the sport of historic errors.'[1] Newfoundland's diplomatic legacies must be taken into account in any systematic attempt to compare her development with that of the other British North American colonies. Thus, if the explanation for New-foundland's slower pace of development lies primarily in the factors of geo-graphical isolation and marginal resource endowment, the factor of historical adversity must also be considered.

I

Of the two international fishery questions that many Newfoundlanders came to perceive during the nineteenth century as victimizing them, the older and more tortured by far was that relating to the French Shore. The origin of this dispute lay in article thirteen of the Treaty of Utrecht of 1713. Under it France had abandoned her claim to Newfoundland, but French fishermen had been 'allowed ... to catch fish, and to dry them on land, in that part only, and in no other besides that, of the said island ... which stretches from the place called Cape Bonavista, to the northern point of the said island, and from thence running down by the western side, reaches as far as the place called Point Riche.'[2] In 1763 the Treaty of Paris extended this advantage; article five of the agreement confirmed the provisions of the 1713 treaty and article six ceded the islands of Saint-Pierre and Miquelon to France, on condition that they not be fortified, to serve as a shelter for her fishermen.[3] Subsequent disputes between British and French fishermen on the Newfoundland coast over their respective rights led to a further definition of the French position in the Treaty of Versailles in 1783.[4] What this agreement did was to alter the boundaries of the French Shore so as to separate more effectively the subjects of the two nations. Historically, English activity at Newfoundland had centred on the east coast of the island from Cape Race northward to Cape Bonavista; beginning with the Guy settlement in Conception Bay in 1610, it was in this region that the various English plantations of the seventeenth century had been founded. Militarily, the French had concentrated their efforts on Placentia Bay, where they had established Plaisance in 1662. But French fishermen were accustomed to working the coast north of Cape Bonavista, particularly along the Great Northern Peninsula, which they knew as 'le Petit Nord.' The Treaty of Versailles acknowledged this rough division of labour which had evolved through time and circumstance. The French Shore was simply shifted northward on the east coast and southward on the west coast; its new limits were set at Cape St John on the one side and Cape Ray on the other.[5]

These eighteenth-century arrangements evoked no opposition from Newfoundland, where the resident population remained small and lived without the benefit of representative institutions. But acquiescence gave way to stridently asserted colonial self-interest during the nineteenth century. A number of factors were involved in this change. By 1827 the population of Newfoundland had advanced to 59,571,[6] and in 1832 a representative system of government was finally established in St John's. Because the imperial authority was anxious to fulfil its international treaty obligations, however, the colonial government was not given effective jurisdiction over the French Shore. By 1855, when responsible government was established in Newfoundland, this denial had become a source of great local frustration, for a multiplicity of causes. In the first place the French fishery was thought in St John's to be posing a severe threat to Newfoundland's international trade. In point of fact the local merchants probably exaggerated the threat of French competition, making it a scapegoat for their own failings and for the vicissitudes of the international marketplace. But there is no doubt that the merchants thought the French were a threat. Nor is their reaction surprising; after 1815 they faced a steady decline in the per capita production of dried salt fish, Newfoundland's most important export commodity.[7] This decline in combination with rapid population growth eventually posed severe economic problems for the colony; in the mid-1890s it precipitated a shattering financial crisis which saw the administration of Newfoundland's public finances pass into the hands of the foreign Bank of Montreal. In retrospect it can be seen that the rise of the Norwegian fishery and the tariff policies of the fish-importing countries were important factors in the situation,[8] but it is easy to see why the merchant elite of Newfoundland should have seized on the highly visible French as the principal source of their adversity.

After the signing of the treaty of 1783 French fishermen had returned to Newfoundland waters in large numbers, but the outbreak of war between Great Britain and France in 1792 had once again led to a British monopoly. During the long Anglo-French and Anglo-American conflicts that followed, the nascent mer-cantile elite of St John's assumed the economic leadership of the fishery from West Country interests. Between 1792 and 1817 the number of ships coming from England declined from 276 to 48, while at the same time St John's enjoyed a considerable wartime boom.[9] In 1815 'not fewer than four hundred sail of British ships, of which a very large portion were fitted out from St John's and the adjacent ports, fished upon the Banks, and not fewer than one hundred thousand quintals of fish were exchanged by British subjects to France alone.'[10] After the war the French, encouraged by a system of bounties (introduced by their government in 1767 to build up its fishing industry and provide a training ground for its navy), returned in force to the northwest Atlantic area. Saint-Pierre, far away from the French Shore, was the centre of the French fishing operations. The French islands saw a steady expansion in population during the nineteenth century; in 1820 their population was only about 500 but by 1870 it had reached nearly 5,000.[11] By 1858 there were six mercantile houses at Saint-Pierre involved in the fishery. When Captain Granville Loch of HMS *Alarm* visited Saint-Pierre in June 1848 he found it a bustling port: 'I found the outer roads and the inner harbor filled with shipping. There were one hundred and thirty-three French vessels averaging from one hundred to three hundred and fifty and four hundred tons; one hundred of these were Bankers [vessels that fished the offshore banks], chiefly brigs, lately returned with cargoes.' Loch concluded that the French had 'established and systematised a large fleet of vessels, which now no unaided individual enterprise can successfully compete with.'[12]

To the rising mercantile elite of St John's this situation was scandalous, the more so since French fishermen enjoyed advantages, both licit and illicit, in the territo-rial waters of Newfoundland itself. Their attempts at retaliation can be seen in the fishery and foreign policies of successive Newfoundland governments. The colony's strategy had four objectives: to restrict the French supply of bait; to prevent French encroachment in Newfoundland territorial waters; to have the fishing concessions given the French in the eighteenth-century agreements establishing the treaty shore interpreted in such a way as to keep French privileges at a minimum; and to prevent the negotiation of any new Anglo-French agreement that would assist the French enterprise.

The first of these had its *raison d'être* in the fact that much of the bait used in the French fishery was obtained from Newfoundland fishermen living on the south coast of the island. English subjects had been forbidden by law to sell bait to foreigners as early as 1786, but the trade had continued.[13] A further attempt to control the sale of bait was made in 1845 when the colonial government, at the behest of the dominant merchant lobby, placed an export tax of 3*s* per hundred-weight on bait fish.[14] The effect of this tax was simply to shift the locale of the trade; instead of French ships coming to Newfoundland for bait, Newfoundland fishermen carried it to Saint-Pierre.[15] Thus the bankers Captain Loch observed in Saint-Pierre in 1848 were waiting to be supplied with Newfoundland bait:

They had taken in their salt, and were waiting for bait (caplin), which they told me would strike into the Bays of St. Pierre's and Miquelon in a day or two. This prophecy (whether likely to prove true or not) was merely mentioned to deceive me, as it is well known the supply afforded round their own Islands is insufficient to meet the great demand. The next morning I observed boats discharging caplin into the Bankers, which I ascertained had been brought over from our own shores during the night in English boats.

This observation led Captain Loch to a conclusion that had already become an obsession in the St John's business community:

It is obvious that by withholding from the French the supply of bait from our own shores, their success upon the Grand Bank would sensibly diminish, and the advantages the fish merchants at present derive from their bounty granted by their Government over other competitors, could not increase the trade beyond the limits controlled by the comparatively very scanty supply of Caplin afforded by their own coasts and islands.[16]

The policy advocated here was simple, but its enforcement on the rugged coast of Newfoundland was exceedingly difficult. A significant portion of the south coast population was deeply divided in its loyalties between St John's and Saint-Pierre. The area was in effect a frontier between two contending commercial systems. Politically, it was governed from St John's, but economically the attractions of the French islands were great. In 1855 provisions and clothing could be obtained 60 to 70 per cent cheaper at Saint-Pierre than in the neighbouring parts of Newfoundland; hence it is not surprising to find that it was common practice for merchants on the French island to give Newfoundland fishermen provisions in return for bait and dried codfish.[17] Nor is it surprising to find that the bait trade survived into the 1860s despite intense opposition in the Newfoundland capital. The failure of the Newfoundland government to enforce its will in the south coast area is illustrative of a theme that runs through the French and American shore questions: the conflict of nationalism and regionalism. As a rising metropole, the interest of St John's clearly lay in a policy of restriction, but the capital met with stout local resistance in its attempts to organize its far-flung hinterland in support of this and other 'national' objectives. In this instance, as in many others, the metropolitan reach of St John's exceeded its grasp. Localism remained a powerful force in the interplay of metropolis and hinterland in Newfoundland history. In the case of the Burin Peninsula region, the area of the nineteenth-century bait trade, its continuing independence of St John's was dramatically illustrated in the referenda of 1948 on Newfoundland's constitutional future when it voted overwhelmingly for union with Canada while St John's, true to its mercantile past, voted for continued independence.

Newfoundland's other initiatives with respect to the French 'menace' also met with only limited success. The efforts of the colonial government to prevent French encroachments on Newfoundland territorial waters faced the same problems of geography, communications, and local opposition that made the bait trade policy so difficult to enforce. Nevertheless, the effort in this area was intensified in 1851 when the French bounties were increased.[18] Bounties, it was argued, allowed the French to employ 'large seines and numerous bultows'; the system enabled French fishermen 'to carry on their fishery in a manner that speedily gives them the command of the whole ground to which they may resort, and in a short time, makes a nominally concurrent fishery exclusively their own.'[19]

On the diplomatic front Newfoundland displayed a remarkable tenacity despite the notable chink that the localism of the south coast area made in the 'national' armour. In 1836 in a letter to Lord Palmerston, who was then foreign secretary, Count Sebastiani, the French ambassador in London, claimed for his country the exclusive right of fishing on the French Shore. Accordingly, he requested the British government 'to disavow the claim of British subjects to a right of fishery upon the coasts in question concurrent with the right of the subjects of France.' Palmerston rejected this demand; although in practice, he replied, Great Britain had recognized as exclusive the French privilege of drying fish on the treaty shore during the fishing season, she had never recognized any exclusive French right of fishing off the shore.[20] Subsequently, France continued to press this claim but, equally, Great Britain, faced with an ever more vociferous colonial lobby, continued to deny it. Negotiations between the two countries failed to resolve the issue until 14 January 1857, when a new agreement was signed in London.[21]

Under the terms of this agreement the French were to have during the fishing season the exclusive right to fish and to use the strand for fishery purposes from Cape St John to the Quirpon Islands on the northeast coast and from there to Cape Norman on the north coast. The same exclusive privileges were also to be theirs at five harbours between Cape Norman and Cape Ray: Port au Choix, Small Harbour, Port au Port, Red Island, and Codroy Island. Along the rest of the coast between these two points there was to be a concurrent French and British fishery but during the fishing season the French were to have 'the exclusive use of the strand for fishery purposes' from Cape Norman to Rock Point in the Bay of Islands. A concurrent fishery was also to be established at Belle Isle and on the coast of Labrador from Blanc Sablon to Cape Charles. Moreover, France was to have complete freedom to purchase bait on the south coast and French naval officers were to have the authority to enforce French exclusive rights when no British officer was available. In return for all this Great Britain was to have a concurrent right to fish on the west coast from Cape Norman to Cape Ray except in the five ports where the proposed agreement gave the French exclusive rights. British subjects were also to have the exclusive use of the strand from Rock Point to Cape Ray with a like exception. In effect, these terms represented a considerable retreat by Great Britain from her historic claim to a concurrent right of fishing on the entire treaty shore. Why the Foreign Office chose this course is not entirely clear, but the alliance with France in the Crimean War was likely a factor in the situation. Whatever the British motive may have been, the agreement was clearly a diplomatic triumph for France; accordingly, it met with fierce colonial opposition.

Fortunately for Newfoundland a vehicle of protest was at hand; the agreement required legislation 'by the Imperial Parliament of Great Britain and by the Provincial Legislature of Newfoundland.' In keeping with a British commitment to attempt to bring the agreement into effect on or before 1 January 1858, Governor Charles Darling referred the matter to the Newfoundland House of Assembly on 6 February 1857.[22] It evoked a storm of protest and a select committee was formed immediately to 'draft resolutions and addresses in relation to the said subject.'[23] This committee heard evidence from twenty-two people and received written answers to questions it circulated from twenty-two others. The response was unanimous. The Roman Catholic bishop of St John's, John Mullock,[24] a strong supporter of the governing Liberal party and a leading figure in the recent divisive struggle over responsible government, summed up the prevailing feeling in St John's in these words:

the Treaty is drawn up solely and entirely in favour of France; we receive no equivalent of any sort; it is a cession of almost the whole Island to a Foreign Power. If put into execution Newfoundland must cease to be a British colony; it will become a desert, a fishing station for France, or be united to the States, for if the French are allowed to monopolize the Northern,

Western, and Labrador Fishery, and the Southern Fishery, by taking bait, which is but another name for a fishery, the people cannot live; they may struggle for a few years in the Bays of Placentia, St. Mary's and Fortune, but as sure as the French are allowed to fish there, and taking bait is fishing, they must leave it and ship under the United States flag.[25]

The select committee which solicited this opinion reported to the house on 26 February 1857. Its resolutions formed the basis of an address to the secretary of state for the colonies protesting the convention and requesting the imperial government not to bring it into effect: 'we therefore earnestly entreat that the Imperial Government will take no steps to bring this Treaty into operation, but will permit the trifling fishing privileges that remain to us to continue unimpaired.'[26] Later the house also adopted an address to the assemblies of the neighbouring colonies of Nova Scotia, Prince Edward Island, New Brunswick, and Canada seeking their support against the convention.[27] Moreover, John Kent and Frederick Carter,[28] both destined to hold the office of first minister, were appointed by the assembly to go to these colonies to advance the Newfoundland cause. In March when the house closed, P.F. Little,[29] the premier, and H.W. Hoyles,[30] the leader of the opposition, went to Great Britain for the same purpose.

Faced with this militant response from the colony, the imperial authorities gave way. On 26 March 1857, Henry Labouchere, the secretary of state for the colonies, wrote to Governor Darling as follows:

The proposals contained in the Convention having been unequivocally refused by the Colony, they will of course fall to the ground. And you are authorised to give such assurance as you may think proper that the consent of the community of Newfoundland is regarded by Her Majesty's Government as the essential preliminary to any modification of their territorial or maritime rights.[31]

His dispatch was hailed in St John's as a 'Magna Carta'; it represented a complete victory for the local view and established a precedent which the Newfoundland mercantile elite never allowed the Whitehall mandarinate to forget.

The 1857 episode is also significant as an indicator of the extent to which the existence of a real or imagined external threat produced a sense of struggle among Newfoundlanders and a combative style that worked to hold their shaky political edifice together. After the establishment of representative institutions in 1832 Newfoundland had presented a political spectacle with religious, regional, occupational, and economic differences working to rend its constitution asunder. The next decades saw several turbulent political struggles before the establishment of responsible government in 1855. Thereafter an uneasy truce was slowly and painfully worked out between the various organized and combative elements in the

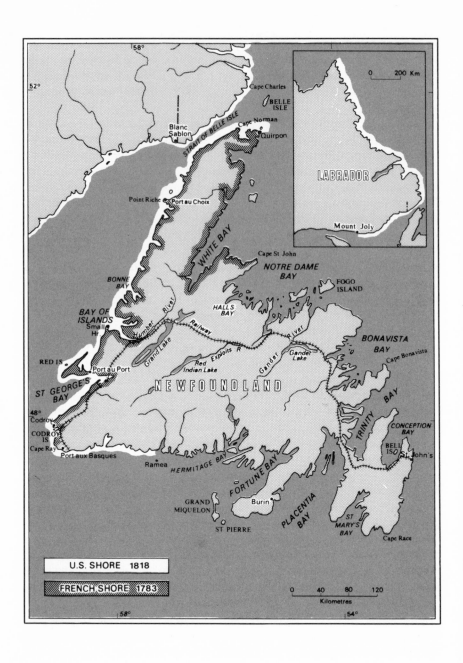

52°

58°

Cape Charles

BELLE
ISLE

Blanc
Sablon

Cape Norman
Quirpon

STRAIT OF BELLE ISLE

200 Km

LABRADOR

Point Riche • Port au Choix

WHITE BAY

Cape St John

NOTRE DAME
BAY

FOGO
ISLAND

Mount Joly

BONNE
BAY

HALLS
BAY

BAY OF
ISLANDS
Smalle
Hr

River

Humber

Railway

Exploits R

River

Gander

BONAVISTA
BAY

Cape Bonavista

RED IS

Port au Port

Grand Lake

Red
Indian Lake

Gander
Lake

NEWFOUNDLAND

ST GEORGE'S
BAY

TRINITY
BAY

48°
Codroy

CODROY
IS
Cape Ray

CONCEPTION
BAY

BELL
ISO St John's

Port aux Basques

Ramea

HERMITAGE BAY

FORTUNE BAY

GRAND
MIQUELON

Burin

PLACENTIA
BAY

ST PIERRE

ST
MARY'S
BAY

Cape Race

U.S. SHORE 1818

FRENCH SHORE 1783

0   40   80   120
Kilometres

58°

54°

Newfoundland political mosaic. The method by which this truce was effected was elite accommodation; in the case of religious differences, for example, this involved a careful distribution of patronage on a denominational basis. The French Shore question provided a common ground which allowed this process to go forward. It provided an issue around which people otherwise badly divided could unite. Only the hardy fishermen who openly traded back and forth to Saint-Pierre prevented complete national unity on the issue, but their dissent was by no means insignificant. That Little and Hoyles could together represent Newfoundland in London was a striking example of the way in which this issue worked to overcome local differences; on the question of responsible government two years earlier they had been implacable opponents. Seen at one level the events of 1857 seem to represent the triumph of an incipient nationalism over partisan politics. But at another and perhaps deeper level they show how a nascent nationalism could be mobilized in the service of elite consensus. In Newfoundland nationalism would be used for the most part to support the compromises worked out after the intense struggle over responsible government and to strengthen the hand of vested interest. In short it would be mainly a conservative force.

II

In the quarter century after the Labouchere dispatch the French Shore question entered a new and more complex stage. Essentially, there were two reasons for this, both relating to the rapid growth of Newfoundland's population, from 122,638 in 1857 to 217,037 in 1901. This growth led to the occupation of fishing sites which had hitherto either been vacant or not fully utilized and to the shift in population away from the area between Cape Race and Cape Bonavista, the historic base of the English speaking population. As table 1 shows, the population of that part of the French Shore extending from LaScie around the Great Northern Peninsula and as far south as Trout River increased from 1.3 to 3.7 per cent of the total Newfoundland population between 1857 and 1901. In the same period the population on the remainder of the west coast rose from 1.4 to 4.2 per cent of the total population.

The increasing local pressure on the inshore fishing ground along the French Shore necessarily increased the danger of conflict between British and French nationals. But increased competition for access to good fishing grounds was not the only way in which demographic change in Newfoundland affected the French Shore question. By the late 1860s there was a growing feeling in the colony that the population of the island would soon outstrip the ability of the fishing resource to sustain it, and that in consequence economic diversification was an urgent necessity. Emigration from the island to the North American continent, combined with the

TABLE 1
Population of the French Shore, 1857–1901

	French Shore			St Barbe District			St George's District		
	Population of the Island of Nfld	Population	Percentage of the Nfld population	Population	Percentage of the Nfld population	Percentage of the French Shore population	Population	Percentage of the Nfld population	Percentage of the French Shore population
1857	122,638	3,334	2.7	1,589[a]	1.3	47.7	1,745	1.4	52.3
1874	158,958	8,654	5.4	4,362	2.7	50.4	4,292	2.7	49.6
1884	193,124	11,973	6.2	6,500[b]	3.4	54.3	5,473[c]	2.8	45.7
1891	197,934	13,322	6.7	6,690	3.4	50.2	6,632	3.4	49.8
1901	217,037	17,234	7.9	8,134	3.7	47.2	9,100	4.2	52.8

SOURCE: Newfoundland census returns, Memorial University of Newfoundland

[a] St Barbe and St George's districts first appeared as census divisions in the census of 1884. The figures given here for 1857 and 1874 refer to the areas later incorporated into those districts.

[b] St Barbe District extended from LaScie to Trout River.

[c] St George's District extended from Cape Gregory to Red Rocks.

sizable sums expended by successive governments on relief to the able-bodied poor, provided stark evidence that this might indeed be the case. But beyond this seemingly Malthusian dilemma there was yet another factor pushing Newfoundland in the direction of economic diversification, namely, the increasingly visible North American standard of material success. Newfoundlanders lived in comparative isolation, but their isolation was not so great that they could not measure their achievements, at least to some extent, against those of other North Americans; moreover, as time passed and communication facilities improved, their ability to make this comparison improved immeasurably.[32] Hence, even among those who had something to gain by preserving political independence, the notion that the integrity of Newfoundland society required a standard of material achievement comparable to that of North America generally caught hold at an early date. Increasingly, Newfoundlanders would give their loyalty to politicians who promised to steer them in a North American direction. This in turn gave rise to the tradition in Newfoundland politics of the charismatic leader-developer, a tradition that begins with William Whiteway[33] and extends through Edward P. Morris,[34] Richard Squires,[35] and Joseph Roberts Smallwood, its most notable examplar, to the present-day Progressive Conservative government of the province. The connection between the French Shore question and the growth of a developmental outlook in Newfoundland was both immediate and direct: Newfoundlanders began to think in terms of a more effective occupation of the northern and western reaches of the island and the exploitation of the agricultural and, more importantly, the mineral and forest resources of those regions. These, of course, were the very areas where French rights existed. The thrust to open up the country, as Edward P. Morris described it, necessarily made Newfoundlanders more determined than ever before to rid themselves of an ancient obstacle to their progress.[36]

The emergence of a developmental mentality in Newfoundland and the appearance of political leaders who articulated this point of view also made the French Shore question for the first time a partisan issue within the colony. Thus, while the Tory merchant tradition remained one of implacable opposition to any concessions whatever to French pretensions, the politicians whose primary concern was with industrial and resource development were willing on occasion to bend to French and imperial wishes, particularly on the bait question, to clear the way for the investment they so ardently desired. The difference between these two groups was always one of degree, but it was often sufficient to bring to the surface the vindictive and venal strain already established as a hallmark of local politics. The developing divergence of interest between those elite elements whose economic interest lay in the traditional fishing economy and those whose interest lay in modernization heightened the intensely combative style which the sense of struggle against an external danger had already firmly implanted in the Newfoundland political culture. A report commissioned by the imperial government in the late 1890s found that 'two parties existed in the colony: the merchants who cared only for bait and the export trade of the fishery, and the development party who cared little for either of these but much for industrial expansion, mainly in the west.'[37] This was, of course, a simplification of the situation; Newfoundland had not yet become sufficiently pluralistic that the developers could ignore or systematically manipulate the traditional merchantocracy, the guardians of the national grail. Yet it had more than an element of truth in it and it gave an accurate forecast of the way Newfoundland society would develop in the twentieth century. Increasingly, the mercantile elite that arose in the early part of the nineteenth century would find itself dominated in both Liberal and Tory parties by the political architects of industrialism.

III

The material progress desired by the proponents of a new industrial Newfoundland came but slowly. Mining was started on a modest scale in the 1850s and was considerably augmented when the Bell Island iron ore mines began production in 1895. In the 1880s the first government of Sir William Whiteway launched the construction of the long projected trans-island railway. This project, which set the pattern for the symbiotic relationship between politicians and developers that has persisted to the present day, was not completed until 1897. Four years later a new census showed that St George's district on the French Shore was the fastest growing district on the island, though this had little to do with railway development. It was with evident satisfaction that the author of the introduction to this census noted 'that the two Districts covering that part of the coast known as the Treaty Shore evidence a large increase in population. They lead the whole Colony in the per centage of increase, and, what is more important, manage to retain their people within their own borders; while St. George's attracts some from the outside as well.'[38] At the turn of the century 'the new Newfoundland' was not all that its publicists might have wished nor was the pace of change in the way of life of the island comparable to that occurring in Canada. Yet the changes were sufficient to alter the nature of local society, to accelerate the trend on the island towards North American values, and to make the settlement of the French Shore question more imperative than ever before.

The diplomatic and imperial consequences of Newfoundland's new economic ambitions became evident in the 1860s when the colony began an agitation for permission to make land grants on the French Shore and to appoint resident magistrates there. In 1864, while serving as administrator of the colony, Laurence

O'Brien, the president of the Legislative Council, raised the land grant question with the secretary of state for the colonies, Edward Cardwell. The occasion was the application by a resident of the Bay of Islands named Kennedy for a grant of land. O'Brien could see no objection to such a grant provided its seaward boundary 'be at such a distance from the strand (say 100 yards) as will preclude interference with the rights of the French ... to erect stages, and other buildings for the purposes of the fishery.'[39] Cardwell rejected this view in a dispatch to an ambitious new governor of Newfoundland, Anthony Musgrave,[40] dated 7 October 1865. 'I do not think in the present unsettled state of the fishery question,' he wrote, 'that it will be expedient to make any grants of land on the "French Shore".'[41]

Musgrave questioned this decision, reminding his superior of the growth of population on the shore, the absence of government there, and the economic potential of the area. The population of the region had either to be removed or else placed under the authority of the Newfoundland government:

if it is to be formally acknowledged that these settlements are not subject to the jurisdiction of the local Government and Legislature, and it is practically impossible at the same time to remove them, they will become more decidedly than ever the refuges of the outcasts of the neighbouring Colonies of Canada, Nova Scotia and New Brunswick, and it ought not to occasion surprise if the result should be a condition of affairs amounting to a national scandal.[42]

Concerning the resources of the area Musgrave argued 'that all endeavour to utilize these materials for prosperity and progress must be abandoned if an objection in perpetuity is to be admitted against the settlement and legal government of the territory adjoining the "French Shore".' The Newfoundland government had already received applications for timber rights in the Humber Valley and for licences to search for minerals on the coast near St George's Bay. If such licences were granted and the subsequent explorations proved successful, there would be a demand for mining leases and for the right to establish settlements. The findings of the government geologist, Alexander Murray,[43] had already indicated a substantial mineral potential in the area adjoining the treaty shore. Moreover, the land there was better suited for agriculture than most parts of the colony. Then there was the proposal to build a railway across the island which would necessarily skirt the French Shore. Everything considered, Musgrave took the view that the right to use and occupy the land on the French Shore should be distinguished from the fishery question in the same way 'as the right to take Salmon in a Scotch River is from the title to cultivate the fields on its banks.' The governor's spirited intervention enabled him to persuade his Executive Council not to raise the subject for discussion at the 1866 session of the legislature. But on 20 May 1866, the Executive Council itself petitioned the secretary of state for the colonies on the matter:

The Executive Council would respectfully invite ... the attention of the Secretary of State for the Colonies to the serious inconvenience arising to parties applying for licenses and grants to search for and work Mines and Minerals in parts of the Island within the coast limits assigned to the French by Treaty for the temporary exercise of fishing privileges; and the great loss resulting to the Colony in suspending the action of these parties in the investment and application of capital for mining purposes, thus affording profitable employment to many of our people together with other material advantages to the Colony.[44]

Private protests were also heard from Newfoundland. In June 1866 Stephen Rendell, the president of the Chamber of Commerce, wrote to the colonial secretary of Newfoundland protesting conditions on the treaty shore.[45] In November 1866 Charles Fox Bennett,[46] Newfoundland's biggest mining promotor and a future premier, wrote to Musgrave protesting Cardwell's decision on land grants.[47] He informed the governor that he had been encouraged by the land act of 1860 to renew his search for minerals in the colony. He had visited various parts of the island during the summers of 1864, 1865, and 1866, and in the autumn of 1866 had made applications in accordance with the provisions of the 1860 legislation for licences to search in the area of the French Shore. These had been refused because of the ban imposed by Cardwell. Bennett complained that the money he had spent on exploration would be wasted if title to land could not be established. He also saw dangers in adopting the course of granting land with a proviso guaranteeing French treaty rights. Outside capital might well be suspicious of such a provision, which could be interpreted as meaning that Newfoundland was in doubt about its territorial control over the whole island.

The protests coming from Newfoundland induced a new colonial secretary, the Earl of Carnarvon, to reconsider Cardwell's ruling, but his review led him to the same conclusion. 'Her Majesty's Government,' he wrote to Musgrave in December 1866, 'much regret the unsettled state of this question and the serious inconvenience to which this leads. But it would be a far greater evil to embroil the Government of England in a dispute with that of France on grounds which a careful consideration of existing Treaties did not clearly justify.'[48] During the 1868 session of the Newfoundland legislature the question of land grants was again discussed in both houses and separate petitions forwarded to London. The petition of the Legislative Council asked for the 'speedy withdrawal of a prohibition fraught with such injurious consequences to the people of this Colony.'[49] The prohibition, it was argued, prevented the investment of capital and thus deprived people 'in a state of almost utter destitution' of the means of employment. In July 1868 John Kent, then a member of the Executive Council, sent his own petition to the Colonial Office.[50]

Under this renewed Newfoundland pressure, the imperial government finally retreated. In December 1868 Carnarvon's successor, the Duke of Buckingham, informed Musgrave that grants could be made in the territory adjoining the French Shore provided that no grant was made that would enable buildings to be erected on the shore itself or cause the French any apprehension.[51] The governor was invited to suggest limits for such grants. In March 1869, Musgrave was informed that he could make grants up to half a mile from high watermark on those parts of the coast not occupied by the French.[52] In areas where the French fished, grants were not to be made. This information was passed by the Foreign Office to the French government with the assurance that Great Britain had been 'especially careful of the interests of French subjects.'[53] Newfoundland had scored a point but only after a long struggle. Moreover, the full sovereignty she sought was still a distant prospect, though Whiteway was able to make further gains on the land question in the 1880s.

The struggle over the appointment of magistrates on the French Shore was, if anything, even more frustrating from the Newfoundland point of view. In 1849 the imperial government had authorized the governor of Newfoundland to appoint a civil magistrate at St George's Bay.[54] Two magistrates had been subsequently appointed – one honorary and the other stipendiary. But the office of stipendiary magistrate had been annulled in 1853 when the Newfoundland assembly had refused to vote the necessary stipend.[55] In the meantime, law and order on the French Shore had been maintained on an *ad hoc* basis by officers of the Royal Navy who toured the area each summer. In 1865 thirty residents of St George's Bay petitioned Governor Musgrave for the appointment of a stipendiary magistrate and a constabulary force.[56] One of the signers of this petition was H.H. Forrest, who had been named honorary magistrate under the terms of the abortive 1849 arrangement. The petition decried the existing state of affairs on the French Shore: 'This portion of Newfoundland is and has been, for years past, without the protection of law. Property and personal security are therefore at the mercy of the evil disposed, the malicious and the turbulent.' The petitioners expressed a willingness to contribute to the cost of government in Newfoundland and asked for the appointment of a revenue officer. Not everyone in St George's Bay agreed with this petition. In the same month a counter-petition signed by forty-one residents was forwarded to Governor Musgrave. It complained that the petition seeking a magistrate had been secretly forwarded to St John's and that it was 'understood to have been signed simply by a few young individuals, that could not perceive their errors, and headed by one or two merchants.' In keeping with the deeply rooted individualism of outport life, these petitioners argued that the residents of the area could not afford the expense of government:

> our Inhabitants are at present reduced to such an extreme state of poverty, owing to the failure of the fisheries since some years back, that if they are compelled to pay Duties, Taxes and such other levies as are generally required by Her Majesty's Representatives, that starvation will undoubtedly and certainly take place by the greatest part of the population of this District.[57]

Instead of more control from St John's, they wanted less; they asked that the region be declared a 'Free Port.'

Cardwell was more receptive to the idea of appointing a stipendiary magistrate than he was to allowing land grants but he was unwilling to allow Newfoundland a free hand:

> I shall be ready to consider any proposal for the appointment of a judicious person to act as Magistrate in that part of Newfoundland provided it is clearly understood that his proceedings will be under the personal control of the Governor. A matter which cannot but touch the execution of Treaties cannot be treated as one of local administration.[58]

Governor Musgrave saw the weakness of this plan: the Newfoundland legislature was unlikely to accept a method of appointing officials on the French Shore which differed from that followed elsewhere in the colony and would probably refuse to pay a magistrate appointed in the manner suggested.[59] During the summer of 1866 Musgrave visited parts of the French Shore, travelling on a government steamer. His purpose was to 'obtain some personal information as to the character and condition of the settlements on the French Shore which circumstances are now forcing upon the consideration of the local Government.'[60] On his return to St John's he gave the new colonial secretary, Lord Carnarvon, a glowing account of the west coast region: 'It would be well,' he wrote, 'for a large proportion of our fishing population on the East Coast if they enjoyed half the substantial prosperity which I saw surrounding settlers on the Banks of the Codroy who live entirely by farming.'[61] But Carnarvon was even less sympathetic than Cardwell had been to the appointment of resident magistrates in the area. On 23 November 1866, he informed the governor that he could not agree to the appointment of magistrates while the fishery question was still in dispute.[62] This issue was to remain in abeyance for the next twelve years while Newfoundland grew more and more restless.

During this time the imperial government tried to extricate itself from a situation of growing complexity by again attempting to negotiate with France a general settlement of the issues in dispute. But this initiative was no more successful than its predecessors and in 1877 the Colonial Office had to give ground on the question of law enforcement. On 23 January 1877 Carnarvon informed the governor of Newfoundland that he would allow resident magistrates on the French Shore if the colony would agree to leave their selection and appointment to him, conditions that only intensified the squabbling between London and St John's.[63] Finally, on 10 November 1877, Captain William Howarth, a naval officer who had served on the Newfoundland station, was appointed to the position of magistrate on the west coast of the island. Half his salary of £500 per year was to be paid for four years by the imperial government, and he was required to collect customs duties in the vicinity of his post. He was also ordered by Whitehall 'to abstain from adjudicating upon any point in which the interpretation of any Treaty is involved or any point which is disputed or under discussion.' If any such case did arise, he was to 'take the instructions of Her Majesty's Government through the Governor of Newfoundland.'[64] The new magistrate left England for Newfoundland on 13 November 1877.[65] France was presented with a *fait accompli*, and for once her protests fell on deaf ears in London. Newfoundland had scored another point in the long diplomatic war of attrition, but in terms of her territorial ambitions her success was marginal and had been realized only after years of frequently rancorous agitation.

During the next quarter century, particularly after the launching of the railway scheme, Newfoundland became much less patient. In 1878 colonial legislation to extend the franchise to residents of the treaty coast was disallowed by the imperial government. During the same year the Newfoundland legislature passed resolutions favouring the construction of a railway from St John's to St George's Bay; these were objected to by the Colonial Office on the ground that the proposed line would terminate on the treaty shore.[66] Subsequently, the Whiteway government revised its plans and chose Halls Bay as the terminus. While the railway issue was in contention the preliminary steps were being taken in yet another round of Anglo-French negotiations. This time the initiative came from France and for the first time Great Britain considered the possibility of purchasing the French rights. In 1881 Whiteway visited London in connection with the renewed negotiations; while there he was able to win new concessions for the colony, including the right for the colonial government to appoint magistrates.[67] So great was his success indeed that he was able to face the electorate in 1882 on a platform which Lady Glover, the wife of the governor of the day, described as 'Newfoundland for the Newfoundlanders.'[68] In the meantime the French Shore problem had been linked in the negotiations to a territorial difference which existed between Great Britain and France in the Pacific. This was the first occasion on which the Newfoundland negotiations had been made part of a larger diplomatic package and the precedent pointed the way to the eventual settlement of the dispute. On 26 April 1884 a new agreement was signed but the combination of an economic decline and the return of sectarian violence in Newfoundland forced the resignation of the cooperative Whiteway government. When a Tory merchant government led by Robert Thorburn[69] was enthroned in St John's, the agreement was lost. The hardened Newfoundland attitude was well summed up by the *Harbour Grace Standard*: 'We want the whole of Newfoundland for Newfoundlanders, nothing more, nothing less.'[70]

The colonial government followed its rejection of the agreement with a renewed effort to bring the bait trade under control.[71] The legislation introduced for this purpose touched off yet another row between St John's and London. Eventually, however, it was allowed to stand and came into effect on 2 January 1888. Yet another abrasive argument followed over the respective rights of British and French subjects to build and operate lobster-canning factories on the French Shore. This issue had been in dispute since the early 1880s but came to a head at the end of the decade. In 1890 Great Britain and France concluded a *modus vivendi* on the issue whereby 'no lobster factory not in operation on July 1, 1889' would be permitted 'unless by the joint consent of the British and French senior naval officers.'[72] This arrangement met with the same strenuous objection from Newfoundland. A petition of protest containing 12,000 signatures was forwarded to London, and a Newfoundland Patriotic Association was formed in St John's. But as had so often been the case in the past on other issues, 'national unity' on this matter was anything but complete. The disruption of the bait trade on the south coast had resulted in a larger French fishing operation in St George's Bay to the great annoyance and detriment of local fishermen. This in turn had produced a strong feeling on the west coast against the policies of the government in St John's – one more illustration of the tension between nationalism and regionalism that runs through so much Newfoundland history. On 24 May a public meeting was held in St George's Bay at which a decision was made 'not to pay duties or taxes, or to recognize St. John's officials until wrongs were rectified, and compensation paid to those who had suffered.'[73] So alienated had the area become that the resident magistrate saw in these events 'a revolutionary movement' and 'an embryo republic.'[74] All of this is further proof that the metropolitan design of St John's was being continually undermined by what F.F. Thompson has called 'the centrifugal forces at work in the colony – the east attached to European trade, the south coast drawn by St. Pierre, and the west by the Canadian Maritime Provinces.'[75] Yet on the issue of the *modus vivendi* Newfoundland was able to fight a considerable rear-guard action, since the imperial government did not have the legislative authority to enable naval officers to enforce its will on the Newfoundland coast.[76] When the imperial authorities introduced legislation to remedy this situation, the colonial legislature reacted furiously. A factor further complicating this situation was Whiteway's growing ambition to bolster the sagging fortunes of his railway venture with an imperial loan.

In 1893 Whiteway's second government introduced bait regulations under which 'licences were allowed to all foreign vessels for bait and ice at specified ports,'[77] a change which provoked the full wrath of the obscurantist merchant and Tory elements. Again, the contract this same government concluded with the Reid Newfoundland Company in May 1893 for the extension of the railway to Port aux Basques was objected to by France, though in this instance Newfoundland enjoyed the approbation of the Colonial Office. In 1897 the Tories regained power in St John's and towards the end of that year the new premier, James Spearman Winter,[78] and his leading supporter, Alfred B. Morine,[79] went to London to discuss the grievances of the colony. This time it was the turn of the Liberal opposition to beat the nationalist drum; thus Winter and Morine were castigated for not having obtained legislative approval for their mission.[80] Liberal opportunism was rewarded when the Newfoundland emissaries succeeded only in arranging for a new imperial commission of enquiry into the problems of the French Shore. Sir John Bramston and Sir James Erskine, the two commissioners named to the enquiry, subsequently toured the French Shore with Morine. Their report is notable for its revelation of the extent of the decline of French activity on the treaty shore. In 1829, 9,378 French nationals had fished between Cape St John and Quirpon; by 1898 this figure had declined to 133.[81] On the west coast of the island the equivalent figures are 1,182 and 158. That France should have gone to such lengths to defend the interest of so few people is a measure not of the worth of the treaty shore itself but of the value of the French rights as a bargaining weapon in the economically much more important bait question. Here the future of Saint-Pierre was at stake. The Bramston-Erskine report was never tabled in the House of Commons. Moreover, a new Liberal premier of Newfoundland, Robert Bond,[82] failed in an attempt to have the French Shore question discussed at the 1902 Colonial Conference.[83]

Nevertheless a settlement satisfactory to all parties was close at hand, thanks to the developing international friendship between Great Britain and France. In 1904, as part of the negotiations that produced the *entente cordiale*, the Newfoundland question was linked to an Anglo-French difference in West Africa, and through a policy of mutual concession a settlement of both questions was effected.[84] France renounced her rights under the Treaty of Utrecht, but she was guaranteed an equal right of fishing during the summer season on the old treaty shore. Ports on the shore were to be open to French fishermen to obtain supplies, bait, and shelter subject to colonial law. In a note accompanying the agreement France was guaranteed that the colony would not be allowed to cut off bait supplies to her fishermen on the treaty shore by refusing them licences. In return for these concessions, which did not satisfy the extreme merchant-Tory elements in Newfoundland, France received territorial concessions in Nigeria, Gambia, and Îles de Los. After some initial hesitation, the Liberal government of Robert Bond accepted the agreement enthusiastically and was able to carry public opinion with it despite the motion of censure against the imperial government that Morine brought into the legislature.[85] Momentarily enjoying political stability and economic security, most Newfoundlanders were content to view the convention as a happy omen for the new century.

IV

One ancient difference had been settled but another remained. When the 1904 agreement was signed, attention in Newfoundland was focused more on American than French fishing rights. Indeed, since the accession to power of the Bond Liberal government in 1900, Newfoundland had come to pose a serious obstacle to the progress of Anglo-American friendship, the complement in British foreign policy of the *entente* with France. The origin of the American fishing rights now in dispute lay in the Treaty of Versailles. That agreement had accorded Americans

the right to take fish of every kind on the Grand Bank, and on the other banks of Newfoundland; also in the Gulph of St. Lawrence, and at all other places in the sea where the inhabitants of both countries [Great Britain and the United States] used at any time heretofore to fish

and the

liberty to take fish of every kind on such part of the coast of Newfoundland as British fishermen shall use (but not to dry or cure the same on that island) and also on the coasts, bays, and creeks of all other of His Britannic Majesty's dominions in America; and ... to dry and cure fish in any of the unsettled bays, harbours and creeks of Nova Scotia, Magdalen Islands, and Labrador, as long as the same shall remain unsettled ...[86]

These arrangements lasted until the outbreak of war in 1812. As a result of that conflict, Great Britain insisted that the liberties (but not the rights) she had recognized in the Treaty of Versailles were automatically forfeited.[87] At the close of the war Great Britain refused to return to the *status quo ante* in relation to the fisheries, and it was only after a protracted controversy between the two countries that the liberties which American fishermen had enjoyed between 1783 and 1812 were partially restored by a convention signed on 20 October 1818. By this agreement the liberty that American fishermen had enjoyed to fish within the three-mile limit in the territorial waters of British North America was restricted to three specific areas: the south, west, and north coasts of Newfoundland from the Ramea to the Quirpon islands; the coast of Labrador from Mount Joly 'Northwardly indefinitely' (but 'without prejudice ... to any of the exclusive Rights of the Hudson Bay Company'); and the Magdalen Islands in the Gulf of St Lawrence. In addition the liberty they had enjoyed to land and dry fish in unsettled places was limited to the south coast of Newfoundland from the Ramea Islands to Cape Ray and to the coast of Labrador. Elsewhere the United States renounced 'any Liberty, heretofore enjoyed or claimed ... to take, dry or cure Fish on, or within three marine Miles of the Coasts, Bays, Creeks, or Harbours.'[88]

For more than half a century American rights, though disputed in meaning, did not occasion any serious controversy in Newfoundland. There were good reasons for this. In the first place American fishermen, unlike those of France, did not compete with Newfoundlanders in European fish markets; their enterprise was directed at the supply of their large and growing domestic market. Moreover, the continuing interest of the New England fishing industry in the British North American fisheries could be used to extract trading advantages from the United States. Thus Newfoundland was included in the tariff concessions granted by the United States to British North Americans in the Reciprocity Treaty of 1854. In the negotiations leading up to this agreement the colony had been willing to see its interest submerged in the general British North American interest. This was also the case in the negotiations leading up to the Treaty of Washington in 1871. It was only after the latter agreement that the issue of American rights really began to heat up in Newfoundland. One of the provisions of the Treaty of Washington required the appointment of an Anglo-American commission to determine the amount of cash compensation the United States should pay for the fishing concessions being given her above and beyond those she possessed under the convention of 1818. This commission eventually met in Halifax in 1877. Its award of $5.5 million – $4.5 million of which was paid to Canada and $1 million to Newfoundland – aroused great indignation in the United States. Accordingly, when in January 1878 a number of American fishing vessels were interfered with at Fortune Bay on the south coast by local fishermen, Washington reacted angrily.[89] Newfoundland refused, however, to compensate the American fishermen, on the ground that they had been breaking colonial law. Eventually, the imperial government paid the compensation demanded by the United States, but the question of Newfoundland's jurisdiction over Americans fishing within her territorial waters was left unsettled. While Great Britain claimed that Newfoundland had the right to enforce 'reasonable regulations' on American fishermen, the United States insisted that their activities could be regulated only 'by a common or joint authority.'[90]

Dissatisfied with the Halifax award and angered by the Fortune Bay incident, the United States abrogated the fisheries articles of the Treaty of Washington on 1 July 1885, the earliest date on which it was possible to do so. In the meantime, however, an Anglo-American *modus vivendi* had been negotiated whereby American fishermen retained the privileges they had enjoyed under the Treaty of Washington; in return President Cleveland agreed to recommend to Congress the appointment of a new commission to be 'charged with the consideration and settlement, upon a just, equitable, and honorable basis, of the entire question of the fishing rights of the two Governments and their respective citizens on the coast of the United States and British North America.'[91] Cleveland's recommendation was however rejected by the Senate. In retaliation Canada began excluding American fishermen from her territorial waters, thereby precipitating the first serious difference in Anglo-American relations since the settlement of the Alabama claims in 1871. During the summer of 1886 there were seizures of American fishing vessels on both the Canadian and Newfoundland coasts; when Canada amended her customs regulations in November of that year so as to restrict the use of her ports by American fishermen, retaliatory legislation was introduced in Congress.[92] Ultimately, the crisis was resolved by the appointment of a joint high commission of the type the Senate had earlier refused. The commissioners – Joseph Chamberlain for Great Britain and Thomas F. Bayard for the United States – met in Washington from 22 November 1887 to 15 February 1888. The agreement they proposed would have defined the three-mile limit established by the convention of 1818 and accorded American fishermen the full use of Canadian and Newfoundland ports. In return for the latter concession the United States would have been required to remove 'the duty from fish-oil, whale-oil, seal-oil, and fish of all kinds ... being the produce of fisheries carried on by the fishermen of Canada and Newfoundland.'[93] The commissioners also negotiated a *modus vivendi*, pending the ratification of the general agreement. The *modus vivendi* gave American fishermen, in return for an annual licence fee, the privileges that would be theirs when the general agreement came into effect.[94] But in April 1888 the Senate rejected the Chamberlain-Bayard Treaty. Canada responded to this slap in the face by turning the other cheek. She did not return to the coercive policy she had adopted after the events of 1885 but continued, albeit reluctantly, to observe on a voluntary and purely informal basis the terms of the *modus vivendi* Bayard and Chamberlain had concluded.

After this fiasco Newfoundland decided to follow an independent policy in commercial and fishery negotiations with the United States. This decision complemented the strategy of resource development to which the colony had turned under Whiteway's leadership. The most ardent advocate of the new policy was

Robert Bond, then a rising young minister. In 1890 Bond scored a singular success when he managed to negotiate a reciprocity agreement with the United States secretary of state, James Blaine.[95] But this agreement was overruled by the imperial government at the behest of Canada, much to the disgust of Newfoundlanders. When Bond became premier of Newfoundland in 1900, he took up the question of reciprocity with the United States once more. He was able to overcome the imperial veto and in 1902 successfully negotiated a new agreement with the American secretary of state, John Hay. This time his ambition was frustrated by Senator Henry Cabot Lodge of Massachusetts, who was under pressure from New England fishing interests that feared the consequences of the agreement. Bond attempted to bring the American opponents of the agreement into line by disrupting the New England fishing operation on the Newfoundland coast. But this strategy only provoked the wrath of the imperial government, which intervened in support of the American fishermen and on behalf of Anglo-American friendship. Bond's retaliatory policy also revived the latent regionalism of Newfoundland life. His 'national' policy met with bitter opposition on the west coast in particular, where the American presence meant a sure supply of ready cash and a release from the iniquitous local truck system. Needless to say, this split among Newfoundlanders did not pass unnoticed either in Whitehall or Washington. Ultimately, Bond's foreign policy precipitated his political downfall; in 1907 Edward P. Morris, one of his strongest ministers, broke with him and later formed a new political party. The new party was able to exploit imperial dissatisfaction with Bond's performance to gain power in 1909 after a series of tumultuous political events. In the meantime the various matters in dispute under the convention of 1818 had been referred to the Hague Court where a settlement was effected in 1910.

Taken together, the French and American shore questions illuminate some of the most important themes of nineteenth-century Newfoundland history. The French Shore problem originated in the transfer of control of the British fishery from the West Country to St John's and the subsequent attempt of the local merchantocracy to extend its economic hegemony over the whole island. The policies of protectionism and economic nationalism that successive Newfoundland governments pursued at the behest of this group met with only limited success. In part this was owing to the regionalism of Newfoundland itself, particularly of the south coast of the island. But the tendency of the merchant elite to attribute to the French presence problems that were either domestic in nature or beyond the control of any Newfoundland government was also an important factor. If Newfoundland's nineteenth-century nationalism was motivated basically by merchant interest, it also had an element of self-delusion about it. Thus although France undoubtedly contributed something to Newfoundland's international trading problems, there were many other factors at work, most notably the poor quality at times of the Newfoundland product and the growth of the fishing industries of Norway and other countries. To the extent that their obsession with the French Shore problem led the merchants to imagine that their difficulties had a simple solution, it was an irrational and retarding force on Newfoundland's development.

By the 1870s the pressure of population on the fishery resource and the influence of North American material success had cleared the way for politician-developers in the North American mould who would ultimately challenge the merchantocracy for control of Newfoundland political and economic life. These leaders were concerned with the development of the resources of the land itself. Accordingly, while they genuflected to the tribal symbol of the French Shore question, they tended to be more flexible in negotiations than those who gave the sea primacy in Newfoundland life. This split made the French Shore question a partisan issue in Newfoundland for the first time. In the long run the developers got their way, but like the old elite they were challenging they never achieved complete success. The fishery became the sick man of the Newfoundland economy, performing at a lower level of economic achievement than the industrial sector and offering much smaller rewards. But though weak in economic power and dependent on transfusions from the industrial sector, the fishing economy continued to occupy a part of the population with great potential for political power. The large percentage of the population that remained in the fishery was a measure of the limited success of Newfoundland's industrial strategy. It was also a guarantee that the relationship between the traditional and modern economies would be symbiotic and that the successful Newfoundland leader would be one who could mobilize the support of fishermen while pursuing the elusive goals of modernization and industrialization.

Ironically, the builders of the new industrial Newfoundland were confronted by the same problems of regionalism that beset the old merchantocracy of the sea. The uproar on the west coast over the policies of the Bond government was but the first illustration of the regional fact in twentieth-century Newfoundland life. In the 1960s the process of modernization and industrialization would produce in Labrador the first political party in Newfoundland history to be unashamedly regional and exclusive. Both the new and the old Newfoundland project images of adversity, with overtones of victimization and defensive inferiority on the one hand and mission and moral superiority on the other. S.F. Wise has observed that the 'fears and emotions' projected by Canadians in the nineteenth century revealed 'their sense of living in a hostile world ... their anxiety for their own survival, and ... their uncertainties about their special place in North America.'[96] By this standard, Newfoundlanders were close to the main stream of British North American life indeed.

NOTES

1 Salisbury in House of Lords, 19 March 1891, *Hansard*, 3rd series, vol. 351, 1411.
2 F.F. Thompson, *The French Shore Problem in Newfoundland: An Imperial Study* (Toronto 1961), appendix 1, 191.
3 Ibid.
4 See A.H. McLintock, *The Establishment of Constitutional Government in Newfoundland, 1783–1832: A Study of Retarded Colonization* (London 1941), 41–3.
5 Thompson, *French Shore Problem*, appendix 1, 191–2.
6 See Shannon Ryan, 'The Newfoundland Salt Cod Trade in the Nineteenth Century,' above; Gertrude Gunn, *The Political History of Newfoundland, 1832–1864* (Toronto 1966), 205.
7 Ryan, 'Newfoundland Salt Cod Trade.'
8 Ibid.
9 *In the Matter of the Boundary between the Dominion of Canada and the Colony of Newfoundland in the Labrador Peninsula*, 12 vols. (London 1927), 4: 1961.
10 *JHA*, 1857, 45–52.
11 Harold A. Innis, *The Cod Fisheries*, rev. ed. (Toronto 1954), 378.
12 *JHA*, 1848–49, appendix, 408–24, Report of Captain Granville G. Loch on the Fisheries of Newfoundland.
13 Great Britain, *Statutes*, 26 Geo. III, c.26.
14 *Statutes of Newfoundland*, 8 Vict., c.5.
15 See *JHA*, 1857, appendix, 225–8, Darling to Labouchere, 9 June 1856.
16 *JHA*, 1848–9, appendix, 408–24.
17 *JHA*, 1856, appendix, 91–2, Report of Commander R. Purvis on the Fisheries on the South West Coast of Newfoundland.
18 See Innis, *Cod Fisheries*, 392–5.
19 *JHA*, 1857, 45–52.
20 Ibid., 175–9.
21 Ibid., 261–7.
22 Ibid., 17–18.
23 Ibid., 20.
24 See above, 91 n34.
25 *JHA*, 1857, 311–14.
26 Ibid., 42–52.
27 Ibid., 58–60.
28 See above, 89 n9.
29 Philip Francis Little, born Prince Edward Island, 1824; lawyer and politician; premier, 1855–8; chief justice, 1858–66; died Dublin, 1897.
30 See above, 89 n1.

31 PANL, dispatches from CO, 1857.
32 For an interesting discussion of this point see James Hiller, 'Whiteway and Progress,' *NQ* 68, no. 4 (1972): 15–18.
33 See above, 38 n20.
34 Edward P. Morris, born St John's, 1859; lawyer and politician; prime minister, 1909–17; created Baron Morris, 1918; died London, 1935.
35 Richard Squires, born Harbour Grace, 1880; lawyer, first elected to assembly, 1909; minister of justice, 1914–17; colonial secretary, 1917–19; prime minister, 1919–23, 1928–32; died St John's, 1940.
36 See John P. Greene, 'Edward Patrick Morris, 1886–1900' (unpublished paper, Centre for Newfoundland Studies, Memorial University 1968).
37 Thompson, *French Shore Problem*, 165.
38 *Report of the Census of Newfoundland, 1901*, x–xi.
39 CO 194/173, O'Brien to Cardwell, 3 Oct. 1864.
40 See above, 90 n17.
41 Dispatches from CO, 1865.
42 CO 194/174, Musgrave to Cardwell, 24 Nov. 1865.
43 See R.D. Hughes, 'Alexander Murray (1810–1884),' Geological Association of Canada, *Proceedings* 23 (1971): 1–4.
44 CO 194/175, Minutes of the Executive Council, 20 May 1866, enclosed in Musgrave to Cardwell, 11 June 1866.
45 PANL, Records of the St John's Chamber of Commerce, Minute book, 1860–66, Rendell to Bemister, 16 June 1866, 58–9.
46 See above, 92 n60.
47 CO 194/175, Bennett to Musgrave, 8 Nov. 1866.
48 Dispatches from CO, 1866, Carnarvon to Musgrave, 7 Dec. 1866.
49 *JHA*, 1868, 41–2, 60–1.
50 CO 194/177, Kent to Buckingham, 13 July 1868.
51 Dispatches from CO, 1868, Rogers to Musgrave, 9 Dec. 1868.
52 Dispatches from CO, 1869, Granville to Musgrave, 10 March 1869.
53 CO 194/178, Draft dispatch to Lyons from Foreign Office.
54 Thompson, *French Shore Problem*, 38.
55 Ibid., 39.
56 *JHA*, 1865, 933–4.
57 Ibid., 935–6.
58 Dispatches from CO, 1865, Cardwell to Musgrave, 7 Oct. 1865.
59 CO 194/174, Musgrave to Cardwell, 24 Nov. 1865.
60 CO 194/175, Musgrave to Cardwell, 10 July 1866.
61 Ibid., Musgrave to Carnarvon, 8 Aug. 1866.

62 PANL, Secret and confidential dispatches from CO, 1838–76.

63 Dispatches from CO, 1877, Carnarvon to Glover, 23 Jan. 1877.

64 Ibid., Malcolm to Howorth, 10 Nov. 1877.

65 Ibid., Herbert to Glover, 13 Nov. 1877.

66 Thompson, *French Shore Problem*, 45–6.

67 Ibid., 52.

68 Ibid., 53.

69 Robert Thorburn, born Scotland, 1836; merchant and politician; premier, 1885–9; died St John's, 1906.

70 Thompson, *French Shore Problem*, 70.

71 Ibid., 74–92.

72 Ibid., 110.

73 Ibid., 112.

74 Ibid.

75 Ibid., 117.

76 Ibid., 120–49.

77 Ibid., 157.

78 James Spearman Winter, born Lamaline, 1845; lawyer and politician; premier, 1897–1900; died Toronto, 1911.

79 Alfred B. Morine, born Nova Scotia, 1857; journalist, lawyer, and politician; Tory leader, 1900–6; died Toronto, 1944.

80 Thompson, *French Shore Problem*, 162.

81 Ibid., 163.

82 Robert Bond, born St John's, 1857; independently wealthy; politician; prime minister, 1900–9; died Whitbourne, 1927.

83 Thompson, *French Shore Problem*, 180.

84 Ibid., 183.

85 Ibid., 184.

86 U.S., 61st Congress, 3rd Session, *Senate Document* 870, vol. 2, 24.

87 Ibid., 240–61.

88 Ibid., 25.

89 See *Parliamentary Papers*, 1878–9, vol. 77 (C. 2184); William G. Reeves, 'The Fortune Bay Dispute: Newfoundland's Place in Imperial Treaty Relations under the Washington Treaty, 1871–1885' (unpublished MA thesis, Memorial University 1971).

90 *Senate Document* 870, vol. 3, 655, 713.

91 Ibid., vol. 2, 35.

92 Ibid., 96–7, 137–8.

93 Ibid., 43.

94 Ibid., 44–5.

95 For the history of this agreement and Bond's later career, see Peter Neary and S.J.R. Noel, 'Newfoundland's Quest for Reciprocity, 1890–1910,' in Mason Wade (ed.), *Regionalism in the Canadian Community, 1867–1967* (Toronto 1969), 210–26. See also D.J. Davis, 'The Bond-Blaine Negotiations, 1890–1891' (unpublished MA thesis, Memorial University 1970).

96 S.F. Wise and R.C. Brown, *Canada Views the United States* (Toronto 1967), 97.

The Railway and Local Politics in Newfoundland, 1870–1901

JAMES HILLER

By the time that the first rails were laid in Newfoundland in 1881, the Intercolonial Railway was completed and the Canadian Pacific under construction. This late entry into the railway age can be explained by the island's isolation from the continental pulls that had initiated major railroad ventures on the mainland. Politically independent, and with an economy reliant on European, West Indian, and South American fish markets, Newfoundland traditionally had an Atlantic orientation and was maritime in its industry and means of transportation. When the colony did begin railroad building, it was not primarily in response to continental pressures, but because the traditional, fish-based economy was not sufficiently productive to give most Newfoundlanders an adequate level of employment and income.[1] First and foremost, the railway was to be a development road – a wand of progress – that would open the country, stimulate mining, agriculture, and lumbering, and free Newfoundland from its retarding dependence on one unpredictable staple.

The idea of economic diversification, and various means to that end, had been under discussion for at least twenty years before the first railway contract. Governments of various complexions in the late 1850s and 1860s had sought to encourage agriculture, through the provision of bounties and other inducements, in the hope that, even if specialization did not develop, a considerable number of families might move from the coastal fringe to relatively fertile areas at the heads of the bays and combine fishing with farming and lumbering. Thus stronger, more self-reliant local economies would be created, which would no longer come begging to St John's for poor relief. In 1864 a geological survey had begun under the able direction of Alexander Murray,[2] a veteran of the Canadian survey; it was hoped that he would locate areas for agricultural and lumbering industries, as well

A version of this paper was presented at the 1974 Atlantic Canada Studies Conference.

as minerals. The agricultural incentives were not a great success, and few outports with mixed economies emerged. Most Newfoundlanders remained on the outer coast, relying as always on the sea, the merchant, and the government. The only non-maritime economic venture that had any great success in this period was the copper mine at Tilt Cove in Notre Dame Bay, where population growth was rapid. The success of Tilt Cove, followed by the Geological Survey reports, stimulated considerable interest among local businessmen in mineral exploration, and they began actively to take out licences in likely coastal areas. On the whole, however, they had neither the expertise nor the surplus capital to proceed, and it seems that most options were acquired for speculative purposes. 'For the most part,' an assembly committee grumbled in 1869, 'the habits and pursuits of the men of capital and enterprise are not adapted to enquiries connected with mines, agriculture and forests.'[3]

By the 1870s, therefore, no significant visible changes had occurred in Newfoundland's economic structure, and the pressure of population on the fisheries was becoming more acute. The overwhelmingly anti-confederate decision of the electors in 1869 made it clear that Newfoundland's future was as an independent country, and that the problem of economic development would have to be faced and solved without Canadian support. Urged on by Murray and his friend Moses Harvey,[4] the Presbyterian-minister-turned-journalist, some local politicians began in the 1870s to consider seriously a railway as the solution to the colony's economic ills. Less sceptical of the colony's economic potential, less fish-bound and maritime in outlook than most of the business community, these men – lawyers and other professionals – tended to agree with and magnify the optimism expressed by Murray in his survey reports. Thus in 1875 the Conservative government led by Frederick Carter[5] announced that it intended to begin serious studies, and obtained authorization for a loan to finance a survey for a trans-insular railway.

This survey was carried out with the help and advice of Sandford Fleming, who since 1864 had been advocating the idea of a Newfoundland line forming part of a short route between London and the major North American cities – an idea which, in turn, derived from John Poor's proposition at Portland in 1850 that Halifax be the American terminus for such a route.[6] In Fleming's vision St John's would become the terminus for fast steamers from Ireland; passengers would then travel by railway from St John's to St George's Bay to connect with ferries running to Shippigan. He estimated that by this means, fog and ice notwithstanding, four days could be saved on a journey from London to New York. A preliminary exploration of a possible route across Newfoundland had been made at Fleming's expense in 1868.[7] In effect, the Newfoundland railway would become an extension of the Intercolonial, part of the all-red trunk line across British North America to the Pacific; its effect on the economic development of Newfoundland was entirely secondary. The colony's politicians evidently were seduced by Fleming's dream, for the 1875 survey followed his proposed route, tracing a line from St John's, through the Avalon Peninsula to Come by Chance, thence north to the Gander River and west via the bottom of Red Indian Lake to St George's.[8] For much of the distance from the Isthmus of Avalon to the west coast, the survey line passed far from inhabited areas and crossed barren lands entirely unsuitable for settlement.

The local railway enthusiasts must have envisaged branches feeding the main line, for although they stressed the virtues of the short route across Newfoundland, and fervently hoped that the imperial government would help pay for it, they based their case on the promise of economic development. Railways, they said, would open up agricultural areas for use by 'our hardy, sober, industrious peasantry, and our fishermen ... We want the people to have homesteads of their own, where they may live comfortably in their old age ...'[9] One MHA envisaged 'railways ... snorting across vast areas of cultivated land, well water-margined and timber-borded.'[10] Others thought that the railway would give St John's a non-coastal hinterland and Newfoundland a west. If Murray was to be believed, the west coast was potentially rich, with good farm land, minerals, and forests; link it with the metropolis, and a microcosm of the Canadian strategy would be achieved with agriculture in the west, mining in the north, manufacturing and shipping in the east. It was a heady brew: the railway would put Newfoundland onto the march of progress, and give it those symbols of modernity and nationhood that her neighbours possessed, but that she lacked. 'It means the opening up of this great island –,' declaimed Moses Harvey in 1878,

the union of its eastern and western shores – the working of its lands, forests and minerals; its connection with the neighbouring continent. It means the increase of population; the conversion of the country into a hive of industry; the commencement of a material and social advance to which at present no limits can be set ... Once it is built, all things are possible. Hail! to the great Hereafter ...[11]

Nevertheless, the railway question was approached most gingerly. Confederation had been the ultimate cure for Prince Edward Island's railway fever and was a fate most Newfoundlanders were determined to avoid. Murray and Harvey rather hoped that confederation would be the end result for Newfoundland as well, but politicians dared not flirt with so dangerous an idea. Fear of the expense involved – the 1875 survey envisaged a total cost of about $8.5 million for a standard-gauge line – was general, especially among anti-confederate politicians who otherwise supported any scheme likely to strengthen the island's economy. The short line idea was attacked as impractical; some argued that the colony's resources were not so great as the railway prophets supposed – that the whole scheme was based on false premises and was no more than a utopian vision devised by eccentrics like Murray and promoted by certain politicians for the purpose of vote gathering. Harvey recollected that in the 1870s 'it required some nerve and moral courage to give utterance to such heretical opinions' as those quoted above.[12] Within the government, only William Whiteway and Ambrose and Edward Shea[13] espoused the railway with great enthusiasm. Carter, temperamentally cautious, recoiled from implementing so grandiose an operation and refused to allow Whiteway to make it a party issue.[14] Murray, frustrated and outspoken, complained to Fleming that 'The system of our local Government is such that any attempt to improve or advance is utterly hopeless, however well intended; and some of its present leaders – Carter in particular – are not simply indifferent but obstructive. *Monopoly* is their password – Fish, Fish and Fish is their cry.'[15] He told the St John's Athenaeum that 'It has often struck me as very remarkable that the people most difficult to persuade that anything good can come out of Newfoundland, are Newfoundlanders.' Unless good lines of road were built, he went on, the colony would relapse into 'the old state of mesmeric indifference which has kept the land at least a century behind the rest of the civilised world.'[16]

Murray was an old man in a hurry, and his strictures on the government at least were not altogether fair. For besides having to contend with local political and financial factors, it had to face the impediments placed in the way of a trans-island railway by the Colonial Office, which did not relish the prospect of a terminus on the French Shore.[17] The 1875 survey plans were taken to England by Governor Sir John Glover in 1876, and deposited at the Colonial Office where, it was thought, interested parties could have easy access to them.[18] It soon emerged that access was anything but easy, since the office feared that tacit approval of the project might upset the French at a time when negotiations were in progress, and so render a permanent settlement of the shore question even more difficult. Carter was content enough with this state of affairs, and was in any case preoccupied with obtaining permission for the appointment of French Shore magistrates. But in 1878 he resigned as premier, to be replaced by William Whiteway, a fifty-year-old lawyer, described by Governor Glover as ''An able and energetic man dissatisfied with the condition of Newfoundland ...'[19] He had been a confederate in 1869 (like Carter and the Shea brothers); failing in this campaign, he turned his frustrated ambition to another goal: the development of the colony through railway building. Murray wrote enthusiastically that under Whiteway 'a new order of things has at length been to an extent inaugurated; and hopes may be entertained of the colony steadily if slowly, advancing in civilisation and progress.'[20]

Late in the pre-election session of 1878, Whiteway moved resolutions offering land grants and an annual subsidy of $120,000 to a company willing to build the trans-insular line, and was opposed only by that veteran anti-confederate and ex-premier Charles Fox Bennett. In London, as authorized by the colonial government, Fleming began to press the Colonial Office to place the survey plans on public exhibition and allow the publication of advertisements calling for tenders.[21] After some prevarication the office refused both requests, fortified in their decision by Glover's opinion that Whiteway would be only too glad to see the scheme withdrawn because he feared electoral opposition, and would welcome the chance to blame London.[22] By this time, Glover viewed Whiteway with deep suspicion; the latter had had the temerity to speculate in the governor's presence on the possible advantages to Newfoundland of leaving the empire, and Glover's judgment of the man and his political position were seriously distorted.[23] Whiteway protested the Colonial Office decision at once and went on to win a quiet general election with little difficulty or opposition.[24]

In the summer of 1879, Whiteway went to London himself to press not only for permission to build the railway but also for financial aid in building both it and a large drydock at St John's. In his submission to Hicks Beach, Whiteway argued that Newfoundland deserved special consideration from the imperial government, a note that was sounded often over the following years. 'When ... the British subsidy for Mail Communication paid to Messrs. Cunard and Co. was cut off,' he wrote, 'the small body of military ... withdrawn and the fortifications in St. John's dismantled, it seemed like severing us from the Mother Country and it appeared as though the only visible link remaining was the Imperial appointment of a Governor ...' Besides neglect, Newfoundland had to bear the burden of French treaty rights and the fishery clauses of the Treaty of Washington, which were then thought to be detrimental to local interests.[25] 'All that we now solicit is a fair consideration as an integral part of Her Majesty's Dominions.'[26] The Colonial Office was in fact anxious to do what it could for Whiteway, if only to induce a more reasonable local attitude towards a French Shore settlement and, if possible, confederation. But the Admiralty saw no need to provide funds for a dock, and the proposed railway could not realistically be viewed as of imperial importance, even if it was decided to brave French objections. Whiteway had to return home empty-handed. It was now clear that if the interior was to be developed the colony would have to find the means itself, and that a railway would have to avoid the French Shore.

The government therefore fell back on a plan for a local railway, rather than the trunk route, based on predictions being made by Murray and a local mine manager, F. Ellershausen, about the future of Notre Dame Bay as a mining region. The latter stated, and Murray agreed, that 'in his opinion, *the whole present population of Newfoundland*, or say 250,000 souls might be employed all the year round either directly or indirectly with the mines.'[27] Mining, they thought, would be the island's greatest industry and would stimulate agriculture and manufacturing.

They both advocated, therefore, a railway from either Halls Bay or Green Bay (inlets of Notre Dame Bay) to Bay of Islands or St George's: a line that would cross and open up the so-called fertile belt drained by the Humber River, and give access to areas where coal deposits and timber were known to exist. It could also form part of the short line trunk route, when it was built.[28] But a west coast terminus was politically impossible, and a line that would not be directly advantageous to the mass of voters on the Avalon Peninsula politically unwise. Whiteway therefore decided to build a line from Halls Bay to St John's. It would link the actual and future centres of population, tap the heads of the eastern bays where potentially good farm land had been reported, and stimulate lumbering on the Gander and Gambo rivers. Further, it would provide St John's with an alternative hinterland, if it was to be denied the west, and provide an attractive number of jobs. The proposal for this 350-mile railway, to be built narrow gauge at an estimated cost of $4 million, was put to the legislature in 1880 and accepted.

The Railway Act of 1880 was an explicitly temporary measure. It authorized the raising of a $5 million loan, and the appointment of railway commissioners to supervise initial work before tenders were called. The report of the joint select committee on which the act was based has been quoted often enough, but it bears repeating, if only because it sums up so neatly the thinking that led Newfoundland into the railway age:

The question of the future of our growing population has, for some time, engaged the earnest attention of all thoughtful men in this country, and has been the subject of serious solicitude. The fisheries being our main resource, and to a large extent the only dependence of the people, those periodic partial failures which are incident to such pursuits continue to be attended with recurring visitations of pauperism, and there seems no remedy to be found for this condition of things but that which may lie in varied and extensive pursuits ...

It is evident ... that no material increase of means is to be looked for from our fisheries, and that we must direct our attention to other sources to meet the growing requirements of the country. Our Mining industry may now be regarded as an established fact ... and there is every reason to believe from recent explorations that a great amount of wealth in copper and other ores is waiting the application of enterprise and capital to bring them into profitable use. Our Agricultural industry ... is yet susceptible of very enlarged development. Vast stretches of Agricultural land ... need only the employment of well-directed labor to convert them into means of independent support for thousands of the population ...

But to what end do these elements of wealth exist if they continue to remain neglected? For they will as before be outside the reach of the people if some energetic effort be not made to render them accessible to our centres of population. We have means of remunerative employment in those dormant resources, coincident with the spectacle so often about us of unemployed labor ...

Your Committee believe that no agency would be so effective for the promotion of the objects in view as that of a Railway; and when they consider that there is no Colony of equal importance under the Crown without a Railroad, and the advantages thereby conferred elsewhere in the enhancement of the value of property and labor, it is felt that in our circumstances no effort within the means of the Colony should be wanting to supply this great *desideratum.*[29]

There was little opposition to the railway proposal in the legislature. Since confederation had been buried as a live political issue in the early 1870s and Charles Fox Bennett's anti-confederate coalition allowed to dissolve, party lines had reverted to a denominational basis for want of any other. The majority Conservatives were mostly Protestants, representing predominantly Protestant constituencies; the minority Liberals, led in 1880 by J.I. Little,[30] were mostly Catholics and held the predominantly Catholic ridings of St John's and the southeast. These denominational parties had no denominational battles to fight. It had been tacitly agreed in the 1860s that the patronage cake would be shared fairly among members of all churches, and the denominational school system was firmly entrenched. The leading men of both parties, able to forget about denominational rivalry, found common cause in positive, nationalistic policies, and neither Carter nor Whiteway had cause to fear the Liberals, as long as they did nothing to raise a confederation scare and saw that Catholics were not discriminated against. Signs of what was to come were provided, however, by some of the merchant members of the legislature. None of them voted against the Railway Act; but in the Legislative Council Robert Thorburn,[31] a member of the select committee, made it clear that he and some others were prepared to accept the railway policy only so long as it proved to be within the means of the colony.[32]

There can be little doubt that many of the larger fish merchants viewed the railway with grave misgivings. They feared increased labour costs, increased taxes, loss of coastal trade for their ships, and eventual colonial bankruptcy and confederation. It seemed to represent a parting of the ways, 'an experience so new, so expensive, so divergent from our ordinary habits and wants, and at the same time so irretrievable in its results for good or evil.'[33] Stephen Rendell, manager of the large Water Street firm of Job Brothers, complained bitterly that the 'visionary pictures of unbounded prosperity' conjured up by the railway enthusiasts were 'all clap-trap and nonsense, calculated to lead the people astray, make them discontented with their present lot, unsettle their minds, and make them worse off than before.'[34] By the early summer of 1880 the railway question was being debated in the local press with far more fervour than the legislature had shown, as the St John's elite woke up to the fact that Whiteway was about to translate the idea about which they had chuckled for so long into actual fact. The *Public Ledger* noted in

July 'a general murmur of discontent' and a grumbling that the benefits of the railway would not balance the financial outlay, and a visiting journalist was surprised 'to find men of intelligence and position disapproving of [it].'[35] One merchant stood at the head of his wharf telling people that a toll-gate would be erected on the road from Conception Bay into St John's to force them onto the railway.[36] He and another merchant went around the bay to spread this and other equally sensational rumours, with the result that when the location surveyors reached Foxtrap towards the end of July they were halted by a noisy mob, armed with sticks and sealing guns, the women's aprons filled with stones. That energetic magistrate (and future historian) D.W. Prowse[37] led the constabulary into action and so managed to end what is remembered as the 'Battle of Foxtrap.' The surveyors proceeded to the accompaniment of no more than a stream of rich abuse.[38] By the fall, newspapers hinted that mercantile opposition was to find expression in a new political party.[39]

The government was unperturbed and by early 1881 was considering two tenders for the construction of the Halls Bay railway. Although the details of the negotiations can be passed over, it is worth noting that one of the tenderers refused to consider a narrow-gauge line on the grounds that its operation would be too costly.[40] The question of gauge, therefore, became an important element in the heated debate over which tender to accept. Whiteway refused to change his opinion that narrow gauge was quite sufficient for a local railway, besides being much cheaper, and he backed the other tender, made by a New York syndicate represented by one A.L. Blackman. Glover and others suspected that Whiteway had less worthy motives as well. In 1880 an American company known as the Newfoundland Consolidated Copper Mining Company, whose local directors were Whiteway and A.W. Harvey,[41] had purchased the mining properties operated by Ellershausen in Notre Dame Bay. It was suspected that the capitalists behind this company were identical to those tendering for the railway contract, and that Whiteway was therefore in a position of conflict of interest. There is little evidence on this point, but what there is suggests that the rumours had a basis in truth.[42] In the event Blackman's syndicate received the contract and formed the Newfoundland Railway Company. It was to build a railway to Halls Bay with a branch to Harbour Grace within five years; the government was to provide an annual subsidy of $180,000 for 35 years, land grants of 5,000 acres per mile, to admit construction materials duty free, and to lend the company $90,000 towards the cost of the right of way. As Whiteway noted, it was a deal similar 'in principle and construction' to the CPR contract of 1880.[43]

The contract did not pass the legislature without stormy debate. Indeed, the assembly began discussion of the railway before the government had decided which tender to accept, prompted by a petition signed by Charles Fox Bennett and seventy-one St John's businessmen praying that the question be put to the electorate.[44] Whiteway's reply was an attack on the structure of the local economy; faced by the conservatism of its guardians, he found himself forced, social conservative though he was, into a populist position. There was something 'radically defective in the state of the country,' he said, when its economic situation appeared generally healthy, merchants accumulated wealth, and yet fishermen so often went hungry and idle. His task was to build the railway, develop the land, and raise 'the working class to their proper position in the body politic.'[45] It was the first time that blame for backwardness had been placed overtly upon the management of the fisheries, as well as on the failure to diversify, and the speech can only have strengthened his opponents in their conviction that the railway represented a serious threat to the traditional way of life. Even so, most business-men in the legislature supported the contract; its few but vociferous opponents based their case not so much on economic or social grounds as on the terms of a contract that they felt gave an alien syndicate of dubious origins too many concessions and the colony too little protection.[46] The 1881 debates made it plain that the railway was now the central issue of local politics, and that new political alignments were the likely result.

In the summer of 1881 the company floated mortgage bonds in London through the agency of Melville, Evans and Company, deposited the necessary $100,000 security, and in August began work in St John's. Early in 1882, other aspects of its plans became clear. In March, Blackman's syndicate petitioned for incorporation in Newfoundland as the Great American and European Short Line Railway Company. Sandford Fleming's dream had returned. The company projected a direct, standard-gauge line from a point in Bonavista Bay to Cape Ray, where ferries would connect it to a proposed line through Cape Breton, joining the Eastern Extension railway at Canso.[47] It was incorporated by Nova Scotia in 1881 and by the federal government in 1882, receiving from the latter a subsidy to build a line from New Glasgow to Oxford. An enthusiastic supporter at Ottawa was Sir Charles Tupper.[48] The Newfoundland government was asked to provide land grants and to guarantee bonds to the extent of at least $3 million. Although the legislature was enthusiastic about the prospect of a direct line, it refused the promise of bond endorsement, and Blackman had to be content with a charter promising land grants only.[49] The legislature did, however, approve financial guarantees and support for a large drydock to be built in St John's by the company's former chief engineer, aided by several of the company's directors. The *Evening Telegram* accurately called it Blackman's 'Consolation Contract.'[50]

Mines, railways, the dock: the syndicate had effectively absorbed all aspects of the Conservative government's development policy, and Whiteway had cause to rejoice. But his failure to obtain the short line bond guarantee from an assembly anxious to do no wrong in an election year led to a distinct diminution in the syndicate's interest in its Newfoundland operations. Its major concern, the centre-piece of its schemes, was the short line route, and this was, for the time being, an impossibility. The syndicate therefore decided to transfer the Atlantic terminus of the route to Louisbourg or Sydney, and appears to have concentrated most of its evidently exiguous resources in work on the mainland. So far as Newfoundland was concerned, it seems the railway company decided to build no further than Harbour Grace; and even that work progressed at a snail's pace, only 45 miles of track being laid by the end of 1882. In St John's rumours flew, claiming that the railway company was nearly bankrupt, which the government press indignantly and confidently denied: for the railway and the contract were the central election issues.

Whiteway's Conservatives, now in open alliance with the Liberals, faced an amorphous New party composed of those who, for one reason or another, were disenchanted with the government. Carter noted that though 'the present party with the Government have usually had the sustainement of the Mercantile Community,' the new projects had raised the fear 'among many commercial capitalists of considerable general influence' that the colony was pledged beyond its means.[51] Most of the Water Street merchants did give open or tacit support to the New party: a few of them ran as candidates, joined by most of the politicians who had opposed the Blackman contract. The most prominent of these were A.J.W. McNeily,[52] formerly speaker of the assembly, and his father-in-law, J.J. Rogerson, formerly receiver general. If a mercantile orientation was one characteristic of the New party, another was its Protestantism. Virtually all its supporters were Protestant, most of them nonconformist, and its campaign efforts were almost entirely concentrated in Protestant constituencies. Whiteway's alliance was predominantly Anglican and Catholic, which gave it a strong base in the Avalon Peninsula. It was not totally bereft of mercantile support, since a few large St John's firms and all of the important outport firms remained loyal. Given this degree of support, railway patronage, the failure of nonconformist voters to rally to the New party, and a stream of propaganda starkly defining the issue as 'Progress' versus 'Stagnation and Starvation,' it is not surprising that Whiteway was returned with twenty-seven of a total of thirty-three seats.

Whiteway's second ministry was less happy than his first. The Blackman syndicate faded from the scene; the railway reached Harbour Grace in the fall of 1884, heralding the Newfoundland Railway Company's bankruptcy soon after. Until 1896 the line was operated by the receiver in the interests of the bondholders. The dock contract was transferred to J.E. Simpson and Company of New York in 1883. It was a sad anticlimax to the fine rhetoric of a few years before. Instead of the 350-mile development railway to Halls Bay, the colony had only 84 miles of track across the largely barren Avalon Peninsula, built at a cost of about $21,000 per mile. This was hardly a development road. 'Where are the smiling hamlets?' asked the sardonic Thomas Talbot[53] in 1889, 'the ample sheep walks, the well-stocked pastures, the waving fields of corn, which the magic influence of the railroad was going to create into life? Have the people settled along the line ... ? Are those already resident within the points of termination ... more comfortable, more independent ... ? Is there less poverty ... ? No.'[54] Nevertheless, the Harbour Grace railway was useful, running as it did through the most densely populated area of the island, and it soon began to show a modest profit.[55] But the interior was as closed as before, the west still inaccessible; and the apparent failure of the 'Policy of Progress' only served to strengthen the prejudices of those who had grave doubts about Whiteway as a leader, and about railway building as a cure for the colony's economic ills.

The New party did not die out with its ignominious defeat. Its merchant members may have retired to their counting houses, but within them they were becoming increasingly obsessed with the expanding French bank fishery, whose product appeared to them to be driving the Newfoundland product out of European markets and lowering prices to ruinous levels. For this problem Whiteway had no answer; the merchants thought the solution was to prevent bait fishes caught within Newfoundland waters from reaching the French bankers. Whiteway's attitude was that the French should be allowed to continue obtaining bait, if in return they would allow industrial use of the west coast, and thereby make a trans-island railway possible. To the merchants it appeared vital that they take over the government. McNeily began to concoct an appropriate strategy: the use of the rural Orange Order as the basis of a sectarian attack on Whiteway's political reliance on the Catholic, urban southwest. Moves to implement this policy were already under-way, when on 26 December 1883 an Orange-Catholic affray at Harbour Grace led to the deaths of four Orangemen and one Catholic.[56] The sectarian animosities latent in Newfoundland society were at once aroused, and opposition forces set about reaping political advantage from the resulting tension within the governing coalition. It was not until the February 1885 session, after a number of the Catholic rioters indicted for murder had twice been acquitted in Catholic St John's, that the St John's Orangemen, now working closely with the New party merchants, made their move. By pressing an overtly sectarian amendment to the throne speech, they created a Protestant-Catholic polarization in the assembly which forced the Liberals to break their alliance with the Conservatives and revert to an independent position. The Protestants, for the time being, remained split between those belonging or looking to the New party, and those remaining loyal to the non-Orange Whiteway, who spent the summer of 1885 fighting for his political life. In the early fall, with an election imminent, he gave up. He agreed to retire from politics, in return for the promise of the chief justiceship, and to amalgamate his faction with the Reform party (as the New party was now called) – an agreement that was repudiated by most of his few remaining supporters. He was replaced as premier by Robert Thorburn and as attorney general by James Winter,[57] the Orange grand master. In the ensuing election the Reformers swept all the Protestant seats bar two: the Liberals all the Catholic seats bar one. The 1885 election was perhaps the most predictable in nineteenth-century Newfoundland.

The Reformers had run a virulently anti-Catholic campaign under the slogan 'No Amalgamation with the Roman Catholics.' But they had no intention of maintaining an exclusively Protestant government after the elections were over. The small print of their manifesto promised Catholics 'a full measure of justice in relation to their political and civil rights,'[58] and arrangements for a future coalition had been made between Reform and Liberal leaders before the election took place. As Prowse put it, the Reformers stood for government 'worked on sound commercial principles ... a new reign of moderate progress and economy ...'[59] Denominational composition was of secondary importance; the primary object was to return power to those who felt they could use it more responsibly than Whiteway, and do something to alleviate the acute problems of the fish trade in a period of strong market competition and falling export prices. In the 1886 session the Reform government refused to consider requests that the Halls Bay railway should be continued. Instead, reverting to the policies of the mercantile governments of the 1860s, it proposed a road-building program geared to the encouragement of agriculture – diversification at the local rather than the national level. The trade, it argued, could afford no more. To counter the supposed fisheries threat from the French, it rejected an Anglo-French agreement approved by Whiteway which essentially traded bait for the opening of the west coast, and passed the famous bill to regulate the export of bait.[60]

The Bait Act, Water Street's economic panacea, was eventually approved by the imperial government in 1887, and put into operation against the French in 1888. For years afterwards fish merchants were to argue that it achieved its object of relieving pressure on European fish markets and thus improving prices. The available evidence, however, points to a different conclusion. The French banking vessels soon found that they could carry on without bait caught on Newfoundland's south coast, the French bank catch did not suffer (apart from the first voyage of 1888), and it is noticeable that fish prices began to climb in 1887, a year before the act was enforced. Those who suffered were the fishermen of the south coast, and the merchants of the French colony of Saint-Pierre. The Bait Act did nothing to reduce market competition, and it is arguable that the Reform government would have been better advised had they tackled some of the fundamental domestic problems that plagued the fishery. The cure of the annual catch was always uneven, often careless, and its shipping and marketing was erratic and uncontrolled. But instead of putting their own basically anarchic trade in order, the merchants chose to strike out at a competitor. It was a policy of desperation.[61]

Failure in this policy was accompanied by the Reform government's inability to maintain its promise of thrift and caution in the use and expenditure of public funds. It came into office in the midst of, and partly as a result of, economic depression; ironically it was that depression which forced the government into large expenditures to provide work and relief. There were as well purely political pressures for such spending, since part of the price demanded by the Liberals when they amalgamated with the Reform party in 1886 was the building of a branch railway to Placentia, the heart of an important Catholic district.[62] By the end of 1886 the government had spent almost half a million dollars on direct and disguised relief, $30,000 of it on the Placentia line. Whiteway had never been so generous. Similar or higher expenditures followed in the next three years. The Placentia branch eventually cost $500,000, double the original estimate. Borrowing was heavy. The Reformers floated the colony's first direct foreign loans, and by the end of 1889 the public debt had doubled since 1885, standing at $4,133,202.43. It was a strange record for a businessmen's government pledged to financial conservatism. Stranger still was the decision reached late in 1888 to recommence the Halls Bay railway. The main reason was undoubtedly political. Eighteen eighty-nine was an election year, and a revived Whitewayite party, firmly committed to a railway development policy, was poised for a comeback. It could be expected to revive the 1882 cry that merchants opposed progress, and it was therefore up to the Reformers to provide tangible evidence that Whiteway did not have a monopoly on it. Having failed to implement an alternative economic policy, they felt that they had to meet Whiteway on his own ground. It was no longer a question of whether or not railways should be built, but a question of who was to build and control them. This is clear from the Reform party election propaganda. Its newspaper, the *Evening Mercury*, urged repeatedly that the merchants were now 'in the van of progress,' that they had become 'out-and-out Newfoundlanders.'[63] But it was to no avail. The Whitewayite press scoffed at the apparent change in attitude: the Reformers were still merchants, still basically reactionary. 'Vote for the Friend of the Workingman and the Apostle of Progress,' 'Vote for Whiteway and $1.25 a day!' cried the *Evening Telegram*;[64] and vote for him the electorate did. In a result that surprised all observers, the Reformers salvaged only seven seats, the entire cabinet going down to defeat.

The Whitewayite party – now adopting the Liberal label – was mostly composed of men new to politics. Only eight of its twenty-nine MHAs had had previous experience, and Whiteway alone had held executive office. Like the coalition of 1882, the party was firmly based on the support of the major denominations and the southeastern constituencies. Its policies were similar to those of previous White-way governments. The railway was to be completed, the French Shore opened to industrial use, and the interior settled as its resources were made accessible. To this familiar mix were added two new elements. First, bait was not to be given the French for any concession other than the abolition or modification of their bounty system; second, the colony would seek to negotiate a separate reciprocity treaty with the United States. These policies were in fact legacies from the Reform government, and were championed in the Liberal cabinet by A.W. Harvey who, for all his support of railways, was an authentic Water Street voice. He was joined, especially in his advocacy of reciprocity, by Robert Bond.[65] Whiteway differed from them in that he appears to have questioned the value of enforcing the Bait Act against the French and the advantages of reciprocity. Further, although he believed in the ultimate desirability of confederation, Bond and Harvey did not. But Whiteway was ageing, and less sure of himself since the debacle of 1885, and so he allowed his senior ministers to carry him along.

The government's first priority was the railway. The colony had tried a CPR-style contract and burned its fingers; it had tried managing construction itself and found this extravagant; the Liberals therefore decided to employ a contractor to build the line for a fixed price. In June 1890 a contract was signed with Robert G. Reid[66] of Montreal and G.H. Middleton of Toronto, who agreed to complete the line to Halls Bay for $15,600 per mile, payable in 3.5 per cent government debentures.[67] Middleton dropped out of the partnership in 1892, but Reid proved himself a reliable engineer and pushed the line rapidly north. The method of financing construction created a large annual addition to the public debt, and the servicing of that debt would have to be met either by higher taxation or through an expanding economy. The only other solution was to try, once again, to obtain an imperial guarantee on a development loan.

Bond and Harvey evidently hoped that reciprocity, through providing new markets for Newfoundland produce, would be an economic tonic, which would enable the colony to meet its new obligations with ease. In the fall of 1890 Bond successfully negotiated a convention with Secretary of State James Blaine in Washington, whereby free bait for American fishermen was traded for free entry of Newfoundland fish and minerals.[68] The reaction of the Canadian government was extremely hostile; as a result the imperial government refused ratification, to the great and vehemently expressed mortification of the Newfoundlanders. The Colonial Office took this decision with great reluctance, not wanting to take any action which could make the colony unwilling to cooperate on French Shore matters. In particular, the imperial government wanted Newfoundland to pass legislation giving effect to the operation of the Anglo-French treaties and the *modus vivendi* governing the French Shore lobster fishery, legislation which Newfoundland was most reluctant to pass, and which it refused when the Bond-Blaine convention was not immediately ratified. The Colonial Office therefore dangled a carrot before the colony. If it would cooperate on the French Shore legislation, and if the state of public finances was judged satisfactory, the imperial government would guarantee the $10 million development loan for which Whiteway had applied in July 1890. By the summer of 1891 these terms had been accepted; but in the session of 1892, the assembly rejected both the legislation and the carrot.[69] For additional revenue, therefore, Whiteway had to look to the tariff, and for interior development future governments had to look to large, outside corporations.

Reid cannot have been alarmed that these developments would in any way affect the colony's credit and so impair his ability to dispose of the bonds with which he was paid. In the election year of 1893 he agreed to continue the railway across the island from the Exploits River to Port aux Basques on the same terms as before.[70] Since Notre Dame Bay had not lived up to Murray's expectations as a mining area, it was not thought worthwhile to continue north to Halls Bay. Port aux Basques was chosen as terminus both because it was the point closest to the mainland, and because it was outside the French limits. The line itself was designed to touch the west coast as little as possible. It is interesting that Whiteway did not consult London before making this agreement. After some initial consternation the Colonial Office decided that the legislation could be allowed – an indication of how far its position on the French Shore question had altered over the years. In a second contract in 1893, Reid agreed to operate the Placentia branch and the railways he was building for ten years, in return for a land grant of 5,000 acres per mile operated.[71] He refused a longer period, being fearful that operating losses would become too onerous when they could no longer be offset by the profits of construction.[72] On their side, the government was confident that by 1903 the line would be a paying proposition.[73] In any case, they could not leave the line dangling at Exploits or Halls Bay, a line to nowhere.

Although the opposition, now known as the Tory party, increased its strength by four in the 1893 election, establishing a strong base in the northern districts, the Liberals had little trouble in maintaining themselves in power. But early in 1894 the colony was plunged into political chaos by the filing of successful election petitions against seventeen Liberals, including the entire cabinet except Harvey, who sat in the Legislative Council. This is not the place to describe the in-fighting of that incredible year.[74] Its effect was to precipitate a financial crisis when, in December, both the local banks stopped payment. For the first six months of 1895 the colony hung on the edge of bankruptcy. Confederation negotiations at Ottawa failed.[75] Salvation came through Bond's success, against heavy odds, in raising sufficient money in London to shore up both the treasury and the government-controlled Savings Bank. The collapse caused much heart searching and recrimination. What had been its cause? The Liberals claimed that it was the result of the fish-exporting firms, who controlled the banks, being overextended, and, in the short term, of political sabotage by the Tories. The latter laid most of the blame on the railway, which they claimed had overtaxed the trade and strained the colony's financial resources to breaking point. On balance, the Liberals had the better of the argument, since there is no denying that the crisis was basically commercial. But the Tories had a valid point, in so far as increased tariffs had placed an additional strain on a trade already beset by a multitude of problems, but against this should be set the fact that the prices of most imports were falling in the 1880s and 1890s.[76] Since 1890 the railway had been pushed forward virtually regardless of what the colony could afford in a period of economic depression. Fish prices fell from a high of $4.20 per quintal in 1889 to $3.29 in 1894, and this fall, together with that in commodity prices, meant that the government's revenue had barely maintained its average level of $1.5 million. Borrowing to cover deficits and public works accompanied the sale of railway bonds, and by the end of 1894 the public debt stood at $9,116,534.73 – an increase of almost $5 million since 1890. To many contemporaries it must have seemed that the railway, the whole 'Policy of Progress,' was the architect of their misfortunes, and that the failure of that policy to ameliorate economic problems was very apparent.

The gap between utopian rhetoric and economic reality caught up with the Liberals in 1897 when, in spite of the completion of the railway to Port aux Basques that year, they suffered a crushing electoral defeat. Like the Reformers in 1889, they became the scapegoats for continuing poverty and depression. In their place was installed a Tory ministry led by James Spearman Winter and the party's *éminence grise* Alfred B. Morine.[77] They were not to know that they were entering office at the turning point of the depression; all they could see was that the fish trade was still in trouble, that colonial finances were precarious, and that the future of the railway posed immense problems. Like their Reform party predecessors they did what they could to straighten out government finances, and in an effort to help the trade sent a mission to Europe to report on market conditions and established, at long last, a Department of Marine and Fisheries. The railway now snaked in a huge arc from St John's to Port aux Basques through land that was as yet almost totally undeveloped. Reid's operating contract was due to expire in 1903. If the present state of affairs were to continue, how could the colony possibly afford to operate a line which was almost certain to run at a loss, and how was the colony to stimulate the economic developments which alone could make it pay? Reid himself provided an answer, which was eagerly grasped by the government and incorporated in the celebrated contract of 1898. For an additional land grant of 5,000 acres per mile, Reid would operate the entire railway system – the Harbour Grace line having been purchased by the colony in 1896 – for fifty years; at the end of that period the railway would become the property of his heirs, and for that reversionary interest he would at once pay $1 million and return 2,500 acres per mile to the colony. Additional clauses provided that Reid would purchase and operate the drydock and, in return for subsidies, operate the Cabot Strait ferry, the coastal steamship service, and the telegraphs.[78] Newfoundland was to have its own CPR. A French newspaper spoke of Reid as another Cecil Rhodes; a more analogous figure might be K.C. Irving.[79]

The Tories argued that the contract would provide immediate financial relief and future prosperity, that it was, in effect, a logical continuation of the 'Policy of Progress.' The colony's outlay on communications would be substantially reduced; the millstone of the railway would be hung around Reid's neck; and economic diversification would become a reality at last, since at his own expense and risk Reid would have to develop his landholdings, totalling some four million acres, to make any money at all. This reasoning was supported by a section of the Liberal opposition led by Edward P. Morris,[80] whose constituency of St John's West stood to gain by the proposed transfer there of the railway machine shops hitherto situated at Whitbourne. The other Liberals under Bond, the official leader since Whiteway's defeat in 1897, vigorously opposed the contract. The taxpayers had paid for the railway, and their representatives in government should control it, not a Canadian businessman. The contract to them represented a monstrous and unjustified sell-out, the creation of a dangerous monopoly. In the small world of Newfoundland Reid would become too powerful, possibly dominant, threatening the colony's future independence of action. This possibility was too high a price to pay for immediate industrial development. These objections were never successfully countered by the Tories, who could only repeat that the end justified the means – an argument scorned by the Bond Liberals, and by the Colonial Office. On Joseph Chamberlain's instructions, the office sent the colony a scathing dispatch, which Morine called 'a deadly blow' to the government.[81]

In the summer of 1898 Bond and other Liberals began a public campaign against the contract, and the then governor, Sir Herbert Murray and the Catholic bishop of St John's, M.F. Howley,[82] were both associated with the campaign. Numerous signatures were collected to petitions calling for imperial action to prevent the contract legislation from becoming law, and for the retention of the governor – whose term of office was coming to an end – in the colony. If London chose not to intervene but allowed him to remain in Newfoundland, Murray intended to dismiss the Winter government on the grounds that it had lost public confidence.[83] In the event, Chamberlain chose neither to extend Murray's term nor to intervene; the best Murray could do was fire a parting shot at the ministry by dismissing Morine on the grounds that he had been in receipt of a retainer from Reid at the time the contract was negotiated – a fact of which he had been aware since the previous

February.[84] In the face of the widespread unpopularity of the contract and of by-election losses in 1899, the Tory government began to fall apart, resolving itself into two factions led respectively by Morine, who craved the premiership, and Winter, who wanted to elevate himself to a safe seat on the bench but wavered before mercantile demands that he remain premier to keep Morine out. Unable to reunite, the government was defeated in the assembly early in 1900. Bond agreed to form a government, but being refused an immediate dissolution by Governor Sir Henry McCallum, he had to come to terms with Morris over the contract issue in order to gain a majority. After some haggling a compromise was reached: the contract would be modified.[85]

On this platform the Liberals went to the country in the fall. All that was left of the Tories was the Morine faction, since Winter and most of his supporters dropped out of politics in 1900. Water Street did not like Morine – he was a confederate and too clever by half – and most of the traditionally Tory merchants stood aloof from the contest. However, backed by the Reids, Morine was able to mount a spirited campaign in support of the 1898 contract. Allow Reid to fulfil his obligations, cried the Tories, and the new Newfoundland promised for so long would finally emerge. Reid's trains and steamers carried Tory colours, and his sons appeared on Tory platforms. But this blatant association of the party with the Reids made it most vulnerable to a nationalistic Liberal attack, which created out of 'Czar Reid' a bogey figure as potent as the menacing Canadian conjured up by the anti-confederates of 1869. Like confederation then, the 1898 contract was represented as a sell-out by place-seekers:

Will you let Reid's hireling lawyer [Morine]
Barter homes and hearths away?
Will you let him sell his country
Sell you all for place and pay?[86]

Bond was returned with an overwhelming majority. The Tories salvaged only four seats. 'I feel *deeply grateful to God* for having saved our poor old country,' wrote Bishop Howley, 'And I had no scruple in having the prayers of the Church offered up in sincere thanksgiving ...'[87]

Bond at once began negotiations with Reid, and these proved long and difficult. It was not until July 1901 that a new contract was agreed upon. The colony bought back the reversionary interest of the railway, by returning to Reid his $1 million plus interest, and resumed control of the telegraphs.[88] In return for $850,000 (or 30¢ an acre) Reid gave up the lands to which the 1898 contract had entitled him. Otherwise the contract was unchanged; the newly created Reid Newfoundland Company was to operate the railway until 1951, to continue the steamship service, keep the drydock and the St John's tramway.[89] Though the contract did not go as far as Bond would have liked in limiting the Reids' power, it nevertheless represented a realistic compromise between his desire to maintain the independence of the colony and its legislature, and the necessity of the Reids' maintaining an operation large enough to have a chance of paying its way. The Reids remained a powerful force in Newfoundland, but their wings had been clipped. Morine regarded the 1901 agreement as a virtual repeal of the 1898 contract, because it had forced the Reids to abandon their plans to diversify independently into lumbering, paper manufacturing, and mining. The loss of the reversionary interest in the railway, of the telegraphs, and some lands had apparently been sufficient to prevent Reid raising any large amount of development capital.[90] The Reids had to be content to manage the railway and steamers, and hope to attract others to exploit their lands – a hope that was in part fulfilled with the establishment of the Grand Falls and Corner Brook paper-mills in 1905 and 1923 respectively.

The 1901 contract marks the end of the initial phase of Newfoundland's development strategy. D.G. Alexander has pointed out how the early twentieth century sees a shift away from infrastructure development 'to the search for foreign direct investment firms to develop modern resource industries,'[91] and the question which remains to be answered here is how far that infrastructure contributed to the colony's economic growth. This is a matter that awaits detailed analysis, and what follows must therefore be general and tentative.

The construction of the railway did not make a major contribution to the economy in the period 1881–98. Although over two thousand men were employed during the peak years of construction after 1890, and a demand was created for locally produced timber, the effect was only to help alleviate conditions in a bleak economic period. No doubt, without the railway work, both unemployment and emigration would have been greater; there is evidence to suggest that the cash placed in circulation added to what has been described as 'the fictitious prosperity' that followed the St John's fire of 1892 and ended with the bank crash of 1894.[92] But the crash itself indicated that railway construction alone was insufficient to offset the colony's deeper economic problems. The return of relative prosperity to Newfoundland at the turn of the century coincided with the end of railway construction, but had nothing to do with it. The end of the so-called Great Depression and the upturn in primary product prices had far more effect on the colony than the few saw-mills that had sprung up near the railway, or even the newly opened iron mines on Bell Island. The large interior developments occurred when the colony's timber lands came into demand, and not before; and capital came because there were trees, not because there was a railway. The railway of course made operations in central and western Newfoundland easier, but it was not a necessary condition of their inception or their success.

A failure in economic terms, the railway was also a loss in accounting terms. If the figures of the Reid Newfoundland Company are to be believed, the railway never made a profit, the total loss for the period 1901–21 being approximately $6 million. A railway expert reported in 1922:

The expectation of the parties to the original contract, as to amount of traffic, has not been realised; and the Reid Newfoundland Railway has always been, and for a long time will be, a line of extremely light traffic, requiring the maintaining of large mileage of track for the handling of small tonnage of freight and a limited number of passengers. These conditions are the result of small population; but still more to the character of the country and the nature of the colony's chief industry: viz, fishing. A very great proportion of the traffic of the small population can be better handled by water than by rail, and at much less expense.[93]

He went on to remark on the excessive grades of the narrow-gauge track, which resulted in a high cost operation; while it cost the CPR 0.78¢ to move one ton of freight one mile, it cost the Newfoundland railway 7.5¢. Low tariffs embedded in the contracts, and unremunerative political branch lines built after 1908, added to the Reids' problems. In 1919 the CPR was earning $15,917.61 per mile; the Newfoundland railway was earning $1,542.70.[94] In 1923 the Reids thankfully sold out to the government for $2 million.[95]

Moses Harvey had predicted that the railway would cause the colony to 'blossom like the rose'; Whiteway had envisioned 'trains laden with minerals, timber and agricultural produce, passing from the smiling fields and gardens of the west on their way to market in the metropolis.'[96] In terms of these expectations, the railway was a failure into which, by 1929, the colony had poured approximately $40 million[97] – a monument to the fact that in the nineteenth century 'so happily [was] the Newfoundland mind constituted that if nothing [could] be got out of the topsoil immediately it conclud[ed] that great riches [were] underneath.'[98] The railway debt was undoubtedly one of the factors contributing to the financial collapse of the 1930s, in this sense justifying the worst fears of Bennett and the New party merchants. Yet the Newfoundland Railway became a much-loved local institution, as individualistic as the island it traverses. Like all railways it was a great connector, helping to unify the country, break down local particularism and prejudice, and creating greater labour mobility. It gave the colony a firm link with the mainland, hastening its gradual move from the Atlantic to the North American orbit. Its social impact must have been as great in its day as was the completion of the trans-island highway in 1965. The joint select committee of 1880, with its strong merchant contingent, had predicted that the railway would not pay; it went on to justify the enterprise in words that can serve as an apt conclusion:

as the work of the country, and in its bearing on the promotion of the well-being of the people, in which the returns are alone sought and will be found, it eminently commends itself to our judgement. In this sense we believe that, in time, it will amply repay its cost, and that the consequent advance in the comfort and independence of the people will fully attest the wisdom of its establishment.[99]

NOTES

1 See Shannon Ryan, 'The Newfoundland Salt Cod Trade in the Nineteenth Century,' and David Alexander, 'Newfoundland's Traditional Economy and Development to 1934,' above.

2 For a sketch of Murray's career, see R.D. Hughes, 'Alexander Murray (1810–1884),' Geological Association of Canada, *Proceedings* 23 (1971): 1–4.

3 *JHA*, 1869, appendix, 677. The Tilt Cove mine was started by C.F. Bennett (see above, 92 n60).

4 See above, 5.

5 See above, 89 n9.

6 G.R. Stevens, *Canadian National Railways*, 2 vols. (Toronto 1960–2), 1: 63; G.P. deT. Glazebrook, *A History of Transportation in Canada*, 2nd ed., 2 vols. (Toronto 1964), 1: 149.

7 L.J. Burpee, *Sandford Fleming, Empire Builder* (Oxford 1915), 84–8; Stevens, *Canadian National Railways*, 1: 186–7.

8 A.R. Penney, 'The Newfoundland Railway: Newfoundland Epic,' in J.R. Smallwood (ed.), *The Book of Newfoundland*, vol. 3 (St John's 1967), 473. This article is a most useful source of factual detail.

9 J.J. Rogerson in assembly debate, 7 April 1880 (Public Ledger (St John's), 20 April 1880).

10 J.J. Dearin in assembly debate, 10 April 1878 (ibid., 14 May 1878).

11 Moses Harvey, 'This Land of Ours,' lecture to the St John's Athenaeum, 11 Feb. 1878, printed in his *Newfoundland as It Is in 1899* (London 1899), 81.

12 Harvey, *Newfoundland in 1899*, 83.

13 See above, 89 n10, 90 n12.

14 Carter in assembly debate, 11 April 1878 (*Public Ledger*, 21 May 1878).

15 Public Archives of Canada, Sandford Fleming papers, Murray to Fleming, 29 May 1877.

16 Alexander Murray, *Roads: A Popular Lecture delivered before the Athenaeum Institute on March 26th, 1877* (St John's 1877), 11, 15.

17 On the French Shore question in general see F.F. Thompson, *The French Shore Question in Newfoundland: An Imperial Study* (Toronto 1961).

18 PANL, Series G 3/77, E.D. Shea to Glover, 11 Jan. 1877

19 CO 194/195, Glover to Hicks Beach, 1 May 1878.

20 Sandford Fleming papers, Murray to Fleming, 25 July 1878.

21 CO 194/196, Fleming to Hicks Beach, 24 June 1878, to Pennell, [1878], and to Dealtry, 21 June 1878.

22 CO 194/195, Hicks Beach to Glover, 14 Aug. 1878; Glover to Hicks Beach, 6 Aug. 1878.

23 Ibid., Glover to Hicks Beach, 30 May 1878.

24 Ibid., Whiteway to Glover, 21 Aug. 1878, enclosed in Glover to Hicks Beach, 22 Aug. 1878.

25 On this point see W.G. Reeves, 'The Fortune Bay Dispute: Newfoundland's Place in Imperial Treaty Relations under the Washington Treaty, 1871–1885' (unpublished MA thesis, Memorial University 1971).

26 CO 194/198, Whiteway to Hicks Beach, 18 June 1879. Whiteway also asked for an imperial contribution to the mail subsidy paid by the colonial government to the Allan Line. This request was eventually granted in 1887.

27 Sandford Fleming papers, Murray to Fleming, 14 Dec. 1878.

28 Ibid.; PANL, G 3/78, Ellershausen to Glover, 19 Aug. 1878; Murray to Glover, 25 Nov. 1878.

29 *JHA*, 1880, 126–9.

30 J.I. Little, born Prince Edward Island, 1835; brother of P.F. Little (see above, 119 n29); judge of the Supreme Court, 1883–1902; chief justice, 1898–1902; died St John's, 1902.

31 See above, 121 n69.

32 Thorburn in Legislative Council debate, 12 April 1880 (*Public Ledger*, 17 April 1880).

33 James Murray, *The Commercial Crisis in Newfoundland: Cause, Consequences and Cure* (St John's 1895) 13.

34 Rendell in Legislative Council debate, 31 March 1881 (*Public Ledger*, 22 April 1881).

35 *Public Ledger*, 6 July 1880; W. Fraser Rae, *Newfoundland to Manitoba, through Canada's Maritime, Mining and Prairie Provinces* (New York 1881), 28.

36 Information given by D.W. Prowse to J.G. Millais and recorded in the latter's *Newfoundland and its Untrodden Ways* (London 1907), 80–1.

37 See above, 6.

38 *Morning Chronicle* (St John's, 29 July 1880; Millais, *Newfoundland*, 80–1.

39 *Patriot* (St John's), 30 Aug. 1880; *Morning Chronicle*, 7 Sept. 1880.

40 PANL, S 2/107, E.W. Plunkett to E.D. Shea, 14 Feb. 1881.

41 A.W. Harvey, born Bermuda, 1839; merchant; member of Legislative Council; died St John's, 1903.

42 CO 194/201, Glover to Kimberley, 2 April 1881. The directorates of the copper and railway companies were distinct. However, it is known that Erastus Wiman, president

of the copper company, was also behind the Great American and European Short Line Railway Company, which made no secret of being the Newfoundland Railway Company under another name.

43 CO 194/201, Whiteway to Glover, 10 May 1881, enclosed in Glover to Kimberley, 11 May 1881. The contract can be found in *JHA*, 1881, 162–7.

44 *JHA*, 1881, 45. The text of the petition and a list of signatures can be found in *Public Ledger*, 22 March 1881.

45 Whiteway in assembly debate, 10 March 1881 (Public Ledger, 15 March 1881).

46 See the protest of the minority in the Legislative Council, 9 May 1881, which summarizes the opposition arguments, *Journal of the Legislative Council*, 1881, 76–7.

47 CO 194/204, Blackman to E.D. Shea, 19 Sept. 1882, enclosed in Carter to Kimberley, 16 Dec. 1882.

48 See, for example, Tupper in Canada, House of Commons, *Debates* 12 (1882): 1521, 5 May 1882.

49 *JHA*, 1882, 213–16, Report of Select Committee, 28 April 1882. The Colonial Office decided to postpone formal confirmation of the legislation until it became clear what works were proposed for the French Shore.

50 See assembly debate, 26 April 1882 (*Public Ledger*, 5 May 1882); *Evening Telegram* (St John's), 25 April 1882.

51 CO 194/204, Carter to Kimberley, 10 Oct. 1882.

52 A.J.W. McNeily, born Ulster, 1845; lawyer and politician; died St John's, 1911.

53 See above, 71.

54 Talbot in Legislative Council debate, 27 May 1889 (*Evening Mercury* (St John's), 12 June 1889).

55 For the period 1885–95, the company made an average annual profit of $3,270. It is less certain that the social rate of return was also positive.

56 On this crisis see Elinor Senior, 'The origin and political activities of the Orange Order in Newfoundland, 1863–1890' (unpublished MA thesis, Memorial University 1959), 139–98; and James Hiller, 'The Political Effects of the Harbour Grace Affray, 1883–85' (unpublished lecture, Newfoundland Historical Society 1971).

57 See above, 121 n78.

58 See *Colonist* (St John's), 2 June 1886.

59 D.W. Prowse, *A History of Newfoundland from the English, Colonial, and Foreign Records*, 2nd ed. (London 1896), 514.

60 See Thompson, *French Shore Problem*, ch. 3, 4.

61 For the detailed history of the trade see Shannon Ryan, 'The Newfoundland Cod Fishery in the Nineteenth Century' (unpublished MA thesis, Memorial University 1971).

62 The amalgamation of 1886 marks the end of the old Catholic Liberal party. The Catholic members split on the issue, and henceforth there was no specifically Catholic political party.

63 *Evening Mercury*, 27 July, 15 Oct. 1889.

64 *Evening Telegram*, 28 Aug., 26 Oct. 1889.

65 See above, 121 n82.

66 Robert G. Reid, born Scotland, 1841; trained as stonemason. He built many railway bridges in the United States and Canada, built the CPR section north of Lake Superior, and supervised the building of the railway through Cape Breton. He was reputed to be a millionaire by the time he came to Newfoundland. He died in Montreal in 1908.

67 The contract can be found in *JHA*, 1891, appendix, 407–31.

68 See D.J. Davis, 'The Bond-Blaine Negotiations, 1890–1891' (unpublished MA thesis, Memorial University 1970); and Peter Neary and S.J.R. Noel, 'Newfoundland's Quest for Reciprocity, 1890–1910,' in Mason Wade (ed.), *Regionalism in the Canadian Community* (Toronto 1969), 210–26.

69 See Thompson, *French Shore Problem*, ch. 5, 6.

70 The contract can be found in *JHA*, 1893, appendix, 360.

71 *JHA*, 1893, appendix, 360.

72 A.B. Morine, *The Railway Contract, 1898, and Afterwards* (St John's [1933]), 8–9.

73 Bond in assembly debate, 25 Feb. 1898 (*Evening Telegram*, 1 March 1898).

74 For details see St John Chadwick, *Newfoundland: Island into Province* (Cambridge 1967), ch. 5; James Hiller, 'A History of Newfoundland, 1874–1901' (unpublished PH D thesis, Cambridge University 1971), ch. 7.

75 See Harvey Mitchell, 'Canada's Negotiations with Newfoundland, 1887–1895,' in G.A. Rawlyk (ed.), *Historical Essays on the Atlantic Provinces* (Toronto 1967), 253–9.

76 The ratio of duties collected to total imports is as follows: 1876–80, 12.21 per cent; 1881–5, 13.29 per cent; 1886–90, 19.97 per cent; 1891–5, 24.67 per cent. I am grateful to Mr John Joy for these figures.

77 See above, 121 n79.

78 CO 194/240, contract enclosed in Murray to Chamberlain, 25 Feb. 1898.

79 *Dépêche coloniale*, 2 Feb. 1899, quoted in Chadwick, *Newfoundland*, 83.

80 See above, 120 n34.

81 CO 194/240, Chamberlain to Murray, 23 March 1898; Morine, *Contract*, 23.

82 Born in St John's in 1843, M.F. Howley became bishop (later archbishop) of St John's in 1894. He died in 1914.

83 PANL, G 3/22, Memorandum by Murray, 29 Dec. 1898.

84 CO 194/241, Chamberlain to Murray, 5 Dec. 1898; Birmingham University Library, Chamberlain papers, Murray to Chamberlain, 27 Feb. 1898.

85 See E.B. Foran, 'Battle of the Giants: Bond and Morris,' in Smallwood (ed.), *Book of Newfoundland*, 3: 155–7.

86 *Evening Telegram*, 3 Oct. 1900.

87 Bond papers (in possession of F.F. Thompson), Howley to Bond, 16 Nov. 1900. Quoted by permission.
88 The government eventually paid Reid $1.5 million in compensation for loss of the telegraphs.
89 CO 194/248, contract enclosed in Boyle to Chamberlain, 22 July 1901.
90 Morine, *Contract*, 34.
91 See above, 29.
92 P.T. McGrath, 'The Railway Question in Newfoundland,' *Canadian Magazine* 16, no. 4 (February 1901): 331.
93 *JHA*, 1922, appendix, 112, Report of R.C. Morgan, Esq., on Railway Operation in Newfoundland, 20 Jan. 1922.
94 Ibid., 133, 117.
95 Penney, 'Newfoundland Railway,' 497.
96 *Evening Mercury*, 21 Aug. 1882; Whiteway in assembly debate, 17 May 1893 (*Evening Telegram*, 1 July 1893).
97 *JHA*, 1929, appendix, 296, Budget speech by Hon. P.J. Cashin, 13 May 1929.
98 PANL, Society for the Propagation of the Gospel Papers, microfilm, Series E, Report by Rev. C. Jeffery, St George's, to society.
99 *JHA*, 1880, 128.

W.F. Coaker and the Balance of Power Strategy: The Fishermen's Protective Union in Newfoundland Politics

IAN MCDONALD

In the early years of this century the Fishermen's Protective Union (FPU) emerged as a vital third force in Newfoundland politics, one intent on creating an economic, social, and political revolution. For almost twenty years it was the predominant factor in Newfoundland society, after which it faded from the scene. An understanding of why the FPU met the fate it did can be gained by examining the challenges it presented to Newfoundland society, and how those challenges were met by established institutions, and by analysing the balance of power strategy adopted by the FPU. Like the populist movements that arose in Canada at this time, the FPU represented an economic and regional revolt. But although the political attitudes it adopted were in many respects similar to those of the other movements, in many respects they differed. For example, unlike the experience of the Canadian movements there was little public debate about the union's political philosophy or its political strategy.

Not burdened by a political ideology as rigid as Henry Wise Wood's doctrine of 'group government' or as vague as George Keen's thoughts on how the cooperative commonwealth might finally be achieved, the FPU leaders were pragmatic in their political thinking. What political theory the FPU did possess was adapted – never completely successfully – to the changing exigencies of the union's political situation. This failure can in large part be explained by the hostile stance adopted towards the FPU by two of Newfoundland's most powerful institutions – the Roman Catholic Church and a significant section of the business community. Yet to understand the reasons for their opposition to the FPU and the impact of that opposition on the FPU's political theory, one must first examine the society and conditions that spawned the union and provoked its program.

At the turn of this century the vast majority of the population of Newfoundland lived in over 1,200 small fishing settlements that clung to the island's 6,000-mile

This paper was presented at the 1974 Atlantic Canada Studies Conference.

coastline. The people earned a subsistence living by exploiting the ocean's resources and supplemented it with the produce of small vegetable gardens. If fortunate, a family might also own a cow or a few sheep. Most of the other necessities of life were imported from the United Kingdom and North America and were distributed to the fishermen by merchants who supplied them with provisions on credit and took their fish in exchange.

In the spring the population of Conception Bay and the northeast coast took part in the seal fishery after which the summer was spent either at the shore fishery, in easy daily reach of the fishing crews, or at the Labrador schooner fishery. Similarly, those on the south coast worked at the shore fishery or at the schooner fishery on the Grand Banks. The autumn months were used to repair houses, hunt, gather firewood, and if a fisherman was located near one of the paper-mills, perhaps earn a few dollars logging. In the winter, nets and gear were put in good order and preparations made to begin the cycle anew.

A glance at this pattern of outport life in 1900 might lead the casual observer to assume that there had been no fundamental change in it for half a century. But over that period profound changes had occurred in the economic and social structure of Newfoundland. The principal hallmark of these alterations had been St John's rapid rise to ascendancy over the island's commercial affairs, a process which further augmented the capital's social and political supremacy. The chief instrument of this process was the new technology of steam.

During the mid-nineteenth century Conception Bay and the northeast coast had played the major role in the creation of a fleet of 400 sealing schooners, which by 1857 were employing 14,000 men and producing products that accounted for 21 per cent of the value of the colony's exports.[1] With the expansion of this fleet there had grown up a prosperous class of sealing skippers, who either commanded their own vessels or managed those of others. At the same time a relatively large artisan class of shipwrights, coopers, sail-makers, and blacksmiths thrived on the maintenance of the fleet. Several outport centres in the area were thus freed from overwhelming dependence on the vagaries of the cod fisheries and carried on a significant foreign trade independent of St John's.[2]

But as the century advanced the sailing schooners were gradually driven out of the seal fishery by steamers whose ownership was concentrated in the capital. Lacking either the capital or the entrepreneurial skills to respond to the new challenge, Conception Bay and the northeast coast by 1884 saw the once proud schooner fleet reduced to fifty vessels by the arrival of twenty-one steamers – seventeen of them controlled by St John's.[3] The number of sealers fell to 6,000, sealing skippers and schooner owners were bankrupted, outport seal-oil refineries shut down their vats, and the artisan class found itself reduced to the ranks of the fishermen. The shock to outport interests was brutal and the social upheaval great.[4]

This setback was aggravated by the fact that the sealing schooners had also been used to develop the Labrador fishery to the point where it accounted for 25 to 30 per cent of the colony's codfish exports, and their demise meant the absorption of much of the Labrador fishery by St John's.[5] Thousands of men formerly tied to the schooners now became independent small boat fishermen who now outfitted in St John's and had their craft freighted back and forth to the Labrador by the city steamers. Not only did the outport centres see their supply trade dwindle but their curing and transshipment roles diminished as increasing amounts of Labrador fish were shipped past them to St John's or direct to Europe from Labrador.

Although these developments affected Conception Bay and the northeast coast in particular, the island in general was beset by the problem of a population whose rate of growth was greatly outstripping the volume and value of codfish exports.[6] The undercapitalized commercial community, upon whose credit the fishermen depended, turned increasingly to the colony's two banks for ever larger loans based on inadequate collateral – transactions perhaps eased by the fact that some of the largest borrowers were also directors of the banks.[7] The not altogether surprising result was the bank crash of 1894. Yet, the bank crash did bring in its wake two further changes in domestic trade patterns that would ultimately benefit the St John's business community.

First, although several established city and outport firms went to the wall and others were compelled to close down branch operations and sell their outport premises at sacrifice prices to a new generation of outport businessmen, the rise of the latter group insulated the city houses from the credit needs of the fisherman.[8] By 1914 it could be remarked that 'the old fashioned supplying system has become almost a thing of the past, two firms only in St. John's doing business in the old way.'[9] Secondly, and as a corollary to this development, as the city houses withdrew from the direct retail supplying of the fishermen they capitalized upon improved steamer and rail connections to expand greatly their wholesale supplying of the new outport merchants.[10] In addition, because many of the new outport merchants were too weak financially to secure their own vessels for the overseas trade, St John's garnered much of the trade of the outport houses that had formerly dealt directly with Europe.[11] Thus while it might have appeared that the bank crash had impaired the capital's commercial influence, direct domination of the outports had been replaced by a less obvious, more indirect, yet more powerful control of rural commerce.

The growth of St John's at the expense of the outports did not go unremarked by the latter who looked upon the city's increasing monopolization of the colony's trade with a jaundiced and bitter eye. With the crash of 1894 the politicians of the St John's establishment saw 'the whole scheme and system of their public life, suddenly, and without any apparent reason crumbled into dust.' The bank crash shook 'the confidence of outport people in the business integrity and stability of the commercial community,' but St John's still flourished.[12] The resentment of the ourports was further heightened by the capital's resistance to outport attempts to encroach upon the profitable wholesale trade and by the outport contention that city interests were being catered to at their expense by unduly high tariffs designed to protect the newly founded manufacturing firms of St John's capitalists.[13]

St John's, replete with its insurance brokers, commission agents, bankers, traders, lawyers, and shippers, was seen as having a stranglehold on the colony's credit and distribution facilities, as acting as a channel through which ever larger amounts of the island's goods must pass. In the process those goods were rendered more expensive by city businessmen determined not to surrender the functions that facilitated the exaction of tribute.

Their commercial power having so visibly declined, their social and political stature having been undermined, the older outport mercantile centres reacted with the anguished cry that in St John's

there has been an abnormal and monstrous growth ... of idle and (comparatively) luxurious intermediary classes, who under the wing of the so-called general government farm the outports ... for their own advantage, and have so enormously over-weighed ... this fishing country with the extraordinary expenditure super-imposed upon the producers, that the outside members of the body whose soul and centre is St. John's, are literally consumed by its trunk.[14]

This complaint, which would be a major thread in the propaganda of the FPU, could not have been more clearly articulated by its founder himself.

But much more important for the welfare of the colony was the fact that the growing financial stature of St John's was not matched by a similar increase in willingness to discharge the responsibilities that resulted from its improved stature. During the last quarter of the 19th century, technological advances and the changing commercial patterns of the fishery seriously undercut the quality of Newfoundland's saltfish and helped to render its marketing system almost chaotic. As the productivity and profitability of the cod fishery declined in the latter half of the 19th century, specialist shore crews, whose job was to cure the fish, became uneconomic and disappeared. Their function was assumed by untrained women and children with a predictable drop in the quality of fish produced.[15] The invention of the cod trap and increasing use of seines exacerbated the problem by producing large catches that left insufficient time for curing.[16]

The element of time became even more important with the introduction of the large capacity steamers that had enabled St John's to absorb so much of the trade of the seal and Labrador fisheries. Since the first fish to reach the foreign markets received a premium price, exporters on the Labrador coast began buying fish tal qual (that is, ungraded and at a flat price for later grading) in order to speed up the process by which it could be handled and raced to market.[17] The fisherman was therefore deprived of the critical incentive to devote extra time producing superior quality, because he no longer received a price differential to reward his efforts.[18] Quality and price dropped accordingly.

Equally seriously, instead of scores of small-capacity schooners straggling to Europe and slowly feeding the markets, foreign buyers were now met by one, two, or three steamers arriving in the same port at about the same time and creating artificial gluts that forced prices down. With the establishment of direct steam charters from St John's the 'rush to market' fever and tal qual buying made rapid inroads into the shore fishery as well, until by 1913 the Newfoundland Board of Trade was found complaining there was no longer any cull of fish, 'all fish being bought tal qual.'[19] So critical did the problem become that in 1915 a government-appointed fishery commission was driven to conclude: 'The deterioration in the cure ... so noticable in recent years, is one of the most serious factors – if not the most serious factor – in the commercial life of the colony ... It is not too much to say that ... this evil ... is threatening the very existence of the colony.'[20]

Quality control and orderly marketing had also been adversely affected by the fragmentation of the trade resulting from the bank crash. As the older and larger city and outport firms, which had practically monopolized the fishery, sold off their branch premises, they were replaced by inexperienced local merchants unfamiliar with the varied requirements of overseas customers and by an equally inexperienced, but less scrupulous, group of fish speculators concentrated in the capital. Unable to meet the demands of foreign customers for specific grades and cures of fish, an increasing number of exporters resorted to falsifying bills of lading.[21] This practice, the general decline in quality, and the constant overstocking of markets finally led foreign buyers to cut outright sales in favour of a consignment system that would allow the fish to be inspected in the markets before any sales were completed.[22] A Newfoundland Board of Trade fish inspection scheme, aimed merely at confirming that bills of lading accurately corresponded to the fish they described, was set up in 1909, but at no time during the five-year life of the scheme was more than 10 per cent of Newfoundland's fish exports submitted to it.[23]

Compounding these difficulties was the notorious competitiveness of Newfoundland exporters, who avidly underbid one another in the markets. Commenting on this trait one of their number lamented:

Every shipper wants to supplant his neighbour ... Everything of common interest is sacrificed to feed our internal disputes and jealousies ... We ... would sooner cut the throat of a rival than share in a common profit and the same 'happy-go-lucky' mode collectively of trusting to chance for a bare market or a glutted one afflicts us still ... some other authority must intervene ... or else the whole industrial structure must cease to be.[24]

Marketing procedures were further confused by the exporters' dependence upon the four Canadian chartered banks in the colony for the credit necessary to purchase the fish and carry them over until its final sale overseas, often as long as six months later. Lacking any knowledge of the intricacies of the trade, the bankers were understandably often overanxious when they saw their funds tied up in a perishable commodity vulnerable to the unpredictable oscillations of half a dozen foreign exchange rates. If for any cause, based upon rumour or reality, bankers became nervous, credits to exporters would be tightened, and pressure placed on them to sell, despite the requirements of their individual situations and the potentially negative effects of such sales on the prospects of their colleagues.[25] Often prices already reduced by poor quality or a glut in the market were further depressed by a needlessly induced downward spiral of panic selling.

Yet although exporters could console themselves at the thought that they could soften the blow of any untoward losses by the fixed profits they made on the supply of provisions, no such recourse was open to the fisherman, who suffered most from these chaotic marketing procedures. Tied to the merchant by the credit system of supply, the fisherman, more often than not in debt, did not dare challenge the merchant's low fish prices or excessive supply prices.[26] To the fisherman, the fish-buying tactics of the merchants seemed arbitrary and erratic, governed by no discernible rationale. Even when fish was bought at a tal qual (average) price, that price could be adjusted by the merchant's culler to suit his employer's interests by basing the prices on dubious claims that the fish was sour, sunburnt, not dry enough, of an average small size deserving a smaller price, poorly split, or simply by giving short weight. The fact that such calculations varied from culler to culler, and were altered by how great the demand was for fish in any given season, did much to fuel the fisherman's sense of victimization and frustration.[27] Nor did it help matters when fishermen tied to a merchant saw independent fishermen getting better prices by selling to the collecting vessels of St John's speculators. Such occurrences, combined with the fact that few merchants provided fishermen with written accounts, gave rise to a conviction among fishermen that they were constantly being cheated.

But if the fisherman felt himself a pawn in the economic system, he also saw himself in the same role in the social and political systems. Although it was true that the scattered pattern of settlement made the provision of even rudimentary government services inordinately expensive, for example, in the field of education this difficulty was intensified by the strict enforcement of a state-subsidized, denominational educational system that often resulted in the waste of limited resources by the three major churches. Such factors (along with educational spending one-third per capita that of Ontario's[28]) resulted in an illiteracy rate of 28 per cent and trapped the fisherman on the bottom rung of the social ladder.[29] Medical facilities were almost totally lacking in rural Newfoundland, there being but one public hospital and that of course in St John's.

Largely because of the administrative savings involved, it had become both natural and customary for successive governments to adopt a subsidization policy that allowed them to delegate their most important responsibilities to other agencies: education and many health services to church and missionary organizations, coastal steamer and railway transportation services to the Reid Newfoundland Company. The distribution of public works moneys, relief, and welfare benefits was assigned by the government to assembly members, local clergymen, magistrates, government heelers, and politically appointed relief officers. It is true that in most cases the inadequate tax bases of rural settlements had resulted in there being no local government outside St John's, but the practice of having the central government or church authorities control all appointments to local road and church school boards did much to sharpen the authoritarian and remote image the government projected to the ordinary outporter.[30] Not surprisingly, there existed in the outports a deep resentment of having their destinies controlled in all things, no matter how indirectly, by a distant and alien capital that financed itself through a heavy and severely regressive customs tariff, which impinged most on those least equipped to bear it.[31]

Yet because the outports lacked adequate educational facilities and local government, which might encourage local talent, rural Newfoundland was compelled to look to the legal and commercial ranks of St John's for political leadership. But even that narrow leadership base was further reduced by the fact that a large part of the business community had never resigned itself to the responsible government system, with the scope it allowed the strident forces of democracy, and pined instead for a return to the crown colony system that had permitted that community so much sway. Its representatives' direct involvement in government was generally limited to the Legislative Council, through which it could exert sufficient negative influence on any measure seen as detrimental to its interests.[32] The eighteen constituencies that returned the island's thirty-six assembly members were not unlike spokes radiating from a wheel; at the hub the representatives, like so many ambassadors from satrapies, battled with each other for a share of the patronage that was essential to their maintenance in office.[33] With district pitted against district, the emergence of any sense of national community was retarded in favour of a crude set of regional interests, and the discussion of those issues most relevant to the needs of the fishing community was seriously inhibited. Because the influence of the St John's establishment rested upon the maintenance of such artificial barriers and on an overcentralization of power, only the mobilization of the island's fishing population along class lines could break the hold of the capital's elite on the apparatus of the social, political, and economic systems. It was this task the Fishermen's Protective Union set out to accomplish.

In 1908, conditions in the fishery were particularly favourable to the establishment of a fishermen's union. An unusually large catch coupled with disordered overseas marketing produced a temporary but harsh depression that saw fish prices in many cases cut by half, leaving thousands of fishermen angry and frustrated. That depression, however, was only the occasion for the union's creation, for the underlying tensions upon which it fed had long existed. As one of the first union politicians later observed, 'The time was overripe: for years before it would have started if a leader had been forthcoming.'[34] In 1908 that leader emerged in the person of William Ford Coaker, a dynamic 37-year-old farmer who did more than anyone to channel the frustrated energies of the fishermen and to shape their future course.

The son of a carpenter, Coaker had been born in St John's. The economic necessities of his family forced him to leave school at the age of fourteen, after which he worked as an outport clerk for a city firm at one of their small branches near Herring Neck in Notre Dame Bay.[35] In 1892 Coaker bought out the same branch premises but lost everything in the bank crash two years later. Abandoning the fish business, Coaker supported himself by farming on an island near Herring Neck and by working intermittently as a telegraph operator. During these years Coaker was well schooled in the inequities suffered by the fishing population, and as he promoted the interests and defended the rights of his fishermen neighbours, he repeatedly found himself embroiled with the merchants of Herring Neck.[36]

In 1903 he established a telegraphers' union, but characteristically he used the pages of its tiny monthly newspaper to devote as much attention to the plight of the fishermen as to the interests of the telegraphers.[37] A year later, Coaker, a former party worker for Sir Robert Bond, used the paper to oppose the re-election of Bond's Liberal party which, he contended, had ignored outport interests. When the Liberals were returned to power, Coaker did not wait for the expected dismissal notice but resigned his job and retreated to his farm.[38] There he spent the following four years brooding about the position of the colony's fishermen and drawing up repeated drafts of a constitution and program for the union he eventually founded at Herring Neck on 2 November 1908.[39]

The motto chosen for the FPU by Coaker, 'To each his own,' placed in sharp relief the central thrust of his message. Coaker argued that the fishermen were exploited by a manifestly unjust economic system, that deprived them of their fair rewards by placing so much arbitrary power in the hands of the merchants. The commercial class along with the government was attacked for its failure to come to grips with the problems of fish quality and international marketing and for failing to improve the working conditions of loggers and sealers. Those failures, claimed Coaker, could be explained by the fact that the party machines catered to the St John's businessmen who financed them while both dictated to a hireling press dependent on government and commercial advertising.[40] In his eyes St John's was the centre of monopoly capitalism, using its influence over the government to maintain high tariffs at the fishermen's expense. By losing their position in the seal and Labrador fisheries the outports had become mere 'tributaries to St. John's capitalists.'[41] Had the farmers of the Canadian west, with their demands for reciprocity and complaints against central Canadian manufacturing interests, onerous freight rates, and avaricious grain companies, been aware of Coaker's activities, they would quickly have recognized in him a soul mate.

The churches too came in for criticism. Coaker claimed that in order to maintain their special status – a status that allowed them to 'jointly control the whole social fabric of Newfoundland life' – the clergy had failed to provide leadership to improve the moral tone of public life. More often than not, he maintained, clergymen would sooner see education grants spent on church buildings than on schools which would educate the fishermen the merchants sought to keep illiterate.[42] All these groups were seen by Coaker as being essentially parasitic since they did not make the contributions to society that they claimed to make. Yet they received more than their 'own.' On the other hand, Coaker scathingly asked if the fisherman received his 'own,' when

he boards a coastal or bay steamer, as a steerage passenger and has to sleep like a dog, eat like a pig, and be treated like a serf? ... does he receive his own at the seal fishery where he has to live like a brute, work like a dog and be paid like a nigger? Do they receive their own when they pay taxes to keep up five splendid colleges at St. John's ... while thousands of fishermen's children are growing up illiterate? Do they receive their own when forced to supply funds to maintain a hospital at St. John's while fishermen, their wives and daughters are dying daily in the outports for want of hospitals?[43]

To redress the balance Coaker made a far-reaching set of proposals.[44] He called for free and compulsory education, outport night schools, non-denominational schools in settlements not large enought to support separate schools, small rural hospitals, and universal old age pensions. Significant amounts of power were to be transferred to the outports, and thus to the fishermen, by the election of all road boards and school boards. Conflict of interest legislation and various devices like the referendum were to be instituted to permit a more thorough monitoring of the behaviour of politicians. Legislation providing loggers and sealers with sickness and accident insurance and improved working conditions was also demanded.

To improve the economic lot of the fishermen in particular and the colony in general, Coaker and the FPU sought to rationalize and modernize the fishery. Quality was to be guaranteed to foreign customers and justice was to be accorded the fishermen through the abolition of the tal qual system, which would be replaced by a government legislated standardized cull rigourously enforced by government paid cullers. The consequent rise in quality would produce higher prices, which would be passed on to the fishermen. The creation of a state trust fund to issue fishery supply loans was also advocated as a means of making the fishermen less dependent on the merchants. The fisheries department was to be thoroughly reorganized and upgraded; overseas trade commissioners were to be appointed to cater to established markets and to develop new ones. Market gluts were to be ended by the timing and regulation of shipments, an innovation Coaker was prepared to let the exporters oversee. Conservation was proposed for various fish species to protect the fishermen's income base, and that base was to be enlarged by the readjustment of the tariff in the fishermen's favour at the expense of overprotected home manufacturers.

Although the foregoing proposals might have caused the commercial community some discomfiture in the short run, it can hardly be doubted that they would have redounded to the greater benefit of the trade. This was not the case with Coaker's program for ending the credit supply system. Realizing that the mentality of dependence fostered by that system reinforced the tradition of intellectual and social submissiveness nurtured by the churches and bureaucracy, Coaker planned on removing the fishermen from the established commercial system. This would be done by having the union import wholesale provisions in bulk. Force of competition would lower prices at merchants' stores, the fishermen would be introduced to the cash system, and as the savings on these provisions mounted, they would be able to accumulate a cash reserve that would enable them together to hold their fish back for better prices. Thus would the fishermen be rendered independent.[45] But underlying these plans and central to their success was the presupposition that Coaker's quality and fish-marketing reforms would be implemented to secure a higher cash return to the fishermen.

While the businessmen of St John's, the large commercial centres of Conception Bay, and outport merchants in general looked upon the FPU's plans with a mixture of scepticism and amusement, the rapid expansion of the union soon compelled them to treat it as a deadly threat.[46] In 1910 pressure from hostile businessmen and politicians on a newspaper that had opened its columns to Coaker succeeded in having him excluded from them and led to the establishment of the *Fishermen's Advocate* – a journal that probably had more influence amongst Newfoundland fishermen than did the *Grain Grower's Guide* amongst western farmers.[47] The company publishing the paper was set up as a limited liability firm whose shares could be purchased only by union members. All subsequent union companies were established along the same lines.[48] The following year the Union Trading Company (in many ways analogous to the Grain Growers' Grain Company) was created to sell supplies to fishermen and to buy and export fish. In 1916 the union built headquarters at Port Union to serve as the collection and distribution centre for forty union 'cash stores' dotting the northeast coast. A local union electric company was also established there along with a large schooner-building company. By 1919 the Union Trading Company had 4,421 shareholders and was carrying on an annual business of $3 million.

The sources of Coaker's social and economic ideas are not easily traced, but he exhibited great intellectual curiosity for a man of his limited educational background. As a young man he was apparently heavily influenced by the novels of Dickens, and later he displayed a familiarity with the British and Australian labour movements.[49] But his references to them were infrequent. North American labour and farmers' movements elicited little comment from him, though the *Fishermen's Advocate* would later follow with interest the activities of Aaron Sapiro, the prophet of the western wheat pools. Having proposed the establishment of a single outport cooperative store in 1896, Coaker was probably aware of the principles of Rochdale cooperation but evidently, and undoubtedly correctly, rejected them as unsuitable in the Newfoundland context, where the fishermen were ill equipped to run a type of operation that depended so much on local commercial skills.[50]

The core of the movement was, of course, the union itself – a democratically structured body in which all power flowed upward from the local council to the district councils (which had the same boundaries as the electoral constituencies in which the union operated) and thence to the Supreme Council which met yearly in annual convention.[51] Restricting membership to fishermen and loggers, Coaker trusted 'to class feeling and interest, to consolidate and unite our ranks.'[52] That militant class consciousness was nurtured by the *Fishermen's Advocate*, by all the paraphernalia of a fraternal organization, and by Coaker's weekly circular letters that were discussed in the local councils and were intended to prompt recommendations for Supreme Council action. This extremely effective information network would make Coaker the best-informed public figure in Newfoundland and provide one of the most important bases for the FPU's power. The question remained, however, in what fashion would that power be exercised?

Since Coaker saw his fishery reforms and a stable overseas marketing pattern as the major premises of the FPU success, he intended from the outset that the FPU play an active role in politics. But that role was to be strictly defined. Although he wanted to see the fishermen represented in the assembly by members of their own class, he did not want the union of become too embroiled in the murkier aspects of political life. Certainly he did not want FPU politicians responsible for the expenditure of local district grants.[53] Since the FPU was a young organization with several other spheres of activity to attend to, it could not afford to dissipate its inexperienced and limited human resources; nor could its fishermen-politicians be expected to possess the skills necessary to administer government departments. The problem, then, was how to exert sufficient direct political pressure to achieve FPU goals without committing the organization to taking over the government apparatus wholesale.

Coaker's solution, contained in section 63 of the union's constitution, proposed the formation of a union political party, which

shall not hold more than sufficient seats to secure the balance of power between the Government and Opposition Parties, and no Union member of the Assembly shall be permitted to hold his seat if he sits on the side of the Government or Opposition, or receive any position from the Government, or any payment except the sessional grant that the Supreme Council may grant him.[54]

The source of Coaker's strategy was not difficult to discern. It was his wish that 'the Union party will act exactly as the Labour Party in England – support the Government that will do their utmost for the masses.'[55] Coaker's use of the term 'exactly' was appropriate in so far as the Labour party even after the 1906 election was seen by British union officials as essentially 'a pressure group on the floor of the House of Commons rather than a national political party with aspirations of governing the country.'[56] But the FPU party was not in fact intended to act 'exactly' like the British Labour party because the former had expressly formulated a balance of power strategy while the latter had not. Furthermore, FPU leaders claimed that the FPU had no party politics, whereas the British Labour party maintained strong links with the British Liberal party.[57]

Amongst near-contemporary populist movements in Canada, the FPU did share in the faith of the Non-Partisan League, that the evils afflicting the democratic structure of government could be eradicated by the use of such devices as the referendum and the recall, conflict of interest legislation, and the use of recall pledges or oaths to be obtained from prospective candidates.[58] Like the Non-Partisan League, the FPU conceived of itself as a third political party, but unlike it, the FPU saw its own growth as strictly limited by the balance of power principle. Another difference between the Non-Partisan League and the FPU was that, whereas the Non-Partisan League was 'reluctant to exclude members on the basis of employment or occupation,' such exclusiveness was demanded by the FPU constitution.[59] In this respect the FPU more closely resembled the ideal of Henry Wise Wood in that it claimed to represent first and foremost, though not exclusively, the interests of Newfoundland's fishing population. Such emphasis on occupational representation by the FPU, however, did not rest on any elaborate theory such as that of Wood's concept of group government, which advocated the replacement of political parties by organized economic interest groups using the legislature to settle their class differences.[60]

The FPU's reason for insisting on occupational membership in the union and occupational representation in the party was to ensure that the party would always be the creature of the FPU and would not fall prey to the designs of professional politicians. Coaker did not advocate the abolition of the traditional party system, which is what Wood's doctrine implied; indeed, the success of the balance of power strategy was based on the assumption of its continued existence. Nor did Coaker espouse any ideas such as those of the Non-Partisan League's plan to end cabinet domination of parliament – by introducing proportional representation into the cabinet, and by ceasing to regard virtually every motion as a vote of confidence.[61]

Coaker promoted no such ideas with their weighty implications for the parliamentary system of responsible government. He believed that by tinkering with the existing system it could be made to serve the interests of his followers quite well.

Coaker's political strategy was not the product of any profound musings about the workings of the party system or responsible government. Its strongest inspiration was his own sense of pragmatism and his sense of urgency. Convinced that the colony was 'passing through a period of revolution in cure and markets and foreign competition,'[62] he saw Newfoundland as a society not only under intense economic pressure but riven by debilitating class divisions fostered by the commercial system. Angered by the government's and the business community's failure to cope with the challenges facing the colony, which indeed threatened its economic survival, Coaker was driven by the urge to achieve sufficient influence to see the FPU's solutions to those challenges implemented. This sense of urgency was the key to his political strategy and it explains his subsequent modifications of the balance of power idea as he edged closer and closer to the centre of power.

Almost from the beginning the efficacy of the FPU's balance of power strategy was cast in doubt by the relationship of the Liberal party to the People's party and by the influence of the Roman Catholic Church upon that relationship. Because Coaker was a former Liberal and eventually joined in an electoral alliance with that party, it is easy to forget his tacit support in the elections of 1908 and 1909[63] of the People's party led by Sir Edward Morris.[64] That Coaker was drawn in that direction is not surprising since Morris, a former Liberal who had broken with Bond in 1907 to establish his own party the following year, appeared to bear more credibly the stamp of Liberalism. Whereas the cautious and conservative Bond had campaigned in the 1908 general election on the basis of his government's record after eight years in office, Morris, who could with ease adopt the role of the people's tribune, had placed before the electorate a bold and exciting program. Among other things it proposed the construction of branch railways, agricultural development, old age pensions, reduced taxation, outport hospitals, night schools, and increased educational spending – in short a policy of 'something for everyone' as it has aptly been described.[65] But in the eyes of Coaker, the program included above all an imaginative fisheries policy, which promised the appointment of foreign trade agents and legislation to deal with the problem of a standardized cull of fish.

Relations between Prime Minister Morris and Coaker were initially cordial, with the *Fishermen's Advocate* on occasion commending the government for some of its early legislation. After several meetings between the two men, it was agreed in 1910 that Coaker would be appointed to a planned new fishery board, though the appointment was subsequently vetoed by the cabinet.[66] This incident, Morris' failure to pay heed to a constant stream of union memorials, his failure to implement his fishery policy, and his refusal to curb the activities of timber-land speculators led Coaker to become highly critical of the government. Yet as late as June 1911 the *Fishermen's Advocate* promised that, if Morris were to alter his policies to accord with the wishes of the FPU, 'the FPU will aid him and his rule will be upheld.'[67]

When later that year the government ignored union appeals to intervene against a St John's fish-buying combine, the possibility of securing any accommodation from Morris rapidly faded in Coaker's eyes. On 26 November 1911, Coaker privately proposed to Bond an agreement according to which FPU members of the assembly would support any government formed by Bond after the next election in return for the passage of certain FPU legislation. The suggestion was fruitless. Bond refused to consider any such proposal and dismissed Coaker's balance of power strategy, with its attempts to further the specific interests of the union, as a barefaced attempt to coerce parliament.[68] Shortly thereafter any possibility of an arrangement with Morris was absolutely precluded by the FPU's repeated attacks on the prime minister for his failure to demand the resignation of his attorney general, Donald Morison, who had been seriously compromised in a timber-land speculation scandal.[69] The attorney general, who represented a district on the northwest coast and had a great deal of influence there, was too important to sacrifice. Not only was he a former grand master of the Orange Lodge, but he had played a critical role in persuading the opposition Conservative party to allow itself to be swallowed up by Morris' People's party in 1908. Morris' reaction to the attacks was unequivocal, the governor reporting in May 1912 that 'Morris has burned his boats as to Coaker ... and ignores him in all public affairs.'[70]

Given the political circumstances of the day, the prime minister's decision was anything but unreasonable. Of the assembly's thirty-six seats, Morris held twenty-seven representing all regions of the island, only seven of them being amongst the twelve seats on the northeast coast that the FPU could hope to win.[71] Bond on the other hand was in a much more vulnerable position since of the nine seats he controlled, five were in union areas, three were in St John's, and one was on the south coast.[72] It was thus to the Liberals that the FPU posed the greatest threat, a threat intensified by Bond's ill health, lack-lustre leadership, and the almost total absence of organization within the Liberal party.[73]

Since the FPU had failed to expand beyond the northeast coast, Morris could afford to write off his seven seats there while retaining enough seats elsewhere to hold onto office. The uninspired opposition of the Liberals and the fact that the FPU had only gained ground in the north made distinctly possible the success of Morris' policy of distracting the non-union sector of the electorate from the scandals of his administration by wooing them with increased government spending. As for the fourteen FPU candidates Coaker talked of running in union areas, government strategists were quick to point out that they could only be elected by defeating Liberals or by Bond's agreeing to accept FPU candidates in union areas. This, the government correctly believed, Bond would be extremely reluctant to do since it would weaken his position in any government vis-à-vis Coaker. With a Liberal-Union alliance thus written off, the government could look forward to a three-way fight from which it might derive considerable advantage.[74] But although Bond's jealous regard for the prerogatives of leadership constituted a sound reason for thinking a Liberal-Union alliance improbable, a much more important one stemmed from the attitude of the Roman Catholic Church towards the FPU.

Because of the lack of local government in Newfoundland, it had become traditional for clerics of all denominations to assume a large administrative role on behalf of the government. Regularly consulted on political matters, acting as chairmen of local school and road boards, as poor relief officers and power brokers between their parishioners and the 'outside' government, the clergy's influence often rivalled and exceeded that of the local merchants, their spiritual authority enhanced by their secular influence.[75] Coaker with his call for elected school and road boards, his contemptuous dismissal of excessive 'denominational nonsense' and his proposal of nondenominational schools in small outports was seen as a challenge to the paternalism of clerical influence that went hand in glove with the authoritarian economic order.[76]

Amongst the Protestant denominations, the Anglican-sponsored Society of United Fishermen – a benefit society with a large Methodist membership – condemned Coaker's activities, on the grounds that he was probably a self-interested adventurer, and warned the fishermen that nothing could affect the unalterable law of supply and demand in the fishery.[77] Owing to the overlapping of the Methodist and Anglican denominations along the length of the northeast coast and Coaker's practice of playing their clerics off against one another if they publicly opposed the FPU, it was difficult for the clergy of these groups to make their influence against the union felt.[78] Such was not the case with the Catholic church with its tradition of obedience to hierarchical authority, the convenient geographic concentration of the Irish on the Avalon Peninsula, and its adherents' exaggerated respect for the church's temporal leadership as a result of the active role it had played in securing their civil and political rights in the mid-nineteenth century. Given the views of the Catholic archbishop, M.F. Howley,[79] who had publicly thanked God that the colony's commercial system still retained elements of the 'old feudal and paternal system,' which insulated the fishermen from Europe's godless materialism, it was hardly surprising that he would look with disfavour on the FPU.[80]

When, within months of the union's establishment, fishermen in the Catholic district of Ferryland took it upon themselves to organize eleven FPU councils, the reaction of Howley was swift and uncompromising. Howley banned the union on the grounds that its oath of loyalty made it a secret society, and subsequently on the basis of its social philosophy. He railed against the objects of the FPU as being

of a most insidious nature; such as are calculated to cause great confusion, and an upheaval of our social fabric; to set class against class, and to end in the ruin and destruction of our commercial and business system ... they cover the most dangerous ideas ... namely to set ... fisherman against the merchant; the labourer against the employer; the outport man against the St. John's man, all of which things are fraught with mischief for our peace and prosperity.[81]

Though Howley later rescinded the ban when Coaker dropped the FPU oath, the damage had been done. The archbishop's views were well known, the union remained informally proscribed, the eleven FPU councils in Ferryland disbanded themselves, and Coaker, who had already conceded to Howley that the latter's opposition would make further organizational efforts in Catholic areas pointless, made no further attempt to encroach on Catholic districts.[82]

It was this development especially which had made a Liberal-Union compact so unlikely. For the previous two decades Newfoundland Catholics had traditionally supported the Liberal party, though in the elections of 1908 and 1909 they had, along with Protestant districts, deserted Bond for Morris. Any alliance of the Liberals with the union would thus risk the irretrievable loss of Bond's Catholic support in the south while the hostility of St John's (with its six seats) to the FPU provided a further important incentive to avoid such an agreement. The attitude of the church also explained why Morris had declined entertaining any thoughts of an electoral alliance with Coaker. As Morris' six northern seats fell prey to the union, he could hardly afford to risk jeopardizing his southern support in Catholic constituencies.

By 1912 it had become clear to Coaker that the FPU's plan of achieving influence over government, by exercising the option of playing two roughly equal parties off against one another, was no longer realistic. The option did not exist; it had been destroyed by the Roman Catholic hierarchy. In addition, it was also manifest that the Liberal party's health was so grave that the union would have to abandon its position of official neutrality to prop up the Liberals and help fill the vacuum created by its organizational weakness. At the FPU convention of 1912, that part of section 63 of the constitution relating to the operation of a balance of power strategy was deleted from the constitution. Power – albeit limited – not theory was paramount in Coaker's thinking.[83]

Following intensified pressure from his Liberal colleagues, who apparently were not sanguine about retaining the south in any case, Bond reluctantly consented to enter into discussions with Coaker concerning an electoral alliance. After three months of exceedingly tortuous negotiations, an agreement was hammered out according to which five Liberals were allowed to run in union areas.[84] The results of the election were anticlimactic. The Liberal-Union alliance won a majority of the votes cast but only fifteen of the assembly's seats, twelve of them in union-dominated areas. Of the seven seats won by the Liberals, four were in union areas.[85] The result for the Liberals might have been more heartening had Bond chosen to campaign on the vital middle ground of Conception Bay, where Morris won seven of nine seats, instead of campaigning only in his own northern district of Twillingate. As it was, he found his personal position intolerable in the light of the union's success and shortly thereafter resigned from political life to be replaced as leader of the opposition by J.M. Kent,[86] his deputy leader.

Given the anaemic state of the Liberal party in 1913, the relative strength of the Morris government in the south, and the fact that Coaker had committed himself and the FPU to occupational representation in the house, it seemed Coaker had little other choice than to abandon the balance of power strategy and the union's early stance of official political neutrality. As he explained to a disgruntled FPU candidate forced to step down for a Liberal in the election, 'If we were able to fight Morris and had the learning to run a government ... we would not trouble to make terms with any party, but our best policy now is to work in cooperation with the Liberals for a time.'[87] The difficulty, added Coaker, was that 'The only alternative was to lead myself and face only Union districts, which would have placed us as an opposition party and be powerless to accomplish anything.'[88]

This initial, and unsuccessful, attempt at applying the balance of power strategy is critically important because it discloses how the Roman Catholic Church could shift the fulcrum of the political system so as to make that strategy futile. It revealed the Roman Catholic hierarchy to be a basic obstacle that might frustrate the FPU's attempts to apply the same sort of leverage in the future. Nonetheless, although there was no longer any public mention of the balance of power principle, the fact that Coaker did not regard the union's alliance with the Liberals as necessarily permanent, as well as the fact that he never attempted to field more than a dozen union candidates, indicates he continued to hope some modified version of the balancing principle might be sufficient to obtain FPU goals. Yet even this more limited strategy presupposed the freedom to tilt towards either of the two established political parties. A survey of the union's subsequent political career will show, however, that this presupposition would not obtain in Newfoundland.

Despite the fact that a Liberal replaced Bond as official leader of the opposition, the Liberal party never recovered from the loss of Bond. In 1916 the party was dealt a critical blow when Morris appointed Kent, the Liberal leader, to the Supreme Court. As the governor of the day noted, the effect of the appointment was to deprive 'the Opposition of the natural heir to the traditions of Sir Robert Bond and the Liberal Party.'[89] Lacking another leader of equal national stature and recognizing that the basis of power resided with the FPU, the Liberals voted to join the union members of the assembly in forming a united opposition group calling itself the Liberal-Union party and led by W.F. Lloyd,[90] a Liberal.[91]

The diminished role of the Liberals was further reflected in the fact that at the 1916 FPU convention Coaker proposed the further amendment of section 63 of the constitution to allow union assembly members to accept ministerial portfolios.[92] In this respect it is worth noting that, in his discussions with Bond in 1913, Coaker had requested the appointment of two FPU ministers without portfolio, presumably wishing the union to be privy to the inner workings of government without having to accept departmental responsibility. By 1916, however, it appeared that parliamentary experience had increased Coaker's confidence to the extent that he felt the FPU could assume such responsibility. It is also probable that Coaker felt the relative weakness of the Liberals would make the acceptance of cabinet posts by union representatives necessary following the election of 1917. Once more circumstances dictated that the FPU be drawn closer to the vortex of power, and again Coaker altered his strategy accordingly, the attainment of direct political influence acting as his guiding principle.

As early as 1914 Morris had privately admitted that he had little chance of winning the next election, and the following three years saw nothing to improve his prospects.[93] Wartime-profiteering scandals, Morris' inability to prevent the Legislative Council's blocking of popular union-sponsored legislation, and the need to increase taxation to pay for the free spending of earlier days placed the opposition in a highly favourable position. But rather than face the electorate, Morris had secured assurances from the Colonial Office that if the Newfoundland assembly passed a bill extending the life of parliament by one year, the royal assent would be forthcoming.[94]

It was this weapon (along with a number of concessions, including the promise of his retirement before the year's end) that Morris used to convince the opposition to join his party in forming a national government on the basis of full equality in the division of cabinet seats. What is significant in this development in terms of the options open to Coaker is the fact that Morris had persuaded the leaders of two of the major denominations to make public announcements favouring the election's postponement if Morris so requested. In view of the known antipathy of the Roman Catholic hierarchy to the FPU and certain oblique references made by Coaker,[95] it seems highly probable that one of the church leaders involved was the new Roman Catholic archbishop, E.P. Roche.[96] Roche, who had told the governor more than once that he viewed 'with concern the growth of the spirit of independence amongst the fishermen which had been fostered by the Fishermen's Protective Union,' was not long in giving concrete expression to his concern.[97]

When Morris resigned as promised in December 1917 and recommended Lloyd, the Liberal-Union leader, as his successor, the archbishop told Sir Michael Cashin,[98] the leading Catholic politician with the People's party, that he would prefer to see Sir Robert Bond summoned from retirement to become prime minister or the reorganization of the government under another leader.[99] Roche was much disturbed at the enhanced position of the Liberal-Unionists and thought Coaker and the union 'likely to become a menace to the well-being of the island.'[100] Cashin, however, decided to test the new prelate's mettle and declined to act upon his suggestion. Roche would have to wait for more fortuitous circumstances to make his will felt.

The debilitating rivalries of partisanship having been smothered, the national government responded to pressure from the Liberal-Union party and acceded to its demands for a business profits tax, a bill limiting the powers of the Legislative Council, legislation establishing a Food Prices Control Board, an income tax measure, and action against a seal-oil refiners' combine. In addition, it had solved a major shipping and insurance crisis, which threatened the successful marketing of the output of the 1917 fishery, though, to the chagrin of exporters, Coaker had insisted government insurance of cargoes be extended only to those willing to pay fishermen a minimum price for their fish.[101]

Angered by this FPU-inspired 'class legislation,' the business community, through its friends in the Legislative Council, seriously considered forcing an election in 1918 by blocking a further bill extending the life of parliament.[102] Since Coaker had just reneged on a pledge to his followers that he would support a military conscription bill only if it was endorsed by a national referendum, he and the union politicians would suffer severely were such an election held; Coaker himself thought sentiment in the colony was running two to one against conscription.[103] Only Sir Robert Bond's refusal to mobilize the opposition forces against the government dissuaded the Legislative Council from pursuing the matter.[104] By thus demonstrating its continued readiness to throw its weight behind any party hostile to the union, the business community revealed how its countervailing use of political leverage might well offset that of the union after the war. In late March 1919, a cabinet decision was made to take the national government to the polls as a unit,[105] and the country was so informed by the prime minister on 2 April 1919.[106] The government's decision is not surprising. Its members had worked well together and there was virtually no organized opposition to contend with. Through its relationship with the FPU, the People's party had done much to reduce its unpopularity while its leaders perhaps hoped that by containing Coaker in a coalition they would be better able to restrain his more radical impulses. Coaker's strength in the north was well appreciated, as was the fact that the FPU had substantial support in Conception Bay. This, combined with the People's party's base in the south and its share of Conception Bay support, seemed sure to guarantee that the government would be easily returned, and that the People's party could therefore afford to ignore the hostility of the business community towards the government.

For Coaker especially, the decision must have seemed ideal.[107] Coaker had worked well with his Liberal colleagues, yet they remained insufficiently strong allies on their own. By remaining within the national government he could maintain the FPU's links with them and could retain the influence in government that his modified balance of power strategy had secured for the union. The FPU in turn would not have to bear a large share of the ministerial responsibility that a Liberal-Union alliance alone might have imposed on it. Another important consideration was that Coaker and the union politicians were frequently distracted by the FPU's commercial activities. Coaker's cabinet colleagues had proved receptive to several FPU proposals, and he could have good reason to believe that they would prove equally sympathetic to his cherished fishery reforms, since a severe crisis in the Italian market had recently spurred a major initiative of government in the organizing of fish marketing.[108] Yet whatever influence the FPU hoped to exercise, it was not destined to be wielded within the framework of a re-elected national government. Other forces were at work.

As previously noted, the Legislative Council, which contained several prominent members of the commercial establishment, had considered striking at the FPU and the national government by blocking the parliamentary extension bill the previous year. But that group, whose interests had been further flouted by the People's party's decision to maintain the national government, now found a powerful ally in Archbishop Roche, who was again reiterating privately 'that he is greatly opposed to the influence of Mr. Coaker.'[109] When the Archbishop had attempted to frustrate Lloyd's assuming the prime ministership, members of the People's party had been reported very upset at the archbishop's attitude, feeling he could 'play a large part – in fact the largest part' in their re-election.[110] Their alarm having been diminished by Roche's apparent loss of interest in the matter, these politicians were now confronted by his spirited pursuit and promotion of Sir Robert Bond in opposition to them.

Although these men could to some extent discount the business community's antagonism toward the government, they could not afford to do so when it was coupled with the much more pervasive influence of Archbishop Roche. Roche's activities were sufficiently unnerving to spur the Cashin wing of the government into out-voting the Liberal-Unionists in order to defer the 1919 election for six months, and five weeks later into bringing about a complete rupture with the FPU that ended in the collapse of the national government and the formation of a new ministry led by Cashin.[111]

Not only had the FPU been thwarted again, but it had been hobbled just as a crisis of major proportions faced the fishing industry. Because Newfoundland's most important competitors had been forced out of the markets by the war, the colony had been able to neglect all the pre-war marketing and quality problems that had so gravely afflicted the industry and in large part prompted the establishment of the FPU. If those problems were not now speedily solved, Newfoundland would not be able to withstand the onslaught of renewed competition. To make matters worse, heavy overinvestment in the industry by Newfoundland merchants and fishermen during the war meant that a collapse, should it come, would be substantially more damaging than in the pre-war period.[112] Within the national government the FPU had been well placed to help mitigate and perhaps stave off such a collapse, but the activities of the Roman Catholic hierarchy and a large part of the business community had successfully removed it from that position. Obsessed by the problems of the fishing industry, in which by now the FPU was heavily involved in a direct commercial sense, Coaker was in no frame of mind to remain barred from the centre of power at this critical juncture. In order to regain a share of government influence Coaker reluctantly joined in an alliance with Richard Squires,[113] an opponent of the national government and an erratically brilliant and unscrupulous politician who had appropriated the mantle of Liberal leadership shed by Lloyd and left unclaimed by Bond.[114] The partnership between the FPU and the supporters of Squires, styling itself the Liberal-Reform party, was not a happy one.

This alliance of interests succeeded in winning twenty-four of the assembly's thirty-six seats in the election of 1919, but from the beginning and throughout its term of office it was repeatedly on the verge of collapse owing to internal dissensions stirred by the irresponsible behaviour of Squires, the prime minister. Over the first eighteen months of the government's life an attempt was made to implement Coaker's fishery reforms, but they were frustrated by partisan opposition, government instability, and antagonistic exporters. As the government lurched from one crisis to another against a backdrop of growing economic depression, severe unemployment, extravagant relief projects, and increased government borrowing, Coaker began to despair and expressed growing concern at his inability to restrain Squires.[115] He complained that the FPU was able to exert only minimal influence on government policy and that when the cabinet did fall in with union proposals it was often 'because of fear rather than conviction.'[116]

Of the eleven FPU members in the assembly, only Coaker and one other were in the cabinet, and although the rest were honest and hard-working men, they were unequal to the task of checking the activities of Squires and his closest colleagues.[117] Coaker himself was in little better position to exercise more control, distracted as he was by his attempts at fishery reforms, by the need to devote close attention to the union's commercial activities and to make frequent visits to the fish markets, and by his deep involvement with plans to establish a new pulp- and paper-mill on the island's west coast. It was only the prospect of securing the latter development that bound Coaker to Squires during the election of 1923. In the meantime, Coaker had recognized that the FPU was suffering from an alliance with individuals it could not effectively influence but for whose acts the FPU had to bear a share of the responsibility. As a number of union politicians became increasingly discouraged by the trend of government and indicated their desire to retire from public life, Coaker began yet another reappraisal of the union's political strategy.[118]

At the union's annual convention in 1922 Coaker announced that he would resign from the cabinet before the impending 1923 election and not re-enter it afterwards, claiming that the restraints of collective responsibility hindered his freedom of action and prevented him from criticizing the government more effectively.[119] A few months later, Coaker suggested that a number of radical changes in the political role of the union be discussed at the convention following the election.[120] One of the changes suggested was that, under the leadership of a new non-political president, the FPU would withdraw from direct political involvement and revert to the pre-1912 role of a militant extra-parliamentary pressure group with no formal ties to any party. Instead the FPU would exert its political influence by voting for independent but sympathetic candidates led by Coaker.

This further attempt to define an effective mode for expressing the union's political potential had a number of possible advantages. Former representatives of the union party could remain in politics pressing for reforms while not embarrassing the union if they were unable to secure them. The FPU itself would be much freer to criticize the government without being open to the charge of 'stabbing it in the back.' As for Coaker, he would be freed from the heavy administrative burden of leading the FPU and would be able to manoeuver more effectively in the assembly to secure his reforms. Coaker's intentions were clear even to the opposition press. After the election had given the government a mandate to press on with the west coast paper-mill and the necessary legislation had been passed, Coaker would 'cut himself adrift from the unholy alliance to launch his balance of power party.'[121] Coaker had readopted his original political strategy. The only difference was that it would not be implemented under the guise of a Union party.

In examining this retreat of Coaker to a narrower balance of power concept it is interesting to note the experience of the Canadian Progressives with a similar strategy after the 1921 election made them the second largest group in the federal parliament. A number of reasons have been advanced to explain the Progressives' failure to exploit their position to the fullest advantage, among them the fact that the movement lacked the necessary discipline, that many of its adherents being former Liberals could not readily entertain supporting the Conservatives if tactics demanded it, and the suspicion of the Alberta members of anything smacking of 'partyism' or the caucus.[122] It has also been observed that 'wedded to the balance of power concept as they were, Progressives could think only in terms of supporting their legislative principles as initiated by the older parties.'[123] It was this wish to avoid political responsibility that was largely responsible for the Progressives' refusal to assume the role of official opposition and alternative government.[124]

While the FPU also entered public life tied to such a narrow definition of the balance of power idea, its political odyssey included tacking before changing political winds to achieve its main purpose of influencing government policy, even at the cost of modifying the balance of power strategy. Thus the union had entered a formal alliance with the Liberals in 1913 and later absorbed them in 1916, the same year in which the union's constitution was amended to permit FPU representatives to assume ministerial responsibility. The union insisted on ministerial influence in the governments of Morris, Lloyd, and Squires, though in keeping with some semblance of its early political theory, it did not seek more cabinet representation than it thought necessary to influence some aspects of policy. Similarly, its willingness to hold discussions with the colony's various political groups also showed it did not see itself as being necessarily tied to one party or another.

Nor was it lack of discipline within the FPU that prevented the fullest exploitation of the numerical balance of power it possessed, but lack of discipline among the other parties in the system. Despite the fact that the FPU held eleven assembly seats, the political system was at once too rigid and too fluid for the successful operation of its political strategy, which entailed the sharing of ministerial responsibility: rigid in that the power of the Roman Catholic Church and Water Street seemed insurmountable obstacles blocking union cooperation with opposition elements, and fluid in the sense that Newfoundland politicians were showing an increasing disposition to operate on an individual level. Thus the FPU was either bound to be associated with irresponsible allies or to face continually the probability of coalitions organized on an anti-union basis with Catholic politicians or representatives of the business community as their core. Political parties were increasingly becoming mere aggregates of individuals, who were for the most part unable to define Newfoundland's interests, let alone serve them, and who had settled for maintaining their own self-interest.

Having advanced from a position that rejected ministerial responsibility to one that instead countenanced its partial acceptance, the FPU still had not achieved its basic aim and had sorely tarnished its image. Retreat seemed the only answer, any advance to total ministerial responsibility being blocked by the risk of a major confrontation with the Roman Catholic hierarchy and by the FPU's inability to construct an alternative government from the limited resources of its political personnel.

Whether Coaker's proposals of 1923 would have been any more effective than when they were initially attempted before 1912 seems highly unlikely. In any case, he never had a chance to implement them. Within two months of the 1923 election the Squires government was rocked by scandals that toppled the prime minister. Within the next twelve months, Newfoundland saw the existing party system, such as it was, reduced to a shambles with the advent of four ministries and the demise of three. Coaker, who had resolved to leave political life, did not contest the 1924 election, although a handful of former union politicians ran under the Liberal banner. The government that was elected was made up of representatives of the interests of St John's businessmen, those of the Roman Catholic Church, and the last tattered remnants of the People's party. Selfishly plutocratic in its legislation and administration, and incapable of formulating an alternative program to deal with the colony's basic problems, it proved itself even more incompetent than the Squires government and equally extravagant.[125]

In a last effort to reform the fisheries and save Newfoundland's rapidly disappearing markets, Coaker ran unsuccessfully in a by-election in 1924 but was later elected in association with Squires in 1928. But Coaker ran as a candidate within a political system in which he had lost all faith. In 1925, he had advised an FPU convention that no solution to Newfoundland's ills could be obtained within the existing constitutional framework. The only answer, he suggested, was to elect a nine-man commission of government for a ten-year period to carry out basic reforms, free from the meddling of political adventurers who were too susceptible to the fear of electoral reprisals from voters who were, in turn, demoralized by extravagant public spending.[126]

That Coaker was driven to make this extraordinary proposal is a reflection of the same factors that had undermined his balance of power strategy throughout all its modifications. Newfoundland had a parliamentary party system in which there was only one party in the normal sense of the word. What the FPU confronted were only fluidly changing combinations of men, who lacked any sense of national purpose. The 'chief aim [of many] is to combine their own personal self-interest with a parade of national devotion.'[127] Content to steal a profit through the amateurish supervision of the colony's rudimentary administrative machine, these middle-class politicians were unequal to the task of coping with Newfoundland's monumental social and economic problems. When attempts to do so were made by the FPU, the path was blocked by the social myopia of the Roman Catholic hierarchy. The hierarchy's attitude reinforced the hostile disposition of the business community towards the FPU, thereby ensuring that the union's choice of political allies would be even more sharply attenuated in a society already plagued by a narrow leadership base.

This, indeed, was the real tragedy that lay behind the fall of the national government in 1919. An unusually effective administration, untrammelled by partisanship, it had appeared ideally suited to deal resolutely with the post-war crisis in the economy. But this attempt by the politicians to come to terms realistically with the colony's fundamental problems, far from being encouraged, was undermined by conservative institutions within the community. The influence of these groups upon politics created divisions which might have been contained by a larger, more pluralistic, and more prosperous community, but which were critically disruptive in Newfoundland where political leadership was at a premium and the economic problems prodigious.

The failure of the FPU's experiment with the balance of power idea illuminates the basic social and economic divisions within Newfoundland during the early twentieth century and reveals the faults and crevices in the foundation upon which responsible government in the colony rested. It was Coaker's perception of these structural weaknesses that in 1926 led him to this prediction:

in my opinion the day is not far distant when the country will be forced to decide, probably with its back to the wall, whether it will be governed by a Commission elected by the people, by nominees of the British Government governing as a Crown Colony, or as a poverty stricken Godforsaken Island administered as a province of Canada.[128]

NOTES

1 E.C. Moulton, 'The Political History of Newfoundland, 1861–1869' (unpublished MA thesis, Memorial University 1960), 6–7.

2 The impact of the rise of the seal fishery and its decline is described in D.W. Prowse, *A History of Newfoundland from the English, Colonial and Foreign Records*, 2nd ed. (London 1896), 514.

3 *Census of Newfoundland and Labrador, 1884.*

4 H.A. Innis, *The Cod Fisheries*, rev. ed. (Toronto 1954), 460. See also R.A. Bartlett, *The Log of Bob Bartlett* (New York 1928), 52, 95, 99–104.

5 Innis, *Cod Fisheries*, 459–60. In 1830, however, of about 270 Labrador vessels only 60 to 70 were fitted out in St John's, with the rest being financed mainly by firms in Conception Bay and on the northeast coast (ibid., 309).

6 For details of population growth and export trade, see Shannon Ryan, 'The Newfoundland Salt Cod Trade in the Nineteenth Century,' above.

7 Moses Harvey, 'The Economic Condition of Newfoundland,' Canadian Bankers' Association, *Journal* 3, no. 2 (1896), and 'The Economic Condition of Newfoundland at the Close of 1896,' ibid. 4, no. 5 (1897): 253–67.

8 *Report of the Commission of Enquiry Investigating the Sea-Fisheries of Newfoundland and Labrador other than the Sealfishery* (St John's 1937), sections 65, 136–7.

9 PANL Newfoundland Board of Trade (BT) letterbook, 5/A1, 88, Gosling to Morris, 12 Jan. 1914.

10 Ibid., and BT Report, 1911, 2.

11 Innis, *Cod Fisheries*, 459–60. See also J.M.S. Careless, 'Aspects of Metropolitanism in Atlantic Canada,' in Mason Wade (ed.), *Regionalism in the Canadian Community 1867–1967* (Toronto 1969), 117–18, in which Careless discusses metropolitanism as a pattern of relations through which urban communities dominate and control their hinterlands. In the late nineteenth century St John's improved its position in terms of all the major functions of metropolitan stature as defined by Careless, *viz.* the provision of larger and better facilities for the export and import trade, the processing of imports through its new local manufacturing industries, improved transportation services, and growing financial and banking facilities.

12 *Evening Telegram* (St John's), 16, 18 Oct. 1895.

13 PANL, BT minutes, 5/A1, 82, 13 Feb. 1912.

14 James Murray, *The Commercial Crisis in Newfoundland: Causes, Consequences and Cure* (St John's 1895), 15.

15 *JHA*, 1882, appendix, 615–16, Letter from Mr. Patrick Hogan on the Fisheries of Newfoundland, 27 Feb 1882; and 'Genuine Planter' to *Terra Nova Advocate* (St John's), 6 Nov. 1880.

16 Harvey in Legislative Council debate, 17 Feb. 1881 (*Public Ledger* (St John's), 24 Feb. 1881).

17 Robert Bond (see above, 121 n82) in 1897 complained that Newfoundland was ruining its markets through bad curing encouraged by the competition of steamers to get to market first, and told of Labrador fish being dried for only one day instead of the required

minimum of three. He also commented that flooded markets put Newfoundland exporters at the mercy of foreign buyers and brokers; Bond in assembly debate, 24 March 1897 (*Evening Telegram*, 1 April 1897).

18 For discussions of the long-term impact of tal qual buying see BT *Report, 1913*, 17–18; and *Report of the Commission on Fishery Matters*, reprinted in the *Evening Advocate* (St John's), 15 June 1915.

19 BT *Report, 1913*, 6–7.

20 *Report of the Commission on Fishery Matters.*

21 See, for example, PANL, BT letterbook, 5/A1, 87, Fearn to Morris, 22 Sept. 1910; BT correspondence, carton 7, Fearn to president of BT, 26 Jan. 1915; 'Annual Report of H.A. DeCampos of Alicante,' reprinted in *Trade Review* (St John's), 10 Sept. 1910.

22 James Murray, letter to the editor, *Evening Telegram*, 19 July 1897; 'Tal Qual Gives Endless Dissatisfaction to Buyers Abroad,' BT *Report, 1910*, 8.

23 PANL, BT minutes, 5/A1, 83, 26 June 1914.

24 Murray to editor, *Evening Telegram*, 19 July 1897.

25 CO 687/60, Harris, to Long, 13 Jan. 1919; Dept. of Marine and Fisheries, *Proceedings of the Convention of Licensed Codfish Exporters* (St John's 1920) (hereafter PCLCE), Coaker, 2, 9 Sept.; and BT Feb. Conference, 1920, Monroe, 5, 20 Feb.

26 The operations of the credit system and internal economy of the cod fishery are thoroughly discussed in *Fishery Commission 1937*, sections 135–55, 282–304; and in Cato Wadel, *Marginal Adaptations and Modernization in Newfoundland* (St John's 1969), 16–23.

27 *Trade Review*, 23 Jan., 25 Sept. 1909.

28 *Evening Chronicle* (St John's), 16 March 1912.

29 CO 194/291, Davidson to Bonar Law, 17 May 1916.

30 See C.W. Powell, 'Problems of Municipal Government in Newfoundland,' Institute of Public Administration of Canada, *Proceedings*, 1949, 168–82.

31 St John Chadwick, *Newfoundland: Island into Province* (Cambridge 1967), 124, notes *ad valorem* duties of 40 to 50 per cent on such articles as boots, furniture, and ready-made clothing.

32 '[Among] ... the more solid merchants and older educated families ... there is still a latent conviction that Newfoundland would be better administrated as a Crown Colony' (CO 537/1167, Harris to Long, 23 March 1918). For the persistence of this attitude amongst the mercantile community see the following: Prowse, *History of Newfoundland*, 534; Government House (hereafter GH), St John's, Secret and confidential dispatches, Davidson to Long, 19 March 1917; CO 194/295, Harris to Long, 14 May 1918; Public Archives of Canada, Robert Borden papers, Nicholson letter from Newfoundland, 13 June 1915, 13293–5. In 1913, W.S. Monroe, a prominent businessman and future prime minister of Newfoundland, publicly stated his view, held till the end, that responsible government in Newfoundland was an

'expensive luxury' and that the colony should revert to crown colony status (see L.B. Wheeler, 'Newfoundland: The Loss of Responsible Government, 1933' (unpublished paper, Department of History, Memorial University 1968), 22).

33 Sir Ralph C. Williams, *How I Became a Governor* (London 1913), 414: '... it has been bred in their [the voters'] bones that it is their duty to strive to extract favours from a government whose sole idea they believe to be a desire to deprive them of their rights.'

34 W.B. Jennings, 'The Fishermen's Protective Union,' in Sir W.F. Coaker (ed.), *Twenty Years of the Fishermen's Protective Union* (St John's 1930), 140.

35 For a brief biographical sketch of Coaker see T.E. Clouter, 'The FPU and Its Leader,' in Coaker (ed.), *Twenty Years*, 182. For further information on Coaker's activities to 1906 see Centre for Newfoundland Studies, Memorial University, Coaker papers, 'Memory Book'; W.F. Coaker, 'Joe Batt's Arm Speech, February, 1909,' *Fishermen's Advocate* (St John's), 19, 26 Nov. 1910; 'Autobiographical Sketch,' ibid., 11 May 1921.

36 *Fishermen's Advocate*, 6 Aug. 1910.

37 See, for example, Coaker papers, *Telegrapher* (Port Blandford), January 1904–February 1905.

38 Coaker to Jackman, 6 Dec. 1904, reprinted in *Telegrapher*, February 1905. See also Coaker's editorial in the same issue.

39 For Coaker's account of the evolution of his plan for the union, see the *Fishermen's Advocate*, 22 Dec. 1917.

40 Ibid., 5 Nov. 1910, 7 Oct. 1911.

41 Ibid., 24 Feb. 1912. In 1905 Coaker had proposed the establishment of a new political party to be led by Sir William Whiteway (see above, 38 n20). The party would give much greater recognition to the rights of the outports as against St John's (see Coaker, letter to the editor, *Free Press* (St John's), 20 Nov. 1905).

42 *Fishermen's Advocate*, 23 Sept., 5 Nov. 1911; Coaker to Morris, 9 Jan. 1911, printed in ibid., 21 Jan. 1911. Sir Wilfred Grenfell, the medical missionary who worked in northern Newfoundland, succinctly noted the common attitude to education as, 'Merchants don't want it. Clergy fear it' (Yale University, Grenfell papers, Add. 291, box 11, Newfoundland Notebooks, 1900).

43 *Fishermen's Advocate*, 29 Oct. 1910.

44 The earliest broad statement of Coaker's program may be found in his 'Joe Batt's Arm Speech, February, 1909,' in ibid., 19, 26 Nov. 1910. A more formal presentation of it may be found in Fishermen's Protective Union Convention Proceedings (hereafter FPUCP), 'Memorial to the Government,' 1909, in Coaker (ed.), *Twenty Years*, 7–12; and in the 'Platform of the Union Party,' FPUCP, 1911, in ibid., 40.

45 *Fishermen's Advocate*, 2 Sept. 1911, 24 Feb. 1912; 'Joe Batt's Arm Speech, February, 1909'; FPUCP, 1911, in Coaker (ed.), *Twenty Years*, 33.

46 By 1915, however, Coaker had so securely established the commercial foundations of

the union that one St John's businessman was led to remark that Coaker's 'business and organization in the past five years has astonished everybody ... every merchant was down on him and would boycott anyone who sold to him ... to-day there is not a firm in St John's not after his trade and would give him any terms asked for' (Robert Borden papers, Jennison to Borden, 11 March 1915, 13270, quoting an unidentified St John's businessman).

47 For details of this incident see Wiseman and Buckley, printers of the *Plaindealer* (St John's), to Coaker, 29 March 1909, reprinted in the *Fishermen's Advocate*, 25 May 1912.

48 For details of the union's commercial activities see Ian McDonald, 'W.F. Coaker and the Fishermen's Protective Union in Newfoundland Politics, 1908–1925' (unpublished PH D thesis, University of London 1971), 51–71.

49 See, for example, the *Fishermen's Advocate*, 14 May, 26 Nov. 1910; 27 Jan., 21 Sept. 1912.

50 'Joe Batt's Arm Speech, February, 1909.'

51 Archives of the Roman Catholic Archdiocese of St John's (hereafter AASJ), FPU file, *Constitution and Bye-Laws of the Fisherman's Protective Union in Newfoundland*, 1908.

52 FPUCP, 1909, Presidential address in Coaker (ed.), *Twenty Years*, 1.

53 'Joe Batt's Arm Speech, February, 1909.'

54 AASJ, FPU file, *Constitution and Bye-Laws*, section 63.

55 *Fishermen's Advocate*, 29 Oct. 1910; see also S.J.R. Noel, *Politics in Newfoundland* (Toronto 1971), 87. As noted above, the union party and the balance of power principle were provided for in the union's constitution. Note also these remarks from the 'Joe Batt's Arm Speech, February, 1909': 'We must put ten or twelve Fishermen's Union men in the House of Assembly ... We do not want to run governments, or to manage the affairs of districts – we want no part whatever in expending grants ... The Union candidates must not combine with any other party. No Union member can accept any position in the Government ... If ten Union members were returned they could certainly hold the balance of power between the two political parties, and the party which would do most for the fishermen would receive the informal support of the Union party. The Union party would be constituted much on the lines of the Labor Party in the British Parliament ... We have no party politics ...'

56 Peter Self and Herbert J. Storing, *The State and the Farmer* (London 1962), 282.

57 See above, note 55; *Fishermen's Advocate*, 20 May 1911.

58 Paul F. Sharp, *The Agrarian Revolt in Western Canada* (Minneapolis 1948), 86; FPUCP, 1911, Address in reply in Coaker (ed.), *Twenty Years*, 37.

59 Sharp, *Agrarian Revolt*, 89; W.L. Morton, *The Progressive Party in Canada* (Toronto 1950), 88; AASJ, FPU file, *Constitution and Bye-Law*, section 50.

60 Morton, *Progressive Party*, 92.

61 Sharp, *Agrarian Revolt*, 88.
62 *Fishermen's Advocate*, 23 Sept. 1911.
63 See *Daily News* (St John's), 19 Aug. 1913; Coaker in assembly debate, *Proceedings of the House of Assembly of Newfoundland* (hereafter *PHA*), 28 Jan. 1914. A few years later the government press made good use of Coaker's early predisposition towards Morris and his antagonism towards Bond (see, for example, *Evening Herald* (St John's), 1 May 1913).
64 See above, 120 n34.
65 Noel, *Politics in Newfoundland*, 58.
66 *Fishermen's Advocate*, 26 Feb., 9 April 1910; FPUCP, 1910, President's address in Coaker (ed.), *Twenty Years*, 19. For further indications of Coaker's amicable relations with Morris see Coaker to Morris, 9 March 1909, and Morris to Coaker, 13 March 1909, printed in *Fishermen's Advocate*, 12, 19 Feb. 1910.
67 *Fishermen's Advocate*, 17 June 1911.
68 Coaker papers, Bond to Coaker, 27 Nov. 1911.
69 For the full details of this episode see CO 194/285, Williams to Harcourt, 6 May 1912, and enclosed documents and minutes. A good summary of the same affair and of the sudden rash of timber speculation connected with the Morris government is given in Noel, *Politics in Newfoundland*, 106–11.
70 CO 194/285, Williams to Harcourt, 7 May 1912.
71 Trinity (3), Bonavista (3), Port de Grave (1).
72 The five in union areas were Fogo (1), St Barbe (1), Twillingate (3). The others were St John's East (3), Burin (1).
73 Noel, *Politics in Newfoundland*, 96–8.
74 *Evening Chronicle* (St John's), 16 March 1912.
75 'In everything the clergy are the rulers of the fishing people. The priest or minister is the man to whom they look for guidance upon all questions domestic and public' (L.E.Q., 'Newfoundland and Its Fisheries,' *Tribune Monthly*, August 1889). This article contains a full account of the high social status and influence of the clergy. P.K. Devine in *Old King's Cove* (St John's 1944) noted how the local priest also secured berths for sealers, helped market local garden produce, and disposed of lumber contracts for the government.
76 Coaker to Morris, 9 Jan. 1911, printed in *Fishermen's Advocate*, 21 Jan. 1911. This reaction to Coaker's movement was common amongst clergy of all denominations (interview with Msgr E.J. O'Brien, 15 Dec. 1968). Msgr O'Brien was ordained about the time the FPU was established and opposed it in accordance with the views of his superiors.
77 AASJ, FPU file, Annual Report of the Society of United Fishermen, March 1909. For evidence of the general antagonism of Methodist and Anglican clergy towards the FPU see, for example, *Fishermen's Advocate*, 12 Nov. 1910, 16 March, 25 Nov. 1912.

78 *Fishermen's Advocate*, 16 March 1912.

79 See above, 14 n18; 146 n82.

80 *Evening Chronicle*, 19 Feb. 1912.

81 AASJ, FPU file, M.F. Howley, 'Circular Letter Secret Societies,' 31 March 1909. This 5,000 word letter is undoubtedly the single most important and revealing expression of the social and political philosophy of the Catholic church in Newfoundland during the early twentieth century. See also ibid., St John to Howley, 9 Feb., 26 March 1909; and Howley quoted in *Free Press*, 18 March 1909.

82 AASJ, FPU file, Coaker to Howley, 27 Nov. 1909. Howley's continued opposition to the union is indicated by a 1912 pastoral letter in which in an unmistakable reference to Coaker he inveighed against the false leaders of the poor man, 'who ... instill into his mind sentiments of jealousy, distrust and envy against the possessor of wealth ... and a false sense of ownership degenerating into communistic principles' (*Evening Chronicle*, 19 Feb. 1912).

83 FPUCP, 1912, Presidential address in Coaker (ed.), *Twenty Years*, 45.

84 W.F. Coaker, 'Past, Present and Future,' *Fishermen's Advocate*, 17 Aug. 1932. For the most important details of the discussions leading up to these negotiations and of the negotiations themselves see Coaker papers, Lloyd to Coaker, 21 Nov. 1912; Coaker to Lloyd, 21 Nov. 1912, 16 April 1913; Coaker to Bond, 23 Aug. 1913; Bond to Coaker, 25, 26 Aug. 1913.

85 Trinity (1), Twillingate (2), St Barbe (1).

86 J.M. Kent, born St John's, 1872; lawyer; member for St John's East, 1904–16; Liberal; minister of justice, 1907–9; leader of opposition, 1914–16; judge of Supreme Court, 1916; died St John's, 1939.

87 Coaker to Yates, 26 Aug. 1913, printed in *Evening Herald*, 24 Sept. 1913.

88 Coaker to Yates, 30 Aug. 1913, in ibid., 24 Sept. 1913.

89 GH, Secret and confidential dispatches, 1916, Davidson to Bonar Law, 28 March 1916.

90 W.F. Lloyd, born England, 1864; school teacher, journalist and lawyer; editor *Telegram*, 1905–16; MHA, 1904–19; prime minister, 1918–19; chief clerk and registrar, Supreme Court, 1919; briefly minister of justice in Hickman government, 1924; died St John's, 1937.

91 *Mail and Advocate* (St John's), 25 March 1916.

92 FPUCP, 1916, Presidential address in Coaker (ed.), *Twenty Years*, 107.

93 CO 537/500, Davidson to Harcourt, 10 March 1914.

94 CO 194/292, Davidson to Fiddes, 27 Dec. 1916. See attached minutes and draft telegram, Long to Davidson, 20 Jan. 1917.

95 GH, Secret and confidential dispatches, 1917, Davidson to Long, 15 June 1917; Coaker, 'Open Letter to the FPU,' *Evening Advocate*, 19 July 1917.

96 E.P. Roche, born Placentia, 1874; educated St John's and All Hallows, Dublin; archbishop of St John's, 1915–50; died St John's, 1950.

97 CO 537/1167, Harris to Long, 23 March 1918.

98 Michael Cashin, born Cape Broyle, 1866; merchant; MHA, Ferryland, 1893–1932; left Liberals, 1905; joined People's party, 1907; in cabinet, 1909–19; prime minister, 1919; died St John's, 1926.

99 The details of the archbishop's concern with the realignment of the national government are contained in three letters: AASJ, Cashin file, Roche to Cashin, 8 Jan. 1918; Cashin to Roche, 11 Jan. 1918; and Roche to Cashin, 14 Jan. 1918.

100 Robert Borden papers, McGrath to Cook, early Jan. 1918, 13371–6.

101 FPUCP, 1917, Presidential address in Coaker (ed.), *Twenty Years*, 119.

102 CO 194/295, Harris to Long, 14 May 1918; Lloyd in assembly debate, *PHA*, 23, 26 April 1918.

103 CO 537/1170, Harris to Long, 30 Sept. 1918; Coaker, 'Past, Present and Future,' *Fishermen's Advocate*, 19 Oct. 1932.

104 Gear to Bond, 2 May 1918, and Bond to Gear, 4 May 1918, quoted in Noel, *Politics in Newfoundland*, 139.

105 Noel, *Politics in Newfoundland*, 128.

106 Lloyd in assembly debate, *PHA*, 2, 17 April 1919. See also reports of assembly proceedings, 27 May, in *Daily News* and *Evening Advocate*, 28 May 1919.

107 In keeping with his determination to maintain for the FPU the maximum freedom of action, Coaker at the 1918 FPU convention had requested and received from the delegates full discretionary powers to negotiate for an alliance to fight the 1919 election in conjunction with whatever group was willing to concede the union its fair share of influence (FPUCP, 1918, Address reply, section 17, in Coaker (ed.), *Twenty Years*, 136–7).

108 The details of this incident are discussed in CO 687/60, Harris to Long, 13 Jan. 1919; Harris to Milner, 15, 19 Jan., 29 March 1919.

109 CO 194/296, Harris to Milner, 21 April 1919.

110 Robert Borden papers, McGrath to Cook, 28 Jan. 1918, 13368–9.

111 See CO 194/296, Harris to Milner, 19, 21 April, 23 May 1919.

112 See Harvey in Legislative Council debate, *Proceedings of the Legislative Council of Newfoundland*, 3 Aug. 1917; CO 194/299, Harris to Milner, 30 Sept. 1920; BT *Report, 1918*, 9; BT minutes, 5/A1, 81, 29 Jan. 1918.

113 See above, 120 n35.

114 Coaker papers, '1919 Electoral Agreement between the FPU and the Liberal Reform Party.' This agreement provided for a marked increase in union influence. In union areas three seats formerly reserved for Liberals reverted to the Unionists, giving them twelve candidates and almost certainly the largest single block of influence in any alliance government. Squires was to be prime minister, Coaker acting prime minister, and the FPU was to be allotted four out of nine seats on the Executive Council and was to have equality in the number of government departments. The Executive Council was

composed of the prime minister, who was also colonial secretary, six of the eight ministers heading government departments, and two ministers without portfolio. In the event only two Unionists served in the cabinet, Coaker (minister of marine and fisheries) and Halfyard (minister of posts and telegraphs), although Dr Arthur Barnes, a newcomer to politics and confidant of Coaker, may have been a union nominee even though he did not hold a union seat. W.B. Jennings, a Unionist and minister of public works, was one of the two ministers who did not sit on the Executive Council. Coaker's attitude to the alliance with Squires was starkly revealed by his terse explanation to his followers that 'there was no other man in sight' (Coaker papers, C.L. 11, 26 Sept. 1919).

115 CO 194/301, Harris to Milner, 4 Jan. 1921. For a discussion of the attempted implementation of Coaker's fishery reforms and general post-war economic problems see McDonald, 'W.F. Coaker and the Fishermen's Protective Union,' 218–308.

116 Coaker papers, C.L.1, 3 Jan. 1921; C.L.2, 22 April 1922.

117 W.B. Jennings, the Unionist minister of public works who sat outside the Executive Council, was in continual disagreement with the policy and conduct of relief projects being carried out in the name of his department by Dr Alex Campbell, minister of mines and agriculture. It was Campbell, Squires' closest colleague, who prompted Jennings' resignation in March 1923 by overruling him on the purchase of departmental supplies and on land arbitration questions. See Jennings' evidence, 'Hollis Walker Commission,' *Daily News*, 10 March 1924 and relief accounts, 'Hollis Walker Report,' *Evening Telegram*, 21, 22 March 1924.

118 See Abbott and Winsor in assembly debate, PHA, 30 April, 3 May 1920; Scammell and Samson, 25 April 1921.

119 See FPUCP, 1922, Presidential address in Coaker (ed.), *Twenty Years*, 210; Coaker papers, C.L.4, 26 Feb. 1923.

120 *Evening Advocate*, 30 Dec. 1922. For an interesting discussion of the proposed changes and some of the FPU's weaknesses see Coaker papers, J.R. Smallwood to Coaker, 9 Jan. 1932. For a further elaboration of Coaker's plans see ibid., C.L.4, 15 April 1924.

121 *Daily News*, 3 Jan. 1923.

122 Morton, *Progressive Party*, 152; Sharp, *Agrarian Revolt*, 157–8.

123 Ibid., 155.

124 Morton, *Progressive Party*, 148.

125 For a discussion of the Monroe government of 1924–8 see Noel, *Politics in Newfoundland*, 179–85; McDonald, 'W.F. Coaker and the Fishermen's Protective Union,' 332–7.

126 FPUCP, 1925, President's address in Coaker (ed.), *Twenty Years*, 236.

127 CO 537/1167, Harris to Long, 23 March 1918.

128 *Fishermen's Advocate*, 4 Dec. 1926.

Newfoundland Politics in the 1920s: The Genesis and Significance of the Hollis Walker Enquiry

R . M . ELLIOTT

On 21 March 1924, the report of the Hollis Walker Commission of Enquiry was published in all St John's newspapers. It presented to the public of Newfoundland a sweeping condemnation of the way in which the government administered its affairs, and revealed a remarkable state of corruption and graft involving several individual members of the Liberal Reform government of Sir Richard Anderson Squires,[1] including the prime minister himself.

It revealed, among other things, that an associate of the prime minister, John T. Meaney, who had been acting liquor controller, had expropriated over $100,000 in departmental funds, of which over $20,000 had found its way into Squires' own pocket. Squires was also found to have accepted $43,000 from officials of the Dominion Iron and Steel Company (DOSCO), the Canadian based company which conducted mining operations at Bell Island, in return for promises to revise government contracts in that company's favour. The minister of agriculture and mines, Dr Alexander Campbell,[2] the prime minister's closest colleague, was found to have used department funds to defray his transportation expenses during the 1923 election campaign, and his department, which was responsible for most of the relief spending in the colony, was discovered to have abused its responsibilities in a scandalous manner.

The Hollis Walker report has received adequate analysis elsewhere,[3] and the details of its findings are, for the most part, beyond the scope of this paper. But the unfolding of events that preceded the hearings has never been adequately examined. And it is these events which go far to explain some of the more bizarre political contortions that followed the enquiry. Without such explanation the political history of 1923 and 1924 appears absurd, and the actions and statements of some of the leading figures fail to make any sense at all. These events show that the political astuteness and agility of the major political leaders of the day were not impaired by the venality, greed, and grasping ambition rampant among them.

The group which Squires led to political victory, first in 1919 and then in the spring of 1923, was a troubled and divided one from the outset. For despite the comfortable majorities the Liberal Reform party was able to obtain on both occasions, and an outward appearance of stability, its naturally incompatible factions were held together by tenuous bonds. It consisted in the main of old Liberals somewhat in the tradition of Sir Robert Bond, led by W.R. Warren,[4] eleven members representing the interests of the powerful Fisherman's Protective Union (FPU), led by the indomitable and imperious W.F. Coaker,[5] and Squires' own following.[6] The government was essentially a troika, but the two main figures were Coaker and Squires, with Coaker commanding, in terms of unified strength, the greater share of control.

Coaker had been forced into the alliance with Squires, and it had not been to his liking from the outset. He would have preferred to have struck a deal with Warren alone, but Squires had a stronger base and hence was by far the more realistic choice.[7] The basis of Warren's political support was not firm, and he lacked sufficient stature to give adequate strength to the Unionists. But in the political amalgam created by the three, Coaker undoubtedly hoped that his and Warren's combined efforts would be sufficient to keep Squires, ever the political opportunist, in line.[8]

Coaker's decision to throw in his lot with Squires was taken despite a history of intense antagonism between the two, which had developed chiefly out of the conscription crisis of 1918. On that occasion, Squires had attempted to have the date for the application of the National Service Act advanced, a move which would have drained many northern fishermen from the fisheries at a crucial time of the year. Since Coaker had already compromised himself with many of his followers by having supported conscription, despite a pledge that he would never do so, Squires' actions could have injured him profoundly. But the armistice was signed and the war over before Squires' move could be effective.[9] Nevertheless, chords of enmity and mistrust had been unmistakably struck between these two powerful and rather unforgiving men.

Cabinet divisions were aggravated by personality differences among the three. Warren was a relatively inexperienced man, who, although he did not lack political insight, had neither the force of personality nor the tenacity of purpose of the other two. He was more likely to be unnerved by difficult situations than either Squires or Coaker. Warren's two colleagues shared those qualities of driving ambition and singleness of purpose that characterize the successful politician. But their goals were different. Coaker's unfaltering obsession, and his prime reason for having formed the alliance with Squires in the first place, was the maintenance of the political position of the FPU so that he might be able to implement its program for the reorganization of the fisheries, an imperative that was becoming all the more pressing in the light of Newfoundland's faltering economy at the war's end.[10] Squires' ambitions were primarily political, not based on any set of principles other than the paramount one of maintaining his own position and keeping himself in office. In short, the government was an unnatural alliance of personally and politically incompatible individuals, who could hardly be expected to hang together in a serious crisis. As one contemporary observer later remarked:

The Squires-Coaker arrangement never did work well ... it was obvious from the beginning that the political marriage ... could not last ... It was not long after the election before it became apparent that the so-called Squires followers and the so-called Coaker followers especially those in the Cabinet were not always of one mind. Both Squires and Coaker were very able men, both were fond of power. It is doubtful too if Squires had the complete support of his own wing in the Cabinet at all times.[11]

Squires' party had won twenty-three of thirty-six seats in 1919 and again in 1923. Eleven of these seats were controlled by Coaker, and this fact alone cast the stability of the government in serious doubt.[12]

The opposition was not a party at all, but a collection of individual soldiers of political fortune.[13] Their sympathies were generally pro-mercantile, and they numbered among their members the most prominent Catholic politicians of the day, most notably W.J. Higgins[14] and Sir Michael Cashin,[15] leader of the previous Tory administration. The focal point of their antagonism was not Squires but Coaker, whose fishermen's movement was loathed and feared by the mercantile community based in St John's and the Roman Catholic hierarchy of the colony alike. They quite rightly recognized in the Fishermen's Protective Union a threat to their own social and economic dominance among the fishermen of the colony.[16]

Squires' first ministry had been absorbed chiefly by Coaker's futile efforts to impose order and regulation upon Newfoundland's chaotic fisheries industry.[17] The government's fisheries regulation legislation, which had been in effect from 1919 to 1921, was unsuccessful because it was not forceful enough. The cooperation of the fish exporters on the island was essential to any regulation policy, but their shortsightedness, and mistrust of government, precluded the imposition of strong penalties upon those who failed to abide by the legislation. A unified front on the international market on the part of Newfoundland exporters was thus not ensured, and a renegade exporter who panicked or who lacked scruples could cause considerable harm by underselling his fellows. This is eventually what happened, and the events that accompanied the collapse of the policy in 1921 possibly caused more hardship to certain speculative and inexperienced firms than if it had never been instituted in the first place. The result was to heighten the distaste of the mercantile community for Coaker, and to strengthen their conviction that government meddling in the marketplace contravened the Law of Nature, and brought down the wrath of the Almighty on all concerned. The episode engendered an intense and widespread antagonism towards the government and cast its political future in jeopardy.

In the midst of these unfavourable circumstances, the government found political salvation in a project, partly underwritten by the imperial government, to develop a paper-mill on the Humber River in western Newfoundland.[18] This was the issue upon which the members of the government rested their fortunes for a second ministry, and it took them safely through the election campaign of May 1923. The opposition concentrated its campaign efforts on dredging up the ill-fated fisheries legislation. But they could not match the heady prospects of prosperity and employment conjured up by the new paper-mill. The Liberal Reform party was returned to office with its majority intact.[19] All was not well with the party nonetheless. The government had lost some 8 per cent of the popular support it had attracted in 1919. And Coaker continued to brood over the regulations fiasco. He had resigned from the cabinet some months before the election so that he might attend to FPU matters with a freer hand.[20]

Squires announced his cabinet early in June 1923, and launched his new administration in a climate which was calm and full of confidence on the surface.[21] But behind the scenes a storm was brewing which as spring turned into summer would bring the new administration to an abrupt and sensational end as it came face to face with a crisis of political corruption and intrigue involving two of its most prominent figures.

On 7 June the House of Assembly opened, and Warren's junior law partner, H.A. Winter, was appointed speaker. The opposition announced that W.J. Higgins would replace J.R. Bennett, who had lost his seat in the recent election, as their leader, although there was no doubt in anyone's mind that the most powerful man in the party continued to be Michael Cashin. The house promptly adjourned until 13 June.[22] In the meantime, the *Daily News*, which was the mouthpiece for the opposition, continued to criticize the Humber agreement as well as the settlement that the government was negotiating with the object of taking over the notoriously unprofitable railway from its private operators, the Reid family.[23] On 20 June the *Daily News* added a new note to its customary barrage of criticism. It suggested that there was much amiss with regard to government expenditures during the preceding election campaign. Opposition members had been asking for figures from the government, apparently to no avail. But the tempo of events now began to pick up.

Less than a week later, Michael Cashin rose in the house and charged that a minister of the crown had used public funds to pay his election expenses. Cashin now claimed that he had possession of cheques, improperly drawn on the treasury.[24] The government refused to answer the charges. But on 6 July W.J. Walsh, the opposition member from Placentia, demanded to know what action the attorney general intended to take on the basis of Cashin's charges. That very afternoon Walsh brought matters to a head by laying specific charges against Dr Alexander Campbell, the minister of agriculture and mines, and the government's chief dispenser of political patronage. Shortly thereafter Dr Campbell was reported to be en route to Prince Edward Island for an extended holiday.[25]

The Hollis Walker report would later reveal the full extent to which Dr Campbell had abused his office and responsibilities. Some of his breaches of public trust involved relatively petty matters such as charging his transportation expenses during the election campaign to his department. But there were far more serious irregularities in the administration of poor relief in the colony, a task which fell under his direction. Circumstances in Newfoundland at the time to an extent explain, although they do not mitigate, some of Dr Campbell's misdeeds.

The end of World War I brought increasing unemployment, and the accompanying economic misery in time began to reach intolerable levels. The severe drop in the earnings of fishermen crippled retailers and local manufacturers, and brought on further unemployment. The stagnation of trade that was evident by 1920 had become a severe depression by the winter of 1922–3, prior to the spring election, and months before the completion of the Humber project.[26]

Accompanying these difficulties were other problems. The cost of the war was draining the treasury of $1.75 million annually for service charges on debts, and related expenditures, and the railway was costing on the average $1.3 million annually.[27] Most of these expenses were being met through increased borrowing. Increased expenditures on government services were significant as well, and they were being managed inefficiently.[28] The situation was becoming impossible. The only hope was to cut government borrowing, which could not be done without withdrawing certain essential government services.

The Squires government had been forced to meet the immediate emergency by providing relief on a scale never before required in the colony, and here it had faced yet another problem. There existed in Newfoundland no apparatus for effectively distributing relief on such a massive scale. Since the early days of responsible government it had been the practice to distribute funds for poor relief and public works – the latter often a form of disguised relief – through the offices of the colonial secretary and the Board of Works, frequently on the advice of assembly members and political heelers, who saw to it that the money was spent to party advantage. In the early 1920s, these funds were effectively controlled by Squires, who was colonial secretary as well as prime minister, and their distribution became politicized to an unprecedented degree.

To complicate the situation further, the Department of Mines and Agriculture,

Dr Campbell's portfolio, had become responsible for a number of relief projects during this period, among them the purchase of timber to be used as pit-props in mining operations, and the distribution of seed potatoes to stimulate agricultural expansion. And of course Campbell, as Squires' crony, saw to it that his department administered such schemes to the political advantage of the prime minister.[29]

No government had ever attempted the difficult task of developing an administrative structure that could effectively and efficiently distribute money to a scattered population. Instead, governments had come to rely upon established institutions, both private and public, to furnish various services, while subsidizing them for so doing. Thus the government was found to be in the position of paying the piper, but rarely calling the tune. Records, moreover, were poorly kept, and the vast amounts of money dispersed during the post-war years provided opportunities for all the unbusinesslike practices, the wastage, and the jobbery later revealed by the Hollis Walker report. It was all too easy to find in this administrative chaos tempting opportunities to use both public funds and services as vehicles for political aggrandizement.

Increased government expenditures during Newfoundland election campaigns were the accepted practice.[30] The extent to which public funds were distributed as poor relief immediately prior to the election campaign of 1923 was what chiefly distinguished that campaign in the public mind. The people had, by 1919, become well used to viewing the government as the source of political and financial favour, and a system of overt bribery by electorate and elected alike was firmly established. It was the additional strain of severe economic dislocation during the Squires administration that overburdened the inadequate civil service, and the horrendous confusion in the Department of Agriculture and Mines that the 1924 enquiry revealed was the not very surprising result.

A wealth of factors – the failure of the fisheries policy, the continued disruption in fishery production, the decrease in fish prices, the continued necessity to borrow to cover the interest payment on the colony's debt, the increase in unemployment, the lack of administrative services for the distribution of public funds, the unsystematic conduct of relief projects such as the cutting of pit-props and the distribution of seed potatoes, and the irresponsible agitation of the opposition throughout the period – all contributed to the difficulties of the first Squires administration. Severely disrupted internally, it was for most of its duration a government in panic, keeping itself in office by injecting extravagant doses of relief funds into the economy, and by implementing impetuous, ill-thought-out emergency measures meant to forestall catastrophe and quell social unrest.

The government's pathetic efforts to come to grips with the problems facing it were constantly thwarted by the opposition, which used every emergency for political gain.[31] The governor attributed much of the seriousness of the position to the inability of members on both sides of the house to tackle the problem in a businesslike and public-spirited way. And he considered the situation severely aggravated by the vacillation of his ministers, due partly, he suspected, to a desire not to disappoint their supporters, and partly to a natural feeling of humanity which shrank from curtailing expenditures in the face of the hardships being experienced by a large sector of the population.[32] Undoubtedly the terror of public insurrection provided another motive.[33]

But in the early weeks of Squires' second administration in June 1923, public interest was focused on the rumoured troubles within Dr Campbell's department. Behind the scenes, however, a frantic crisis was taking place involving not Dr Campbell, but the prime minister himself. The matter concerned the liquor controller's department, and its roots extended back some considerable time.

In June 1922, John T. Meaney, who was acting liquor controller, abruptly terminated his practice of making payments to Squires out of department funds in exchange for IOUs.[34] Meaney had been a willing conspirator in this arrangement as long as there was a chance that his position would be made permanent. The prime minister had tried to oblige Meaney in this regard, but had run into persistent cabinet opposition. Meaney was not well thought of by some of the more high-minded members of Squires' cabinet.[35] Consequently, relations between Meaney and Squires began to sour, but the former wisely retained in his possession those incriminating IOUs that Squires had failed to redeem.[36]

On 21 June 1923, in the midst of all the speculation concerning Dr Campbell, the papers made brief and offhand mention of a burglary that had taken place some days before at the office of the liquor controller. Meaney was dismissed from his office two days later.[37] On the day of his dismissal, the *Evening Telegram* referred to a burglary that had taken place at the offices of the attorney general, W.R. Warren, some months earlier. On that occasion, the desks and private papers of the attorney general and his deputy were looted. The *Telegram* speculated that the same individual was responsible for both the burglary of the attorney general's office and the recent entry into the liquor controller's office. Certain papers – assumed to be the object of these searches – had apparently not been found in either case.

Someone was clearly looking for something of considerable importance and had reason to suspect that what he was looking for might be in the hands of the attorney general, or if not there, at the liquor controller's department. That 'someone,' Meaney suspected, was Squires himself. But Meaney was a match for his old mentor, and as he later revealed to M.C. Hawco, the minister of posts and telegraphs, he had already removed from his office the papers which Squires wanted.[38]

Meaney's dismissal had been a direct result of the fact that the accounts of his department were overdrawn.[39] The Bank of Montreal had refused to honour any further cheques issued by the department, unless they were countersigned by the auditor general. With an investigation pending, Meaney realized that the prime minister could make no attempt to save him and decided to try to use the evidence he had in his possession to the best possible advantage.[40] He first approached Warren with the papers that implicated Squires but evidently did not receive the vigorous response on which he had counted.[41] He waited for some weeks, and sometime around 18 July went with the evidence to the opposition leader, W.J. Higgins.[42] Undoubtedly he hoped that he could in this way forestall Squires from taking action against him. Meaney engaged Higgins as his solicitor, who approached Warren with the evidence on or about 18 July, and thereby set in motion the events that terminated with Squires' resignation on 23 July.[43]

Sometime towards the end of June or the beginning of July, Warren had conferred with the prime minister about the allegations regarding his involvement in the liquor controller's department, and he had threatened to resign over the matter.[44] Warren's importunities had roused Squires to action, however, and he now began to make desperate efforts to save himself. His lawyer, W.R. Howley, had already approached Warren to implore him to call off an intended investigation into the liquor controller's department, and Squires himself was busy trying to form an alliance with J.R. Bennett, the former leader of the opposition, with a view to having Bennett, and not Warren, called upon to form the next ministry.[45]

But with the evidence of Squires' complicity now in the hands of the opposition, Warren was forced to take some positive action. He twice conferred with Squires, first privately and then together with Coaker.[46] Amazingly, in view of his apparently hopeless position, Squires attempted to bargain for concessions. Refusing to confirm or deny the charges – he claimed he was not shown the evidence – Squires requested that he be permitted to remain in office until the end of the year, so that he might attend the Imperial Conference; that he be retained by the government to negotiate the Labrador boundary dispute; that he be allowed to manage Newfoundland's preparations for the impending British Empire Exhibition; and that he be rewarded financially for the time and effort he might spend on these projects.[47] Warren went to Higgins with these demands, which Higgins, and subsequently Warren, rejected. Finally, on 22 July Warren, with the support of three other ministers, demanded Squires' resignation under threat of his own and those of his supporters.[48] The following morning the ministers did resign; Squires bent to the inevitable and recommended to the governor that Warren be called upon to form a new government.[49]

There is no reason to assume that the four dissenting ministers were seeking Dr Campbell's resignation at this time, and that Squires resigned in defence of his colleague.[50] The evidence from the enquiry clearly establishes that Squires himself was the object of the cabinet revolt. For although knowledge of Campbell's implication in departmental graft had already come to light, it was quickly overshadowed by the evidence against Squires himself. It must be kept in mind, however, that the public was not to know about these events until the hearings took place in the early months of 1924. On the face of it, it is curious that Squires would make such brazen requests to Warren and Higgins. But Squires undoubtedly had something in his possession that allowed him to dally with both the remains of his own party and the opposition with some hope of success. Perhaps it was the knowledge that he was not alone in having used the liquor department to personal advantage.

On 24 July Warren took office. The papers seemed to assume that Squires had resigned because of the pressure of certain ministers, led by Warren, to hold an investigation into Campbell's department.[51] The house adjourned that same day until the following week. In the meantime, several conferences were held between Warren and the opposition, apparently with the intention of forming a coalition.[52] But the opposition's terms were found to be unacceptable by the government.[53] There was no way, of course, that Warren could have known the weakness of his own position during those July days. It was entirely conceivable that the entire administration, himself included, could come crashing down as a result of the scandals. It could only have been to his advantage to seek the good will of the opposition. And this would not have been unpalatable to him, for he numbered many of them among his personal friends.[54] But even allowing for such reasons, relations between the two groups in the house became unusually amiable, and continued so for the remainder of the year, throughout the period of the enquiry itself, and until the tumultuous spring of 1924.

Warren was now faced with the aftermath of the crisis. On 28 July 1923, he announced that there would be a complete investigation into all the alleged scandals. The following day he announced his new cabinet.[55] It included Coaker among its ranks. Warren apparently had persuaded him to make an effort to bolster the new administration by lending his powerful presence to the government. Coaker did so without much enthusiasm, however, and was not involved to any significant extent in the events that were to follow.

At this point Warren had to establish an appropriate apparatus to conduct the investigation he had promised. At first, he considered appointing a local commission, but he was compelled to change his mind. The three men he requested to serve on the commission all refused.[56] Warren therefore turned to the Colonial Office, which chose Thomas Hollis Walker to undertake the enquiry. A sixty-three-year-old barrister of considerable stature, he was reputed to be a skilled cross-examiner with a painstaking and thorough mind. He was to prove himself admirably suited to the task he had been assigned.

The rest of the summer passed uneventfully. But it was soon September, and the terms of reference that were to serve as Hollis Walker's guidelines were still not publicly known. Meanwhile, the *Daily News* continued to give forth its ration of speculation and rumour. One rumour suggested that the scandals involved persons other than Squires and Campbell.[57] The *Daily News* was likely referring to Coaker, and the subsequent enquiry was to prove them wrong on this score. But if the paper had the wrong man, it was certainly on the right track. There were other speculations making the rounds. Some were to the effect that the opposition was not entirely guiltless in the liquor department affair and there was agitation from some quarters that the investigations into the alleged wrongdoings extend back to cover the opposition's dealings as well as those of Squires.[58] The *Daily News* dismissed these rumours as an attempt by Squires and his associates to disperse the cloud of blame which hung over their heads and in this way to blur the outlines of their own misdeeds.

Throughout the autumn the more prominent figures in the episode were doing a great deal of travelling. Squires returned from a visit to Toronto and the United States and by mid-September was prepared to embark again, this time for England. A fellow traveller on this occasion would be his former colleague, and present antagonist, W.R. Warren, who was intending to represent the colony at the Imperial Conference of that year.[59] Apparently they went off on the same vessel. With Campbell, Squires, and Warren out of the colony the investigation had to be postponed until the new year. Prominent opposition members were abroad as well. P.T. McGrath, a well-known opposition journalist, was in London, and Michael Cashin was in Paris.[60] Squires travelled to Paris later, and he had several meetings with Cashin both there and in London.[61] Cashin had also been in touch with Warren. With all the major figures in one place, far from the oppressive scrutiny of rumour-ridden St John's, there was a wealth of opportunity for making deals, pooling interests, establishing cover-ups, and the like.

Throughout October, information regarding the affairs of DOSCO, the mining operation on Bell Island, and its relation with the former Squires ministry began to come to light. The revelations came out against a backdrop of severe labour troubles and extensive layoffs at the mines. By 16 October, the newspapers were maintaining that the commission of enquiry would possibly reveal more about the company's relations with the Squires government and the unsavoury nature of the dealings between them.[62] The rumours were, as usual, correct. The DOSCO involvement, which can be set aside here, would provide Hollis Walker with another important area of investigation.

Warren arrived back in St John's from the Imperial Conference on 21 December.[63] He issued the commission's terms of reference the following day. They were not quite the same as those he had outlined in a rough draft, drawn up before he left for England on 15 September. The clause referring to the liquor department allegations was originally stated thus: 'And whereas similar allegations have been made respecting the amounts due the Treasury of the Colony by the Department of the Liquor Controller ...' The final draft, on the other hand, read: 'Whereas allegations have been made that amounts paid to the Department of the Liquor Controller were not paid into the Treasury but were paid over to private individuals.'[64] On the face of it the change in wording seems insignificant. But in fact it was crucial. The original draft would have provided for a thorough investigation of every aspect of the operation of the liquor controller's department, including the supplying of that department. The final draft which was presented to Hollis Walker, who arrived in St John's early in January 1924, neatly limited the investigation to a specific charge supported by Meaney's specific evidence.

Why would Warren have taken such a step? Warren's own testimony taken during the enquiry sheds some light on the matter. Before he left for England, he had employed an auditor to conduct a preliminary enquiry into the liquor controller's department.[65] This enquiry uncovered a record of wholesale corruption within the liquor department of which Squires' complicity constituted only one part. At the outset of the hearings, W.R. Howley, Squires' very capable lawyer, made a determined effort to persuade Hollis Walker to widen the investigation by demanding that the auditor's report in question be released to the commission. Warren refused, maintaining that it would not be in the public interest to do so. Hollis Walker judged that the terms of his commission bound him to an investigation into the specified charges concerning Squires and Meaney, and that he could therefore not demand that Warren release the report to him.[66] Warren maintained that in any case he had not seen that report before he changed the terms of reference from the original draft to the considerably narrower final version.[67] Perhaps he had not. But it is highly unlikely that the firm he employed to conduct the preliminary investigation would not have volunteered the explosive information their probing had uncovered as soon as he returned to St John's.

The hearings were opened by Hollis Walker on 7 January and continued until 14 March. Throughout that time St John's appears to have been in a state of stupor and shock as Hollis Walker's relentless and incisive cross-examination of witnesses revealed the full extent to which the prime minister and his principal colleague, Dr Campbell, were involved in a morass of political graft and financial chaos. The evidence of each day's hearings was published daily in the papers. It made intriguing reading. Throughout the enquiry Squires continued to make oblique protestations that he was the victim of political intrigue, a plot to discredit him. In view of the overwhelming evidence concerning his own misdemeanours, this was a curious approach to take. Hollis Walker was understandably perplexed. One exchange between the two was as follows:

WALKER

Intrigue with what object? To get rid of you?

SQUIRES

The overthrow of my administration.

WALKER

You did not think it was political intrigue when your attention was brought to it by your colleagues. It must have been personal intrigue to overthrow you. Do you think they would try to overthrow the administration of which they themselves were members?

SQUIRES

My idea is that it was for political re-organization.

WALKER

In which the same party would rule, but you would be out of it?

SQUIRES

The same party but with others.

WALKER

But without yourself?

SQUIRES

Yes.[68]

And later on, there was a terse exchange between Squires and Warren:

SQUIRES

In my opinion the manipulation was under the direction of the opposition.

WARREN

You mean that your own party was being made the tool of the opposition.

SQUIRES

No. But it is quite significant that it was the leader of the opposition whom Meaney had consulted, and who was Meaney's lawyer.[69]

Squires was implying that Warren had plotted with the opposition to overthrow him. But if indeed there had been any such collusion between Warren and the opposition, on what could it have been based? What would each side have had to gain from such a *modus vivendi*? Warren undoubtedly felt that he needed the tolerance and good will of the opposition in order to carry on in office. Coaker had lost a great deal of his former enthusiasm and effectiveness. He was clearly distracted and disillusioned about the FPU's political future, and he was no longer the tower of strength and dynamism that he had formerly been. And Warren's position as leader of a government that had so recently been associated with Squires and Campbell was not strong. A tenacious and antagonistic opposition would have called the government's credibility into question and would have made it difficult, if not impossible, for Warren to govern effectively. Why indeed had the opposition not employed this tactic?

It is likely that Squires knew the answer. The matter was undoubtedly closely connected with the preliminary audit into the liquor controller's department, which Warren had ordered before he left for London in September 1923, and which he refused to release to the commission. Squires was likely aware that the auditor's report would reveal that in 1919 Michael Cashin had imported forty cases of whiskey, and three octaves of rum without paying the appropriate duty of $1,100.[70] Cashin had also made a killing during 1922 and 1923 with Meaney's help. He had been selling liquor to the government at inflated prices, and had been paid by means of cheques made out to an intermediary, but clearly marked for Cashin himself. The amount involved this time was $22,198, and presumably Cashin would have cleared about half of that.[71] A full investigation into the accounts of the liquor controller's department would have made this information public, and thoroughly discredited the opposition. But the terms of reference of the commission of enquiry did not allow for a full investigation. Had Warren deliberately protected the opposition in return for their tolerance towards his administration? It is highly probable that this is exactly what had happened.

Squires had probably been informed by Meaney of the irregularities within the department with regard to the *supplying* of liquor, but saw little reason to act on it, since he had much to hide himself. But undoubtedly this knowledge lay behind his cryptic remarks that he was being made a scapegoat and his air of martyrdom. The auditor's report, which Warren refused to hand over to the commission, would not be made public until two years later. By that time, however, the government of Walter Monroe,[72] including several members of both the present parties, would be busy making itself unpopular with the electorate.

On 21 March 1924, Hollis Walker submitted his report, and promptly left for home. The colony was left to cope with its implications and immediately went into a series of political convulsions that remain unrivalled for their complexity. The papers published the report, and began to make strident calls for action. The ubiquitous Alfred B. Morine[73] presented a long harangue to the *Evening Telegram* on 25 March, in which he maintained that Newfoundland was afflicted with 'moral leprosy.' His suggested cure was a reduction of expenditure, a reform of the civil service, a reduction in the number of cabinet portfolios – he would abolish the fisheries ministry entirely – and a reduction of taxation.

In the meantime, there remained the problem of what action should be taken on the basis of the Hollis Walker report. Sometime earlier, Warren informed the governor that he did not intend to prosecute on the basis of it. Neither he nor the governor believed that a grand jury would find a true bill against Squires, largely for 'sectarian' reasons.[74] Their reasoning requires some explanation, for there had been no overt mention of sectarianism throughout the entire sorry episode. How could Warren have foreseen so accurately that Squires, whose government had never been particularly popular in merchant-dominated St John's, would be able to elicit such overwhelming sympathy there in the light of all the evidence against him? It is likely that there was widespread suspicion that the full story had not indeed emerged from the Hollis Walker enquiry, that it had not been an unbiased and thorough investigation, and that Squires, although undoubtedly guilty of all the charges against him, was, as he had claimed, in some sense the victim of political intrigue. The only 'sectarian' aspect to this was perhaps the speculation or rumour that the most prominent Catholic politician of the day, Sir Michael Cashin, was getting off scot-free while Squires and Campbell were being made to pay for their wrongdoings. Newfoundlanders tended to use the word 'sectarianism' in an imprecise and confusing way, and the word served a multitude of purposes, many of them at odds with each other, within the arena of Newfoundland politics.

Whatever hopes Warren had of riding out the storm were dashed by the strident demands by Unionist members of his cabinet that he proceed with legal action against Squires, Meaney, and Campbell, and that, moreover, the government undertake a wider investigation of the liquor controller's department than that just carried out by the Hollis Walker Commission.[75] The integrity of the Unionist members of the Liberal Reform party had been upheld and vindicated by the recent enquiry, and undoubtedly they were experiencing a somewhat justified sense of self-righteousness in the face of the findings against Squires and the rumoured misdeeds of prominent opposition members. On 9 April 1924 Warren bent to the pressure which certain of his cabinet members and certain sectors of the public were bringing to bear, and he served notice that the Department of Justice would take legal action against Squires, Meaney, and Campbell.[76] That same day it was also announced that a wider investigation into the operations of the liquor controller's department would be undertaken, and the Colonial Office was requested to find another investigator.[77] Immediately and abruptly the tone of the editorials in the opposition newspaper, the *Daily News*, changed. Its conciliatory attitude disappeared, and there was none of the former agitation that justice be served. The 'arrangement' between Warren and the opposition had clearly been terminated.

The political situation now underwent particularly grotesque and rapid alterations. Warren's decision to take legal action against the three main figures, and to proceed with a wider investigation drove Squires and the opposition into an alliance, which destroyed Warren's ministry. Squires, out on bail, defected with four of his followers to the opposition benches, and their combined efforts brought down the Warren administration on 24 April 1924.[78] Warren was granted a dissolution but, unnerved by these events, he abandoned his FPU colleagues, struck a bargain with the opposition himself, and formed a new ministry on 3 May which survived only five days. Coaker was then called on to form a ministry but refused. Finally, A.E. Hickman, a member of the Liberal-Unionist alliance, was summoned. Assuming the leadership of what remained of this group, he fought and lost the election of June 1924 to Walter Monroe.[79]

Squires himself did not run in the election. Warren, however, had been right when he stated that no grand jury would find a true bill against Squires. In October 1924 the grand jury summoned to indict him dismissed the charges categorically.[80] A confidential report, undertaken by the Ministry of Justice into the acquittal of the request of the governor, revealed that the public, or certain segments of it at any rate, considered that justice had not been done, nor had it been seen to be done.[81]

The political profile of Newfoundland had been profoundly altered as a result of the crisis of 1923–4. The FPU had been critically damaged, not only as a result of its association with the Squires' administration, but also because, in the context of 1924, it was unable to find a suitable political ally. The 'Catholic' group, which had been forced into political isolation when Archbishop Roche,[82] motivated by his antipathy towards the FPU, presided over the breakup of the national government in 1919,[83] found itself in comfortable alliance with its former partner, the Water Street business community, which was supporting Walter Monroe. In the election of 1924, the polarization of political divisions along traditional class and social lines was more clearly expressed than it had been for some time, since a merchant party faced its favourite protagonist, the FPU, whose representatives were being led by Hickman, and who were now despondent, with none of their earlier moral aura or populist appeal.

With Warren fighting the election as an independent, and with Squires conveniently out of the running altogether, Monroe concentrated the full force of his attack on Coaker, who ironically was not running for office, and the FPU politicians, all of whom had been exonerated by the Hollis Walker enquiry. Coaker was presented by the Monroe party as an *éminence grise* controlling the Hickman party from the sidelines.[84] Emphasizing his own business-like qualities, and his lack of political finesse, Monroe stressed his directness of manner and his honesty, which he embodied in his campaign pledge to 'Clean up; keep clean and give a square deal to all.'[85] Squires was relegated to the role of scapegoat – a victim of political intrigue as he had claimed – and the full blame for public wastage and extravagance was unfairly laid on Coaker's shoulders. Monroe attacked the regulations policy of 1919–21, but he offered no alternative to it. Corruption and unrestrained government spending were effectively presented as the chief ills facing the colony, and a businessman at the helm, it was suggested, would chart the proper course. The impression was being created that retrenchment and honest government would solve the colony's underlying economic problems, whereas in fact these two approaches could only have had a minimal effect. The Hollis Walker enquiry, however, had created fertile soil for such suggestions, and the Monroe party returned from the polls with resounding success.[86]

The Monroe administration made no attempt to deal with the continuing problems in the fisheries or to establish a sound administrative system, and soon found itself as unable to cope with the morass in which it found itself as the Squires' administrations before it.[87] Borrowing to meet the island's annual deficit continued as before. The income tax that had been levied during the war was repealed. Tariffs on essential imports were increased, thereby throwing the burden of financing government on the shoulders of those least able to bear it. Projects of questionable merit but prodigious expense were undertaken, and the continuing crisis of unemployment was tackled with the same lack of direction as previously.

An audit of the customs department in June 1924 revealed that merchants were no less inclined to help themselves to public funds than were political opportunists such as Squires and Campbell.[88] The United Tobacco Company, for example, of which J.R. Bennett had been director, owed excise duties on cigarettes of nearly $28,000. In short, events went on much the same as they had before, with only superficial differences of a very shallow kind of integrity distinguishing the Monroe administration from Squires' graft-ridden government. W.J. Higgins, commenting to Coaker on the Monroe administration with which he served, wrote:

It is just a continuing performance here day and night, listening to tales of woe – everyone wanting a job. Where we are going to end the Lord only knows. The country can't exist on building roads and docks. There has got to be production, but unfortunately there seems to be an increasing desire on the part of a number to quit that form of employment and look for what is becoming a permanent institution – government work. It will have to stop, but when and how you can foretell as well as myself. You have been close enough to it to understand ... Revenue is up – but how much of it is false. Are we not simply living on our capital, by way of borrowed money.[89]

By 1928 the Monroe government was itself experiencing political bankruptcy, for it too had failed to find solutions for difficulties arising from an administrative system overburdened by a rudimentary economy in need of drastic reorganization. The result was another opening for the astute Squires who carried the general election of that year handily. But his new administration provided more of the same; the deficit financing and borrowing that had started in 1920 continued unabated, and led in 1932 to the financial crisis that resulted in the collapse of responsible government.

The Amulree[90] Royal Commission, which was appointed in 1933 to enquire into the financial embarrassment facing the colony at that time, produced a report that vigorously repeated the moral condemnation which had so pervaded the Hollis

Walker report. It established the premise upon which it would examine the financial position of Newfoundland in the following terms: 'The broad facts of the financial position in Newfoundland are unfortunately all too plain. Ever since the war, the country has been living beyond its means, and the budget has not been balanced since 1920.'[91] It would have been more accurate to say that Newfoundland was living beyond its means throughout the 1920s largely as a result of the war. The conclusion reached by the commission that the colony had profited from the war is only superficially true; prices paid for Newfoundland fish soared and brought a temporary wave of prosperity. But Newfoundland had borrowed $13 million to finance her war effort, and with increased costs of pensions, rehabilitation of veterans, compensation to widows and orphans, and the additional burden of servicing the debt, the capitalized cost of the war reached $35 million and throughout the 1920s was draining the treasury of close to $2 million annually, a figure roughly equivalent to the island's average annual deficit on current account.[92]

The railway accounted for the largest portion of the debt. By 1919 government investment in the railway accounted for a little less than half of Newfoundland's $42 million debt. From 1920 to 1923 the railway had been responsible for the addition of a further $18 million, with the result that by 1923 close to 40 per cent of Newfoundland's staggering $100 million debt could be attributed to the railway.[93] In short, the war and the railway together constituted the 'reckless disregard of the dictates of financial prudence' which led to the eventual collapse in 1933.[94] The underlying problem remained the steady erosion of the fisheries industry, with no sound alternatives to replace or supplement it.

But the Amulree Royal Commission came to far different conclusions: sound administration, an efficient public service, a respite from divisive and corrupting politics, and the application of Westminster standards of orderly government and fiscal probity would go a long way towards curing Newfoundland's problems.[95] The record of commission government shows quite clearly, however, that all these innovations had only a meagre effect on the colony's progress towards solvency. For that government too had to carry substantial deficits,[96] and the unemployment problem remained so severe that public order was again threatened.[97]

One member of the Amulree commission privately disagreed with the premises of the report that was finally issued. One month before the final drafting, the Canadian government's representative on the commission, Charles A. Magrath, wrote to Lord Amulree stating his objections:

The Newfoundlander is a North American whether he likes it or not, though many of those people round St. John's do not seem to appreciate it. Our great neighbour to the south of us, with the tremendous prosperity that they enjoyed for years, leading to vast public expenditures influences us in Canada as well as those in control in Newfoundland. In fact, loose spending seems to have been the order of the day in all countries in recent years ... If I am to be critical as to what happened in the past, I feel I would pay some attention to that section of the people who had the greatest opportunities, with corresponding obligations as citizens. The main trade of that Island has been its fisheries, and those operating between the fisherfolk and the markets of their products abroad, should have sufficient influence on the Island to have restrained the activities of the politicians they now complain of.[98]

On the question of the extent to which graft, stupidity, or corrupt government was responsible for Newfoundland's collapse, he said: 'Frankly it is a subject in which I am not interested. Every nation seems to go through a certain amount of it before becoming more or less competent.' He continued: 'It looks to me as if we are not giving sufficient weight to world factors which have brought about business and governmental difficulties in Newfoundland as in all other countries.' Perhaps Magrath's own North Americanism gave him a particularly clear vantage point. In any case, his views were remarkably incisive and forthright. Rather than jeopardize the colony's chances of acquiring a conversion loan, however, he decided to preserve the unanimity of the commission's findings, and he maintained silence.

A strong case for honourable default on Newfoundland's part in 1933 was expounded in 1937 by A.F.W. Plumptre. He too deplored the idea of placing most of the blame for Newfoundland's difficulties on the shoulders of 'reckless and extravagant' politicians:

It is important to realize that what precipitated the suspension of responsible government, recommended by the Commission, was the imminence of default; it was not the inefficiency of the economic system, nor the corruption of politics. Once the Commission had been appointed, these served as strong arguments in favour of drastic political changes: but if default had not threatened, the Commission would never have been requested by the British, Canadian, and Newfoundland governments.[99]

Plumptre correctly assumed that the report was based on one imperative, that under no circumstances could the Newfoundland government default because of the adverse effects this would have on the credit of the empire. What he could not have known was that the commission's conclusions had been drawn up in Whitehall,[100] largely at the instigation of British Treasury officials, before the commission had issued its report.[101] The document itself was an attempt to justify, to rationalize, measures that had already been decided upon. And the justification used, the one thought most likely to be accepted by the Newfoundland people, was their ineffectiveness in a working democracy, and the continuing carelessness and venality of their leaders. So willing were they to accept this judgment of themselves, that the possibility of default was only briefly considered. Instead, with almost shameless docility, even eagerness, the Newfoundland government accepted the recommendations of the commission on behalf of the people of the colony, and made themselves a party to the suspension of responsible government and democratic government. And although it is not possible to quantify degrees of community despair, one can justifiably assume a close connection between that sorry red herring of 1924 – the Hollis Walker enquiry – and the unquestioning acceptance of the Amulree commission's findings against the Newfoundland people in 1933. The profound sense of moral inferiority and ineptitude that was established in 1924 left little doubt in the minds of the colony's people that they were indeed unfit to govern themselves, particularly since it was again being stated explicitly before all the world in 1933.

The Hollis Walker enquiry thus assumes an importance far beyond a gothic tale of political machinations. It was another milestone along the road to lost economic and political independence for Newfoundland, a country which had seemed to have a fairly promising future at the turn of the century. It is doubtful if the Hollis Walker enquiry had any salutary effect upon the colony. A thorough investigation – one which would have enabled Hollis Walker to give the inner workings of the civil service a thorough perusal, and the misuse of public funds a full, politically untramelled airing – might have provided a chance to make one last unsullied attempt to clean up the mess and get on with the job of governing the colony. As it turned out, the political scheming that accompanied the episode could only add to the cynicism and despair of an already dispirited people. The contention, already commonly accepted among Newfoundlanders, that in politics one lot is as good as the next could only have been reinforced by the events that preceded and followed the hearings.

Lofty standards of public morality among a people and their leaders are certainly to be desired. But they are no substitute for a sound administrative and economic structure. 'Honest merchant administrations' led by 'plain men of business' result in only superficial change where the standard of wholesale unadulterated venality on the part of the many is substituted by the equally repulsive one of wholesale unadulterated greed and exploitation on the part of the few. In recent times these two concepts of government have generally been the only ones presented to the Newfoundland people by its politicians, and together they constitute our political party system: what is referred to as liberal populism on the one hand and toryism on the other. In terms of the development of adequate political ideologies, little has changed in Newfoundland since the days of Richard Squires and Walter Monroe, despite two momentous commissions of enquiry, a lengthy suspension of democratic institutions, and confederation.

Political purges and their accompanying cathartic effects, even sound administrative measures and standards of fiscal sobriety, such as those established by the
commission government in 1934, were insufficient to compensate for economic
problems of overwhelming dimensions which continued to be overlooked. The
problems left unsolved by the Squires administration and the Monroe administration continued to plague Newfoundland until World War II, after which confederation brought temporary surcease. Indeed they are still present. The political
scandals revealed in 1924 gave rise to a distortion of the underlying problem and
provided a way of avoiding the essential difficulties, which were thought to be
beyond the capacity of the community to solve. As long as the problem was
thought to be one of moral and intellectual ineptitude, the Newfoundland community continued to fail to look for a sound economic base on which to rest the
aspirations of its people.

NOTES

1 See above, 120 n35.
2 Alexander Campbell, born Souris, Prince Edward Island, 1876; Quarantine Office,
   1909–25; minister of agriculture and mines, 1919–23.
3 See S.J.R. Noel, *Politics in Newfoundland* (Toronto 1971).
4 W.R. Warren, born St John's, 1874; lawyer; MHA Trinity, 1902–4, 1908–13, and for
   Fortune Bay, 1913–24; minister of justice, 1919; prime minister, 1923–4; judge
   Supreme Court, 1926–7; died St John's, 1927.
5 See above, 148–9.
6 CO 194/297, Harris to Milner, 14 Nov. 1919.
7 Ibid. See also Ian McDonald, 'W.F. Coaker and the Fishermen's Protective Union in
   Newfoundland Politics, 1908–1925' (unpublished PH D thesis, University of London
   1971), 196–8.
8 McDonald, 'W.F. Coaker and the Fishermen's Protective Union,' 197.
9 Ibid., 166–8.
10 Coaker had demanded that prices be fixed and marketing procedures regulated, and had
    been pressing for government action for some time (see Centre for Newfoundland
    Studies, Memorial University, Coaker papers, Circular letters, June–October 1919).
    The opportunity to implement the FPU program must certainly have been the chief
    factor that made the alliance with Squires palatable in the light of the recent antagonism
    between them.
11 Cheeseman notes, 21 Aug. 1965 (private collection in the possession of Mr Roy
    Cheeseman, St John's). J.T. Cheeseman was a close personal friend of Coaker and had
    been a member of Squires' party in 1919.

12 Governor Harris, who was an astute and concerned observer of political events in the colony during his sojourn there, found the coalition between Coaker and Squires inexplicable from the beginning (see CO 194/297, Harris to Milner, 14 Nov. 1919).

13 McDonald, 'W.F. Coaker and the Fishermen's Protective Union,' 109–10, 200–1.

14 W.J. Higgins, born St John's, 1880; lawyer; MHA for St John's East, 1913–28; speaker, 1918–19; colonial secretary in Warren's four-day government, 1924; minister of justice in Monroe government, 1924–8; judge Supreme Court, 1928–43; died St John's, 1943.

15 See above, 179 n98.

16 McDonald, 'W.F. Coaker and the Fishermen's Protective Union,' 63, 83–91, 179.

17 A detailed account of the imposition and the eventual collapse of the fisheries regulation policy instigated by Coaker can be found in ibid., 218–70.

18 CO 194/303, Harris to Churchill, 11 Feb. 1922.

19 *Daily News* (St John's), 31 May 1923.

20 *Evening Advocate* (St John's), 6 June 1923.

21 *Evening Telegram* (St John's), 6 June 1923.

22 *Daily News*, 8 June 1923; *Evening Telegram*, 7 June 1923.

23 See, for example, *Daily News*, 9, 11 June 1923.

24 Ibid., 27 June 1923.

25 *Evening Telegram*, 6, 14 July 1923.

26 The situation by January was aggravated by the closure of the mines at Bell Island, which threw over two thousand miners out of work. They were not reopened until March (see CO 532/237, Allardyce to Devonshire, 16 Jan., 7 March 1923).

27 McDonald, 'W.F. Coaker and the Fishermen's Protective Union,' 276.

28 Ibid., 277.

29 'The Hollis Walker Report,' findings on third allegation. On 21 March 1924, the report was published in all St John's newspapers.

30 See, for example, John P. Greene, 'Newfoundland: The Election Scandals of 1894, By-products of the Administration of Local Affairs' (unpublished paper, Department of History, Memorial University n.d.). See also Gertrude Gunn, *The Political History of Newfoundland, 1832–1864* (Toronto 1966), 157–8.

31 See CO 194/301, Harris to Churchill, 19 Dec. 1921. Commenting on the session which had just ended, the governor told of mobs invading the floor of the assembly and successfully intimidating the government into further expenditures on relief: 'In this they were encouraged by leaders of the Opposition ... In all cases, the action seems to have resulted in expenditure of public money which would not have been granted in the ordinary course of events.'

32 CO 194/303, Harris to Churchill, 11, 29 July 1922.

33 On several occasions the cabinet anticipated civil disorder, and during the period in question the imperial government was issued with several requests for British warships

to visit St John's in the event of riot (see CO 194/301, Harris to Churchill, 22 Oct. 1921; CO 194/303, Harris to Devonshire, 30 Dec. 1922).

34 PANL, Hollis Walker evidence, vol. 1, Meaney's evidence, 7 Jan. 1924.

35 McDonald, 'W.F. Coaker and the Fishermen's Protective Union,' 319.

36 Hollis Walker evidence, vol. 1, Meaney's evidence, 7 Jan. 1924.

37 *Evening Telegram*, 23 June 1923.

38 Hollis Walker evidence, vol. 1, Meaney's evidence, 7 Jan. 1924.

39 Ibid., vol. 2, Squires' evidence, 15 Jan. 1924.

40 Ibid., vol. 1, Meaney's evidence, 7 Jan. 1924.

41 Ibid., vol. 9, Warren's evidence, 21–4 Feb. 1924.

42 Ibid., vol. 1, Meaney's evidence, 7 Jan. 1924.

43 Ibid. There is considerable confusion concerning the date on which Meaney went to Higgins with the evidence. Meaney mentioned 18 July but thought that it could have been 15 July, or 20 July. Hollis Walker in his comments to Squires assumed that the period during which Squires dallied with Warren over his resignation was from a week to ten days (see ibid., vol. 2, Squires' evidence, 17 Jan. 1924).

44 Ibid., Squires' evidence, 15 Jan. 1924.

45 *Daily News*, 28 Feb. 1924 (proceedings of the Hollis Walker enquiry); 27 Feb. 1924.

46 Hollis Walker evidence, vol. 2, Squires' evidence, 17 Jan. 1924.

47 Ibid.

48 The three other ministers were W.W. Halfyard, minister of marine and fisheries, Dr Barnes, minister of education, and S.J. Foote, minister without portfolio (see *Evening Telegram*, 25 July 1923). Halfyard was a Unionist. Barnes represented a Unionist district.

49 CO 532/257, Allardyce to Devonshire, 23 June 1923.

50 The evidence from the inquiry given by Meaney, and the chief protagonists, Squires and Warren, establishes quite plainly that the pressure brought to bear upon Squires after 18 July had nothing directly to do with Dr Campbell. See Noel, *Politics in Newfoundland*, ch. 12.

51 See, for example, *Evening Telegram*, 24 July 1923.

52 *Daily News*, 31 July 1923.

53 Ibid. These terms were that a thorough and searching investigation be made into all the scandals, and that opposition strength should not be less than the government's. Since the opposition could assume that the second term would be totally unacceptable to most government supporters they could assume that the coalition proposal would not come to anything. Under these circumstances it was not at all dangerous to call for a 'thorough investigation,' which, if it had indeed been undertaken, would have been highly detrimental to the public image of certain opposition members.

54 'Memoirs of Harry Anderson Winter,' pts 1 and 2, *NQ* 72, no. 2 (1976): 18.

55 *Daily News*, 28, 30 July 1923.

56 *Evening Telegram*, 10 Aug. 1923. The three men were Messrs Fenelon, Blackwood, and Knight.

57 *Daily News*, 3 Sept. 1923.

58 Ibid., 10 Sept. 1923.

59 *Evening Telegram*, 11 Sept. 1923.

60 *Daily News*, 16 Oct. 1923, 21 Nov. 1923.

61 Ibid., 21, 29 Nov. 1923.

62 Ibid., 16 Oct. 1923.

63 *Evening Telegram*, 21 Dec. 1923.

64 Hollis Walker evidence, vol. 10, Howley's cross-examination of Warren, 27–8 Feb. 1924.

65 Ibid.

66 *Evening Telegram*, 10 Jan. 1924 (proceedings of the Hollis Walker enquiry).

67 Hollis Walker evidence, vol. 10, Howley's cross-examination of Warren, 27–8 Feb. 1924.

68 Ibid., vol. 2, 17 Jan. 1924.

69 Ibid.

70 *Proceedings of the House of Assembly*, 28 April 1926, 534–5.

71 *Daily News*, 29 April 1926.

72 Walter Monroe, born Dublin, 1871; merchant; prime minister, 1924–8; appointed to Legislative Council, 1929; died St John's, 1952.

73 See above, 121 n79.

74 CO 532/275, Allardyce to Masterson-Smith, 17 March 1924.

75 See *Daily News, Evening Telegram, Evening Advocate*, 21 March to 9 April 1924.

76 *Daily News*, 9 April 1924.

77 CO 532/275, Allardyce to Thomas, 9 April 1924.

78 Ibid., Allardyce to Thomas, 10 May 1924.

79 Ibid.

80 CO 532/310, confidential report from P.J. Summers to Allardyce, undated, enclosed in dispatch, 7 Jan. 1925. A true bill was found on two counts against Dr Campbell, but he was eventually acquitted.

81 Ibid.

82 See above, 178 n96.

83 McDonald, 'W.F. Coaker and the Fishermen's Protective Union,' ch. 5.

84 *Evening Telegram*, 15 May 1924.

85 Ibid.

86 CO 532/275, Allardyce to Thomas, 3 July 1924.

87 Noel, *Politics in Newfoundland*, 179–85.

88 *Daily News*, 19 April 1926. Report of an audit into the affairs of the Department of Customs prior to 1925, initiated by the Monroe administration, 27 June 1924.

89 Coaker papers, W.J. Higgins to Coaker, 30 June 1925.

90 William W. Mackenzie, Baron Amulree, born Scotland, 1860; lawyer and industrial arbitrator; raised to peerage, 1929; secretary of state for air, Macdonald government, 1930–1; died 1942.

91 Dominions Office, Newfoundland Royal Commission, *Report*, 1933 (Cmd. 4480), section 121.

92 McDonald, 'W.F. Coaker and the Fishermen's Protective Union,' 276.

93 1933 Commission *Report*, section 180.

94 Ibid., section 120. On this point see also above, 142–3.

95 Ibid., section 634.

96 PANL, *Accounts of Consolidated Revenue Fund and Appropriation Accounts, 1933–39*.

97 Noel, *Politics in Newfoundland*, 233–4.

98 Amulree papers (private collection), C.A. Magrath to Lord Amulree, 3 Oct. 1933.

99 A.F.W. Plumtre, 'The Amulree Report (1933): A Review,' *CJEPS* 3 (1937): 58–71.

100 Public Record Office (London), Cab. 24/225, C.P. 321 (31), memorandum by Neville Chamberlain, 14 Dec. 1931; Cab. 24/243, C.P. 203 (33), proposal by Chamberlain for dealing with the financial position by Newfoundland, 21 Aug. 1933.

101 Public Record Office, D.O. 35, box 413, F. 11754/98, unsigned memorandum to Harding, 4 Nov. 1932; Cab. 24/244, C.P. 273 (33), note by Chamberlain, 14 Nov. 1933, referring to proposal mentioned in note 100 above.

Party Politics in Newfoundland, 1949–71: A Survey and Analysis

PETER NEARY

Looking back at the post-confederation political history of Newfoundland, it is now possible to delineate three distinct periods, each marked by a dramatic opening event. A first period obviously began with the completion of confederation and the accession to power in St John's of Joseph Roberts Smallwood. A second period can be said to have started with the Progressive Conservative victory in the federal general election of 1957 – an event which drastically altered the realities facing Smallwood and the provincial Liberal party. A third period, it could be argued, began with the sweeping Conservative victory in Newfoundland in the federal election of 1968, the first Conservative electoral victory in the province's post-confederation history. Running through these periods is a common theme: the continuing erosion of the traditional, staple, subsistence, outport economy of Newfoundland by the forces of urbanism and industrialism.

1949–57

Although a number of the members returned in the first provincial election, held on 27 May 1949, had been active in party politics before the loss of responsible government in 1934, the basic determinant of party affiliation in the immediate post-confederation period was attitude towards the issue of union with Canada. The Liberal party arose naturally out of the political machine which Smallwood and others had built up to fight the referenda campaigns of 1948 and with which they had ultimately secured union with Canada; the Progressive Conservative party inherited the support of most of those who, for one reason or another, had opposed confederation.[1] Smallwood became premier first and party leader second. The first post-confederation cabinet was sworn in on 1 April 1949, its number

Reprinted with minor editorial changes from *Journal of Canadian Studies* 6, no. 4 (1971): 3–14; 7, no. 1 (1972): 3–21, by permission.

including Leslie R. Curtis and William J. Keough, both of whom, like Smallwood, held office continuously into the 1970s. On 28 April 1949, the founding convention of the Liberal party assembled at the Church Lads Brigade Armoury in St John's which had been decorated for the occasion with flags and bunting scavenged from the convention that the previous year had chosen Louis St Laurent leader of the national Liberal party.[2] On 30 April, this convention unanimously selected Premier Smallwood to be leader of the provincial wing of the party.[3] F. Gordon Bradley, who had been closely associated with Smallwood in the struggle for confederation, was 'unanimously selected to be the Newfoundland Liberal Party head in the federal field.'[4] The St John's *Evening Telegram* captured something of the reforming zeal and brimming self-confidence of the 1949 generation of Newfoundland Liberals in this account of remarks made by Smallwood about the convention: 'For the first time in history ... a party is being born in this convention by the hand of the people. This was no small hole in the wall affair held in a back room. People from every bay and district of Newfoundland were here to launch a party. They were the blood and sinew of Newfoundland, for the people make a country.'[5] In the event the Liberal party of Newfoundland, which Smallwood described in one of his most memorable phrases as the party of the 'toiling masses,' was not to meet in convention again for over twenty years.

During the founding convention of the party Smallwood announced that the first provincial election would be held on 27 May. Needless to say, his political opponents had been organizing for some time in anticipation of this announcement. On 8 April, H.G.R. Mews, who had opposed union with Canada, had been chosen leader of the provincial Progressive Conservative party at a meeting in St John's.[6] His election had been followed by a visit to the province of the national party leader, George Drew, who thus became the first important 'mainland' politician to venture onto the hustings in the new province. His visit did not bode well for the future of his party there. While in St John's he stated that, although he was not opposed to the union of Newfoundland and Canada as such, he objected to the procedure by which union had been effected.[7] In the circumstances the approach taken by the Conservative leader could hardly have been more inappropriate. Obviously, if the Conservatives were to advance in Newfoundland, they would have to forget about the confederation issue and concentrate on producing alternative policies to those of the Liberals within the context of Canadian federalism. Drew's strategy merely encouraged the already popular view, cultivated by Smallwood and the Liberals at every opportunity, that the Conservative party was founded upon obscurantist anti-confederate sentiment. Rightly or wrongly, the Conservatives were identified with this origin until a new generation of Newfoundlanders came of age in the 1960s. In view of the obvious and immediate economic benefits of confederation, the identification of their party with the old anti-confederate cause was a great liability to the Conservatives during the first years of union.

That the political future belonged to the heirs of the confederate movement was made abundantly clear by the result of the first provincial election: the Conservatives were unable even to hold all the constituencies which had voted against union with Canada. The 1949 election gave the Liberals an overwhelming majority in the House of Assembly and set the electoral pattern for the province for the next twenty years. Of the twenty-eight members elected, twenty-two were Liberals and only five were Progressive Conservatives. The one remaining seat was captured by an independent, Major Peter Cashin, who had been the most bellicose and obscurantist of the anti-confederates. Ferryland, the constituency which voted independent, had a generation before been the political base of Sir Michael Cashin, Major Cashin's father and prime minister of Newfoundland briefly in 1919.[8] In the 1948 referenda on the constitutional future of Newfoundland, its electors, who were almost all Catholic and of Irish descent, had led their countrymen in support for the proposition that the pre-1934 constitutional system should be restored. The extent of the Liberal sweep in 1949 is evident in the fact that the party polled over 90 per cent of the popular vote in five constituencies and over 80 per cent in another seven. Overall the Liberal share of the popular vote was 65.5 per cent, while that of their Conservative opponents was a modest 32.9 per cent. Clearly, the electorate had taken to heart one of the Liberal slogans, 'Let Joe finish the job.' Geographically, the Conservatives were able to win seats only in St John's and its immediate hinterland. This identification with the capital, which historically had been the object of great resentment and jealousy in the outports, was yet another Conservative liability in the 1950s. The 1949 election result cannot, however, be explained in terms of a simple rural-urban split. Thus, while it is true that the Liberals carried most of the constituencies where the traditional outport way of life was strong, they also carried the urban constituencies of Grand Falls and Humber, where the principal economic activity was pulp and paper manufacturing and where industrialism had made a great impact on the new province.

Yet another prominent feature of the 1949 result was an obvious religious split carried over from the struggle between confederates and anti-confederates. Anti-confederate sentiment had been strongest on the Avalon Peninsula and it was in this area, where there was a high concentration of Catholic voters, that the Conservatives had their greatest success in the first provincial election. This was a pattern that was also to endure and was a striking contrast to the situation elsewhere in Canada. It was not until 1962 that the Conservatives were able to win seats off the Avalon Peninsula. Moreover, of the eighteen Newfoundland Conservatives who sat in the House of Assembly in St John's or the House of Commons in Ottawa between 1949 and 1965, seventeen were Roman Catholics, as were four of the first five leaders of the opposition Smallwood faced.[9] In a province that in 1949 was still largely preindustrial and where sectarian loyalties were still deeply felt, so strong an association with a particular religious group was an obvious handicap to the Conservatives. Yet a good case could be made for the view that geography and real or imagined economic interest had been more important than denominational affiliation in determining the outcome of the 1948 referenda.[10] Thus, there were Avalon Peninsula districts where Catholics were not in a majority which had voted against confederation, while there were districts away from the Avalon Peninsula where the percentage of Catholic voters was high which had voted for confederation.

The overwhelming Liberal victory in the provincial election was repeated in the federal election which followed. Since Newfoundlanders had no experience of federalism and were concerned above all else with their immediate social and economic problems, it is not surprising that the 1949 federal campaign was decidedly 'provincial' in tone. The same politicians who had a few weeks before battled for control of the House of Assembly in St John's now fought over the seven seats allocated to Newfoundland in the House of Commons, and the same factors which had influenced the outcome of the first contest were decisive again in the second. What the 1949 federal campaign showed above all else was that federal politics in Newfoundland would be a mere adjunct of provincial politics and that the real political sovereign of the province would continue to reside in St John's. Although F. Gordon Bradley, who had been sworn into the federal cabinet on 1 April 1949, as secretary of state, had been chosen by the founding convention of the Newfoundland Liberal party to lead its federal wing, no attempt was made to create a separate federal organization for the province. Instead the management of the federal constituencies was left to Smallwood and his provincial organization, and there was no doubt that the victory which followed was of the provincial party's making. The serious battling in the 1949 campaign was confined to the two St John's seats, which on this occasion were carried by the Conservatives. Until 1968 the only debatable point about the outcome of any federal election in Newfoundland was whether 'Joey' would win five, six, or all seven of the seats in the province. St Laurent toured Newfoundland during the 1949 campaign but he did so under Smallwood's patronage and had no significant following or independent standing in the province, as no mainland politician, with the possible exception of J.W. Pickersgill, has ever had since. The relationship between the federal and provincial Liberal parties which was fixed in the early months of union and which endured essentially intact until 1968 was a striking example of the phenomenon of elite consensus at work in the Canadian party system. The federal leadership accepted Smallwood's lead in Newfoundland affairs and when in power channelled federal patronage to the province through him. In return Smallwood

209 Party Politics, 1949-71

delivered in election after election a minimum of five of Newfoundland's seven seats to his Ottawa allies. St Laurent and Pearson got the seats and Smallwood made the announcements. The political importance of this arrangement to Small-wood cannot be overestimated, since 'Uncle Ottawa,' as he affectionately came to describe the federal government later on, alone could provide the improved standard of living which the proponents of confederation had promised and on which the fortunes of the Liberal party in the province soon became dependent.[11] Until the Conservatives came to power in Ottawa in 1957 Smallwood was in the enviable position of being associated politically with every federal program in Newfoundland – an enormous asset in a province where, because of historical conditioning, economic expectation was low and even the most modest material gain in 'mainland' terms seemed an impressive economic achievement.

Unquestionably, the most significant party political development in the first years of Newfoundland's Canadian history was the growth of Smallwood's personal political power. By the close of a decade of union his mastery of his immediate political following and his standing with the electorate was such that one might well look to the third world rather than the other Canadian provinces for a suitable standard of comparison. Many factors contributed to this development. The mood of Newfoundland in the 1950s was one of great optimism and a notable contrast to that of Nova Scotia after its entry into confederation. For almost everyone in the new province confederation meant immediately more cash in hand. The extension of the Canadian welfare state to Newfoundland instantaneously improved the provincial living standard, while the elaboration of a comprehensive provincial social welfare system during the 1950s gave further relief to a people who had always lived close to the economic abyss and who were still haunted by the memory of the economic catastrophe of the 1930s. Materialism, no bad thing in itself, was initially on the Liberal side. Social welfare and the promise of greater economic security lay at the root of Smallwood's political power. Any people's estimate of its political leaders is likely to be a function of comparison – comparison with its past condition, or with the fortunes of others, or with what it believes to be possible. In the immediate post-confederation period of Newfoundland's history, comparison was all on Smallwood's side. The recipients of family allowances and old age pensions, the parents who sent their children to a transformed educational system, and the beneficiaries of a greatly expanded public health service had no doubt about the wisdom of the course which had been taken in 1949. A decade after the decisive second referendum of 1948, in which over forty-seven per cent of those voting had opposed union with Canada, it would have been difficult to find an opponent of confederation in the province.

Dramatic material advance such as Newfoundlanders experienced in the first years of confederation would perhaps have brought political success to any political leader associated with it. But the extent and durability of the power Smallwood achieved can only be understood when other considerations relating to the unique historical experience of Newfoundlanders and his own skill as a political manager are taken into account.

For a variety of social and economic reasons Newfoundlanders had not developed a very deep understanding of or attachment to democratic values.[12] In 1934, in the face of the crisis of the Great Depression, responsible government had actually been abandoned in favour of government by a commission appointed by the British government. Between 1934 and 1946, when delegates were elected to a 'national convention' to consider the constitutional future of the country, no official had been elected in Newfoundland, except at the municipal level. Moreover, local government, which has done much elsewhere to cultivate respect for representative institutions, was not extensively developed in Newfoundland until the post-confederation period was well advanced. Hence, there was much in their history that had conditioned Newfoundlanders, especially those who lived in the tradition-bound outports, to expect authority to flow from above. Accordingly, the lack of democratic structure in their political parties meant little to most Newfoundlanders until recently, and there is reason to suspect how much it means even now. The centralization of power which occurred in the Liberal party after 1949 was clearly facilitated by the special character of the Newfoundland political culture. Beginning with the provincial election campaign of 1951, the common practice of the party was for Premier Smallwood to announce the names of the Liberal candidates, both federally and provincially. Only after the debacle it suffered in the federal election of 1968 did the Liberal party in Newfoundland begin to acknowledge in practice the need for democratic candidate selection procedures at constituency level.

As a political manager, Smallwood was in a class by himself in the province after 1949. A man of enormous energy and application, he seldom found himself on the defensive before the severe setback his party suffered in the federal election of 1968 and even after that he conceded little to his opponents. In his debating skill and ability to use the mass media effectively he had political gifts of incalculable worth. His public speaking technique, refined through the years, placed great emphasis on the repetition of essential facts and ideas. To the ears of educated listeners with middle-class aspirations this approach often seemed patronizing, vulgar, and simple-minded, but in the 1950s there were few middle-class Newfoundlanders. Smallwood spoke in a language the common people could understand and was a born entertainer and storyteller in a society where these skills were still highly valued. Like William Aberhart he was well known as a radio personality before he achieved success in politics. 'The Barrelman,' a program he began in 1937 to 'make Newfoundland better known to Newfoundlanders,' had given him a command of the medium which no other local politician could match.[13] As a member of the National Convention, Smallwood had virtually ceased to address himself to his fellow delegates, concentrating instead on using the convention as a platform to bring the gospel of confederation to the people via radio. In the immediate post-confederation period the radio spectacular, in which the premier would announce the details of some new social welfare, health, educational, or industrial advance, became a regular feature of Newfoundland political life. The fact that Smallwood made virtually all major announcements himself placed his ministers in a position of great inferiority to him in terms of public esteem and concentrated party control ever more tightly in his hands. When television was introduced to Newfoundland in 1955, Smallwood proved himself almost as adept a performer on the new medium as he had been on the old. In the 1960s his remarkable versatility as a radio performer was again evidenced by the ease with which he adjusted to the demands of the 'open-line' situation.

The position Smallwood achieved can, then, be related to his unique insight into the outlook of Newfoundlanders and his ability to apply that insight, through the mass media, to the service of political power. In his political style he attempted to combine the roles of 'man of the people' and 'visionary' leader. The familiar phrases of the common people of Newfoundland were never far from his lips; yet he was careful to distinguish himself sharply, even in his dress, from those around him. He sought through his rhetoric to communicate to the people a sense of destiny, to make them feel that through him and his government they were participating in a great historical drama – the building of what he had called 'the new Newfoundland.' Smallwood's instinctive theatrical sense found political employment in this work: prestige projects were given high priority by the government and public demonstrations to celebrate the people's progress became part of his standard political repertoire. Perhaps the most famous of the latter was the public celebration which he organized in 1961 to mark the opening of the new campus of Memorial University. Once again the parallels that come to mind are from the third world – as any visitor to Newfoundland who sees the prestige buildings of the party grouped together along the Prince Philip Parkway, Smallwood's creation, might readily attest.

But Liberal power and Smallwood's domination of his party could not have been founded on rhetoric and skilful public relations alone. In the area of electoral strategy few tricks were missed on the government side during the first years of confederation. In particular the changes made in the electoral system after 1949 clearly favoured the continuance of Liberal rule. Historically, governments in Newfoundland had maintained as one of the objectives to be achieved in the determination of constituency boundaries the equitable representation in the legislature of the various religious groups into which the population was divided.[14]

TABLE 1
Each party's percentage of popular vote and of members elected in all constituencies, exclusive of those won by acclamation, in Newfoundland provincial elections, 1949–66

	L	PC	CCF/NDP	UNP
1949*	65.5/78.6	32.9/17.9	–	–
1951	63.6/78.3	34.4/21.7	–	–
1956	66.3/90.6	30.9/ 9.4	1.7/——	–
1959	58.0/85.7	25.3/ 8.6	8.0/——	8.2/5.7
1962	58.7/79.5	36.6/17.9	3.5/——	0.5/——
1966	61.8/92.3	34.0/ 7.7	1.8/——	–

SOURCE: Newfoundland election returns, *Parliamentary Guide*;
Evening Telegram
*Includes Labrador

TABLE 2
Each party's percentage of popular vote and of members elected in constituencies contested by it, exclusive of constituencies won by acclamation, in Newfoundland provincial elections, 1949–66

	L	PC	CCF/NDP	UNP
1949	65.5/78.6	32.9/17.9	–	–
1951	63.6/78.3	36.4/23.8	–	–
1956	66.3/90.6	34.3/10.7	6.2/——	–
1959	67.0/93.7	27.3/ 9.4	13.0/——	24.5/22.2
1962	58.7/79.5	40.1/20.0	29.7/——	14.7/——
1966	61.8/92.3	35.5/ 7.9	21.0/——	–

SOURCE: Newfoundland election returns, *Parliamentary Guide*; *Evening Telegram*

This was so, even though, as the 1948 referenda had shown, voting had by no means strictly followed denominational lines. Originally, the denominational principle had been introduced to rectify a grievance felt by the Roman Catholic part of the population which, before the introduction of responsible government in 1855, had been virtually excluded from public office. In practice, as labour mobility had increased, its application had become more and more difficult. Nevertheless, it was used by Smallwood to justify changes in the electoral system which were made in 1955 and 1962. In 1955 the membership of the House of Assembly was increased from twenty-eight to thirty-six, a change which, in the premier's words, 'made twelve Roman Catholic Districts, twelve Church of

TABLE 3
Liberal and PC members elected by number of electors on official constituency voters lists in Newfoundland provincial elections, 1949–66

	1949*		1951		1956		1959		1962		1966		Total	
	L	PC	L	PC	L	PC	L	PC	L	PC	L	PC	L	PC
1,000–1,999					2		2		2				6	
2,000–2,999			1		2		2		2		3		10	
3,000–3,999	1		1	1	4		4		8	1	7		25	2
4,000–4,999	4		4		8		7	1	8		8		39	1
5,000–5,999	6	1	7		4		4		4	1	6	1	31	3
6,000–6,999	5		5		9		8	1	5		3	1	35	2
7,000–7,999	1		1		3	1	4		2	3	6		17	4
8,000–8,999						2		1	1	1	1		2	4
9,000–9,999		2	1	1	1				2	1	2	1	5	6
10,000–	4	2	3	3							3		10	5
Total	21	5	23	5	32	4	31	3	34	7	39	3	180	27

SOURCE: Newfoundland election returns, *Parliamentary Guide*; *Evening Telegram*
*Does not include Labrador

England Districts and twelve Nonconformist Districts.'[15] A second principle used to defend the changes made in 1955 was that the electoral system should be weighted in favour of rural voters since, as Smallwood disarmingly put it, 'the people of the countryside, what we call the outports, are socially sounder than the people of the cities and urban areas.'[16] In 1962 the number of seats in the assembly was enlarged to forty-two with the same principles of redistribution being followed. The deviation of the electoral system from the democratic precept that all votes should be of equal worth is apparent in tables 1, 2, and 3.

That Smallwood should have glorified the rural voter in this fashion is ironic since he had maintained from the moment he became premier that the path of progress for the province lay through 'make or break' industrialization.[17] The economic history of Newfoundland during the previous half-century encouraged this strategy. During that time the demography of Newfoundland had been radically altered, owing to the movement of people out of the outports to become either full-time or part-time wage workers in an expanding 'modern' sector of the local economy or migrants to the United States or Canada. Thus, although the popular image of Newfoundlanders, perhaps even to themselves, remained at mid-century that of a fishing people, other forms of economic activity had easily supplanted the fishery in economic worth. Between 1891 and 1895 fishery production had accounted for 84 per cent of the value of all production in the major commodity-producing fishery, mining, and forestry sectors of the economy; the comparable figure for the 1936–40 period was 22.7 per cent.[18] During the Second World War the relative decline in the economic importance of the fishery had been temporarily reversed, but after confederation the trend of the inter-war years reasserted itself. During the period 1946–8, while the effects of the war were still being felt, fishery production accounted for 43.7 per cent of the value of all commodity production in the primary industries mentioned above. But over the period 1958–63 this figure was reduced to 16.4 per cent.[19] It has been estimated that in 1956 the primary fishing industry contributed only 4 per cent and the fish processing industry 2 per cent of the gross provincial product.[20] Yet these industries still engaged about 15 to 16 per cent of the labour force. This disparity showed that, despite extensive out-migration of population, the 'modern' sector of the economy had never been capable of absorbing all the surplus labour available in the fishery. This in turn reflected the fact that the 'modern' sector was built on extractive resource industries, heavily dependent on external demand and limited in their ability to expand by the availability of resources. Because of its geographical disadvantages little secondary industry had been established in Newfoundland and this remains true to the present.

The situation facing Smallwood on his accession to power was, therefore, not unlike that which had faced many recent third world leaders.[21] The intervention of outside capital and the needs of more developed economies had made serious inroads into the traditional outport society which had grown up around the fishery. This in turn had created in Newfoundland a 'dual' economy: a low-productivity, tradition-bound, outport sector, which supported a large part of the population but at a low standard of living; and a 'modern' sector, based on mineral and forestry resources, service industries, and, after the Anglo-American 'destroyers for bases' deal of 1940, the employment provided by American bases. The 'modern' sector accounted for most of the wealth created in the economy but had a growth potential limited by the availability of resources and the vagaries of external demand.

Initially, because of his close association with the immediate economic benefits which confederation brought to all groups of Newfoundlanders, Smallwood enjoyed widespread support in the areas of the province which belonged to the 'modern' sector of the economy, St John's included. But the referenda results of 1948 and the provincial and federal elections of 1949 all showed that, in general, his support was greatest where the outport way of life remained strong. It was Smallwood's good fortune that the electoral map he inherited in 1949 was weighted in favour of the areas from which he drew his greatest support. Not surprisingly, the result of the redistribution he executed in 1955 was to transfer even more power to the outport constituencies. He rewarded his outport supporters with the benefits of the Canadian welfare state and with various support payments to bolster their low incomes from fishing. It has been estimated that by 1961 'the more direct forms of support to the Newfoundland fishing industry had risen to an amount that equalled ... 65 per cent of the total income generated in the combined fishing and fish processing industry.'[22] The support or transfer payment which perhaps yielded the greatest political return was unemployment insurance, which was introduced for fishermen in 1956. In return for the unprecedented largesse that Smallwood provided, outport Newfoundlanders gave him their loyalty and asked few questions.

With a secure electoral base in the outports and strong support in the rest of the province Smallwood set as the first priority of his new government the expansion of the 'modern' sector of the economy through industrialization and the exploitation of resources which had not hitherto been developed or fully utilized. Accordingly, the attention he gave to the 'traditional' economy can be seen as largely a holding operation to tide the fishing population over while the alternative sources of employment were being created which would end forever the stranglehold of the capricious fishery on the economic furtunes of the Newfoundland people. The duality of the Newfoundland economic and social context helps explain the curious blend of 'progressive' and 'reactionary' elements which Smallwood has exhibited. His political circumstances required him to be at home equally in a board room in New York or an Orange Lodge in Bonavista Bay.

In 1951 Smallwood made the issue of industrialization the focus of his second provincial election campaign. The previous year a Latvian economist, Alfred Valdmanis, had arrived in St John's as economic adviser to the government. A rapid series of negotiations aimed at the establishment of a number of small industries had followed. The culmination of these developments was the surprise announcement by Smallwood on 1 November 1951 that he intended to seek immediately a new mandate from the people in support of the course of development the government was following.[23] The announcement of the election caught his Conservative opponents almost totally unprepared. The first Conservative leader, H.G.R. Mews, had suffered personal defeat in the 1949 election and had subsequently abandoned the party leadership for a career in St John's municipal politics: elected mayor in 1950, he held this office continuously until his retirement in 1965. In the absence of Mews, the leadership of the small Conservative group in the House of Assembly had passed to John G. Higgins, a St John's lawyer. When Higgins decided not to seek re-election in 1951, the Conservatives entered their second provincial campaign without a leader and with very little opportunity to find one before the voting was held, since Smallwood had scheduled the election for 26 November. In the circumstances, the direction of the campaign was assumed by Gordon Higgins, the member of the federal House of Commons for St John's East.[24] This time the party was unable to field a full slate of candidates: five seats were conceded to the Liberals by acclamation and in two others the challenge to the government was left to independent candidates. The election produced another Liberal rout. On a reduced turnout the Conservative share of the popular vote rose slightly but the party's standing in the Legislature remained the same, and the five members it elected were again all from St John's and its immediate hinterland. When the House of Assembly met again, the leadership of the Conservative group was assumed by Peter Cashin, who had abandoned the seat he had won as an independent in 1949 and successfully contested St John's West for the Conservatives.

Since political success implies political failure, Smallwood's strength can only be fully understood when the weakness of his opponents is also considered. The Conservatives in Newfoundland clearly laboured after 1949 under many disadvantages, not least among them Liberal control of patronage, a potent political weapon in a community where every job counted and a significant proportion of the population was directly dependent on the Government for its livelihood. But the malaise which descended on the Conservatives after their second defeat was partly of their own making. While it was wrong to say that the party harboured a desire to reverse the union of 1949, it had inherited, as would become clear in the *annus mirabilis* of 1959, something of the social and economic conservatism and parochialism that had made the anti-confederate cause so strong. After 1951 defeatism spread in the party, candidates became hard to find and defections began to occur. Except for a token presence which it maintained in a few of the larger centres away from the Avalon Peninsula, the Conservatives virtually retreated into St John's to await the death of the government by its own hand. Except at election time, outport Newfoundland became for the party almost a *terra incognita*. When the long series of post-confederation Liberal victories was finally broken in the federal election of 1968, most observers agreed that the result was an 'anti-Joey' rather than a pro-Conservative vote.[25] Significantly, at the moment of their first electoral success, the Conservatives had still to finish the job of establishing constituency associations throughout the province.

During his early years as premier, Smallwood was probably given worse moments by defections from his own ranks than he was by the opposition. The first defection from the government occurred in March 1951, when Edward Russell, the minister of natural resources, resigned.[26] This resignation proved to be of little practical significance, but it was symbolically important since Russell was a strong supporter of the cooperative movement and a figure out of Smallwood's 'socialist' past. Harold Horwood, a close associate of Smallwood in the struggle for confederation and member of Labrador from 1949–51, also broke with the government.

In his 'Political Notebook,' which he began publishing in the *Evening Telegram* in 1952, he became one of Smallwood's sternest critics. A potentially very dangerous situation for the government arose in April 1954 when Alfred Valdmanis, who Smallwood once said would, as an economic developer, be 'worth his weight in gold to Newfoundland,' was arrested and charged with fraud in connection with his work for the government.[27] Valdmanis was subsequently tried, found guilty, and sentenced to a four-year prison term at hard labour. A year after the sensational Valdmanis arrest, Dr Herbert L. Pottle, the minister of public welfare and an ordained minister of the United Church of Canada, left the government over the conduct of the economic development program.[28] Unlike Russell, Pottle had not let his cabinet colleagues know in advance that he was contemplating resignation and his announcement caught Smallwood completely by surprise. Pottle had a well established public reputation, a good ministerial record, and, seemingly, the ambition to lead an uprising against the premier. After leaving the cabinet he stated that he intended to remain in the House of Assembly as a Liberal but not as a Smallwood Liberal.[29] He failed, however, to rally much support against the government and three months after his resignation left the province.

The Valdmanis scandal and the doubt cast upon the government's economic development by the Pottle resignation gave the Conservatives promising campaign material, but the third provincial election, which was held on 2 October 1956, left them farther behind the Liberals than ever. Far from damaging Smallwood, the Valdmanis episode and its sequel required a new definition of his political power. The fact that he came through this period unscathed fed the myth of political invincibility that was growing up around him, both within and without the Liberal party. Among his opponents this fed the defeatism that was already rampant; among his followers it promoted unquestioning loyalty.

The Conservatives were led in the 1956 campaign by Malcolm Hollett, who had entered the House of Assembly after winning a by-election in 1952 in St John's West. In January 1953, Peter Cashin's leadership had been repudiated by his Conservative colleagues in the House of Assembly after he had publicly critized Gordon Higgins, the Conservative federal member for St John's East. Hollett had subsequently been chosen in his stead.[30] Cashin had then run as an independent against Higgins in the 1953 federal election. His intervention had given the Liberals victory in St John's East by splitting the opposition vote there and had allowed Smallwood to sweep the province. St John's West, the other federal constituency the Conservatives had won in 1949, had fallen to the Liberals in 1953 in a straight two-way fight. The outcome of the 1953 federal election had been another staggering blow to Conservative hopes in Newfoundland. Nevertheless, with an established leader they were better prepared, organizationally at least, to fight a campaign in 1956 than they had been in 1951, though three seats were conceded to the Liberals by acclamation and the anti-government fight left to the Co-operative Commonwealth Federation (CCF) in four others. On the Liberal side, although the five-year term of the government was drawing to a close, the timing of the election had been carefully planned. In April the provincial government had introduced a comprehensive medical care program for children of sixteen years and under and in August the federal government had announced that unemployment insurance would be introduced for fishermen. In the context of Newfoundland society these were economic achievements of great magnitude, and against them and the Smallwood slogan of 'The best eight years yet' the Conservative assault foundered. When the votes were counted, the Liberals were farther ahead both in seats and popular vote than ever before.

The timing of the introduction of the unemployment insurance scheme for fishermen was indicative of the close working relationship which had been forged between Smallwood and the federal Liberal leaders. On 12 June 1953, Gordon Bradley had been appointed to the Senate and J.W. Pickersgill had taken his place in the cabinet as secretary of state. At Smallwood's invitation Pickersgill had then contested Bonavista-Twillingate, the constituency vacated by Bradley. His Conservative opponent in the election had been Edward Russell, Smallwood's former cabinet colleague. The premier had campaigned enthusiastically for his federal ally, telling a St John's audience on one occasion: 'By the time I get through with Ned Russell there won't be enough of him left to stuff a thimble.'[31] In the event Pickersgill had won the seat handily. Like all good political deals, the arrangement made between Pickersgill and Smallwood in 1953 was mutually beneficial. The benefit which accrued to Pickersgill was simple: he obtained a safe seat in the House of Commons. Smallwood's return was more complex. Pickersgill had a long record of service to the Liberal party which went back to the King era and, as Smallwood said later, 'knew where all the bodies were buried in Ottawa.'[32] Accordingly, he could command a standing in the cabinet which was beyond the reach of any Newfoundlander and was well qualified, as the introduction of the unemployment insurance scheme for fishermen showed, to act as a lobbyist in the scramble among the provinces for federal funds. By 1953 Smallwood had become very dissatisfied with Bradley's performance in Ottawa and was anxious to have a stronger agent on Parliament Hill.[32] Pickersgill met his requirements perfectly. The fact that he was a 'mainlander,' committed to a career in national politics and without independent standing in Newfoundland, also held advantages for Smallwood, both negatively and positively. Negatively, Pickersgill's occupancy of Newfoundland's seat in the federal cabinet ensured that no Newfoundland Liberal would be able to use Ottawa as a base to challenge the position Smallwood had established for himself in the party. Positively, Pickersgill's obvious dependence on Smallwood's patronage helped ensure that the federal leadership of the party would continue to work through Smallwood in Newfoundland.

1957–68

The accession of the Conservatives to power nationally in 1957 radically altered the circumstances in Newfoundland politics. In the 1957 federal election the Newfoundland Conservatives won back the two St John's seats they had won in 1949 but lost in 1953. One of the Conservatives elected, W.J. Browne, became a minister without portfolio in the Diefenbaker cabinet. To the extent that Smallwood's political power was founded upon his credibility as the indispensable intermediary between the Newfoundland people and the federal government, a great gap in his political defences was opened by these events. If they had the wit to use it, the local Conservatives now had, through their ability to influence federal policy towards Newfoundland, a powerful political lever. The possibilities inherent in the situation for the party were made plain in the federal election of 1958, which ensured that Smallwood would have to fight a provincial campaign while his opponents held power in Ottawa. Not only were the two Conservatives elected in 1957 easily returned, but the party's share of the popular vote rose to 45.2 per cent, the highest percentage popular vote it had ever received in a federal or provincial election in the province. In two constituencies away from the St John's area – Trinity-Conception and Humber-St George's – the party polled respectively 41.4 per cent and 43.2 per cent of the votes cast and was at last within striking distance of the Liberals. Yet when the next provincial election was held in 1959 the party dropped to an all time low in a provincial contest, both in seats and popular vote. The explanation for this decline and for the failure of the Newfoundland Conservatives to exploit the opportunity which the Diefenbaker victory had given them is to be found in two controversies which made 1959 one of the most turbulent years in Newfoundland's troubled political history.

The first of these controversies arose in February 1959 when Smallwood intervened in a strike which had been in progress for some time against the Anglo-Newfoundland Development (AND) Company, one of the two large pulp and paper concerns operating in the province, by a local of the International Woodworkers of America. The IWA had entered Newfoundland in 1956, when an organizing team had been sent to the province. A long inter-union battle had followed between the IWA, seeking to win the support of Newfoundland loggers, and a number of local unions, seeking to maintain the right they had established for themselves to represent the loggers' interests. In this struggle the IWA had been ably led by H. Landon Ladd, a native of British Columbia and the president of district 2 of the union. A tough, experienced and determined unionist, schooled in the militant traditions of the west coast labour movement, Ladd had advanced the cause of the union on many fronts. Newspaper advertising had been used extensively and effectively and a radio campaign for support had been launched through a special program for loggers entitled 'Green Gold.' Finally, in May 1958, local

2-254 of the union had obtained legal certification under the terms of the New-foundland Labour Relations Act as the legal bargaining agent for loggers em-ployed by the AND Company.[34] Another IWA local was later certified as the bargaining agent for loggers employed by the contractors who supplied wood to the other large paper-manufacturing company in the province, Bowater's New-foundland Pulp and Paper Mills Ltd.[35] Once certified, local 2-254 began negotia-tions with the AND Company for a wage and working agreement for its mem-bership. When a stalemate was reached in these negotiations a conciliation board was appointed by the Provincial Department of Labour under the terms of the Labour Relations Act to recommend a settlement.[36] When this board reported, its recommendations were accepted by local 2-254 but rejected by the AND Company. At this point the union did what it had every legal right to do and what any union might be expected to do in the circumstances: on 31 December 1958, it went on strike.[37] The strike proved long and bitter. On the company side there was a grim determination to keep out the IWA whose resources and bargaining power con-trasted sharply with those of the local unions it was seeking to replace; on the union side victory was essential if the IWA was to maintain the foothold it had so painfully bought in the province. Amidst growing tension the deadlock was finally broken when Smallwood sensationally intervened in the strike on the evening of 12 February in a highly emotional speech heard throughout the province.[38] Accusing the IWA of lawlessness and of threatening the provincial economy, Smallwood called on the loggers to drive the union from Newfoundland. In place of the IWA he offered the loggers membership in a new union to be organized immediately by the minister of welfare, C. Max Lane. Throughout this speech Smallwood was careful to distinguish between the 'Newfoundland' loggers and the 'outside' leaders who had misled them. In language strikingly reminiscent of the nativism which had surfaced during other great confrontations between capital and labour in Canadian history, Smallwood characterized the IWA as a subversive outside influence incom-patible with the Newfoundland way of life. 'How dare these outsiders,' he declared, 'come into this decent Christian Province and by such desperate, such terrible methods try to seize control of our Province's main industry.' History and geography had combined in Newfoundland to produce a strong particularism, and Smallwood's emotional appeal swept all before it. His intervention caused anger and dismay in areas of the province where the IWA was strong, but away from those areas the few voices raised in support of the union were, for the most part, lost amidst the shrill rhetoric of its opponents. There was even an attempt by students at Memorial University to organize a demonstration against the union. Smallwood's ability to use the mass media was never more in evidence than during this strike. Moreover, the local press, led by the St John's *Evening Telegram*, the newspaper with the largest circulation in the province, lined up solidly behind him in the stand he had taken.[39] For a time the questioning voice of Ed Finn was heard in the *Telegram* and its sister paper, the Corner Brook *Western Star*, but he resigned from the managing editorship of the latter paper when the *Telegram* organization persisted in its pro-government policy.[40] In combatting the unfavourable publicity which its labour policy attracted on the mainland, the government had the able assistance of Newfoundland's leading TV personality at the time and a future minister in the Trudeau government, Don Jamieson.

The political implications of the government's intervention in the strike situation began to unfold on 23 February when Smallwood introduced a resolution in the House of Assembly condemning 'the International Woodworkers of America for its conduct in Newfoundland' and declaring 'that, by this conduct, the said union has become a stumbling block to the pulp and paper industry and a danger to the public interest.'[41] The premier's motion was supported by all four Conservative members. The report in the *Evening Telegram* on the stand taken by the leader of the opposition read in part as follows:

We are on this side ... the natural opponents of that side ... but we are here long enough to know that there are times when to oppose would be the worst thing in the world to do ... I watched a union official of the I.W.A. on T.V. ... I was nauseated. This man ... threatened to destroy the economy of Newfoundland ... to strangle off the life blood of Newfoundland ... I am not prepared to stand by and see even the loggers under the leadership of the I.W.A. disrupt the whole economy of Newfoundland. We of the Opposition cannot do other than agree with the Premier's resolution ... [42]

The result of this development was an immediate split in the ranks of the PC party in Newfoundland. In industrial Corner Brook, where the labour movement was supporting the IWA, the local Conservative association, the second largest in the province, dissociated itself from the stand taken by the Conservative members of the legislature.[43] This split was confirmed when the opposition supported the legislation which the government introduced to give effect to its labour policy, even though this went beyond the decertification of the IWA locals and effected basic changes in the procedures governing all trade union operations in the province.[44] These additional changes were justified by the premier, at least in part, on the ground that they would allow his government to outlaw the Teamsters union in the province. At the time of the IWA strike the agent for this particular union in Newfoundland was the president of the Newfoundland Federation of Labour, which was vigorously supporting the strikers. Describing the leadership of the Teamsters as 'pimps, panderers, white slavers, murderers, embezzlers, extortioners, manslaughters, and dope peddlers,' the premier predicted that Newfoundland would be 'holding a torch to the rest of Canada' in the action it was taking against the union.[45] 'We'll blot it off the face of the good earth of Newfoundland. There will be no Hoffa in Newfoundland. There will be no toehold of Hoffaism in Newfoundland.'[46]

On 11 March, five days after the bills amending the Labour Relations Act and decertifying the IWA had been passed by the House of Assembly, a riot occurred in the small central Newfoundland town of Badger, the focal point of the strike activity, which was continuing despite the hostility of the government. A constable of the Newfoundland constabulary, members of which had been sent to the area from St John's, was fatally injured in this incident. Before this outbreak of violence at Badger the provincial authorities, through the federal minister of justice, had requested the RCMP, which was normally responsible under the terms of a federal-provincial agreement for all policing in Newfoundland outside the City of St John's, to send reinforcements to the province.[47] On the order of the minister of justice, Davie Fulton, the reinforcements requested were now assembled but they were halted en route to Newfoundland after the federal cabinet had met and decided to refuse the Newfoundland request lest the RCMP be used, in effect, to break the strike.[48] A protracted controversy now began between the provincial government, personified by Smallwood, and the federal government, personified by Diefenbaker, over the legality of the federal government's action. This controversy was fed by the resignation of the RCMP commissioner, L.H. Nicholson, who had favoured compliance with the Newfoundland request.[49] The RCMP controversy compounded the problems of the Newfoundland Progressive Conservatives. The Newfoundland representative in the federal cabinet, W.J. Browne, supported the decision of his colleagues but the other Conservative MP from the province, James McGrath, while disagreeing with the methods of Premier Smallwood, declined to endorse fully the actions of the cabinet.[50] On the other hand, the events of 6–11 March also disrupted the Liberal caucus in Ottawa. Canadian opinion generally seemed strongly opposed to what Smallwood was doing to the IWA and his actions constituted a great embarrassment to the federal Liberal leadership. Accordingly, Pearson was under great pressure, both within and without the caucus, to disown his Newfoundland lieutenant.[51] At the same time he was under pressure from Pickersgill and the other four Newfoundland Liberal MPs to do no such thing. In the end it was their view that prevailed. Pearson never took a clear stand one way or the other. On 16 March he said in the house that, on the basis of the information he then had, he 'would be unable as leader of the party to agree with certain of the procedures that have been followed or with certain provisions of the new laws,' but he never went in public beyond these generalities.[52] With both Conservatives and Liberals compromised on the strike issue by their Newfoundland followers, the parliamentary expression of the demand for disallowance of the Newfoundland legislation which was being voiced by many Canadians, both within and without the labour movement, was left to the CCF.[53]

The IWA controversy was still in progress when another issue arose which was to have an even more devastating effect on the fortunes of the Conservative party in Newfoundland. Under term 29 of the terms of union by which Newfoundland had entered confederation, the government of Canada had agreed to appoint, within eight years of the date of union, a royal commission 'to review the financial position of the Province of Newfoundland and to recommend the form and the scale of additional financial assistance, if any, that may be required by the Government of the Province of Newfoundland to enable it to continue public services at the levels and standards reached subsequent to the date of Union, without resorting to taxation more burdensome, having regard to capacity to pay, than that obtaining generally in the region comprising the Maritime Provinces of Nova Scotia, New Brunswick, and Prince Edward Island.'[54] Smallwood was counting on this term of union to bring Newfoundland another 'windfall' from the federal government. In 1953, in anticipation of the appointment of the federal royal commission promised in the ambiguous and densely worded term 29, the provincial government had appointed a royal commission of its own to prepare Newfoundland's case. This commission had delivered its report on the eve of the 1957 federal election.[55] In the meantime, on 21 February 1957, with Smallwood in agreement about its membership, the federal royal commission had been appointed under the chairmanship of J.B. McNair, the chief justice of New Brunswick and a former Liberal premier of that province.[56] The other commissioners named were Sir Albert Walsh, the chief justice of Newfoundland and the province's first lieutenant governor, and John Deutsch of Queen's University. The McNair Commission reported on 31 May 1958.[57] Its implied criticism of the priorities the provincial government had followed in its spending since 1949 and its central recommendation that additional payments be made to Newfoundland in satisfaction of term 29 on a sliding scale, which would begin at $6.6 million in 1957 and be frozen at $8 million annually in 1961, stung Smallwood to the quick. He had expected much more and denounced the commissioners for their findings. He appealed to Diefenbaker to reject the recommendations of the commission and to give the province the $15 million annually it had sought. The decision of the federal government on the McNair commission recommendations was announced by Diefenbaker on 25 March 1959: Newfoundland would not be given a grant in perpetuity in satisfaction of term 29 as the commission had recommended but would be paid $8 million annually until 1962.[58] These payments would constitute the final settlement between the two governments under the terms of union. Smallwood retaliated by launching a campaign against Diefenbaker which was probably his greatest public relations job ever. As he had so successfully done during the IWA controversy, he pitched his appeal to the particularism that still lingered in his province. The disruption of the Newfoundland Progressive Conservative party ensued. Malcolm Hollett had criticized Diefenbaker's decision when it had been announced, but with the two Newfoundland federal Conservative MPs lined up solidly behind the prime minister, he refused to follow Smallwood all the way as he had done on the IWA issue.[59] In this, however, he was unable to carry his colleagues with him. On 18 July the legislation embodying the settlement Diefenbaker had announced was given royal assent. Smallwood now threatened an election if the House of Assembly did not give unanimous support to a motion he intended to introduce denouncing the federal government's decision.[60] At this point two Conservative members of the House of Assembly, A.M. Duffy and James Higgins, left the caucus to sit as members of a new party, which eventually styled itself the United Newfoundland party (UNP).[61] When the vote was taken on Smallwood's strongly worded resolution, Duffy and Higgins voted with the Liberals while their former colleagues cast the only two negative votes.[62]

Needless to say, an election followed. The Conservatives had now to compete for the anti-government vote not only with the 'loyalist' UNP but with a party which was launched during the summer of 1959 by the opponents of Smallwood's labour legislation. The CCF, which had stood up for the IWA in the House of Commons, had had a precarious existence in Newfoundland since 1949. For a brief period in 1955–6, a defector from the Liberal caucus, Sam Drover, had sat in the House of Assembly as a CCF member, but the party had been unable to get anywhere electorally. It had enjoyed the support of a few labour leaders, but the struggling Newfoundland labour movement as such had not lined up behind it. Altogether the CCF had contested fourteen constituencies in federal and provincial elections between 1949 and 1959, but the share of the vote obtained by any of its candidates had never risen above 23.2 per cent in a provincial constituency or 5.8 per cent in a federal constituency. In view of this record, the deeply ingrained 'provincialism' of Newfoundland politics, and the fact that the New party movement was already well advanced nationally, it is not surprising that the Newfoundland Federation of Labour and its allies should have chosen to create a new political instrument when the decision was made to fight the government at the polls. The attitude of the new party, which called itself the Newfoundland Democratic party (NDP) and which eventually became the Newfoundland wing of the New Democratic Party, towards the Conservatives was admirably stated by Harold Horwood: 'The Tory Party in Newfoundland is as useless as a sixth toe.'[63] The new party was led in the campaign by Ed Finn, the former managing editor of the Corner Brook *Western Star*. Its platform promised the restoration of democracy and the immediate repeal of 'the anti-labour laws ... which, if allowed to stand, threaten the welfare of thousands of Newfoundland families and ... the economic welfare of the whole province.'[64] When some Conservatives promised during the campaign a new deal for labour, the IWA called upon the federal government to prove the sincerity of this commitment by disallowing the legislation the Smallwood government had enacted, but its appeal went unheeded.[65] For the moment the division between Newfoundland Toryism and organized labour was irreparable.

The result of the election, which was held on 20 August, was another smashing Liberal victory and the bare survival of the Conservatives as the official opposition. The Liberal popular vote dropped to 58.0 per cent but the true strength of the party was masked by the fact that it did not contest three St John's seats – the constituencies of the two UNP members who had left the Conservative caucus and a third constituency where the UNP was likely to be strong. In the thirty-two constituencies the Liberals did contest, they elected all but one of their candidates and their share of the popular vote was 67.0 per cent. In addition one Liberal member was elected by acclamation. The Conservatives elected three members but their share of the popular vote dropped both overall and in the constituencies they contested to the lowest figures in their history. The Conservative humiliation was made complete by Smallwood's personal defeat of Malcolm Hollett in St John's West. The UNP ran nine candidates, obtained 8.2 per cent of the popular vote, and elected two members, both in St John's. A turnover of seventy-four votes in St John's East, where James Higgins ran, would have placed the party ahead of the Conservatives in members elected. The NDP did not elect any members, but despite its hurried creation, the lack of a well-established labour consciousness in Newfoundland, and the fact that, whether by accident or design, attention had been drawn away from the issue it was seeking to exploit by the emotionalism of the term 29 controversy, it obtained 8.0 per cent of the popular vote. Moreover, in eight of the nineteen constituencies it contested it ran second to the Liberal party.

Luckily for the Conservatives, neither of its two new competitors for the anti-government vote was able to sustain its initial dynamism. Although very different in outlook, both the UNP and the NDP had been founded in the heat of battle and, as the controversies which had given rise to them receded in time, their support dwindled, although the NDP retained a substantial following in the Corner Brook area. The selection of James Greene, who had been the IWA's legal counsel in the province, to succeed Malcolm Hollett helped restore the Conservatives to respectability again in the eyes of the Newfoundland labour movement and facilitated the decline of the NDP. When Smallwood called a snap election for 19 November 1962, while the memory of Diefenbaker's reversal in the federal election of that year was still fresh in the public mind, the Conservatives were able to rally all but 4.7 per cent of the anti-government vote. Only one of the UNP members elected in 1959 stood under that party's label in 1962 and he was defeated. The NDP contested only two seats in the election and its share of the popular vote declined almost to the level of the CCF before 1959. Its best result was in Humber West, where the provincial leader, Ed Finn, was not opposed by the Conservatives and won 47.8 per cent of the votes cast. The Conservatives elected seven members, the largest contingent they had ever returned, and their share of the popular vote rose to 36.6 per cent. Three of the constituencies won by the party – Grand Falls, Humber East, and St Barbe South – were away from the Avalon Peninsula. Still, the Liberals were the easy victors: this time they carried thirty-four seats, three by acclamation, and won 58.7 per cent of the popular vote.

The result of the sixth provincial election, which was held on 8 September 1966, was even more favourable to the Liberals. The party's share of the popular vote rose to 61.8 per cent, while that of the Conservatives dropped to 34.0 per cent. Moreover, the Conservatives lost the three seats off the Avalon Peninsula they had won in 1962. In the meantime, of course, the Liberals had regained power in Ottawa. During the period of minority government between 1962 and 1968 the support the national Liberal party had in Newfoundland became politically more valuable to it than ever before, and Smallwood's stock in Ottawa was accordingly high. In the 1962 federal election the Liberals carried six seats in Newfoundland; in the elections of 1963 and 1965 they swept the province. When Smallwood, after initially seeming to favour Robert Winters, supported the selection of Trudeau as Pearson's successor, the continuity of Liberal power in Newfoundland seemed assured. But in the 1968 federal election the long series of victories the party had won in the province was dramatically broken. In a stunning upset Newfoundlanders voted against the national trend and returned six Conservatives. On a slightly higher turnout than in the election of 1965, the Conservatives' share of the popular vote rose from 32.4 to 52.7 per cent while that of the Liberals declined from 64.1 to 42.8 per cent.

Why did the Liberal party, which seemed so invincible in September 1966, suffer so crushing a reverse less than two years later? There is no simple answer to this question. The dominant position which the party had occupied in the province for so long was the product of the interplay of many factors. Its defeat in 1968 and its radically altered position in the province since then suggests a similar complexity. Thus, the fortunes of the party were probably adversely affected in 1968 both by the politics of the immediate pre-election period and by the cumulative effect of longstanding social, economic, and demographic trends that were working against the maintenance of the political status quo.

The immediate difficulties of the government began in January 1967, when a hospital workers' local of the Canadian Union of Public Employees (CUPE) went on strike at Grand Falls for higher wages. This strike was ended, as the IWA strike of 1959 had ultimately been ended, by legislation. Under the terms of a bill which became law on 27 January, hospital workers were forbidden to strike in future or to continue any strike action then in progress.[66] This legislation renewed the conflict between the government and the labour movement of the province, which had started in 1959 and which had gone on intermittently ever since. On the other hand, the opposition of the Conservative members of the legislature to the action taken by the government against the strikers helped restore the credibility their party had lost in the view of the labour movement in 1959. This was important because the CUPE strike proved not to be an isolated episode but the beginning of a period of labour militancy in which provincial government employees, who constitute a large group in the labour force, have played a leading role.[67]

In January 1966, James Greene had resigned as leader of the Progressive Conservative opposition and had been succeeded by Noel Murphy, a Corner Brook doctor.[68] In May 1967, Murphy, who had been defeated in the 1966 election, was in turn succeeded as leader of the party by Gerald Ottenheimer of St John's.[69] Ottenheimer at once began a campaign to increase the party's strength away from the St John's area. The moment proved opportune: in October, when a by-election was held in Gander, a constituency the Liberals had won handily in 1966, the Conservative candidate was returned.[70] In the meantime, J.W. Pickersgill had resigned both his portfolio and seat in the House of Commons to become the first head of the Canadian Transport Commission. His place as Newfoundland's representative in the federal cabinet had been taken by C.R. Granger, whose resignation from the provincial house had opened the Gander seat. Spurred on by the provincial success in Gander, the Conservatives launched a vigorous campaign to defeat Granger in the seat vacated by Pickersgill, Bonavista-Twillingate, the symbolic heartland of Newfoundland Liberalism. The result of the by-election, which was held on 6 November, was another Liberal victory, but the Conservatives were able to increase their share of the popular vote from the 26.7 per cent they had obtained in 1965 to 42.8 per cent.

The Bonavista-Twillingate by-election was followed by one of the most troubled periods the Liberals had known since their accession to power over eighteen years before. A sudden drop in frozen fish prices led to the closure of two large fish plants and threw the fishing industry into a major crisis early in 1968.[71] While the government was attempting to deal with this crisis, the report of a royal commission which had been appointed in 1966 to study the economic state and prospects of the province cast doubt upon its financial and development policies.[72] Then, on 29 March, less than four weeks before the federal election was called, the government was forced to submit to the legislature for approval what was easily the toughest budget it had ever introduced.[73] Welfare payments were cut, a comprehensive scheme of assistance for university students, which had been introduced in 1966 and given extensive publicity throughout Canada, was drastically curtailed, and a number of consumer taxes, already among the highest in Canada, were increased. While the bad news of the budget was still fresh in the public mind and after the federal election had been called, John Crosbie, the minister of health, and Clyde Wells, a minister without portfolio who had been minister of labour at the time of the hospital workers strike, resigned from the cabinet, the former at the premier's request.[74] Specifically, Crosbie and Wells parted company with the government because they disagreed with a scheme whereby it intended to provide interim financing to a firm led by a New York promoter, John Shaheen, with which it was negotiating for the construction of an oil refinery as part of the industrial development program. But they did not confine their criticism of the government to this one matter. Using arguments similar to those contained in the royal commission report submitted shortly before, they were highly critical both of the government's general administration of the province's affairs and of Smallwood's personal approach to the cabinet system. Smallwood had invited Crosbie and Wells into the cabinet as part of a general program of political fence-mending that he had started to forge links between the government and the rising post-1949 generation of Newfoundlanders, who took confederation and the welfare state which had come with it for granted. Both men had figured prominently in the party's campaign in 1966 and Smallwood and Wells had contested adjoining constituencies in Corner Brook, the latter defeating the incumbent Conservative leader, Noel Murphy. John Crosbie's importance was augmented by the fact that he belonged to one of the most powerful business families in the province. For a variety of reasons, therefore, the departure of Crosbie and Wells was fraught with trouble for the government, the more so since they asserted on leaving the cabinet, as Herbert Pottle had done just over thirteen years before, their right to continued membership in the Liberal party. The explosive potential inherent in the new situation became apparent on 16 May when Smallwood was forced to retract unequivocally charges he had made that Crosbie had used his cabinet position to advance the interests of Crosbie family enterprises.[75] The unaccustomed public humiliation thus inflicted on Smallwood compounded the existing troubles of the Liberal party. Everything considered, the Liberals had never been so badly prepared for an election as they were on 25 June 1968. Still, their defeat in six of the seven Newfoundland constituencies was one of the surprises of election night.

It is one of the historian's articles of faith that events can only be understood in their context, both particular and general. In the case of an election result this means looking not only at the surface politics of the immediate pre-election period in the political community being studied, but also at any well-established historical trends which might be affecting voting behaviour there. A number of such trends in Newfoundland's post-confederation history are highly suggestive with regard to the 1968 federal election result in the province. Demographically, great changes had occurred in Newfoundland since 1949. In the 1951 census Newfoundland's population stood at 361,416. When the interim census of 1966 was taken this figure had risen, despite continuing emigration, to 457,853. Important changes had also occurred in the distribution of population. In the 1951 census 42.83 per cent of the population was classified as urban; by 1961 this percentage had risen to 50.68 and by 1966 to 54.05. This population explosion, in combination with the revolution of rising expectations which confederation had excited, demanded of the Newfoundland economy a high level of performance. The primary responsibility for meeting this demand fell within the context of Canadian federalism to the provincial government. Its answer was the industrialization and resource development program which Smallwood pressed relentlessly forward from the moment he became premier. Implicit in this strategy, which it was always assumed would be effected by private enterprise with whatever government assistance was necessary or could be afforded, were three interrelated objectives: the ultimate rationalization of the fishery and the resolution of the wasteful duality of the Newfoundland economy; the provision of the new jobs demanded by rapid population growth; and the expansion of the tax base to allow the provincial side of the welfare state to continue to advance. As a modernizer Smallwood had his greatest success not on the island of Newfoundland itself but in Labrador. In 1954 large-scale mining of the huge iron ore deposit in central Labrador was started by the American dominated Iron Ore Company of Canada at a moment when high grade deposits of this mineral were being exhausted in the United States itself.[76] In 1967 work was started by the internationally backed Churchill Falls (Labrador) Corporation Ltd, on the harnessing of the Churchill Falls in Labrador, the largest single unused water-power resource of its type in Canada.[77] On the island of Newfoundland itself, the success of the government in promoting resource-based industry was less spectacular but nevertheless important. In 1965 a Newfoundland and Labrador Power Commission was organized. Subsequently, under the direction of this agency, a large hydro-electric development, which greatly augmented the energy supply available on the island, was completed at Bay d'Espoir. The progress of the Newfoundland economy after 1949 is evident in a number of statistics. Between 1951 and 1965 the net value of production in commodity-producing industries rose from $146 million to $368 million, with mining and construction leading the way.[78] This growth was in turn reflected in the gross provincial product, which rose from $393 million in 1958 to $717 million in 1965 and to $949 million in 1968.[79] Economic growth was accompanied by significant shifts in the provincial labour force. As might be expected in a developing economy, the greatest expansion in the work force, both absolutely and relatively, occurred in the construction and service-producing industries. When the 1961 census was taken, the number of construction workers in the province was 74.3 per cent greater than the number recorded in the census taken a decade before; in the service-producing industries the percentage increase over the same decade was 33.1.[80] By the mid 1960s the new economic order was strikingly evident in the popularity of subdivision living among the province's enlarged bureaucratic and professional elites, who were working hard to create a Don Mills by the sea.

Newfoundlanders had come a long way economically in their first fifteen years as Canadians. Yet none of the objectives implicit in the economic strategy their government had followed had been realized. The duality of the Newfoundland economy had manifestly not been overcome; by 1956 the number of fishermen had declined to 14,956, but when the growth rate of the modern sector of the economy slowed during the recession of the late 1950s this figure rose sharply and in 1964 stood at 22,615.[81] After that the number of fishermen has declined, but despite their limited contribution to the gross provincial product, they continued to be the largest occupational group in the province, constituting, as noted above, 15 to 16 per cent of the labour force.[82] A high unemployment rate, a large welfare constituency, and continuing emigration constituted further proof that Newfoundland's economy was not keeping pace with the needs of its burgeoning population.[83] In the mid and late 1960s, moreover, the unemployment problem was compounded by the fact that many jobs were being lost to the economy in some of the older areas of its 'modern' sector. The mechanization and professionalization of the woods labour force led to a reduction in the number of persons employed in the logging industry from a monthly average of 5,600 in 1960 to 3,239 in 1963.[84] In 1966 the Dominion Steel and Coal Corporation's iron ore mining operation at Bell Island, a venture dating back to 1895, went under and brought one of the largest urban centres in the province to its knees. The job situation was also adversely affected by a drastic reduction in the American defence establishment in the province. In 1960 the American base at Fort Pepperall near St John's was closed. This was followed in 1966 by the closing of Harmon Air Base, on which the Stephenville area of western Newfoundland was largely dependent, and by the announcement that the naval base at Argentia, one of the economic mainstays of the Placentia Bay area of the Avalon Peninsula, would be reduced to little more than a token operation by 30 June 1970.

Finally, the lack of sufficient dynamism in the Newfoundland economy showed itself in a period of relative financial austerity which began with the politically disastrous budget of 1968. During the early 1960s the provincial government borrowed heavily to meet its social needs and advance its industrial development program. Between 1958–9 and 1968–9 the debt of the province rose from $104,039,000 to $659,266,000.[85] Deficit financing on this scale could only be sustained by a rapidly growing economy and revenue base or greatly increased direct federal support. When these did not materialize sufficiently, the burden of debt became an increasingly critical factor in Newfoundland's public finance, as it had been before the collapse of responsible government in 1934. In 1967–8 debt charges amounted to 22.5 per cent of provincial revenue.[86] The tight money situation throughout Canada and the United States undoubtedly contributed something to the adverse financial situation facing the Smallwood administration in the late 1960s, but even when this factor was taken into account Newfoundland seemed to be heading for another of the financial crises which have cast such a dark shadow across its modern history. The scenario was familiar, only this time the distress signal was going out to Ottawa rather than to Whitehall.

The political implications of Newfoundland's precarious financial situation were great. As the 1960s progressed, the economic circumstances of the provincial government forced it into many trying decisions. After 1965, for example, the government began urgently pressing forward with federal assistance, a program started in 1953 to move people away from the outports and into urban 'growth' centres.[87] But this program, which its supporters claimed would provide the basis for the long-term solution of the province's economic problems, encountered many difficulties and much criticism. Politically, the resettlement program was a highly dangerous operation for the government, not only because its benefits were not often immediate but because it made demands on the part of the population which had given Smallwood his greatest support and in whose favour the electoral system is weighted. Smallwood's power was built on economic achievement and the optimism which it had engendered. His power began crumbling when the economic problems of the 1960s restricted his freedom of manœuvre, ended the bonanza politics on which he had thrived during the 1950s, and spread disappointment and concern among his constituents.

The economic problems which were weakening Smallwood's grip on the Newfoundland electorate in the late 1960s brought into question the whole strategy of economic development the province had been following since 1949. The capacity of their resource-based economy to meet the needs of the Newfoundland people was clearly circumscribed by two factors: the availability of resources and the external demand for those resources. The strategy of mobilizing international 'private' capital to advance resource development brought striking immediate gains but in the long run could only bring limited success. Primarily, the multinational businesses which were attracted to Newfoundland sought not to maximize local employment opportunity, but as the Labrador iron ore development clearly showed, to supply the needs of more developed economies. The disabilities inherent in undue reliance on imported private capital were, moreover, compounded in Newfoundland's case by the fact that she was and continues to be in a weak bargaining position among the provinces vis-à-vis international finance. After the initial construction boom was over, the return in jobs and tax revenue from many resource developments contrasted sharply with the value and extent of the resources being exploited. When Smallwood inaugurated the Churchill project in 1967, he stirringly proclaimed: 'This is our land, this is our river, this is our waterfall. Newfoundland first, Quebec second, the rest of the world last.'[88] Yet, ironically, when the construction boom at Churchill ended in the mid 1970s Newfoundland inherited only a tiny fraction of the power generated annually on the site. The capital for an alternative strategy of public ownership and development of natural resources might have been mobilized by the federal government but this course was never contemplated either in St John's or Ottawa. What Newfoundland's post-confederation history perhaps demonstrated above all else was how a decentralized federalism facilitated the progress of foreign capital in Canada.

1968–72

The Liberal defeat of 1968 was followed by a period of intense factionalism and party strife reminiscent of the troubled politics of the late 1920s and early 1930s. For some time before the election Smallwood had been mentioning the possibility of his own retirement from politics and the summoning of a convention of the party to choose his successor. Whether he was really serious about this must remain a matter for speculation, but the events of June 1968 strengthened the hand of his critics and forced him to act. On 8 July 1968, he announced that a convention would be held before the end of 1969 to choose a new leader for the party. This announcement was followed by a cabinet shuffle, which may have been inspired by fear on Smallwood's part of further defections from the Liberal caucus. In August, Crosbie, Wells, and another dissident Liberal backbencher, Tom Burgess, the member for Labrador West, announced that they were forming a movement to democratize the Liberal party. Relations between Smallwood and his two former cabinet colleagues took a new turn in September 1968 when a formula was agreed upon whereby Crosbie was able to attend a meeting in Grand Falls to which Smallwood had invited five hundred Liberals to draft a constitution for the party. At this meeting, from which Clyde Wells was excluded, Smallwood announced that he intended to retire from politics once the reorganization of the party had been completed and the way cleared for the announced leadership convention. After the Grand Falls meeting, Liberal constituency associations were organized throughout the province and by early 1969 the Liberal leadership race was on with a vengeance. John Crosbie was an obvious contender. Another was Fred Rowe, the minister of education and a cabinet veteran, who announced his candidacy on 30 January. Later an abortive campaign was launched by Richard Cashin, one of the Liberals defeated in 1968, to draft Don Jamieson, Newfoundland's representative in the federal cabinet. Still the contest had an air of unreality about it since there was widespread scepticism about Smallwood's retirement plans. This scepticism was fed by the knowledge that Smallwood was determined not to allow the leadership of the party to fall into 'the wrong hands,' by which he clearly meant John Crosbie. Accordingly, there was no great surprise when in June 1969 Leslie R. Curtis, perhaps Smallwood's closest cabinet associate, circulated a petition among the Liberal members of the legislature in favour of Smallwood's continued leadership. Yet the events of 1968 had so altered the context of Newfoundland politics that it was immediately clear that a convention could only be denied at a considerable price, and in July Smallwood finally took the plunge. On the fourth he announced that a convention would be held in November, though he specified neither whether this would be a leadership convention, nor whether he would be a candidate if the leadership were in fact to be put on the line. These points were finally clarified for an expectant province by the premier on 15 July. The convention would indeed be a leadership convention. As for himself, he would resign as party leader on the opening day of the convention but would accept nomination for the office again. The leadership race now polarized into a two-way fight between Smallwood and Crosbie, with Fred Rowe throwing his support behind the premier. The election of delegates at the constituency level began on 29 September and was fiercely contested by both sides. By the time this process was completed just under three weeks later the atmosphere within the party, if two such disparate groups could now be referred to as such, had deteriorated badly. On 13 October, eighteen days before the convention was to assemble at the St John's Memorial Stadium, T. Alec Hickman, the minister of justice, entered the field, offering himself as a 'compromise' candidate. Hickman's announcement of his candidacy was followed shortly by his resignation from the cabinet. Three other candidates – Randolph Joyce, a Memorial University student, Vincent Spencer, the mayor of the town of Windsor, and Peter Cook, the son of a prominent Crosbie supporter, also secured nomination at the convention, but none had any significant following among the delegates. Cook's candidacy proved nominal but Joyce and Spencer seized the opportunity presented by the convention to speak from a platform on which the attention of the whole province was focused.

The delegates who formed the convention presented a study in contrasts and a microcosm of the 'new Newfoundland' – the traditional salt and pepper cap of the Jack-of-all-trades bayman representing one extreme of the social spectrum and the buttoned-down shirt of the *arriviste* the other. The ironies and paradoxes of the convention were in a sense epitomized in the two leading personalities – Smallwood and Crosbie. Smallwood had been one of thirteen children, had had little formal education, and had clawed his way up from the ranks. His rhetoric was and always had been that of the champion of the 'toiling masses.' His proudest boast was the social service state he had helped create. Yet he was now pilloried by his opponents as the authoritarian linchpin in a corrupt and inefficient administration, the creature of unscrupulous businessmen, 'the king of cost-plus' – in short, an obstacle to the further development of the province. The irony surrounding Smallwood was intensified by the fact that some of his leading assailants were people who had benefitted enormously from the system he had created or into which he had drifted. John Crosbie, on the other hand, had been born into every privilege his society had to offer. The product of a private school, university educated, a lawyer, he had entered provincial politics not at the bottom but at the top. Yet his rhetoric was that of 'planning,' 'priorities,' and a 'democratic' party structure. In the event Smallwood was the easy victor, obtaining 1,070 votes to Crosbie's 440, Hickman's 187, Joyce's 13, Cook's 3, and Spencer's 1. But the tumultuous finale of the convention, in which scores of Crosbie's supporters giving the fascist salute rushed towards the dais on which Smallwood was standing in triumph, suggested that if one round in the battle that had started in 1968 had ended another was about to begin. Nevertheless, Smallwood was once again master in his own house and was now able, without fearing further defections from the ranks of his supporters among the Liberal MHAS, to concentrate his attention on preparing for the provincial election which would have to be held before the close of 1971. Through obfuscation, delay, and astute political management, he had withstood the greatest challenge he had ever faced.

The convention was followed by an important realignment of political forces. Altogether eight of the MHAS elected as Liberals in 1966, five of them with cabinet experience, had opposed Smallwood's candidacy. Within forty-eight hours of the convention H.V.R. Earle, the minister of finance, and the only sitting member of the cabinet who had not followed the premier's lead, had his portfolio snatched from him. Earle and Alec Hickman, whom he had supported for the leadership, both eventually found their way into the Conservative caucus. In the meantime, after a period of intense speculation about his next move, John Crosbie had decided to sit as an Independent Liberal. Since Clyde Wells was already sitting under this label and Gerald Mryden, who had supported Hickman at the convention, had announced that he intended to do likewise, Crosbie's decision brought the Independent Liberal total to three. This figure was subsequently raised to four by the addition of B.J. Abbott, a former cabinet minister and a Crosbie supporter at the convention. In April 1970, while the legislature was in session, the four Liberal independents and over three hundred of their supporters met in convention in Gander and formed themselves into a 'Liberal Party Reform Group' under John Crosbie's leadership. The two other members elected as Liberals in 1966 who had later challenged Smallwood's leadership followed different courses. N.S. Noel, the deputy speaker of the House of Assembly and a Crosbie supporter at the convention, remained within the Liberal caucus. Tom Burgess had favoured Hickman for the leadership but had announced well in advance of the convention that he would henceforth sit in the house as a member of a 'New Labrador Party' which he was organizing to advance the interests of the Labrador area. The origin of this party lay in the sense of exploitation which had developed in particular in the affluent but isolated mining towns of western Labrador and which had ample precedent in other Canadian 'frontier' regions. On 18 April, the week before the Gander convention at which the Liberal Reform group was formed, the executive board of the Provincial Liberal Association voted unanimously to expel from the association the seven MHAS who had crossed the house. When the post-convention Liberal shuffling ended, the alignment of members in the House of Assembly was as follows: Liberals 31, Progressive Conservatives 5, Liberal Reform 4, Labrador Rights party 1.

Important changes also occurred in the Conservative party during 1969. On 10 November, nine days after Smallwood's convention victory, Gerald Ottenheimer announced that, for personal reasons, he was resigning both the leadership of the party and his seat in the House of Assembly. After an initial postponement a Conservative leadership convention eventually assembled in St John's on 15 May 1970. Altogether seven candidates contested the leadership. The victor was Frank Moores, a Harbour Grace businessman and a graduate of the same private school – St Andrew's in Aurora, Ontario – as John Crosbie. Moores had been elected to the House of Commons for the constituency of Bonavista-Trinity-Conception in 1968 and had subsequently become national president of the PC party. His total of 425 votes on the first ballot more than doubled the combined votes of the six other candidates, his closest rival, Hubert Kitchen, a Memorial University education professor and former president of the provincial party, obtaining 91. But the transfer of power from Ottenheimer to Moores was not as smooth as these figures suggest. Kitchen had risen rapidly in Newfoundland politics as opposition to Smallwood had spread after the Gander by-election of October 1967. Long established in the political culture as the 'natural' alternative to the Liberals, the Conservatives ascended with this new political stirring, attracting support indiscriminately from the many elements in the population Smallwood could no longer satisfy. As might be expected, this sudden change in fortune created both organizational and ideological problems for the party. Kitchen was involved in both. Like Moores, he traced his origins to the Harbour Grace area, though from the base rather than the apex of the Newfoundland social pyramid. As an educated 'bayman' – one of the many beneficiaries of the Smallwood educational reforms of the 1950s – he typified, at least in some respects, the rising meritocracy of the province. Accordingly, his election to the presidency of the party in October 1968 soon occasioned resentment in the St John's Tory group which had kept the flame of opposition flickering since 1949. Yet his policy outlook was not typical of the 'new class' to which he belonged and which, in general, found in the Conservative party a suitable vehicle for its ambitions. In September 1970 this particular Conservative contradiction was resolved when, after a period of uneasy truce between the new Conservative leader and his foremost convention challenger, Kitchen was expelled from the party.

With an election now at most a little more than a year away, the political temperature remained high. Smallwood had been working hard since his re-election to restore the credibility of his government as an effective instrument of economic advancement. The *cause célèbre* of the stormy 1970 session of the legislature, the longest since confederation, had been the legislation relating to the refinery deal, the interim financing of which had provided the issue for John Crosbie's resignation in 1968. Smallwood vigorously defended the refinery deal with John Shaheen and his associates on the grounds that it would not only be of benefit in itself but would provide the basis for an industrial breakthrough by the province in the petrochemical field. His opponents denounced the deal as epitomizing everything that had been wrong with the government's approach to industrial development. Construction of the huge refinery began before the election, and Smallwood clearly hoped that the employment thus provided, together with the advancement of the industrial program on other fronts, would have a greater impact on the electorate than the rhetoric of his opponents. In his efforts to create a more favourable economic climate in which to go to the people, Smallwood also counted heavily on the provincial programs of the federal Department of Regional Economic Expansion (DREE). The first agreement between Newfoundland and DREE had been completed in 1969, and a year later the department had already acquired something of a 'pork barrel' reputation in the province. But whether Smallwood could derive much political benefit from this particular form of federal spending remained in the immediate pre-election period an open question. The 1968 federal election had clearly ended the 'special relationship' he had long enjoyed with the federal Liberals. If anyone could now lay claim, either explicitly or implicitly, to being the indispensable intermediary between the Newfoundland people and the federal treasury, it was Newfoundland's representative in the federal cabinet, Don Jamieson. The first Newfoundlander to have acquired a major federal portfolio, Jamieson had built an independent political base in Newfoundland and next to Smallwood had for a long time been the best-known public figure in the province. He had attended the Liberal leadership convention in November 1969 but had not publicly declared himself for any candidate. Whether Smallwood would enjoy the association with federal power which had been so important to him in the past would depend on the attitude taken by Jamieson. Smallwood's powers of recovery and manœuverability were legendary, but to the extent that the fortunes of his government were being adversely affected by deep-seated trends which could not be reversed in the short run, he was clearly going into battle this time against poorer odds than he had ever faced before.

The Conservatives meanwhile were better prepared, organizationally at least, for an election than at any time in the past and were confident that the prize was at last to be theirs. Yet the Conservative sky was not entirely clear. If a provincial election had been held on 25 June 1968, and the same voters had shown the same party preference, the Conservatives would have won handily. But there was no guarantee that voters who were willing to rap Joey's knuckles by electing Conservative federal MPs would now go the whole hog and turn him out of office. The electoral map was also fraught with danger for the Conservatives. In the past the electoral system had had the effect of making the percentage of seats obtained by the Liberals in the House of Assembly much higher than their percentage of the popular vote and, conversely, the percentage of seats obtained by the other parties much lower, though it should be noted in this context that the Liberals had always enjoyed majority popular support. But the electoral system was also capable of producing a Liberal majority in the House of Assembly out of a Liberal minority popular vote. Of the thirty-three provincial seats away from the St John's and Corner Brook urban areas, the Liberals carried thirteen in the federal election of 1968. If in the provincial election they could hold these thirteen and win the nine others in this group that they came closest to winning in 1968, they would again have a majority in the House of Assembly but might well not have a majority in the popular vote. Another factor complicating the Conservative position was the competition of three other opposition groups – the Liberal Reform Group and the New Democratic, and the New Labrador parties. The Liberal Reform Group had received massive publicity, appeared to be well financed, and was clearly capable of siphoning votes away from the Conservatives. But the Liberal Reform leaders had their own problems. In addition to facing the usual difficulties associated with the establishment of a new presence in a political system, they were somewhat exposed by the fact of their initial climb in the political world under Smallwood's patronage. On balance it seemed likely that an arrangement of some sort would be made before the election between the Conservatives and the Liberal Reformers so as not to split their vote. The NDP was unlikely to make any such deal but its vote was again generally expected to be small except in the Corner Brook area and one or two other places where the party had been concentrating its efforts. The New Labrador Party was almost a complete unknown in the electoral equation, but in so far as it was appealing to anti-government sentiment its very existence was threatening to the Conservatives.

The 1971 session of the legislature provided a tumultuous climax to the stormy history of the thirty-fourth general assembly elected in 1966. In the absence of

TABLE 4
Percentage popular vote by party in Newfoundland
federal constituencies, 1949–68

	CCF/NDP	L	PC	SC
1949	0.2	71.9	27.9	–
1953	0.6	67.3	28.1	–
1957	0.3	61.9	37.8	–
1958	0.2	54.4	45.2	–
1962	4.9	59.0	36.0	0.1
1963	4.2	64.5	30.0	–
1965	1.2	64.1	32.4	1.6
1968	4.4	42.7	52.8	0.1

SOURCE: *Parliamentary Guide*; *Reports of the Chief
Electoral Officer*

Frank Moores, who retained his federal seat, John Crosbie stood out as the leading figure on the opposition benches. As the session proceeded from excess to excess the Liberal Reformers and Conservatives drew closer together and on 3 June a tacit alliance was sealed when John Crosbie entered the Tory ranks. He passed Hubert Kitchen, whose background contrasted so remarkably with his own, moving in the opposite direction. On 26 July Kitchen entered the Smallwood cabinet as minister of education. In the pre-election manœuvring Smallwood was also able to attract four other new cabinet ministers. These included Bill Adams, the mayor of St John's and a former Liberal member of the legislature, and Noel Murphy, a former leader of the Conservative party and now mayor of Corner Brook.

The final act of the pre-election drama was played during the summer of 1971 against a background of continuing labour unrest in the province.[89] In April the St Lawrence Workers' Protective Union, the only Newfoundland local of the Confederation of National Trade Unions began a prolonged strike against the fluorspar mining operation of the Aluminum Company of Canada. Then in May an electricians' strike began, adversely affecting the important construction industry just as the Liberals were trying to recapture some of the optimism of the past by getting an economic upsurge, however temporary, underway. While this dispute was still in progress, a strike that proved to be long and bitter was started against the American Smelting and Refining Company at Buchans, hitherto one of the most stable industrial communities on the island. But the most explosive and politically most intriguing strike was that started against the fishing operation of Spencer Lake in the isolated south coast town of Burgeo. The union involved in this strike was the recently organized Newfoundland Fish Food and Allied Workers Union. This union had been gaining influence among some outport Newfoundlanders in a

TABLE 5
Statistical summary by party, Newfoundland provincial elections, 1949–66

	1949		1951	
	L	PC	L	PC
Constituencies contested	25	25	25	18
Members elected in constituencies contested by two or more candidates	22	5	18	5
Members elected by acclamation	–	–	5	–
Total members elected	22	5	23	5
Total vote	109,801	55,108	83,628	45,304
% popular vote	65.5	32.9	63.6	34.4
% popular vote in constituencies contested by party	65.5	32.9	63.6	36.4

	1956			1959			
	L	PC	CCF	L	PC	NDP	UNP
Constituencies contested	34	28	10	32	31	19	9
Members elected in constituencies contested by two or more candidates	29	3	–	30	3	–	–
Members elected by acclamation	3	1	–	1	–	–	–
Total members elected	32	4	–	31	3	–	2
Total vote	75,883	35,375	1,877	75,560	33,002	10,391	10,639
% popular vote	66.3	30.9	1.6	58.0	25.3	8.0	8.2
% popular vote in constituencies contested by party	66.3	34.3	6.1	67.0	27.3	13.0	24.5

(*Continued*)

TABLE 5 (*Concluded*)

	1962				1966		
	L	PC	NDP	UNP	L	PC	NDP
Constituencies contested	41	34	5	1	41	37	3
Members elected in constituencies contested by two or more candidates	31	7	–	–	36	3	–
Members elected by acclamation	3	–	–	–	3	–	–
Total members elected	34	7	–	–	39	3	–
Total vote	72,319	45,055	4,374	638	91,613	50,316	2,725
% popular vote	58.7	36.6	3.5	0.5	61.8	34.0	1.8
% popular vote in constituencies contested by party	58.7	40.1	29.7	14:7	61.8	35.5	21.0

SOURCE: Newfoundland election returns; *Parliamentary Guide*; *Evening Telegram*

fashion reminiscent of the beginnings of the important union movement launched by William Coaker in 1908. The slogan of the south coast strikers, 'It started in Burgeo,' clearly harked back to the earlier militancy. By providing an alternative focus for the growing discontents of the embattled and insecure rural population, this new union thrust had created problems for both the Liberal and Conservative parties, since they were now both attempting to be composite, brokerage parties. Both Smallwood and Moores approached the strike situation cautiously. Both in the Kitchen appointment and in some of his comments on the new union movement Smallwood seemed to be showing an inclination to head the Liberal party back towards its radical roots. The Newfoundland Fish Food and Allied Workers Union was after all just the sort of populist thrust he had embraced as a young man and during the summer he talked once more about the dignity of labour and the rights of those 'who work with hand and brain.' For fleeting moments the old radical gleam could be seen in him and one or two of his ministers; but the Liberal ship was now laden down with privilege and encrusted with the barnacles of compromise. Hence when Smallwood finally called the election on October 6 his fate was very much in doubt. In the end, considering the forces that were arrayed against him, he did remarkably well. When the returns were completed on 29 October, the day after the election, the Conservatives seemingly had won 21 seats and the Liberals 20.[90] The one remaining seat was won by Tom Burgess of the New Labrador party. The NDP fell victim to the Liberal-Conservative squeeze and was not a serious challenger anywhere in the province. The election led directly to a constitutional crisis that was ultimately resolved by the resignation of the Smallwood government on 18 January 1972. Where the political ferment which began in the mid-1960s and which was rooted in their economic vulnerability would lead Newfoundlanders was a question that seemed as relevant after these last tragic days of the Smallwood era as before.

NOTES

1 In 1946 a 'national convention' was elected to recommend 'possible forms of future government to be put before the people at a national referendum.' In 1948 this convention recommended that the people be asked to choose between two forms of government: the commission system which had existed since 1934 or the system of responsible government which had existed before then. This recommendation was overruled by the United Kingdom government, which decided that the people should be offered a third choice: confederation with Canada. When the promised referendum was held on 3 June 1948, the result was as follows: for another five years of commission government, 14.32 per cent; for confederation with Canada, 41.13 per cent; for responsible government as it had existed before 1934, 44.55 per cent. Since none of the three options had majority support, the commission government option was dropped and a second referendum held on 22 July 1948. The result of the second referendum was as follows: for confederation with Canada, 52.34 per cent; for responsible government as it had existed before 1934, 47.66.

2 *Evening Telegram* (St John's), 29 April 1949.

3 Ibid., 2 May 1949.

4 Ibid.

5 Ibid., 29 April 1949.

6 Ibid., 9 April 1949.

7 Ibid., 20 April 1949.

8 See above, 179 n98.

9 *Canadian Parliamentary Guide* and biographical information provided by staff, Centre for Newfoundland Studies, Memorial University.

10 G.O. Rothney, 'The Denominational Basis of Representation in the Newfoundland Assembly, 1919–1962,' *CJEPS* 28 (1962): 564.

11 It has been estimated that federal expenditure in Newfoundland during the calendar year 1961 constituted one-fifth of the gross provincial product (see *Report of the Royal Commission on the Economic State and Prospects of Newfoundland and Labrador* [St John's 1967], 407).

12 See Peter Neary, 'Democracy in Newfoundland: A Comment,' *Journal of Canadian Studies* 4, no. 1 (1969): 37–45.

13 For an account of Smallwood's career before 1949 see Richard Gwyn, *Smallwood: The Unlikely Revolutionary*, rev. ed. (Toronto 1972).

14 Rothney, 'The Denominational Basis of Representation,' 557.

15 Ibid., 565–6.

16 Ibid., 566.

17 See Gwyn, *Smallwood*, 138–41, 168–9, 240–1.

18 R.I. McAllister, 'An Outline of the Newfoundland Economy,' in R.I. McAllister (ed.), *Newfoundland and Labrador: The First Fifteen Years of Confederation* (St John's 1966), 70.

19 Ibid.

20 Parzival Copes, 'The Fishermen's Vote in Newfoundland,' *Canadian Journal of Political Science* 3 (1970): 582.

21 See ibid., 580.

22 Ibid., 582.

23 *Evening Telegram*, 2 Nov. 1951.

24 See ibid., 8 Nov. 1951.

25 See, for example, Leslie Harris, 'Newfoundland and Labrador,' in *Canadian Annual Review for 1968* (Toronto 1969), 208.

26 *Evening Telegram*, 24, 27 March 1951. Russell published political memoirs in the *Evening Telegram* on 28 Oct., 4, 11, and 18 Nov. 1966.

27 Ibid., 24 April 1954.

28 Ibid., 22 April 1955.

29 Ibid., 28 April 1955.

30 Ibid., 27 Jan. 1953.

31 Ibid., 3 July 1953.

32 *Globe Magazine* (Toronto), 30 May 1970, 6.

33 See Gwyn, *Smallwood*, 174.

34 *Evening Telegram*, 5 May 1958.

35 Ibid., 26 Nov. 1958.

36 Ibid., 21 Nov. 1958.

37 Ibid., 16, 31 Dec. 1958.

38 Ibid., 13 Feb. 1959.

39 See, for example, ibid., 13 Feb., 6, 12 March 1959.

40 See ibid., 31 Aug. 1959.

41 Ibid., 24 Feb. 1959.
42 Ibid.
43 Ibid., 26 Feb. 1959.
44 For the legislation see *Statutes of Newfoundland*, 1959, 1–7.
45 *Evening Telegram*, 5 March 1959.
46 Ibid.
47 House of Commons, *Debates*, 1959, vol. 2, 1959.
48 See Gwyn, *Smallwood*, 216–17.
49 House of Commons, *Debates*, 1959, vol. 2, 2005–6.
50 *Evening Telegram*, 19 March 1959.
51 Gwyn, *Smallwood*, 219.
52 House of Commons, *Debates*, 1959, vol. 2, 1963.
53 Ibid., 1677, 1779, 1832–3, 1866, 1966, 2132–3, 2227; vol. 4, 4106; vol. 5, 5409. See also *Canadian Annual Review for 1960* (Toronto 1961), 51.
54 *Report and Documents Relating to the Negotiations for the Union of Newfoundland with Canada*, Department of External Affairs, Conference Series, 1948, no. 2 (Ottawa 1949), 22.
55 *Report of the Newfoundland Royal Commission for the Preparation of the Case of the Government of Newfoundland and for the Revision of the Financial Terms of Union* (St John's 1957).
56 Gwyn, *Smallwood*, 187.
57 *Report Royal Commission on Newfoundland Finances under the Terms of Union of Newfoundland with Canada* (Ottawa 1958).
58 House of Commons, *Debates*, 1959, vol. 2, 2215–16.
59 *Evening Telegram*, 26 March 1959.
60 Ibid., 18, 20 July 1959.
61 Ibid., 20 July 1959.
62 Ibid., 28 July 1959.
63 Ibid., 12 June 1959.
64 Ibid., 6 Aug. 1959.
65 Ibid., 10 Aug. 1959. In a message to the voters published in the *Evening Telegram* on 19 August Ed Finn attacked the Conservatives as follows: 'But the main reason why we could not honourably have anything to do with the PC's is because, in their pitiable weakness, they betrayed the working people of Newfoundland – the people who somehow, in spite of oppression and neglect and Smallwood's anti-labour laws, manage to keep the province going. When the Liberal machine, at the request of the paper companies and other big business interests, drafted two of the worst anti-labour laws in the history of western civilization, the PC's not only failed to protest against them, they actively and outspokenly supported them.'
66 *Statutes of Newfoundland*, 1966–7, vol. 1, 51–7.

67 In 1967 the total number of man-days lost in strikes and lockouts in Newfoundland was 10,680. The comparable figures for 1968 and 1969 are, respectively, 32,620 and 85,900 (*Labour Gazette*, Canada, Department of Labour, table G-3). The following table of union membership in Newfoundland, 1965–9, was compiled from the annual survey of trade union membership in Canada contained in the *Labour Gazette*.

	Locals	Locals reporting	Membership
1965	115	108	20,900
1966	114	105	21,488
1967	153	141	23,442
1968	163	140	24,295
1969	172	146	23,649

68 *Evening Telegram*, 17 Jan. 1966.
69 Ibid., 15 May 1967.
70 Ibid., 23 Oct. 1967.
71 See Harris, *Canadian Annual Review for 1968*, 205–7.
72 *Report of the Royal Commission on the Economic State and Prospects of Newfoundland and Labrador* (St John's 1967).
73 *Evening Telegram*, 1 April 1968.
74 Ibid., 14 May 1968.
75 Ibid., 17 May 1968.
76 The Iron Ore Company of Canada's backers included the following American companies: Armco Steel Corporation, Hanna Mining Company, National Steel Corporation, Republic Steel Corporation, Bethlehem Steel Corporation, Wheeling Steel Corporation, and Youngstown Sheet and Tube Company. In 1970 the Canadian participants in the company were Hollinger Mines and Labrador Mining and Exploration Company (see *Survey of Mines, 1970* [Toronto, 1969], 61). The dependence of the United States in this period on outside supplies of iron ore is discussed in Gabriel Kolko, *The Roots of American Foreign Policy* (Boston 1969), 50–4.
77 In 1969 Churchill Falls (Labrador) Corporation Ltd. was 63.3 per cent owned by the British Newfoundland Corporation (*Moody's Industrial Manual*, July 1969, 3290). The British Newfoundland Corporation (BRINCO) was itself founded in 1953 by a syndicate led by N.M. Rothschild and Sons. The other major founding interests were: Anglo-American Corporation of South Africa Ltd., Anglo-Newfoundland Development Company Ltd., the Bowater Paper Corporation Ltd., English Electric Company Ltd., Frobisher Ltd., and Rio Tinto Company Ltd. The Frobisher interest was subsequently bought by the Compagnie Financière de Suez (see Victor Young, 'Analysis of Common Stock' [unpublished paper, Centre for Newfoundland Studies, Memorial

245 Party Politics, 1949–71

University 1966], 69). In 1969 it was reported that Rio Tinto Zinc Corporation and Bethlehem Steel had arranged to acquire about a 50 per cent interest in the corporation (*Moody's Industrial Manual*, July 1969, 3290).

78 *Report of the Royal Commission on the Economic State and Prospects of Newfoundland and Labrador* (St John's 1967), 16.

79 Atlantic Provinces Economic Council, *Atlantic Provinces Output over Income*, Pamphlet no. 15, (May 1970), 9.

80 Census, 1961, *Bulletin 7*, 1–12, 66.

81 Copes, 'Fishermen's Vote,' 580. See also Ottar Brox, *Maintenance of Economic Dualism in Newfoundland*, Newfoundland Social and Economic Studies, no. 9 (St John's 1969).

82 Ibid.

83 The unemployment situation in Newfoundland is discussed in N. Hurwitz, *Seasonal Unemployment in the Province of Newfoundland*, Institute of Social and economic Research, Memorial University (St John's 1968). On page 9 Hurwitz concludes: 'The economy is not able to create sufficient jobs to keep pace with the population force. This further indicates that there is a large volume of disguised unemployment and under-employment in the economy. Diversification of the economy had not proceeded fast enough to absorb a growing working population.' In March 1968, Newfoundland's welfare constituency numbered 87,059: 42,007 persons were receiving long-term assistance; 45,052 were receiving short-term assistance (*Annual Report of the Department of Public Welfare for the Year Ended March 31st 1968*, 74–8). The Dominion Bureau of Statistics estimated Newfoundland's population on 1 June 1968, at 507,000 (DBS 91–201, 1968).

84 Robert D. Peters, 'The Social and Economic Effects of the Transition from a System of Woods Camps to a System of Commuting in the Newfoundland Pulpwood Industry' (unpublished MA thesis, Memorial University 1965), 87.

85 Department of Finance, Government of Newfoundland.

86 *Report of the Royal Commission on the Economic State and Prospects of Newfoundland and Labrador* (St John's 1967), 427.

87 See Noel Iverson and D. Ralph Matthews, *Communities in Decline: An Examination of Household Resettlement in Newfoundland*, Newfoundland Social and Economic Studies, no. 6, (St John's 1968), 2–3.

88 Gwyn, *Smallwood*, xii.

89 The number of man-days lost in Newfoundland in strikes and lockouts rose from 2,300 for the period January to November 1970, to 172,050 for the period January to November 1971 (*Globe and Mail* (Toronto), 11 Jan. 1972.)

90 For more details on the election see my 'Changing Government: The 1971–72 Newfoundland Example,' *Dalhousie Law Journal* 5, no. 3 (1979): 631–58.

The Collapse of the Saltfish Trade and Newfoundland's Integration into the North American Economy

DAVID ALEXANDER

The growth of European population and overseas emigration in the modern period was associated with an expanding international economy.[1] Every corner of the world was given a role to play, from China and India to Tristan da Cunha and Newfoundland. For some of the outposts of this European-centred economy, subsequent redundancy has had bitter consequences. Mauritians, as V.S. Naipaul observed, have been 'left with what they started with: an agricultural colony, created by empire in an empty island and always meant to be part of something larger, now given a thing called independence and set adrift, an abandoned imperial barracoon, incapable of economic or cultural autonomy.'[2] Both Canada and Newfoundland were part of this imperial economic history and neither separately nor jointly have they satisfactorily adjusted, in all respects, to being set adrift from a decaying empire. For Newfoundland the disengagement was exceedingly painful, and there were times when it appeared to be joining the ranks of Naipaul's imperial barracoons.

A major economic problem of the smaller colonies was an inability to escape from foreign trade dependence.[3] They were bound tightly to metropolitan demands for foodstuffs and raw materials, and suffered from wide fluctuations in export earnings. Export specialization deepened during this century, and in twenty-one out of thirty-two British colonies for which there are statistics 'the single most important export accounted for a greater proportion of the total in 1934–8 than it had in 1909–11, and only eleven colonies had a wider export base.'[4] Newfoundland was one of the exceptions, for the average value of its single most important export (fish) fell from 66 per cent of total exports in 1899–1901 to 46 per cent in 1934–8 with the development of mineral and forest product sectors.[5] Nonetheless in the late 1930s this three-product export economy had a ratio of exports to net

Reprinted with minor editorial changes from Canadian Historical Association, *Historical Papers*, 1976, 229–48, by permission.

national income of around 60 per cent.[6] The same ratio in Canada (which is always touted as a highly trade dependent country) was around 20 per cent.[7]

If absolute magnitudes are ignored, it can be seen that Canada and Newfoundland shared international economic characteristics arising from their British North American heritage. The most important was that both sought large trade surpluses overseas in order to balance trade deficits in North America. Until World War II, as table I shows, Newfoundland was somewhat less dependent upon North American export markets than Canada was upon the USA; but on the import side Newfoundland was sharply more dependent upon North America than Canada upon the USA. This reflected, on the one side, the competitive nature of Newfoundland output in North American markets and, on the other, the narrow range of its domestic product. Newfoundland exports, however, were spread among trading partners more widely than Canada's. Comparing the shares of exports going to each country's ten leading markets in 1948, an 'index of dissimilarity' assumes a value of $D = 0.26$. This indicates less export concentration among one or two countries within the ten in Newfoundland's case.[8] If the foreign enclave sectors (forestry and mining) are removed from the Newfoundland export figures the index of dissimilarity rises to $D = 0.44$. This indicates that the indigenous fishing industry was much more oriented to many overseas markets than the Newfoundland or Canadian export sectors in general. But as consumers, Newfoundlanders did not look to exotic lands. For any country, a marked divergence between export and import markets is a matter of concern; but it is especially so for a small and unimportant one which survives only by exporting over half of its national product.

Before World War I Newfoundland and Canada ran negative trade balances as each imported capital to expand productive capacity. Following the war each emerged as a mature debtor, earning large surpluses on their trade accounts to service interest and dividend remittances on the earlier capital inflows. But in Newfoundland the productivity of the investments (and the added burden of external war debt) proved inadequate to service the obligations and maintain personal incomes and public services at adequate standards. The first pair of columns of table 2 shows that following the large capital inflow associated with the Corner Brook paper-mill in the early 1920s, the Newfoundland net trade balance as a percentage of total trade climbed to almost 25 per cent in 1933, in which year the country collapsed. Refinancing of the debt by the United Kingdom, budgetary assistance, and grants from the Colonial Development Advisory Committee[9] eased the requirement for large trade surpluses for the rest of the decade. The second pair of columns indicates that in every year but one Newfoundland's relative surplus on overseas account was significantly larger than Canada's, reflecting its greater need to earn surpluses to cover the North American current deficit and the international indebtedness. The importance of the latter is suggested by the third pair of columns,

TABLE 1
Percentage distribution of trade

	Newfoundland		Canada	
	North America	Overseas	USA	Overseas
EXPORTS				
1945–48	48	52	41	59
1940–44	51	49	38	62
1930–39	33	67	37	63
1923–29	31	69	39	61
IMPORTS				
1945–48	91	9	74	26
1940–44	93	7	77	23
1930–39	71	29	61	39
1923–29	75	25	67	33

SOURCE: Dominion Bureau of Statistics, *Newfoundland, Statistical Background* (Ottawa 1949), and M.C. Urquhart and K.A.H. Buckley (eds.), *Historical Statistics of Canada* (Toronto 1965)

which indicates the large overseas surpluses relative to the North American trade deficit, until military expenditure relieved some of the burden.

Both Newfoundland and Canada depended upon an international trading climate, and a financing mechanism, which would permit imbalances on current and capital account to be adjusted between North America and overseas countries. In this respect they revealed a common heritage in the British-centred international economy of the nineteenth century. Newfoundland acquired its basic population stock and developed its economy in a climate of growing free trade.[10] Shannon Ryan has traced the increasing difficulties of the fishing industry as economic liberalism retreated later in the nineteenth century;[11] but no less important was the slowly weakening position of sterling in this century as an international trading and reserve currency. It was the position of sterling in the world that allowed Newfoundland and Canada to generate trade surpluses overseas against North American deficits. In this respect both countries had a stake in the continued viability of imperial Britain.

I

G.W. Watts wrote in 1950 that Canada had always regarded its overseas exports as more a means of earning dollars than of acquiring goods and services.[12] Overseas

TABLE 2
Newfoundland and Canadian trade balances

	Net trade balance as percentage of total trade		Overseas trade surplus as percentage of overseas trade		Overseas trade surplus as percentage of NA deficit	
	Nfld.	Canada	Nfld.	Canada	Nfld.	Canada
1948	−8%	8%	57%	31%	65%	266%
1947	−13	4	63	49	57	125
1946	−1	11	73	51	93	195
1945	−2	34	79	70	90	6747
1944	−14	32	77	74	58	1631
1943	−16	27	76	71	51	592
1942	26	18	68	62	32	281
1941	−24	6	53	39	33	67
1940	3	5	62	37	113	138
1939	8	11	49	36	156	272
1938	13	11	48	38	207	217
1937	11	11	46	33	187	269
1936	8	20	43	38	155	397
1935	16	15	48	32	272	577
1934	17	11	51	31	245	291
1933	24	14	59	32	308	403
1932	23	5	51	27	576	145
1931	19	−2	57	19	423	80
1930	14	−13	58	16	224	35
1929	11	−5	55	24	117	68
1928	11	5	49	36	206	143
1927	11	6	55	32	172	164
1926	9	12	54	40	157	235
1925	0	17	50	43	100	383
1924	−21	13	20	39	33	279
1923	−14	−16	39	34	59	159

SOURCE: DBS, *Newfoundland, Statistical Background,* and *Historical Statistics of Canada*

trade was simply a financial operation. This was no less true for Newfoundland, and both countries had reason to worry that the Second World War would inflict permanent damage on a trade and payment system upon which they had relied since the Napoleonic Wars.

The financial problems of international payments were set aside during the war in order to maintain a stream of goods moving into the United Kingdom.[13] This was accomplished by strict control on capital movements, trade licensing, requisitioning of British overseas assets, accumulation of sterling balances, and gifts and lines of credit, notably lend-lease after 1941.[14] Avoidance of a Canadian post-war recession, or collapse, was believed to be dependent upon rapid restoration of British imports of Canadian goods for dollars. Because Britain had liquidated a large fraction of its overseas income and built up huge sterling balances overseas, and because it would take time to reorganize the export industries, it was recognized that restoration of the old pattern would not be immediate.[15] Therefore, to maintain exports to Britain in the short term, Canada was obliged to extend lines of credit,[16] but it was expected that the United States would ease difficulties for both Britain and Canada in the longer term. It was a shock for both when lend-lease was abruptly terminated in the summer of 1945.[17] The American credit to Britain of $14.4 billion announced in December of that year was not regarded as generous, particularly since it carried an obligation to make sterling convertible for current transactions a year following ratification, which took place in July 1946. Canada had extended credit to Britain throughout 1945 and early in 1946 offered a loan of $1.25 billion. Britain could draw on this for up to 50 per cent of its net deficit with Canada, the remainder of which was to be paid in US dollars. At the same time, Canada provided $750 million in credits to non-Empire countries for use through 1947.

All of this represented financial band-aids, and few Canadians were prepared to admit the real structural crisis. In a speech in Montreal late in 1945, however, James Duncan of Massey-Harris (one of a handful of overseas-oriented businessmen in modern Canadian history) called upon Canadians to face the fact that Britain would not be able to resume her previous role. It was necessary for this country, he argued, to increase the number and importance of our customers abroad and to purchase freely from those to whom we wished to sell.[18] The need to abandon the old financial orientation towards exporting should have been clear when, at the end of August 1947, the chancellor of the exchequer announced suspension of the sterling convertibility instituted only a few weeks earlier. Both Canada and Newfoundland, which was part of the Canadian dollar system, found themselves in a less favourable payments environment than before the premature restoration of convertibility. They were now excluded from the 'transferable account' group of countries,[19] which provided for the multilateralism within the group and the sterling area on current transactions, and isolated into a 'bilateral' group,[20] where payments were restricted to payees in the sterling area and the individual country concerned, with no transferability within the group. The London *Economist* commented that while many countries had been 'put on the spot,' 'none is in a more difficult spot than Canada.' The only long-term solution for Canada was to reduce the 'triangularity' of its trade and payments by diverting imports from the US to Britain.[21]

By the end of 1947 Canadian gold and foreign exchange reserves had fallen from $1.25 billion at the beginning of the year to $500 million.[22] The reserve position was restored in 1948 by re-establishing US import controls and travel restrictions, and by suspending British drawings on the post-war loan. Encouragement was given to production which would earn or save US dollars,[23] and relief also came through European 'off-shore' purchases in Canada with Economic Cooperation Administration (ECA) dollars. C.D. Howe, the minister of reconstruction, welcomed the announcement of the Marshall Plan as constituting salvation for both Europe and Canada.[24] The availability of ECA dollars for purchases of Canadian products did provide a breathing space in 1948; but British commentators repeatedly stressed that Canada's trade was characterized by structural problems which neither the ECA nor a restored sterling convertibility would resolve: 'The great dilemma can be put in a very simple … form. Will Canada shift its *exports*, sending less to the United Kingdom and other soft currency countries and (if possible) more to the United States; or will it shift its *imports*, buying less from the United States and (if possible) more from other countries?'[25] Despite the temporary controls on American imports, the *Economist* correctly predicted that the growing domination of the Canadian economy by the USA would result in a shift of exports to that country.

Throughout late 1948 and 1949 Canada's trade prospects in Europe deteriorated. The world shortages of food and raw materials began to ease and, despite government exhortations to close the 'dollar gap,' European businessmen showed an understandable preference for trading in soft currency markets. In April 1949 the ECA gave notice that Britain's offshore food purchases were to end, [26] since an American farm surplus was beginning to develop. By mid-summer sterling was under pressure, and Sir Stafford Cripps announced massive cuts in food, timber and paper imports. In September Cripps astounded the world by devaluing 30 per cent against the US dollar. The sterling area followed, as did Holland, Denmark, Norway, Sweden, and Greece. Severe devaluations were announced elsewhere in Europe, and Canada devalued by 10 per cent, leaving an effective sterling depreciation against the Canadian dollar of something less than 24 per cent.[27]

In response to this succession of Britain and European crises, the value of Canada's overseas exports slipped below exports to the United States for the first time. With the surge of American investment in Canada the ratio of exports to GNE fell much more sharply.[28] The brunt of the contraction was experienced by the farm sector and in 1950 the Canadian government was obliged to cover farm losses with export subsidies. Early in 1949 the *Economist* had predicted that 'prodigies of export promotion to Canada will have to be achieved if within three years commercial relations between Britain and Canada are not to be disturbed, to the disadvantage of both parties, by considerable further cuts in British imports from

Canada.'[29] This was not forthcoming and Canada did not make efforts to divert imports from the USA to overseas suppliers. Consequently, the historic triangularity of Canadian trade and payments gave way to a bilateral orientation toward the United States.

Unlike Canada, Newfoundland was in no position to finance exports in order to maintain post-war employment. While the current value of national income more than doubled during the war, it began to slip in 1947, and on a per capita basis Newfoundland was among the poorest of western countries.[30] In 1947 exports from the three resource sectors accounted for almost 70 per cent of net national income,[31] and some 40 per cent of mineral exports, 52 per cent of forest products and 65 per cent of fishery exports were shipped directly to soft currency markets.[32] Fishery exports were most seriously in danger. The industry was the country's most important employer and *directly* supporting over a third of the population. The saltfish industry, which accounted for over half of all fishery exports, was the pivot around which the entire fishing industry revolved. Much of the remaining fishery export represented by-products of the saltfish sector or were fisheries that would not be pursued in the absence of the salt trade. Newfoundland's saltfish producers exported virtually all their output into European or western hemisphere soft currency markets, and consequently post-war exchange and payments problems were of unusual importance to the country.

Poverty in pre-war Newfoundland was widely attributed to dependence upon saltfish. The industry was characterized by low labour productivity and poor market returns.[33] The commission government's program of reconstruction was centred on raising efficiency and diversifying output into less traditional products. This reorganization began in 1934, and by the end of the war the country had the nucleus of one of the world's best fishery services. The Newfoundland Fisheries Board was established in 1936 under the chairmanship of Raymond Gushue, a brilliant young St John's lawyer. The board was granted virtually unlimited regulatory authority over all aspects of production, processing, and marketing,[34] but a special responsibility was to cajole the highly individualistic saltfish exporters into a national cooperative marketing system. Through single-desk selling, it was hoped to improve prices, block consignment sales by weak exporters, halt the drain of false quality claims, and generally to lower marketing overhead costs. Cooperative marketing proceeded in three stages, beginning with the formation of marketing companies, such as the Portugal Exporters Group in 1936,[35] with exclusive licences to export to particular markets. Any exporter wishing to ship to Portugal was required either to be a member of the company or to ship through one of its members. The company would negotiate contracts, pool fish from its members, and distribute the net proceeds to shippers on the basis of their contributions to the pool. By 1941 all major markets had been allocated to such cooperative marketing companies. The second stage in national marketing came early in 1943 with the formation of the Combined Food Board in Washington and the appointment of Raymond Gushue as chairman of its fishery committee. The Newfoundland Fisheries Board then created a marketing administration committee, to coordinate allocations received from Washington and the supplies available from the various marketing companies. The practical effect was to consolidate marketing into European and Western Hemisphere divisions and to push exporters a further step towards single-desk selling. This was finally realized in 1947 with formation of the Newfoundland and Associated Fish Exporters Limited (NAFEL), to which the fisheries board granted an exclusive licence to export. NAFEL had no shareholders and earned no profits; it was a cooperative marketing organization for firms holding a general export licence and paying a $10,000 membership fee.[36] The general manager of the company was the very able F.A.J. Laws, an Englishman trained in the fish marketing business by Hawes and Company of London, who had come to Newfoundland as its representative in the 1920s. In later years NAFEL was attacked as an 'evil cartel' which impoverished fishermen and sapped business initiative; but there was no significant opposition to its formation in 1947. With all of Newfoundland's competitors, except Canada, operating single-desk marketing, and with most of the markets equipped with government or quasi-government buying agencies, it is difficult to believe a return to competitive and unregulated exporting could have been as effective as the NAFEL organization.

While the industry was well prepared to meet the strains of post-war trade, informed opinion was pessimistic about its future. The 'Fisheries Post-War Planning Committee,' chaired by the ubiquitous Raymond Gushue, expected a short boom following the war, and then a slump as European production was resumed.[37] A major worry was that as a member of the Canadian dollar area Newfoundland would not be competitive in soft currency markets. The committee concluded, nonetheless, that it was neither feasible nor effective for the country to establish its own currency linked to sterling, and it saw no alternative to 'further expansion of the frozen industry (for dollar Markets) ... to the greatest extent and as rapidly as possible ...'[38] The fisheries committee of the National Convention reached the same conclusion. It admitted that for the immediate future the saltfish trade would have to assume the burden of employment and income, but in the longer term penetration of the American frozen market was essential.[39] Peter Cashin, the leading anti-confederate, became almost ecstatic over the prospects: '... once we are in a position to market our fresh and frozen fishery products in the United States of America our fishery problems will be finally solved ...'[40] The only realistic assessment of this post-war consensus was, unfortunately, being written in the obscurity of Oxford University. Henry Mayo pointed out that the United States tariff was notably unstable; that Newfoundland's bargaining power in the USA was much weaker than generally assumed; and that technical and economic factors would constrain any rapid transition to fresh-frozen production. What was still worse, Mayo estimated the employment prospects of such an industry to be equivalent to a medium-sized pulp-mill.[41]

Newfoundlanders were not as worried as Canadians about abandoning overseas trade for bilateralism with the Americans. In Canada overseas trade was widely recognized as being essential to the prosperity of certain regions and industries, as well as providing balance against American economic and political power. In Newfoundland realism dictated there was little the country could do to retain overseas markets in the looming post-war economic crisis, and to some extent the old trilateral trade nexus was identified with national collapse. American markets had been seen as a key to national prosperity since the turn of the century and rather than being a threat to independence their development could be a way of avoiding confederation with Canada.

II

Newfoundland's overseas fish trade became embroiled in the same currency and payments problems that beset Canadian exports. NAFEL opened for business at the end of August 1947 with large European forward contracts negotiated for sterling payment. Britain's almost simultaneous suspension of sterling convertibility presented the company with a major crisis. Outport members of NAFEL were telegraphed on 2 September: 'For your information nearly half season's production arranged for sale Spain, Italy, Portugal in sterling. However British Government's alteration exchange regulations prevents conversion of sterling to dollars for business with these countries.'[42] It was expected, however, that Britain would make an exception in Newfoundland's case. Convertibility was fundamental to the country's economic survival, but contributed little to the sterling bloc's dollar problems. Britain, moreover, was still responsible for Newfoundland. But it was difficult for the British to make exceptions in one case without admitting others, and since Iceland and Faroe – two of Newfoundland's European competitors – were members of the sterling bloc, a concession would be especially sensitive. But something had to be done, and at the end of September it was announced 'that arrangements are being made for the dollar resources of the Newfoundland Government to be used for conversion of sterling received for sales of fish in Europe.'[43] This referred to the surplus of less than $30 million built up during the war and deposited in London. The facility was to apply only to 1947 production fish and was not to exceed $6 million. The overseas buyers were to establish sterling credits at a London bank, and once its corresponding bank in St John's took possession of shipping documents, the London bank would pay over the sterling to a Newfoundland government account established by the crown agents for the colonies. The Newfoundland dollar account in London would then be debited, while NAFEL's St John's account would be credited with the dollar value of the sale at the sterling-dollar exchange rate prevailing on the day of the deposit.[44] It was not a happy arrangement. However disguised, Britain was permitting convertibility. The Newfoundland government was accumulating unwanted sterling and depleting its precious dollar reserves. NAFEL and the fish trade had no assurance the currency crisis would ease for the 1948 season, or that conversion facilities would be available in future years. Nonetheless, the facility removed the immediate obstacle and shipments moved out smoothly in the autumn and winter.

With a seller's market in Europe for all foodstuffs, the company was successful in establishing the strong marketing posture for which it had been created. Virtually all sales were f.a.s. or f.o.b. Newfoundland ports for irrevocable bank credits against fisheries board quality inspection certificates. When Spain proved unable to close on its contracts (because the authorities could not, or would not, provide the sterling or dollars) the allocated fish was smoothly shifted into Italy and Greece without panic or depression of prices. But there were signs that NAFEL's longer term position was less strong. It was noted that Greece was now an Icelandic saltbulk market and would accept NAFEL's bank fish or Labrador heavy-salted fish with reluctance. It was therefore unfortunate that the shipment of Labrador which went to Greece in the winter of 1948 received a stormy reception on the Piraeus docks. NAFEL's representative reported the fish was badly split, slack salted, showing pink, and possessing tails like 'damp cardboard.'[45] But Laws refused to meet the claim by the Greek buyers. He was determined to maintain the new selling policy that buyers must accept the fisheries board inspection in Newfoundland as final. The consequence was that the Greek's were convinced Newfoundland fish was no substitute for Icelandic. No commercial sales of any consequence were made with Greece in subsequent years, although since the market was already strongly committed to Iceland a generous settlement on the claim might have made no difference.

Italy was always full of alarums of impending disaster, but the buyers were satisfied with the quality and price of their 1947 imports and they absorbed all the fish NAFEL had to offer.[46] The Portuguese were difficult customers. They complained endlessly that NAFEL did not supply enough large fish, that the company's packages fell apart, and that the Gremio's ships were required to load at too many small Newfoundland ports. But underneath this complaining posture, they too were satisfied with their 1947 transactions.[47] It was Spain that was the real worry. Before the war it was a major consumer of Labrador fish, and this was always difficult to market. Exchange problems blocked shipments to Spain in 1947, however, and the country made no secret of its plans to expand its national fishing fleet.[48] It was a bad sign for Newfoundland when a large and well-established market survived a season without imports, as Spain did in 1947.

NAFEL was free of European competition in the western hemisphere and the Canadians, who were not a great worry, were cooperating with NAFEL to reduce competition. While the Brazilian balance of payments was deteriorating in 1947, the northern plantation market absorbed the expected volume of small Madeira (a good quality Newfoundland shore dried fish). In Barbados, Trinidad, Jamaica, and the smaller West Indian markets the governments maintained systems of import subsidies and retail price control. They fussed about prices, volumes, and exchange, but the population had to be fed and only Newfoundland could supply large volumes of low grade shore fish. Puerto Rico was the largest and most sensitive of the Caribbean markets. Under a system of wartime price controls the importers had switched into Labrador semi-dry, which was cheaper than the Madeira or Thirds (one of the lower grades of Newfoundland shore dried fish) which was traditionally consumed. For NAFEL this new Puerto Rican market for semi-dry was a godsend, since with Spain closed it was becoming extremely difficult to find any market outside Italy for Labrador fish. But there were difficulties. When price controls were lifted the importers might shift back into hard dried shore fish, and the semi-dry frequently deteriorated upon arrival in the hot climate. In 1947 only NAFEL's strong selling position enabled it to resist Puerto Rican claims on poor quality.

The 1948 production year proved unexpectedly easy to market, largely because there was a poor fishing season in Europe and North America. The ECA program also eased Europe's exchange problems and NAFEL was able to reduce its drawings on a renewed sterling conversion facility. At the end of the marketing year the company estimated it 'could have quite easily sold another 100,000 quintals ... if we had had the fish.'[49] In most markets the company had been able to force a price increase, and the strong selling terms were maintained. But there were less satisfactory underlying trends. The Greeks, who were still angry over their 1947 purchase despite a small settlement on the claim, refused to conclude a contract. The Labrador market in northern Italy was beginning to go the way of the Greeks in demonstrating a preference for European saltbulk, and even southern Italy was beginning to wean itself from the ancient taste for hard dried shore fish. Italy also proved unexpectedly short of exchange, despite ECA, and contracts were eventually signed only at 1947 price levels.[50] The Portuguese began negotiations in the spring in a remarkably stubborn mood over exchange, prices, and a host of irritants, and only signed contracts when the Gremio, in a panic, suddenly realized there was a world shortage of saltfish.[51] The Spanish were in the midst of trade talks with the British, who persuaded them to allocate £200,000 for Newfoundland fish; but in the end they again refused to release the exchange.[52] In Puerto Rico the quality problem with semi-dry reached crisis proportions, and the fisheries board representative expressed fears that the market would be lost.[53] Brazil imported larger volumes than in 1947, but it was against a background of deepening payments problems and a major struggle to persuade the Rio authorities to issue import licences. In the West Indies there was strong resistance to price increases, and the various food controllers began searching Europe for supplies of dried scale fish which could be imported for sterling payment.

The world shortage of food supplies had held off the crisis which exploded on the company in 1949. NAFEL opened the year, much like a modern utility company, with brisk announcements to customers that prices would be increased to meet higher production costs: in the end it was a matter of disposing of stocks at any price.[54] Everywhere in Europe the September devaluations made Newfoundland fish much more expensive.[55] In Greece the United States Foreign Trade Administration, which was virtually running the country, was reluctant to authorize the use of aid funds for Newfoundland imports, and the Piraeus importers were not interested in a commercial transaction. The Italian market deteriorated badly. Early in the spring there were signs that northern demand for heavy salted cures would be especially weak,[56] and in July the fisheries board representative reported that the trade authorities had decided not to release dollars for codfish. ECA officials were also strongly opposed to making available any United States aid funds.[57] Early in September a contract for $500,000 of shore fish was finally closed, but at prices below the 1947 level. The lira devaluation in that month wiped out any further hopes of dollar sales, and in the autumn small shipments moved out only through complex and costly barter transactions.[58] Ottawa or London or both had been slow to authorize sterling transactions, but in December permission was finally granted and the pace of sales picked up. But shipments of 1949 fish fell to 3.9 thousand metric tons from 8.8 thousand in 1948, and no Labrador fish was moved into Italy. In Portugal the company opened negotiations, on instructions from Ottawa, for minimum terms of 75 per cent dollars and 25 per cent sterling. Lisbon was completely uninterested and it was not until late September than an authorization was received to negotiate for 25 per cent dollars and 75 per cent sterling.[59] The Portuguese were still indifferent, and a contract was not closed until October, for 100 per cent sterling at 1948 price levels.[60] At the end of the year NAFEL faced a huge stock overhang, and the Portuguese closed another sterling contract at a price discount of 25 per cent.[61] In Spain Ottawa unleashed a trade delegation. Like the British before them they persuaded the Madrid officials to authorize $500,000 for imports of Newfoundland fish, but as in previous years the necessary import licences never reached the importers.

Weakness in European markets inevitably spread to western hemisphere markets. In Puerto Rico the importing group demanded that NAFEL award them the exchange benefit which had emerged with the September devaluation of the Canadian dollar. When NAFEL refused, the Puerto Ricans slowed down the rate of importation to a virtual halt in December. The company had no choice but to award the exchange difference to the importers.[62] In Brazil the long smouldering payments crisis came alight, and the Rio officials firmly prohibited foreign exchange for fish from dollar countries. By the end of the year NAFEL was reduced to shipping on sight draft terms for cruzeiros, with the Exports Credits Insurance Corporation providing reluctant cover.[63] Exports to Brazil in 1949 slipped from 6.1 thousand tons to 2.9 thousand. Even in the West Indies the company was forced to reduce prices in order to keep shipments moving and to fend off emerging European competition.

The modest optimism in which NAFEL had operated during its first two years was broken in 1949, and the company and industry faced two decades of steady decline. Table 3, column 1, shows the precipitous drop in the volume of shipments by 1954/5. The European markets contracted most sharply, and whereas they absorbed over half of output before the war, by the mid-1950s they took less than a quarter. As table 4 indicates, declining volumes found no compensation through rising prices. In current dollars the net returns from the industry fell from around $16 million in 1947/8 to less than $7 million in 1955/6. In constant 1947 dollars both the aggregate return from the industry and the net realization per metric ton were less than two-thirds that of the immediate post-war years. The expansion of the frozen industry, moreover, proved insufficient to compensate for the collapsing salt trade. Table 5 shows that the current dollar value of all fishery output fell during these years, and the industry's contribution to the value of Newfoundland resource output declined from around 46 per cent in 1947 to some 25 per cent in 1954.

The 1949 crisis was the beginning of a long demoralization. The European markets were never recovered, Brazil was lost and the western hemisphere markets severely weakened. In March 1950 one of many trade and provincial government delegations made the journey to Ottawa in search of assistance. In a brief presented to the federal cabinet[64] the trade argued against the inclination to view saltfish as a dying industry. A United States oriented frozen trade, it argued, could never fully employ the fishing labour force, and a failure to market in Europe would represent a disaster for the province's fishermen. NAFEL asked for $12 million sterling conversion for 1950 production and for 'Government to pronounce a policy to overcome the existing currency difficulties so as to bring about a measure of confidence with the resulting capital expenditure to maintain the industry.' But the provincial government was somewhat ambivalent, absorbed as it was with prospects for industrial development and happy to see labour transfers from the traditional occupations. The minister of fisheries, W.J. Keough, stated at Fredericton in February 1950 that Newfoundland's policy was to concentrate on the United States market for fresh fish,[65] and this policy coincided perfectly with the growing Canadian view that the country's exports should be shifted from overseas markets.

The frozen industry expanded sluggishly in the 1950s and 1960s[66] as the old salt sector contracted painfully. The bank fishery disappeared in the 1950s as capital reinvestment in ships and gear dried up and groundfish production was diverted into the filleting plants. This put an end to Newfoundland's best hopes for entering the European saltbulk trade. The Labrador floater fishery was abruptly closed at the end of the 1954 season. Market realizations no longer covered production costs and James Sinclair, the federal minister of fisheries, refused any further subsidies.[67] Saltfish output was therefore cut back to the inshore catch, particularly of the northern bays where filleting plants were scarce and opportunities for a trawler industry limited by winter ice.

With contracting market opportunities and falling prices, the fisherman's troubles were quickly translated into an ugly squabble over NAFEL. The company was seen as a new symbol of oppression by the 'fishocracy' and no amount of explanation by the fisheries board or NAFEL itself could convince otherwise. Premier Smallwood initially provided the company with cautious support. In December 1950 he said, 'I cannot ... regard the NAFEL organization as being perfect. But we would never be willing to see NAFEL go out unless it could be replaced smoothly by an even better organization if such were possible.'[68] But his attitude hardened thereafter, and a few months later the house was advised that 'the outfit called NAFEL contains some of the scum of the earth.'[69] In the election campaign in November 1951 the premier served notice 'that if the Liberal Government is re-elected we intend to improve on NAFEL' by making it more democratic and much more efficient.[70] In the summer of 1952 the widely respected architect of the fisheries board and NAFEL itself, Raymond Gushue, bailed out of the growing mess and accepted the presidency of Memorial University. With his exit there was no one of equal stature to defend what was left. Harold Horwood, the future novelist, offered a sustained attack against NAFEL in his widely read 'Political Notebook' in the St John's *Evening Telegram*, with his demand for a socialist or cooperative alternative to organized marketing.[71] Stewart Bates, of the federal Department of Fisheries, entered the angry debate only to note that NAFEL was not the kind of organization to which Canada was accustomed, but that his department was reluctant to replace it unless Newfoundlanders proposed an alternative.[72] Federal fisheries was not, however, prepared to support the only possible alternative. At the annual meeting of the Newfoundland Federation of Fisheries in November 1953, W.J. Keough presented the provincial government's desire that Ottawa establish a national fish marketing board under the National Products

Marketing Act.[73] With characteristic vigour, Smallwood argued that NAFEL was bringing 'ruin, bankruptcy, disaster and starvation' and that government should 'kick their teeth in.'[74] He was determined to establish a provincial marketing board if Ottawa would not create a national organisation, but J.W. Pickersgill, freshly elected in Bonavista-Twillingate, was exceedingly cool to either proposal. A compromise was reached when Smallwood proposed that marketing responsibility be assumed by C.D. Howe at the federal Department of Trade and Commerce, in whom he had great confidence,[75] with the remaining responsibilities of the Newfoundland Fisheries Board being transferred to the federal Department of Fisheries. This decision was announced in April 1954, together with the news that NAFEL was to remain in existence with reduced powers. The company's control over interprovincial trade was terminated, and this meant that Newfoundland saltbulk could now be freely sold to Nova Scotia processors, but it retained its exclusive export licence for an additional three years.[76]

Mr Smallwood informed the press that it was 'a fine piece of luck for Newfoundland that Mr Howe had agreed to accept the Canadian Government's responsibility for the successful marketing of our salted codfish.' He had no doubt that 'NAFEL will disappear and be replaced by a far superior system of marketing.'[77] The optimism did not prove justified. No serious effort was made to reverse the deteriorating market prospects, and a policy was firmly established not to stimulate the saltfish industry lest this 'prejudice the expansion of the freezing industry.'[78] In other fishing countries the cured and fresh/frozen sectors were not regarded as mutually exclusive and simultaneous development of both was held to be essential to a larger and more flexible fishing economy. Smallwood was also wrong when he predicted NAFEL would be replaced by a national fish marketing board. Instead the marketing system so painfully built up in Newfoundland in the 1930s and 1940s was dismantled once production volume was down to a level where its absence would not produce chaos. On 31 July 1958 NAFEL received notice from the minister of trade and commerce that its exclusive export licence would terminate the following year, and 'no reason was given for this decision.'[79] NAFEL survived as a voluntary association of exporters for another ten years until the establishment of the Canadian Saltfish Corporation, but in 1959 domestic competition for markets was resumed. In 1963 the provincial government tried once again to push Ottawa into an effective fisheries policy, but its carefully prepared *National Fisheries Development* submission received a cool response from the F.B. Finn Commission in the following year.[80] It is hardly surprising, in this atmosphere of growing pessimism, that the major Newfoundland firms began to withdraw from the industry. NAFEL began business in 1947 with thirty-three members and in 1951 it had thirty-four. In that year two firms gave notice of intention to withdraw and by 1958 full membership was down to nineteen. It was the major St John's firms which withdrew most rapidly, and without their influence, capital, and business expertise the whole trade was weakened. It was not, moreover, a case of withdrawing from the salt sector to enter the fresh-frozen, although a few firms made such a transition. For the most part, expansion in the fresh-frozen industry was managed by corporate food conglomerates, while the old Newfoundland firms retired into wholesaling, retailing, and other service industries. Within ten years of confederation Newfoundland businessmen became characteristically Canadian.

III

In his 1956 presidential address to the Canadian Political Science Association, J. Douglas Gibson, the economist and subsequent general manager of the Bank of Nova Scotia, acknowledged the concern some Canadians felt about the reorientation of their economy towards a dependence upon the United States. This was 'primarily the result of fundamental economic changes and not of national economic policies' and for the most part he felt it was a transition Canadians should welcome.[81] Since then a less complacent attitude has grown among many Canadians, if not their bankers, and there is even a growing awareness that the transition from an overseas-oriented economy to an American one has distributed costs and benefits unevenly. For the Atlantic provinces with their long-standing North Atlantic connections, the post-war winding down of overseas trade was especially burdensome and not adequately compensated through expanding continental markets. Nova Scotia was obliged to tear up its apple orchards and plant varieties more palatable to North Americans; the New Brunswick lumber industry fell into several years of depression; and the shipyards and ports of the Maritimes shrank with the decline of the Canadian merchant marine and overseas trade.[82] Prairie and central Canadian farmers also faced transition problems with the shrinkage or disappearance of wheat, livestock and dairy markets in Europe. But it was Newfoundland fishermen – and because of their importance to the province – Newfoundland itself, that felt the most severe and long lasting effects from the disintegration of the old North Atlantic economy.

Gibson was no doubt right that Canada's abandonment of overseas markets was not a matter of national economic policy, but neither was it vigorously resisted. With the passage of time and the growth of US corporate control over Canadian commodity production, the ability and inclination to resume an overseas connection was lost. During the post-war crisis Canada had taken the easy route into the United States market. To maintain goodwill and a presence in overseas markets would have required limiting imports from the USA in favour of overseas suppliers – another 'national policy' and tinkering with market forces which Canadian economists continue to find objectionable.[83] For the Newfoundland fishing indus-

TABLE 3
Saltfish shipments, 1947–55

	Shipments (000 tons)			Percentage	
Year	Total	European	Western hemisphere	European	Western hemisphere
1947	58.7	24.7	34.0	42	58
1948	47.4	17.1	30.3	36	64
1949	47.8	17.6	30.3	37	63
1950	38.1	15.5	22.6	41	59
1951	41.7	11.5	30.2	28	72
1952	39.1	8.8	30.3	23	78
1953	29.2	7.0	22.2	24	76
1954	32.5	7.8	24.6	24	76
1955	22.3	5.1	17.1	23	77

SOURCES: NAFEL, *General Circulars*, 1947–56
NOTE: Totals indicate the disposal of a production year stock. Thus the 1950 sales include disposals in 1950, 1951, and even 1952.

TABLE 4
NAFEL Net realizations on saltfish shipments

	Current values		Deflated values, $1947	
Fiscal year	Net realization $ million	$ per metric ton	Net realization $ million	$ per metric ton
1947/48	$16.1	$300.20	$16.1	$300.20
1948/49	15.3	315.74	12.9	265.22
1949/50	13.3	321.72	10.9	263.81
1950/51	11.6	251.77	8.9	193.86
1951/52	–	–	–	–
1952/53	9.8	275.79	7.1	198.57
1953/54	8.6	267.59	6.3	195.34
1954/55	8.7	265.91	6.5	199.43
1955/56	6.8	282.26	5.0	208.87

SOURCES: Calculated from NAFEL, Chairman's reports, Annual General meetings, and *General Circulars*, various 1947–56
NOTE: Complete data to calculate net realization for 1951/2 are not available. 'Net realization' is the f.o.b. or f.a.s. value of shipments (including the value of packages) less marketing costs and working capital deductions to NAFEL's 'revolving working fund.' In short, it is the net return to fish exporters for sales made by NAFEL. Current values are deflated by the Canadian Wholesale Price Index.

TABLE 5
Newfoundland resource output ($ million)

Year	Forest products	Minerals	Fishery products	Total	Fishery as % of total
1947	$23	$14	$31	$ 68	46%
1948	31	16	29	76	38
1949	46	28	30	104	29
1950	49	26	30	105	29
1951	60	32	29	121	24
1952	62	33	28	123	23
1953	61	34	24	119	20
1954	62	43	28	113	25

SOURCES: *Historical Statistics of Newfoundland and Labrador* (St John's 1970),
vol. 1, table L-1 and M-2; DBS, *Newfoundland, Statistical Background*, table 99; and
Department of Fisheries, 'Summary Statistics of Canada's Fisheries,' *Canadian
Fisheries Annual* (Gardenvale, Que.), 1935–54, table 1B
NOTE: Prior to 1949 shipments are for fiscal years terminating at the end of June.
From 1949 pulp and paper 'shipments' represent value of production (excluding
value added by managerial and sales personnel) and therefore slightly underestimate
the market value of shipments. Fishery exports after 1949 are estimates made by
the Newfoundland Fisheries Board.

try, however, such a policy was essential. The province was centred on a huge
international resource, and if Canada did not produce for overseas markets, then
consuming countries would expand national fishing fleets to supply themselves. In
NAFEL Newfoundland had constructed the nucleus of the kind of organization
needed to enter the international trade in fresh/frozen fish products. It had effectively responded to some of the lessons of the inter-war period; but Canada's
reluctance to support and build on that experience in the 1950s and 1960s contributed to the ruin of the island's rural economy. That ruin is a small monument to
Canada's post-war failure to adjust imaginatively to the withering of the British
empire.

NOTES

1 Much of the research for this paper was done while the author was on sabbatical leave
from Memorial University with the assistance of the Canada Council. I am also indebted
to Mr Bill Gillespie for making available to me some of his research in the St John's
newspapers. Keith Matthews was, as always, generous in sharing his deep knowledge
of the history of the Newfoundland saltfish trade.

2 V.S. Naipaul, *The Overcrowded Barracoon* (London 1972), 270.

3 See W.G. Demas, *The Economics of Small Countries* (Montreal 1965).

4 David Meredith, 'The British Government and Colonial Economic Policy, 1919–1939,' *Economic History Review* 28, no. 3 (1975): 494.

5 Ibid., table 5.

6 Calculated from R.A. MacKay (ed.), *Newfoundland: Economic, Diplomatic and Strategic Studies* (Toronto 1946), appendix B.

7 Calculated from M.C. Urquhart and K.A.H. Buckley (eds.), *Historical Statistics of Canada* (Toronto 1965), series E8 and F243.

8 The following analysis is based upon calculations from *Canada Year Book* (Ottawa 1950), 908, and *Newfoundland Customs Returns, 1947/48*, 7. The index of dissimilarity was used for ease of calculation. It is usually highly correlated with the Gini index, with the value of '*D*' being the sum of positive differences in the rows of two distributions. It assumes values between 0 and 1 for ranks which are respectively identical and totally dissimilar.

9 Meredith, 'British Government and Colonial Economic Policy,' table 3, 491.

10 For a succinct treatment of these international developments, see A.G. Kenwood and A.L. Lougheen, *The Growth of the International Economy, 1820–1860* (London 1971).

11 Shannon Ryan, 'The Newfoundland Cod Fishery in the Nineteenth Century' (unpublished MA thesis, Memorial University 1971).

12 G.S. Watts, 'Some Longer-Term Factors in the Canadian Balance of International Payments,' *CJEPS* 16 (1950): 16.

13 J.L. Granatstein, *Canada's War: The Politics of the Mackenzie King Government, 1939–1945* (Toronto 1975) traces the hard bargaining on both sides that lay behind the common cause.

14 See G. Clayton, 'The Development of British Exchange Control, 1939–45,' *CJEPS* 19 (1953): 161–73, and Alan O. Gibbons, 'Foreign Exchange Control in Canada, 1939–51,' in ibid., 35–54.

15 F.A. Knox, 'Some Aspects of Canada's Post War Export Problem,' *CJEPS* 10 (1944): 312–27.

16 This is described in 'Canadian Export Policy,' *Economist*, 12 Jan. 1946, 59.

17 In these years the *Economist* was highly critical of the United States and appreciative of the enlightened wisdom of Canadian efforts (see 'Dollar Crisis,' *Economist*, 1 Sept. 1945, 289–90).

18 'Canadian Export Policy,' *Economist*, 12 Jan. 1946, 59.

19 This now included Argentina, Belgium, Brazil, Holland, Italy, Norway, Portugal, Spain, and Sweden, several of which were critical export markets for Newfoundland saltfish.

20 Including Austria, China, Denmark (excluding Faroe), France, Greece, Switzerland, and Eastern European countries.
21 *Economist*, 20 Sept. 1947, 496.
22 See J. Douglas Gibson, 'Post-War Economic Development and Policy in Canada,' *CJEPS* 20 (1954): 446–8.
23 Ibid.
24 *Economist*, 6 Sept. 1947, 409. ECA was the Washington arm of the Marshall plan.
25 'Canada's Economic Future,' ibid., 10 Jan. 1948, 45.
26 'ECA and Canadian Wheat,' ibid., 23 April 1949, 760.
27 'The Exchange Adjustments,' ibid., 24 Sept. 1949, 680–1. It was the size of the devaluation which caught the world by surprise, since the forward rate on sterling in New York indicated a discount of no more than 20 per cent. If Britain had devalued by no more than that, it is unlikely the Canadian dollar would have been adjusted from par with the U.S. As it was, the 10 per cent Canadian adjustment represented a departure from the traditional practice of adjusting midway between sterling and the U.S. dollar.
28 See *Historical Statistics of Canada*, series F334–41.
29 'Canadian Loan Freed,' *Economist*, 29 Jan. 1949, 210.
30 In 1947 Newfoundland's net national income per capita was about $300, compared with around $650 (at prevailing exchange rates) in the beleaguered United Kingdom and $825 in Canada. Calculations from Dominion Bureau of Statistics (hereafter DBS), *Province of Newfoundland: Statistical Background* (Ottawa 1949), table 105; *Historical Statistics of Canada*, series E8; and B.R. Mitchell and P. Deane (eds.), *Abstract of British Historical Statistics* (Cambridge 1962), 368.
31 Calculated from DBS *Newfoundland, Statistical Background*, table 99.
32 A large fraction of fish shipments to North America were also destined for soft currency markets as re-exports.
33 Average physical productivity per fisherman persisted for decades at around 45/50 quintals a year.
34 *Statutes of Newfoundland*, Act. no. 11, 1936.
35 The details of the development of co-operative marketing can be traced through the official minutes of the Newfoundland Fisheries Board, held in the Maritime History Group Archives, Memorial University.
36 The extensive company records of NAFEL are held in the Maritime History Group Archives, Memorial University.
37 Newfoundland Fisheries Board (hereafter NFB), *Report of the Fisheries Post-War Planning Committee* (St John's 1946), 71.
38 Ibid., 72.
39 *Report of the Fisheries Committee of the National Convention* (St John's 1947), 7.
40 *Report of the Finance Committee of the National Convention* (St John's 1947), 27.

41 H.B. Mayo, 'Newfoundland and Canada: The Case for Union Examined' (unpublished D PHIL thesis, Oxford University 1948), 202–9.

42 NAFEL, *General Circular*, 5 Sept. 1947.

43 Ibid., 6 Oct. 1947.

44 Most of the details are recorded in NFB to NAFEL, 13 Oct. 1947, C-L (47) 44. The legislation authorizing the conversion was The Salt Codfish (Trade Facilities) Act, 1947, no. 36.

45 Hawes to NAFEL, 19 April 1948, C-F (48) A61.

46 Ibid., 23 March 1948, C-F (48) A66.

47 NAFEL, *General Circular*, 12 Nov. 1947, and various letters of Hawes to NAFEL, C-F (48) A68. The Gremio was the importers' guild.

48 Hawes to NAFEL, various correspondence in C-F (47) 79 and C-F (48) A70.

49 NAFEL, *General Circular*, 30 March 1949.

50 Ibid., 20 Aug. 1948.

51 NFB to NAFEL, 9 OCT. 1948.

52 Hawes to NAFEL, 29 June 1948, C-F (48) A70.

53 E. Templeman in NFB, *Annual Report*, April 1949.

54 The terms of union negotiated with Canada in 1948 provided for a continuation of Newfoundland fishery laws for five years, and under this NAFEL's exclusive trading position was protected.

55 Hawes to NAFEL, 26 Sept. 1949, C-F (49) B37.

56 Hawes to NAFEL, 12 May 1949, C-F (49) A46.

57 Strong to NFB, 7 July 1949, C-F (49) B77.

58 NAFEL, *General Circular*, 19 Nov. 1949.

59 Ibid., 23 Aug. 1949.

60 Hawes to NAFEL, 5 OCT. 1949, C-F (49) B40(1).

61 NAFEL, *General Circular*, 14 March 1950.

62 NAFEL to Badrena, 21 Dec. 1949, C-F (49) B3.

63 H.T. Aitken to NAFEL, 19 Oct. 1949, C-F (49) B19.

64 'A Memorandum Regarding Sterling Convertibility for 1950 Newfoundland Salt Fish Production,' in NAFEL, *General Circular*, 14 March 1950.

65 *Evening Telegram* (St John's) 6 Feb. 1950.

66 The value of fishery exports in 1947 was around $31 million compared with a value of fishery products (less bait) in 1967 of some $59 million. Quite apart from the effects of inflation on real values, the gain is hardly impressive since an equal increment in values had been achieved in the forest products sector by 1949 and in the mining industry by 1954.

67 NFB *Minutes*, 5 July 1954.

68 *Evening Telegram*, 5 Dec. 1950.

69 Ibid., 14 April 1951.

70 Ibid., 10 Nov. 1951.
71 Ibid., 29 Oct. 1952.
72 Ibid., 5 Nov. 1952.
73 Ibid., 2 Nov. 1953.
74 Ibid., 27 Jan. 1954.
75 J.W. Pickersgill, *My Years with Louis St. Laurent* (Toronto 1975), 223–4.
76 An associate membership, with a much reduced entry fee, was also imposed, presumably to soften the 'monopolistic' characteristics of the organization. Few small firms applied for entry under these terms, preferring to continue marketing through the larger firms.
77 NAFEL, E-GM (52) 1.
78 Canada, *Commission of Enquiry into the Atlantic Salt Fish Industry* (Ottawa n.d.), viii–x.
79 NAFEL chairman's report, E-GM (58) 2.
80 Newfoundland, *National Fisheries Development: A Submission by the Government of Newfoundland to the Government of Canada* (St John's 1963), and Canada, Commission to Inquire into the Problems of Marketing Salted and Cured Fish Produced in the Atlantic Provinces, *Report* (Ottawa n.d.).
81 J. Douglas Gibson, 'The Changing Influence of the United States on the Canadian Economy,' *CJEPS* 22 (1956): 422–3.
82 See J.R. Petrie, 'The Impact of the Sterling-Dollar Crisis on the Maritime Economy,' *CJEPS* 16 (1950): 347–52.
83 See R.J. Wonnacott, 'Industrial Strategy: A Canadian Substitute for Trade Liberalization,' *Canadian Journal of Economics* 8 (1975): 536–47.

Select Bibliography

Readers should note that the 'Reference Works' and 'General Accounts' sections of this bibliography contain many items relevant to the more specialized headings that follow.

1 / REFERENCE WORKS

Barter, Geraldine. *A Critically Annotated Bibliography of Works Published and Unpublished Relating to the Culture of French Newfoundlanders.* St John's 1977.

Colombo, John Robert, ed. *Colombo's Canadian Quotations.* Edmonton 1974.

Cooke, Alan, and Caron, Fabien, comps. *Bibliography of the Quebec-Labrador Peninsula.* 2 vols. Boston 1968.

Dictionary of Canadian Biography. 6 vols. to date. Toronto 1966– . An indispensable source for Newfoundland biography.

Encyclopedia Canadiana. 10 vols. Toronto 1957. Deals comprehensively with many aspects of local history. See especially Rothney, Gordon, 'Newfoundland,' vol. 7, 297–320.

Government of Newfoundland. *Historical Statistics of Newfoundland and Labrador.* St John's 1970.

– *Supplement for the Historical Statistics of Newfoundland and Labrador.* St John's 1974.

Greene, John P. 'The Provincial Archives of Newfoundland.' *Acadiensis* 3, no. 1 (1973): 72–7.

Hamilton, W.B. 'Atlantic Canada.' In J.L. Granatstein and Paul Stevens, eds. *Canada since 1867: A Bibliographical Guide.* 2nd ed. Toronto 1977, 181–97.

– *Local History in Atlantic Canada.* Toronto 1974. A useful guide to many aspects of Newfoundland history.

Johnson, J.K., ed. *The Canadian Dictionary of Parliament, 1867–1967.* Ottawa 1968. Useful for post-confederation biography.

Matthews, Keith, 'A "Who was Who" of Families Engaged in the Fishery and Settlement

of Newfoundland, 1660–1840.' Mimeographed. St John's: Memorial University 1971.
– 'Check List of Research Studies pertaining to the History of Newfoundland.' In the
Maritime History Group Archives. 4th edition with accessions since October 1975.
St John's July 1978.
Mitchell, Harvey. 'Archives of Newfoundland.' *American Archivist* 21 (1958): 43–53.
An account of the early days of the Archives.
Morley, W.F.E. *The Atlantic Provinces.* Toronto 1967. A major bibliography.
Ray, Roger B., comp. *The Indians of Maine and the Atlantic Provinces: A Bibliographical
Guide.* Portland, Maine 1977.
Saywell, John T., ed. *Canadian Annual Review.* Toronto 1961–   . Since 1963 this
publication has offered a province by province review of public affairs. The 1963 and
1964 Newfoundland reviews were written by Parzival Copes and W.M. Dobell respec-
tively. Since 1965 Leslie Harris has been the Newfoundland contributor.
Seary, E.R. *Family Names of the Island of Newfoundland.* St John's 1976.
– *Place Names of the Avalon Peninsula of the Island of Newfoundland.* Toronto 1971.
Sterns, Maurice A., comp. *Newfoundland and Labrador Social Science Research: A Select
Bibliography.* St John's 1975.
Story, Norah. *The Oxford Companion to Canadian History and Literature.* Toronto 1967.
Informative 'Newfoundland' and 'Labrador' entries as well as many more specific
references to Newfoundland people and events. See also Toye, William, ed. *Supplement
to the Oxford Companion to Canadian History and Literature.* Toronto 1973.
Thibault, Claude. *Bibliographica Canadiana.* Toronto 1973.
Wallace, W.S., ed. *The Macmillan Dictionary of Canadian Biography.* 3rd ed. Toronto
1963. Covers many Newfoundland figures not yet included in the *Dictionary of Canadian
Biography.*

II / GENERAL ACCOUNTS

Anspach, Lewis Amadeus. *History of the Island of Newfoundland.* London 1819.
Canada and Newfoundland. Vol. 6 of J. Holland Rose, A.P. Newton, and E.A. Benians,
general eds. *The Cambridge History of the British Empire.* Cambridge 1930. A.P.
Newton, 'Newfoundland, 1783 to 1867,' 422–37, and 'Newfoundland, 1867–1921,'
672–85.
Chadwick, St John. *Newfoundland: Island into Province.* Cambridge 1967.
Harvey, Moses. *A Short History of Newfoundland.* 2nd ed. London 1890.
Harvey, Moses, and Hatton, Joseph. *Newfoundland, the Oldest British Colony: its History,
its Present Condition and its Prospects in the Future.* London 1883.
McAllister, R.I., ed. *Newfoundland: The First Fifteen Years of Confederation.* St John's
1966. This useful collection contains sections on 'The Land and the People,'
'The Government,' and 'The Economy.'

MacKay, R.A., ed. *Newfoundland: Economic, Diplomatic and Strategic Studies*. Toronto 1946. This important work, which reflects Canada's wartime interest in Newfoundland, includes papers under the following headings: 'The Economy of Newfoundland,' 'Diplomatic and Strategic Studies,' 'The French Shore,' 'Fishery Negotiations with the United States,' 'Relations with Canada.' The contributors to the volume were R.A. MacKay, S.A. Saunders, A.M. Fraser, Gerald S. Graham, A.R.M. Lower, and G.S. Watts.

MacNutt, W.S. *The Atlantic Provinces: The Emergence of Colonial Society, 1712–1857*. Toronto 1968.

Mannion, John, ed. *The Peopling of Newfoundland: Essays in Historical Geography*. St John's 1977.

Neary, Peter, and O'Flaherty, Patrick, eds. *By Great Waters: A Newfoundland and Labrador Anthology*. Toronto 1974.

Pedley, Charles. *The History of Newfoundland from the Earliest Times to the Year 1860*. London 1863.

Perlin, A.B. *The Story of Newfoundland*. St John's 1959.

Prowse, D.W. *A History of Newfoundland from the English, Colonial and Foreign Records*. London 1895. Reprinted by Mika Studio, Belleville, Ont. 1972.

Rogers, J.D. *Newfoundland*. Oxford 1911.

Rothney, Gordon O. *Newfoundland: A History*. Canadian Historical Association Booklets, 10. 3rd ed. Ottawa 1973.

– 'The History of Newfoundland, 1900–1949: Background Notes.' In Mason Wade, ed. *Regionalism in the Canadian Community, 1867–1967*. Toronto 1969, 198–209.

Smallwood, J.R., ed. *The Book of Newfoundland*. 6 vols. St John's 1937–75.

Sterns, Maurice A., ed. *Perspectives on Newfoundland Society and Culture*. St John's 1974.

Stewart, Alice R. 'A Regional Approach for New England and the Atlantic Provinces.' Canadian Historical Association, *Annual Report*, 1966, 187–91.

Tocque, Philip. *Newfoundland: As It Was and as It Is in 1877*. Toronto 1878.

III / POLITICAL AND CONSTITUTIONAL

Baker, Melvin. 'The Government of St. John's, Newfoundland, 1888–1902.' Unpublished MA thesis, Memorial University 1975.

– 'The Politics of Municipal Reform in St. John's, Newfoundland, 1888–1892,' *Urban History Review* 2-76 (October 1976): 12–29.

Brym, Robert J., and Neis, Barbara. 'Regional Factors in the Formation of the Fishermen's Protective Union of Newfoundland.' In Robert J. Brym and R. James Sacouman, eds. *Underdevelopment and Social Movements in Atlantic Canada*. Toronto 1979, 203–18.

Clark, Richard L. 'Newfoundland 1934–1949: A Study of the Commission of Government and Confederation with Canada.' Unpublished PH D thesis, UCLA 1951.

Cohen, Anthony P. *The Management of Myths: The Politics of Legitimation in a Newfoundland Community.* St John's 1975.

Copes, Parzival. 'The Fisherman's Vote in Newfoundland.' *Canadian Journal of Political Science* 3, (1970): 570–604.

Courage, J.R. 'The Development of Procedure in the General Assembly of Newfoundland.' Unpublished MA thesis, Memorial University 1960.

Cramm, Frank. 'The Construction of the Newfoundland Railway, 1885–1898.' Unpublished MA thesis, Memorial University 1961.

Crosbie, John C. 'Local Government in Newfoundland.' *CJEPS* 22 (1956): 332–46.

Cuff, H.A. 'The Commission of Government in Newfoundland: A Preliminary Survey.' Unpublished MA thesis, Acadia University 1959.

Feltham, John. 'The development of the F.P.U. in Newfoundland (1908–1923).' Unpublished MA thesis, Memorial University 1959.

Fizzard, Garfield. 'The Amalgamated Assembly of Newfoundland, 1841–1847.' Unpublished MA thesis, Memorial University 1963.

Fowler, William A. 'The Growth of Political Conscience in Labrador,' *NQ* 72, no. 4 (1976): 38–40, 42–4.

Fraser, A.M. 'Government-by-Commission (1934–6): A Survey.' *CJEPS* 3 (1937): 71–83.

Greene, John P. 'Edward Patrick Morris, 1886–1900.' Unpublished paper, Centre for Newfoundland Studies, Memorial University.

– 'Newfoundland: The Election Scandals of 1894; By-products of the Administration of Local Affairs.' Unpublished paper, History Department, Memorial University n.d.

– 'The Influence of Religion in the Politics of Newfoundland, 1850–61.' Unpublished MA thesis, Memorial University 1970.

Gunn, Gertrude. *The Political History of Newfoundland, 1832–1864.* Toronto 1966.

Gwyn, Richard. *Smallwood: The Unlikely Revolutionary.* Rev. ed. Toronto 1972.

Harris, Leslie. 'The First Nine Years of Representative Government in Newfoundland.' Unpublished MA thesis, Memorial University 1959.

Hiller, James. 'A History of Newfoundland, 1874–1901.' Unpublished PH D thesis, Cambridge University 1971.

– 'The Political Effects of the Harbour Grace Affray, 1883–85.' Unpublished lecture, Newfoundland Historical Society 1971.

– 'Whiteway and Progress.' *NQ* 68, no. 4 (1972): 15–18.

Innis, Harold A. 'Basic Problems of Government in Newfoundland.' *CJEPS* 3 (1937): 83–5.

Johnson, Jon B. 'The Newfoundland Provincial Election, September 16, 1975.' Unpublished MA thesis, McGill University 1976.

Jones, Frederick. 'Bishop Feild: A Study in Politics and Religion in 19th Century Newfoundland.' Unpublished PH D thesis, Cambridge University 1971.

- 'Bishops in Politics: Roman Catholic v. Protestant in Newfoundland 1860–2.' *CHR* 55 (1974): 408–21.
Kerr, K.J. 'A Social Analysis of the Members of the Newfoundland House of Assembly, Executive Council, and Legislative Council for the Period 1855–1914.' Unpublished MA thesis, Memorial University 1973.
McCorquodale, Susan. 'Newfoundland: Plus ça change, plus c'est la même chose.' In Martin Robin, ed. *Canadian Provincial Politics: The Party Systems of the Ten Provinces.* 2nd ed. Toronto 1978, 138–70.
- 'Public Administration in Newfoundland during the Period of the Commission of Government: A Question of Political Development.' Unpublished PH D thesis, Queen's University 1973.
McDonald, Ian. 'W.F. Coaker and the Fishermen's Protective Union in Newfoundland Politics, 1908–1925.' Unpublished PH D thesis, University of London 1971.
McLintock, A.H. *The Establishment of Constitutional Government in Newfoundland, 1783–1832: A Study of Retarded Colonization.* London 1941.
MacWhirter, W.D. 'A Political History of Newfoundland, 1865–1874.' Unpublished MA thesis, Memorial University 1963.
Matthews, Keith. 'The Class of '32: St. John's Reformers on the Eve of Representative Government.' *Acadiensis* 6, no. 2 (1977): 80–94.
Matthews, Ralph. 'Perspectives on Recent Newfoundland Politics.' *Journal of Canadian Studies* 9, no. 2 (1974): 20–35.
- 'The Smallwood Legacy: The Development of Underdevelopment in Newfoundland, 1949–1972.' *Journal of Canadian Studies* 13, no. 4 (1978–9): 89–108.
Mitchell, Harvey. 'The Constitutional Crisis of 1889 in Newfoundland.' *CJEPS* 24 (1958): 323–31.
Moulton, E.C. 'Constitutional Crisis and Civil Strife in Newfoundland, February to November 1861.' *CHR* 48 (1967): 251–72.
- 'The Political History of Newfoundland, 1861–1869.' Unpublished MA thesis, Memorial University 1960.
Neary, Peter. 'Changing Government: The 1971–72 Newfoundland Example.' *Dalhousie Law Journal* 5, no. 3 (1979): 631–58.
- 'Democracy in Newfoundland: A Comment.' *Journal of Canadian Studies* 4, no. 1 (1969): 37–45.
- 'Party Politics in Newfoundland, 1949–71: A Survey and Analysis.' *Journal of Canadian Studies* 6, no. 4 (1971): 3–14.
- 'Party Politics in Newfoundland: The End of the Smallwood Era.' *Journal of Canadian Studies* 7, no. 1 (1972): 3–21.
- ed. *The Political Economy of Newfoundland, 1929–1972.* Toronto 1973.
Noel, S.J.R. 'Politics and the Crown: The Case of the 1908 Tie Election in Newfoundland.' *CJEPS* 33 (1967): 285–91.
- *Politics in Newfoundland.* Toronto 1971.

Overton, James. 'Towards a Critical Analysis of Neo-Nationalism in Newfoundland.' In
Robert J. Brym and R. James Sacouman, eds. *Underdevelopment and Social Movements
in Atlantic Canada.* Toronto 1979, 219–49.

Paine, Robert. 'Who's a Spoiler? A Note on the Newfoundland Provincial Election of
September, 1975.' *NQ* 72, no. 2 (1976): 33–9.

Panting, G.E. 'Newfoundland's Loss of Responsible Government.' In J.M. Bumsted, ed.
Documentary Problems in Canadian History. Georgetown 1969.

– 'The Fishermen's Protective Union of Newfoundland and the Farmer's Organizations in
Western Canada.' Canadian Historical Association, *Annual Report*, 1963, 141–51.

– 'The People in Politics.' *NQ* 65, no. 4 (1967): 15–17.

Perlin, George. 'St. John's West.' In John Meisel, ed. *Papers on the 1962 Election.*
Toronto 1964.

Pickersgill, J.W. *My Years with Louis St. Laurent: A Political Memoir.* Toronto 1975.

Plumptre, A.F.W. 'The Amulree Report (1933): A Review.' *CJEPS* 3 (1937): 58–71.

Pottle, Herbert. *Newfoundland, a Light that Failed.* Portugal Cove, Nfld 1979.

Powell, C.W. 'Problems of Municipal Government in Newfoundland.' Institute of Public
Administration of Canada, *Proceedings*, 1949, 168–82.

Rothney, G.O. 'The Denominational Basis of Representation in the Newfoundland House
of Assembly, 1919–1962.' *CJEPS* 28 (1962): 557–70.

Senior, Elinor. 'The Origin and Political Activities of the Orange Order in Newfoundland,
1863–1890.' Unpublished MA thesis, Memorial University 1959.

Smallwood, J.R. *I Chose Canada.* Toronto 1973.

Stanley, G.F.G. 'Sir Stephen Hill's Observations on the Election of 1869 in Newfoundland.' *CHR* 29 (1948): 278–85.

Vallis, Fred. 'Sectarianism as a Factor in the 1908 Election.' *NQ* 70, no. 3 (1974):
17–28.

Wells, Elizabeth A. 'The Struggle for Responsible Government in Newfoundland,
1846–1855.' Unpublished MA thesis, Memorial University 1966.

Winter, Harry Anderson. 'Memoirs of Henry Anderson Winter.' Introduction by A.B.
Perlin. Parts 1 and 2, *NQ* 72, no. 1 (1976): 15–24; part 3, *NQ* 72, no. 3: 17–22.

IV / ECONOMIC

Akyeampong, E.B. 'Labour Laws and the Development of the Labour Movement in
Newfoundland, 1900–1960.' Unpublished MA thesis, Acadia University 1970.

Alexander, David. 'Development and Dependence in Newfoundland.' *Acadiensis* 4, no. 1
(1974): 3–31.

– 'Newfoundland's Traditional Economy and Development to 1934.' *Acadiensis* 5, no. 2
(1976): 56–78.

– 'The Collapse of the Saltfish Trade and Newfoundland's Integration into the North

American Economy.' Canadian Historical Association, *Historical Papers* (1976), 229–48.

– *The Decay of Trade: An Economic History of the Newfoundland Saltfish Trade, 1935–1965*. St John's 1977.

– 'The Political Economy of Fishing in Newfoundland.' *Journal of Canadian Studies* 11, no. 1 (1976): 32–40.

Antler, Steven D. 'Colonialism as a Factor in the Economic Stagnation of Nineteenth Century Newfoundland: Some Preliminary Notes.' Unpublished manuscript, Centre for Newfoundland Studies, Memorial University.

Chodos, Robert. *Let Us Prey*. Toronto 1974.

Fay, C.R. *Channel Islands and Newfoundland*. Cambridge 1961.

– *Life and Labour in Newfoundland*. Cambridge 1956.

– 'Newfoundland and the Labrador Potential.' *CJEPS* 19 (1953): 455–61.

Hamdani, Daood Ul Hasan. 'The Role of Public Finance in the Economic Development of Newfoundland, 1949–64.' Unpublished MA thesis, Memorial University 1966.

Innis, Harold A. *The Cod Fisheries: The History of an International Economy*. Rev. ed. Toronto 1954.

Joy, J.L. 'The Growth and Development of Trades and Manufacturing in St. John's, 1870–1914.' Unpublished MA thesis, Memorial University 1977.

McGrath, Sir P.T. 'Newfoundland and the Paper Supply.' *Dalhousie Review* 3 (1923–4): 483–91.

Mathias, Philip. *Forced Growth*. Toronto 1971.

Matthews, Keith. 'A History of the West of England–Newfoundland Fishery.' Unpublished D PHIL thesis, Oxford University, 1968.

Mayo, H.B. 'The Economic Problem of the Newfoundland Fisheries.' *CJEPS* 17 (1951): 482–93.

Neary, Peter. 'Newfoundland and Quebec: Provincial Neighbours across an Uneasy Frontier.' *Bulletin of Canadian Studies* 2, no. 2 (1978): 35–51.

Peters, Robert D. 'The Social and Economic Effects of the Transition from a System of Woods Camps to a System of Commuting in the Newfoundland Pulpwood Industry.' Unpublished MA thesis, Memorial University 1965.

Ryan, Shannon. 'The Newfoundland Cod Fishery in the Nineteenth Century.' Unpublished MA thesis, Memorial University 1971.

Sanger, C.W. 'Technological and Spatial Adaptation in the Newfoundland Seal Fishery during the 19th Century.' Unpublished MA thesis, Memorial University 1973.

Smith, Philip. *Brinco: The Story of Churchill Falls*. Toronto 1976.

Staveley, Michael. 'Migration and Mobility in Newfoundland and Labrador: A Study in Population Geography.' Unpublished PH D thesis, University of Alberta 1973.

Usher, Abbott Payson. 'The Influence of the Cod Fishery upon the History of the North Atlantic Seaboard.' *CJEPS* 6 (1940): 591–99. A review of Harold A. Innis, *The Cod Fisheries: The History of an International Economy*.

V / IMPERIAL AND INTERNATIONAL

Anglin, Douglas G. *The St. Pierre and Miquelon Affaire of 1941*. Toronto 1966.

Brebner, John Bartlet. *North Atlantic Triangle: The Interplay of Canada, the United States and Great Britain*. New Haven 1945.

Campbell, C.S. 'American Tariff Interests and the Northeastern Fisheries, 1883–1888.' *CHR* 45 (1964): 212–28.

– *Anglo-American Understanding, 1898–1903*. Baltimore 1957.

Cave, Joy B. *What Became of Corporal Pittman?* Portugal Cove, Nfld 1976.

Cayley, Charles E. 'The North Atlantic Fisheries in U.S.–Canadian Relations: A History of the Fisheries Problems, their Settlements and Attempted Settlements, with Special Emphasis on the Period since the Establishment of the Dominion of Canada.' Unpublished PH D thesis, University of Chicago 1931.

Davis, D.J. 'The Bond-Blaine Negotiations, 1890–1891.' Unpublished MA thesis, Memorial University 1970.

Gluek, Alvin C., Jr. 'Programmed Diplomacy: The Settlement of the North Atlantic Fisheries Question, 1907–12.' *Acadiensis* 6, no. 1 (1976): 43–70.

Mulock, P.M. 'North-Atlantic Fisheries, 1866–1885; A Study in Canadian and American Relations.' Unpublished MA thesis, Acadia University 1939.

Nicholson, G.W.L. *The Fighting Newfoundlander: The History of the Royal Newfoundland Regiment*. St John's 1964.

– *More Fighting Newfoundlanders: A History of Newfoundland's Fighting Forces in the Second World War*. St John's 1969.

Neary, Peter. 'Grey, Bryce, and the Settlement of Canadian-American Differences, 1905–1911.' *CHR* 49 (1968): 357–80.

– 'The French Shore Question, 1865–1878.' Unpublished MA thesis, Memorial University 1961.

– 'The Embassy of James Bryce in the United States, 1907–13.' Unpublished PH D thesis, University of London 1965.

Neary, Peter, and Noel, S.J.R. 'Newfoundland's Quest for Reciprocity, 1890–1910.' In Mason Wade, ed. *Regionalism in the Canadian Community, 1867–1967*. Toronto 1969, 210–26.

Reeves, William G. 'The Fortune Bay Dispute: Newfoundland's Place in Imperial Treaty Relations under the Washington Treaty, 1871–1885.' Unpublished MA thesis, Memorial University 1971.

Robison, Houston. 'Newfoundland's Surrender of Dominion Status in the British Empire, 1918–1934.' Unpublished PH D thesis, University of Chicago 1949.

Stacey, C.P. 'The Withdrawal of the Imperial Garrison from Newfoundland, 1870.' *CHR* 17 (1936): 147–58.

Stewart, Ian M. 'The "Revolution of 1940" in Newfoundland.' Unpublished MA thesis, Memorial University 1974.

Straus, Richard. 'The Diplomatic Negotiations Leading to the Establishment of American Bases in Newfoundland, June 1940–April 1941.' Unpublished MA thesis, Memorial University 1972.

Tallman, R.D. 'Warships and Mackeral: the North Atlantic Fisheries in Canadian-American Relations, 1867–1877.' Unpublished PH D thesis, University of Maine 1971.

Tansill, C.C. *Canadian-American Relations, 1875–1911*. New Haven 1943.

Thompson, F.F. *The French Shore Problem in Newfoundland: An Imperial Study*. Toronto 1961.

Tucker, Gilbert N. 'Some Aspects of the Battle of the Atlantic.' Canadian Historical Association, *Annual Report*, 1946, 84–91.

– 'The Organizing of the East Coast Patrols, 1914–1918.' Canadian Historical Association, *Annual Report*, 1941, 32–40.

VI / NEWFOUNDLAND AND CANADA

Bridle, Paul, ed. *Documents on Relations between Canada and Newfoundland*. Vol. 1. Ottawa 1974.

Browne, G.P., ed. *Documents on the Confederation of British North America*. Toronto 1969.

Brun, Henri. 'Le Labrador à l'heure de la contestation' (review article). *Canadian Journal of Political Science* 6 (1973): 518–20.

Cashin, Peter, Horwood, Harold, and Harris, Leslie. 'Newfoundland and Confederation, 1948–49.' In Mason Wade, ed. *Regionalism in the Canadian Community, 1867–1967*. Toronto 1969, 227–63.

Christopher, Brother. 'The Influence of Economic Factors on Newfoundland's Entrance into Confederation.' Unpublished MA thesis, University of Ottawa 1957.

Creighton, D.G. *John A. Macdonald*. 2 vols. Toronto 1952–5.

– *Road to Confederation*. Toronto 1964.

Cunningham, W.B. 'Newfoundland Finance, with Particular Reference to the Union with Canada, 1949.' Unpublished MA thesis, Brown University 1950.

Eggleston, Wilfred. *Newfoundland: The Road to Confederation*. Ottawa 1974.

Finkle, Peter Z.R. 'Canadian Policy for Marine Fisheries: An Alternative.' *Journal of Canadian Studies* 10, no. 1 (1975): 10–24.

Granatstein, J.L. *Canada's War: The Politics of the Mackenzie King Government, 1939–1945*. Toronto 1975.

Hayman, Kathryn E. 'The origins and function of the Canadian High Commission in Newfoundland, 1941–1949.' Unpublished MA thesis, University of Western Ontario 1979.

Hiller, James, comp. *The Confederation Issue in Newfoundland, 1864–1869: Selected Documents*. St John's 1974.

Jones, Frederick. 'Newfoundland and Canada in the 1860s.' *History Today* 22 (1972): 420–5.

Longley, J.W. 'Difficulties with Newfoundland.' *Proceedings and Transactions of the Royal Society of Canada* 11, 3rd series (1917), section 2: 253–66.

Mayo, H.B. 'Newfoundland and Canada: The Case for Union Examined.' D PHIL thesis, Oxford University 1948.

– 'Newfoundland and Confederation in the Eighteen-Sixties.' *CHR* 29 (1948): 125–42.

– 'Newfoundland's Entry into the Dominion.' *CJEPS* 15 (1949): 505–22.

Mitchell, Harvey. 'Canada's Negotiations with Newfoundland, 1887–1895.' *CHR* 40, (1959): 277–93. Reprinted in G.A. Rawlyk, ed. *Historical Essays on the Atlantic Provinces.* Toronto 1967, 242–59.

Smith, F.J. 'Newfoundland and Confederation, 1864–1870.' Unpublished MA thesis, University of Ottawa 1970.

Stacey, C.P. *Arms, Men and Governments.* Ottawa 1970.

Stanley, G.F.G. 'Further Documents Relating to the Union of Newfoundland and Canada, 1886–1895.' *CHR* 29 (1948): 370–86.

Waite, P.B. *The Life and Times of Confederation.* 2nd ed. Toronto 1962.

VII / SOCIETY AND CULTURE

Barnes, Arthur. 'The History of Education in Newfoundland.' Unpublished D PAED thesis, New York 1917.

Bellows, G.R. 'The Foundation of Memorial University College, 1919–1925.' *NQ* 71, no. 4 (1975): 5–9.

Brown, Howard. 'A Study of the Curling Area, 1860–1920.' *NQ* 71, no. 3 (1975): 17–25; no. 4: 17–24.

Burke, Louis. 'Some Irish Contributors and Contributions to Newfoundland Education in the Last Century.' Unpublished M LITT thesis, University of Dublin 1975.

Devereux, E.J. 'Early Printing in Newfoundland.' *Dalhousie Review* 43, (1963): 57–66.

Cohen, Anthony P. 'The Definition of Public Identity: Managing Marginality in Outport Newfoundland Following Confederation.' *Sociological Review* 23 (1975): 93–119.

Crumlish, Michael L. 'The Christian Brothers: A Factor in the Development of Education in Newfoundland.' Unpublished MA thesis, Notre Dame University 1932.

Cuff, H.A. 'The Newfoundland Teachers' Association, 1890–1930: Its Founding and Its Establishment as a Stable, Influential and Permanent Professional Organisation.' Unpublished MA thesis, Memorial University 1971.

Dunphy, Mary A. 'The History of Teacher Training in Newfoundland, 1726–1955.' Unpublished B ED thesis, Mount St Vincent University 1956.

Fingard, Judith. 'The Relief of the Unemployed Poor in St. John, Halifax and St. John's, 1815–1860.' *Acadiensis* 5 no. 1 (1975): 32–53.

– 'The Winter's Tale: Contours of Pre-industrial Poverty in British America, 1815–1860.'
Canadian Historical Association, *Historical Papers*, 1974, 65–94.

Halpert, Herbert, and Story, G.M. *Christmas Mumming in Newfoundland*. Toronto 1970.

Hamilton, W.B. 'Society and Schools in Newfoundland.' In J. Donald Wilson, Robert M.
Stamp, and Louis-Philippe Audet, eds. *Canadian Education: A History*. Scarborough
1970, 126–44.

Hammond, James J. 'A Study of the Administration of Education in Newfoundland,
1949–1973.' Unpublished MA thesis, Dalhousie University 1975.

Handcock, Walter G. 'The Origin and Development of Commission of Government Land
Settlements in Newfoundland, 1934–1969.' Unpublished MA thesis, Memorial University 1970.

– 'Spatial Patterns in a Trans-Atlantic Migration Field: the British Isles and Newfoundland
during the Eighteenth and Nineteenth Centuries.' In Brian S. Osborne, ed. *The Settlement of Canada: Origins and Transfer*. Kingston 1976, 13–45.

Howley, Michael F. *Ecclesiastical History of Newfoundland*. Boston 1888.

Howley, J.P. *The Beothucks or Red Indians: The aboriginal inhabitants of Newfoundland*.
Cambridge 1915. Reprinted in Coles Canadiana Collection 1974.

Hughes, R.D. 'Alexander Murray (1810–1884).' Geological Association of Canada,
Proceedings 23 (1971): 1–4.

Jones, Frederick. *Edward Feild, Bishop of Newfoundland, 1844–1876*. Pamphlet.
St John's 1976.

– 'John Bull's Other Ireland – Nineteenth Century Newfoundland.' *Dalhousie Review* 55
(1975–6): 227–35.

– 'The Early Opposition to Bishop Feild of Newfoundland.' *Journal of the Canadian
Church Historical Society* 16 (1974): 30–41.

– 'The Making of a Colonial Bishop: Feild of Newfoundland.' *Journal of the Canadian
Church Historical Society* 15 (1973): 2–13.

Kelly, E.T. 'The Coming of the Newfoundland Irish: The State of the Question.' *NQ* 65,
no. 4, (1967): 18–20; 66, no. 1 (1967): 14–16.

Leyton, Elliott. *Dying Hard: The Ravages of Industrial Carnage*. Toronto 1975.

McCormack, Sister Mary B. 'The Educational Work of the Sisters of Mercy in Newfoundland, 1842–1955.' Unpublished MA thesis, Catholic University of America 1955.

McGee, H.F., ed. *The Native Peoples of Atlantic Canada*. Toronto 1974.

Mannion, John. *Irish Settlements in Eastern Canada: A Study of Cultural Transfer and
Adaptation*. Toronto 1974.

– *Point Lance in Transition: The Transformation of a Newfoundland Outport*. Toronto
1976.

Marshall, Ingeborg, and Springett, Martin. *The Red Ochre People: How Newfoundland's
Beothuck Indians Lived*. Vancouver 1977.

Martin, Anne Elizabeth. 'Up-Along: Newfoundland Families in Hamilton.' Unpublished
MA thesis, McMaster University 1974.

Matthews, Ralph. *'There's No Better Place than Here': Social Change in Three Newfound-land Communities*. Toronto 1976.

Mercer, Paul, ed. *The Ballads of Johnny Burke: A Short Anthology*. Pamphlet. St John's 1974.

Mills, David B. 'The Evolution of Folk Architecture in Trinity Bay.' *NQ* 69, no. 3 (1972): 17–23.

Moyles, Robert G. *'Complaints is Many and Various but the Odd Divil Likes It': Nineteenth Century Views of Newfoundland*. Toronto 1975.

Neary, Peter. ' "Traditional" and "Modern" Elements in the Social and Economic History of Bell Island and Conception Bay.' Canadian Historical Association, *Historical Papers*, 1973, 105–36.

– *Bell Island, a Newfoundland mining community, 1895–1966*. Ottawa 1974.

Nemec, Thomas F. 'St. Shotts in Historical Perspective.' *NQ* 71, no. 3 (1975): 17–22.

– 'The Irish Emigration to Newfoundland.' *NQ* 69, no. 1 (1972): 15–19, 22–4.

– 'Trepassey, 1505–1840 A.D.: The Emergence of an Anglo-Irish Newfoundland Out-port.' *NQ* 69, no. 4 (1973): 17–27.

– 'Trepassey, 1840–1900: The Ethnohistorical Reconstruction of Anglo-Irish Outport Society.' *NQ* 70, no. 1 (1973): 15–24.

Netten, J.W. 'Edward Feild, Protagonist of Denominational Education.' In L.S. Patterson *et al.*, eds. *Profiles of Canadian Educators*. Toronto 1974, 77–94.

O'Dea, Shane. *The Domestic Architecture of Old St. John's*. Pamphlet. St John's 1974.

O'Flaherty, Patrick. 'Looking Backwards: The Milieu of the Old Newfoundland Outports.' *Journal of Canadian Studies* 10 (1975): 3–9.

– Introduction to *New Priest in Conception Bay*, by Robert Traill Spence Lowell. Toronto 1974.

– *The Rock Observed: Studies in the Literature of Newfoundland*. Toronto 1979.

Ommer, R.E. 'Scots Kinship, Immigration and Early Settlement in Southwestern New-foundland.' Unpublished MA thesis, Memorial University 1973.

O'Neill, Paul. *The Story of St. John's, Newfoundland*. Vol. 1, *The Oldest City*. Erin, Ont. 1975. Vol. 2, *A Seaport Legacy*. Erin, Ont. 1976.

Parsons, Jacob. 'The Origin and Growth of Newfoundland Methodism, 1765–1855.' Unpublished MA thesis, Memorial University 1964.

Pastore, Ralph. *The Newfoundland Micmacs*. St John's 1978.

Patterson, George. 'The Beothiks or Red Indians of Newfoundland.' *Proceedings and Transactions of the Royal Society of Canada* 9 (1891), section 2: 123–71.

Pitt, D.G. *Windows of Agates*. St John's 1966.

Raymond, W.O. 'Philip Henry Gosse and *The Canadian Naturalist*.' *Proceedings and Transactions of the Royal Society of Canada* 45, 3rd series (1951), section 2: 43–58.

Rowe, Frederick W. *Education and Culture in Newfoundland*. Toronto 1976.

– *Extinction: The Beothucks of Newfoundland*. Toronto 1977.

– *The History of Education in Newfoundland*. Toronto 1952.

Sheldon, Mary. 'The Establishment of the Denominational School System in Newfoundland with Particular Reference to the Role of the Anglican Church, 1836–1876.' Unpublished MA thesis, University of Toronto 1972.

Sider, Gerald M. 'Christmas Mumming and the New Year in Outport Newfoundland.' *Past & Present* 71, (1976): 102–25.

Smith, Marjorie. 'Newfoundland, 1815–1840: A Study of a Merchantocracy.' Unpublished MA thesis, Memorial University 1968.

Story, G.M. *George Street United Church: One Hundred Years of Service.* St John's 1973.

– 'Judge Prowse (1834–1914),' *NQ* 68, no. 1 (1971): 15–19, 22–5.

– 'Judge Prowse: Historian and Publicist.' *NQ* 78, no. 4 (1972): 19, 22–5.

– 'Newfoundland Dialect: The Historical View.' *Canadian Geographical Journal* 70 (1965): 126–31.

– 'Notes from a Berry Patch.' *Proceedings and Transactions of the Royal Society of Canada* 10, 4th series (1972), section 2: 163–77.

– 'St. John's Balladeers.' *English Quarterly* 4 (1971): 49–58.

Teresina, Sister Mary. 'The First Forty Years of Educational Legislation in Newfoundland.' Unpublished MA (Ed.) thesis, University of Ottawa 1956.

Upton, L.F.S. 'The Beothucks: Questions and Answers.' *Acadiensis* 7, no. 2 (1978): 150–5.

– 'The Extermination of the Beothucks of Newfoundland.' *CHR* 58 (1977): 133–53.

Veitch, N.A. 'The Contribution of the Benevolent Irish Society to Education in Newfoundland from 1823 to 1875.' Unpublished M ED thesis, St Francis Xavier University 1965.

Whiteley, Albert S. *A Century in Bonne Esperance: The Saga of the Whiteley Family.* Ottawa 1977.

Whiteway, Louise. 'Newfoundland in 1867.' *Dalhousie Review* 46 (1966–7): 39–62.

– 'The Athenaeum Movement: St. John's Athenaeum (1861–1898).' *Dalhousie Review* 50 (1970–1): 543–9.

Wicks, Rene. 'Newfoundland Social Life: 1750–1850.' *NQ* 70, no. 4 (1974): 17–23.

Winsor, Naboth. 'Methodism in Newfoundland, 1855–1884.' Unpublished MA thesis, Memorial University 1970.

Winter, Keith John. *Shanaditti: The Last of the Beothucks.* Vancouver 1975.

Zaslow, Morris. *Reading the Rocks: The Story of the Geological Survey of Canada, 1842–1972.* Toronto 1975.

Index

Abbott, B.J. 234
Act for the Encouragement of Manufacturing (1877) 26
Adams, William 238
Alexander, David G. 12, 141
Alsop, Robert 81
American Shore 95–122 passim; and U.S. dispute with Newfoundland 114–18
Amulree Royal Commission (1933) 196–8, 204 n90
Anglo-Newfoundland Development Company (AND): and Grand Falls paper-mill 30; strike against (1958) 219–22
Anspach, Lewis Amadeus 3–4

Baine Johnston and Company 49, 50, 81
Bait Act (1887) 134
Bannerman, Sir Alexander 4, 67
Bates, Stewart 259
'Battle of Foxtrap,' the (1880) 130
Bayard, Thomas F. 116
Bemister, John 80
Bennett, Charles Fox 76, 77, 78, 79, 108; and 1881 railway petition 127–31
Bennett, Sir J.R. 184
Bennett, Thomas 81
Blackman, A.L. 130, 131

Blaine, James G. 117, 136
Bond, Sir Robert 113, 117, 136–41 passim, 161
Bond-Blaine convention (1890) 117, 136–7
Bradley, F. Gordon 206, 208, 218
Bramston, Sir John 113
Brebner, John Bartlet 10
Brennan, Peter 71
Browne, W.J. 219, 222
Burgess, Tom 232, 235, 241

Campbell, Dr Alexander 181, 185
Campbell, C.S. 10
Canadian Saltfish Corporation 260
Canadian Union of Public Employees (CUPE): and 1967 strike in Grand Falls 226–7
Cardwell, Edward 107, 110
Caron, Fabian 13
Carroll, Michael 81
Carter, Frederick B.T. 69, 70–89 passim, 101, 124; and railway 126
Cashin, Sir Michael 166, 183–4, 185, 190, 193–4, 207
Cashin, Peter 207, 216, 217, 253
Cashin, Richard 232

Catholicism, Roman: nineteenth-century
influence of in Newfoundland 14 n18,
67–89, 160–8 passim
Cell, Gillian. T. 9
Chadwick, St John 7, 8
Chamberlain, Joseph 116, 139
Chamberlain-Bayard Treaty (1888) 116
Churchill Falls (Labrador) Corporation Ltd
229
Clift, J.S. 78
Coaker, Sir William F. 31, 182–3; and
alliance with Liberal party 163–7, 181–
4; and balance of power strategy in early
twentieth century 148–80; biography of
155; and Fishermen's Protective Union
148–58, 169–71; relations with Edward
Morris 161, relations with Robert Bond
161–2
Coal Development Act (1910) 30
cod fishery: and bye-boat fishery 41–2; decline of 40–66, 75, 151–2, 246–67;
Harold A. Innis on 10; and Labrador
fishery 45–7, 51; and Newfoundland's
nineteenth-century competitors 57–9;
and Newfoundland's nineteenth-century
conditions of trade 59–62, 151–3; and
resident fishery 41–7 passim; and seal
fishery 44–5; as source of employment
and market income 19–22, 23, 47–57;
technological developments in 50;
twentieth-century legislation re 31; and
West Country fishery 3, 19, 41–2,
47, 97
Commercial Society 69, 79
Companies Corporation Act (1873) 26
Cook, Peter 233
Cooke, Alan 9; and Fabian Caron 13
Crosbie, John 228, 232, 233, 234, 238
Curtis, Leslie R. 206, 233

Dalton, John 72
Darling, Charles 100
Deutsch, John 233
Dawe, Robert 80
Drew, George 206
Dominion Iron and Steel Company (DOSCO):
bribery and 181, 190
Drover, Sam 224
Duffy, A.M. 224
Duncan, James 250

Earle, H.V.R. 234
Edward Duder and Company 50
Erskine, Sir James 113
Evans, Edward 82

Fay, C.R. 9
Finn Commission 260, 267 n80
Fishermen's Protective Union (FPU) 148–
80, 163, 183; and erosion of its influence
in 1920s 169–71; and merchant opposition to 166–8; organization of 158; platform of 156–7, 158; political, social,
and commercial reasons for formation of
148–56; and 1913–23 political
involvement 164–9; and proposed 1923
reorganization of 169–70; relationship
with Liberal party of Robert Bond 162;
comparison with Non-Partisan League
159–60; and Roman Catholic and Protestant opposition 162–5, 183
Fleming, Sandford 124–5
Forrest, H.H. 109
Fraser, A.M. 11
Frecker, J.P. 82
French Shore 44, 48, 85, 95–122; and
Bramston-Erskine enquiry 113; and
1836 French claim 99–100; legislation
re 96; and lobster-canning and bait

dispute 113–14; magistrates for 109–11, 126; and opposition of St John's merchants to French fishing 98–9; and 1857–1901 pressure of Newfoundland population re 103–6; settlement re between France and Britain 113–14
Fulton, Davie 222

Gibson, J. Douglas 261
Glen, Thomas 84
Glover, Sir John 126
Gosling, W.G. 14, 15 n19
Graham, Gerald S. 8
Granatstein, J.L. and Paul Stevens 11
Granger, C.R. 227
Green, W.S. 80
Greene, James 225, 227
Gremio (Portuguese importers' guild) 256, 257
Gunn, Gertrude 8
Gushue, Raymond 252, 253, 259

Hamilton, W.B. 11
Harris, Sir C. Alexander 8
Harris, Leslie 12
Harrisse, Henry 9
Harvey, A.W. 136
Harvey, Moses 5–6, 124, 125
Hawco, M.C. 187
Hay, John 117
Hickman, Albert E. 195
Hickman, T. Alex 233, 234
Higgins, Gordon 216, 217
Higgins, James 224, 225
Higgins, John G. 215
Higgins, W.J. 183, 184, 188, 196
Hill, Stephen 79, 85
Hiller, James 9
Hogan, Patrick 43

Hollett, Malcolm 217, 224, 225
Hollis Walker, Thomas. See Walker
Homestead Law (1873) 26, 76
Horwood, Harold 216–17, 224, 259
Howe, C.D. 260
Howley, James P. 8, 14 n18
Howley, Michael F. 139, 140, 163
Howley, W.R. 188, 191
Howarth, William 111
Hoyles, Hugh W. 67–70, 101

Innis, Harold A. 10
International Woodworkers of America (IWA): in Newfoundland 219–22

Jamieson, Donald 221, 232–3, 236–7
J. and W. Stewart Company 81
Job Brothers and Company 49, 78, 81
John Munn and Company 50
Jones, Bertram 75
Jones, Frederick 9
Joyce, Randolph 233
Judah, Charles B. 9

Kavanagh, John 71
Kent, John M. 67–73, 101, 164
Kent, Robert 83
Keough, William J. 206, 259–60
Kirwin, William 12
Kitchen, Hubert 235–6, 238
Knight, Thomas 80

Labrador Rights party. See 'New Labrador party'
La Morandière, Charles de 9
Ladd, H. Landon 219
Lane, C. Max 220
Liberal party (post-confederation): 1949–57 history of in Newfoundland 205–18;

and 1959 controversies 219–26; and
1966 election 226; and 1968 election
226–32; and 1970 Independent Liberals
and 'Reform Group' 234–5, 237
Little, J.J. 128
Little, Philip F. 101
Lloyd, Sir W.F. 165
Loch, Granville 97, 98
Lodge, Henry Cabot 117
Lounsbury, R.G. 9–10

McCallum, Sir Henry 140
McDonald, Ian 8
Magrath, Charles A. 197–8
McGrath, James 222
McGrath, P.T. 190
MacKay, R.A. 11, 83
McLintock, A.H. 8
McNair Commission 223–4
McNair, J.B. 223
McNeily, A.J.W. 132, 133
MacNutt, W.S. 10
Mannion, John 10, 12
March, Stephen 81
Matthews, Keith 9, 12
Mayo, Henry B. 9, 253–4
Meaney, John T. 181; dismissal of as
acting liquor controller 187–8
Mews, H.G.R. 206, 215
Middleton, G.H. 136
Mitchell, Harvey 12
Model Farm Act (1908) 31
Monroe, Walter 193–6
Moores, Frank 235, 238
Morine, Sir Alfred B. 113, 138, 140, 141,
193
Morison, Donald 161
Morley, W.F.E. 11
Morris, Sir Edward P. 105, 117, 139; and

relations between FPU and People's party
160–1
Morton, W.L. 9
Muir and Duder Company 80
Mullock, John 71, 72, 100–1
Munn, John 80
Murphy, Noel 227, 228, 238
Murray, Alexander 107, 123–4, 126
Murray, Sir Herbert 139–40
Musgrave, Anthony 69, 107, 110
Myrden, Gerald 234

Napoleonic Wars: influence of on
Newfoundland 44, 48, 55, 56, 58
National Fishing Company (Portugal) 61
'New Labrador party,' the (Labrador Rights
party) 235, 237
Newfoundland
agriculture in 26–7; commission government in 36, 171; and confederation
– Commercial Society and 69, 79
– confederates' attitude towards 75
– 1869 Canadian government attitude towards Newfoundland and 67, 85–6
– 1869 rejection of 67–94, 123–47
– fishery merchants' attitude towards
73–5, 77–8, 96–7
– Protestants' attitude towards 79–81
– Roman Catholic attitude towards 69–
83 passim
– terms of 209, 223
and denominational struggles 67–94
passim, 129, 132–4, 207–8, 211–13;
and development of manufacturing in
26–7, 29–32; employment in 19–22,
23, 29, 33–4, 229; and Fishermen's Protective Union 162–3, fishery in, in sixteenth century 18; and growth of
population 19, 21, 23–5, 32, 41–2, 51,

75, 96, 103–4, 229; and growth of St John's as retail centre 149–51; and McNair Commission report (1957) 223–4; nineteenth-century written history of 3–7; and 1957–68 political situation 219–32; and 1949–57 political situation 205–18; and 1968–72 political situation 232–41; and 1969 agreement with federal Department of Regional Economic Expansion (DREE) 236; and 1920s political situation 185–7; and outport life 148–9, 153–5, and the railway 25, 26, 123–47; responsible government in 25, 35, 77; and shipbuilding 26; twentieth-century written history of 7–13. *See also* American Shore, cod fishery, Fishermen's Protective Union, French Shore, International Woodworkers of America, Liberal party, Napoleonic Wars, Peninsular War, Progressive Conservative party, seal fishery, Teamsters Union, Treaty of Utrecht, Treaty of Versailles, War of 1812
Newfoundland and Associated Fish Exporters Ltd (NAFEL) 253–63 passim
Newfoundland Consolidated Copper Mining Company 130
Newfoundland Democratic party (NDP) 224–6, 237
Newfoundland Fish Food and Allied Workers Union: and 1971 Burgeo strike 238, 240
Newfoundland Fisheries Board 252, 253
Newfoundland Pulp and Paper Mills Ltd 220
Newfoundland Railway Company 130
Newman and Company 48–9, 75, 81
Newton, A.P. 8
Nicholson, L.H. 222

Noel, N.S. 234–5
Noel, S.J.R. 9
Non-Partisan League 159–60
Noonan, J.L. 81

O'Brien, Lawrence 106–7
O'Dea, Agnes 13
O'Flaherty, Patrick 12
Ottenheimer, Gerald 227, 235

Parsons, Robert 71, 89
Pedley, Charles 4
Peninsular War (1808–14): influence of on Newfoundland 42, 56
People's party 160, 161, 165–8, 171
Perlin, A.B. 7–8
Pickersgill, J.W. 218, 227, 259
Pinsent, R.J. 80, 83
Pitt, D.G. 12
Plumptre, A.F.W. 198
Pottle, Herbert L. 217
Prendergast, J.L. 80
Progressive Conservative party: 1949–57 history of in Newfoundland 206–7, 215–17, 219; and 1959 decline and failure 219–26; and 1966 election 226; post-1968 history of 226–32, 235–7; and United Newfoundland and New Democratic parties 224–5
Prowse, Daniel W. 5, 6–7, 130, 134
Prowse, Robert 79
Punton and Munn 57

Quinn, David 9

Railway Act (1880) 128
Reeves, John 3
Reid Newfoundland Company 113, 140–1, 142, 154

Reid, Sir Robert G. 136, 137, 140
Rendell, Stephen 78, 81, 108, 129
Ridley, Thomas 81
Roche, E.P. 166, 168, 195
Rogers, J.D. 7
Rogerson, J.J. 132
Rothney, Gordon O. 8, 11, 12
Rowe, F.W. 10, 232
Russell, Edward 216, 218
Ryan, Michael 81
Ryan, W.F. 14 n18

Saint, Jabez 81
St Lawrence Workers' Protective Union:
  and 1971 strike against Aluminum Company of Canada 238
St Pierre and Miquelon: and Newfoundland
  trade 81–2; nineteenth-century popula-
  tion of 97; and Treaty of Paris (1763)
  96. See also French Shore
seal fishery: decline of 75, 149; growth of
  44–5, 49. See also cod fishery
Seary, E.R. 12
Shaheen, John 228, 236
Shea, Ambrose 69, 70, 71, 79; and support
  for railway 126
Shea, Edward D. 69, 70, 72; and support
  for railway 126
Simms, James 48
Sinclair, James 259
Smallwood, Joseph R. 105, 205–41 passim, 260. See also Liberal party
Smith, T.R. 81
Society of United Fishermen 162
Spencer, Vincent 233
Squires, Sir Richard A. 105, 168–71, 183;
  and breakdown of Liberal Reform party
  181–95; and Hollis Walker Commission
  of Enquiry 181–204; and 1928 re-
  election 196

Stabb, Nicholas 83–4
Stevens, Paul 11
Story, G.W. 12

Talbot, Thomas 71–2, 133
Tansill, C.C. 10
Thibault, Claude 11
Teamsters Union: in Newfoundland 221–2
Thompson, F.F. 9, 112
Thorburn, Robert 50, 112, 129, 134
Tocque, Philip 5
Tourist Commission Act (1927) 31
Treaty of Utrecht (1713): influence of on
  Newfoundland 96, 113
Treaty of Versailles (1783): influence of on
  Newfoundland 114
Treaty of Washington (1871): influence of
  on Newfoundland 116, 127

Union Trading Company 158
United Newfoundland party (UNP) 224–6

Valdmanis, Dr Alfred 215, 217

Waite, P.B. 11
Walker, Thomas Hollis 189
Walker Commission of Enquiry, (1924)
  181–204
Walsh, Sir Albert 223
Walsh, W.J. 185
War of 1812: influence of on
  Newfoundland 42
Warren, William R. 182, 187–9; and Hol-
  lis Walker Commission of Enquiry 189–
  96; and 1924 defeat 194–5
Watson, Ellis 81
Wells, Clyde 228, 232, 234
White, Edward 83
Whiteley, George 64 n27
Whiteley, W.H. 50, 65 n28

Whiteley, William H. 12, 65 n28
Whiteway, Sir William 25, 38 n20, 80, 105; government of 113–14, 132–4; and support for railway 126–32

Williamson, J.A. 9
Winter, H.A. 184
Winter, James Spearman 113, 134, 138
Wise, S.F. 118

Contributors

DAVID ALEXANDER was born in British Columbia, and educated at the universities of Victoria, Washington, and London. He is currently a member of the Maritime History Group at Memorial University.

R.M. ELLIOTT was born in St John's, Newfoundland, and educated at Memorial University. She is currently an MA candidate at Memorial University.

JAMES HILLER was born in England, and educated at Oxford, Memorial, and Cambridge universities. He teaches in the History Department at Memorial University.

IAN MCDONALD (1942–77) was born in Montreal, and educated at Memorial, Oxford, and London universities. He was a member of the History Department at Memorial.

PETER NEARY was born on Bell Island, Newfoundland, and educated at Memorial and London universities. He is chairman of the History Department at the University of Western Ontario.

SHANNON RYAN was born in Harbour Grace, Newfoundland, and educated at Memorial University, where he is a member of the History Department. He is a research student at London University.